The Colonial Caribbean in Transition

The Colonial Caribbean in Transition
Essays on Postemancipation Social and Cultural History

edited by
Bridget Brereton and Kevin A. Yelvington

The Press University of the West Indies
Barbados • Jamaica • Trinidad & Tobago

University Press of Florida
Gainesville • Tallahassee • Tampa • Boca Raton • Pensacola • Orlando • Miami •
Jacksonville

Published by The Press University of the West Indies
1A Aqueduct Flats   Mona
Kingston 7   Jamaica
ISBN 976-640-030-X (paper)

Published simultaneously in the United States of America by The University Press
of Florida
15 NW 15th Street, Gainesville, FL 32611
ISBN 0-8130-1696-7 (cloth)

CATALOGUING IN PUBLICATION DATA (UWI)

The colonial Caribbean in transition :
essays on postemancipation social and
cultural history / edited by Bridget
Brereton and Kevin A. Yelvington.
p. cm

Includes bibliographical references and
index.
ISBN 976-640-030-X
1. West Indies — History — 1810-1945. 2.
West Indies — Social conditions. 3. Social
integration — West Indies — History. 4.
West Indies — Economic conditions. 5.
Wood, Douglas. I. Brereton, Bridget. II.
Yelvington, Kevin A. III. Wood, Donald.
IV. Title.
F1621.C65 1999   979.9-dc20

LIBRARY OF CONGRESS CATALOGING IN
PUBLICATION DATA (UPF)

The colonial Caribbean in transition :
essays on postemancipation social and
cultural history / edited by Bridget
Brereton and Kevin A. Yelvington.
p. cm
Includes bibliographical references.
ISBN 0-8130-1696-7 (cloth: alk. paper)
1. Caribbean Area—Civilization. I.
Brereton,
Bridget, 1946- . II. Yelvington, Kevin A., 1960- .
F2169.C66 1999   972.9-dc21
98-53065
CIP

Set in Garamond
Book design by Errol Stennett
Cover photograph: Women in a tenement in Bridgetown, Barbados, a century after the
end of slavery and apprenticeship. Source: Public Record Office, Colonial Office 950/
826, photographs from the Moyne Commission, 1938-39. Courtesy of the Public Record
Office.

for Donald and Susan

Contents

Contents

Illustrations and Tables

Illustrations

Tables

Preface: A Tribute to Donald Wood

This volume of essays on the social and cultural history of the Caribbean after the end of slavery was inspired by the life and work of Donald Wood, Reader Emeritus in History at the University of Sussex, Britain. It was conceived and planned as a tribute to him.

With some difficulty, the editors managed to persuade Donald to write a short autobiographical note, which follows this preface. Fascinating as it is, it does not, perhaps, quite explain why we and our contributors were moved to pay tribute to him through this book.

Donald's book, *Trinidad in Transition: The Years After Slavery* (1968) is unquestionably a classic of Caribbean historiography. Along with books by Philip Curtin and Douglas Hall on Jamaica in the same period, it opened up the study of the Anglophone Caribbean in the postemancipation decades, and it pioneered the social history approach. It has been immensely influential, and several subsequent works on Caribbean society in the nineteenth and early twentieth centuries have been modelled on it.

But Donald's influence on the writing of Caribbean history far transcends his fine book. For three decades, and up to the time of this writing, he has been the mentor, guide and friend of countless men and women engaged in researching the history of the region. Graduate students working in Britain, historians based at the University of the West Indies or the University of Guyana, American, British, and Caribbean academics visiting London on research trips – all have benefited from Donald's knowledge, his diffidently offered advice, his warm friendship and hospitality.

Donald personally supervised several important doctoral dissertations at Sussex, starting with those by Kamau Braithwaite (which became *The Development of Creole Society in Jamaica, 1770–1820* [1971]) and Robert J. Moore, who has contributed to this volume. But he extended his help and advice to many graduate students who were not his supervisees, such as Yelvington; and he served as mentor and inspiration to many who never studied at Sussex or even in Britain, such as Brereton.

His close links with the University of the West Indies and the University of Guyana ensured that he played an important role in both institutions' graduate and research programmes in history. He served as external examiner for the taught master's courses at both universities, and was positively exploited in the frequency with which he was asked to examine research theses (as we write this, he is serving as external examiner for a St Augustine doctoral thesis). His reports and advice have always been immensely thorough, conscientious and useful.

Donald and his wife Susan befriended, it seems to us, nearly everyone spending time in London, or Falmer, with an interest in Caribbean history and society. He nurtured people he helped with his interest, his warmth, his erudition (never on display), his fundamental decency. He is still doing it. And in these ways – in addition to his published research and his decades of teaching at Sussex – Donald has been a significant and wholly positive influence on Caribbean studies.

Donald Wood: An Autobiographical Note

I was born in London on 17 October 1923 and went to Latymer Upper School in Hammersmith from 1935 to 1941. While there my contemporaries and I realized that we would go to war as our fathers had done. We joined the school on 10 September 1935, the day before the huge Nuremberg rally, and we left in the Summer of 1941 just after the Germans invaded Russia. By then I had sat the Higher School Certificate in English, History, French, German and Latin.

We thus did not have the problem of wondering what to do next. I had always quite fancied the idea of a nautical life and I volunteered for the Navy. My sea time on the lower deck was spent in destroyers, mainly on convoy duty in the North Sea and the Channel, the Atlantic and the Arctic. This is possibly why later I was drawn to more balmy climes. In early 1944 I was commissioned. My first appointment was to an American assault ship preparing for the Normandy invasion. We put ashore some of the first wave of infantry on D-Day on Utah Beach. Living in this ship was my baptism into the complexities of race relations. The rest of my seafaring was spent in a light cruiser in the Mediterranean: sailing around this ancient sea and its wounded shores awakened my dormant sense of history. The ship took part in the invasions of Southern France and Greece and helped clear out the Germans from the Aegean islands. I was not to know when landing in Athens that my future wife, when a child, had been one of the last British civilians to escape in a fishing boat when the Germans had arrived there three years earlier.

The final stage of my nautical life was spent in naval parties in Lubeck and Kiel. We were first engaged in reopening and administrating these devastated harbours, disarming the Kriegsmarine and handing over some of its ships to the Russians. I had other interesting duties such as travelling around Western Germany, or swanning as it was enviously called by others, with British naval scientists seeking their opposite numbers. A highly satisfactory task was helping to restart German fishing in the Western Baltic. But one also discovered something of the foulness of Festung Europa as it collapsed into chaos and

Donald Wood

recrimination. The population was starving and demoralized amidst their ruined cities. The British and American zones were awash with refugees and defeated soldiers, and we learned about concentration camps. We helped to evacuate survivors of Belsen to Sweden, and I went to a war crimes trial.

I did not then know that such turmoil around the Southern Baltic littoral had happened before, at least from the time of the Thirty Years War.

In October 1946, a fortnight after being demobbed, I went up to Cambridge to read History at Fitzwilliam House and I was to stay there for eleven good years. A warm, hard working and sometimes boisterous atmosphere prevailed as we tried to come to terms with peace. Fitzwilliam was crammed in 1946 with ex-warriors ranging from those from the British forces to a few from the Polish Navy and the French Foreign Legion. Indeed it was an ex-legionnaire at Fitzwilliam, first met in the Mediterranean, who had persuaded me to consider going to university. He had sent me an telegram when I was on leave earlier saying that he had arranged an immediate interview. On the train I decided that, if selected, I would read History, having flirted with English and Modern Languages at breakfast. I have never regretted my choice.

I got a First in both parts of the Historical Tripos and stayed on for research and, after a while, some college teaching. I had been impressed by Professor Herbert Butterfield's lectures on the History of Science – the atomic bomb as well as the concentration camps were raising sombre questions in people's minds – and it seemed important just then to work in this field. My PhD thesis (1949–52) was on "Practical Mathematics in Elizabethan England". Looking back I see that it gave me a sound training in scholarship, although I was quite glad that my surveyors, gunners and navigators had barely got up to decimals by the end of my thesis, however fluent in Latin some of the real mathematicians were.

The Geographical Tripos was being refashioned at that time. One of the innovations was the introduction of some history courses. I was invited in 1952 to conduct them, and for five years I was a demonstrator, as it was called then, or assistant lecturer, and lectured on European Expansion, the History of Geographical Thought, and the historical geography of the oceans. One of the significant stepping stones in my intellectual development came when I was asked by a student if I was doing anything particular in the long vacation. I thus unsuspectingly became the graduate member of a Cambridge expedition to North Borneo or Sabah as it is now; really asked I now realize, to add *gravitas* to the social and professional proceedings of the scientific undergraduate members. A memorably uncomfortable time was had by all. It was my first experience of the tropics. In studying and living in a rice growing community in a remote valley in the rain forest I glimpsed some problems of what was beginning to be called the Third World; it became an abiding interest in my career.

After my time was up I moved out of the academic life for some years. First I became a talks producer for the BBC World Service. My task after training was putting together the commentary after news bulletins and compiling feature programmes. It was a cultivated, cosmopolitan scene shattered by frenzied moments. My office was near that of Henry Swanzy, the producer of "Caribbean Voices" which, had I but known it, was leaving its seminal mark on West Indian literature. My secretary, Genevieve, was friendly with a Barbadian broadcaster called Tom Adams whom she later married. So I was moving nearer to an interest in West Indians who were becoming frequently seen on London streets.

My next career move was unexpected. I was coming to the conclusion that I did not want to spend all my life in radio, as stimulating as it was. The chance came in September 1958 to be deputy director in the Institute of Race Relations in London. It had just become independent after being a department of the Royal Institute of International Affairs or Chatham House. Independence was in the air elsewhere in those times. Ghana had become independent within the Commonwealth in March 1957, and soon after, so it seemed, every few months a new African and, a little later, a West Indian state would be fledged into the Commonwealth after an uneasy incubation in constitutional conferences in Lancaster House just down the road. In cooperation with Chatham House I organized joint lunch time meetings to hear, amongst others, nationalist leaders such as Tom Mboya, Odinga Oginga, Hastings Banda, Michael Blundell, Norman Manley and Grantley Adams.

The tarnished side of all this were the race riots in Nottingham and London in the late summer of 1958. Europe's inner demons had not been exorcized in 1945. Outbreaks like these as well as, for example, the urgent problems of the Federation of Rhodesia and Nyasaland gave the study of race relations a new edge.

There were various tasks to be done in the institute. I collected the core of a library before handing over thankfully to a professional librarian – when she could be afforded. I was also the founder editor of the journal *Race* and directed one of the first surveys of Britain's new immigrant population (*Coloured Immigrants in Britain*, 1960). During my travels around the country for this survey and also for lecturing and conferences I met a wide range of West Indians. I decided that when the opportunity arose, I would return to the historian's trade; and as one living through years of decolonization and new ocean migrations reminiscent of those of the 1840s, I would examine some of the past moves in the game leading up to the contemporary state of play. And thanks to Naipaul's early novels, which I was avidly choosing for the library, and people I met, I thought of Trinidad.

The opportunity came in 1961 with a research fellowship at the Institute of Commonwealth Studies in London University. Together with the Public

Record Office when it moved to Kew, it became the scholarly and social Mecca in London for researchers in Caribbean studies. It had a fine and growing library, which was soon to house the famous collection of the West India Committee. It mounted, as indeed it still does, a range of postgraduate seminars and conferences about all parts of the Commonwealth; visiting scholars could be heard and based there; research students could test out their ideas before an informed audience. It was in this congenial base that I wrote my book about Trinidad after emancipation.

Reflecting back, I realize that those years were a time of transition in several ways. On a personal note, we had a first son and one surveys the world from a more actuarial and sober perspective as a father. I first read the Colonial Office files amidst the Dickensian shadows at Chancery Lane rather than surrounded by the pampered luxury and technology of Kew. And as a matter of course in those days, the family went to Trinidad by sea. The Victorian experiences of the voyage still echoed faintly around the ship – the leaving of Liverpool, our diverse fellow passengers in steerage, the storm tossed arrival at Madeira, increasingly clement days and velvety night skies, the Trade winds, the first flying fish, the West Indian landfall at Barbados. The decline of the passenger carrying steam ship with its bittersweet imperial memories of departure and arrival coincided with the end of the seaborne empire and the coming of the jumbo jet. I sailed once more to the West Indies in a cruise ship as a lecturer; it was a contrast rather like that between Chancery Lane and Kew.

But in Eric Williams' phrase, it was time to put my bucket down. With a growing family I wanted permanency rather than the uncertainty of three- or five-yearly appointments. And I put my bucket down with a resounding clank when appointed to be a lecturer in History in the new University of Sussex. I was a founder member of its School of African and Asian Studies and taught there for twenty-five years from 1964 until 1989 when I retired as a reader emeritus in History. Sussex in those halcyon and almost legendary years of university expansion in Britain, nourished by innovation and ample funding, emphasized tutorials and seminars more than lectures. These were given but usually by a circus of people; indeed the only full course of university lectures that I ever gave again, apart from extramural ones, was in Cambridge when someone was on a sabbatical. The other important characteristic of the map of learning, as we called it, was that our students took two kinds of courses: those in their main subject or major and a few interdisciplinary ones or contextuals. It is plain now that Caribbean studies can be enriched by an interdisciplinary approach; to some people it seemed rather odd.

Although we always played second fiddle numerically to African and Indian studies in the school, a core of Caribbeanists gradually emerged. It included Gerald Moore (English Literature), Richard D.E. Burton (French Studies) and David Harrison (Sociology). I always enjoyed the cut and thrust of teaching all sorts and conditions of undergraduates. We all taught at various times an introductory and interdisciplinary course on Caribbean Societies. From the earliest days I taught major history courses on the British Caribbean and on European Expansion and a long-lived contextual, pioneered by Gerald Moore and myself, on slavery and its consequences in the Americas. These were followed by a contextual course on the impact of missions. I had seen Christianity at work in Sabah, East Africa and the Caribbean and felt that its study would fill an intellectual gap in a school devoted to the developing world. Towards the end of my time when some African historians retired or moved elsewhere without being replaced I took on some of the teaching on West African history.

Then there were the research students. There always seemed to be a few doctoral Caribbeanists of various nationalities. My first were the historians Kamau Brathwaite and Bobby Moore, later Guyanese High Commissioner in Canada. Through Dr Moore and Professor Menezes a long connection with the History department at the University of Guyana began when I was the first external examiner of its MA course. I have been an external off and on ever since both there and at the University of the West Indies. Much of what I know about the Caribbean comes, I suspect, from these research students from the West Indies or elsewhere, as one tried to nudge their ideas through the joys and miseries of scholarship onto the pristine pages of a completed dissertation.

On my retirement I was touched to be given an honorary research fellowship back at the Institute of Commonwealth Studies. This provides, as it did long years ago, an hospitable academic focus, as it were, amidst the beguiling distractions of retirement; but shorn now of committees, administration, and reproachful piles of unmarked essays. I am preparing a book about Berbice, a place which won my heart after hospitable visits to its villages and polders. I try to keep up with Caribbean studies by seminars, reading and in meeting old friends.

London
September 1996

Contributors

Bridget Brereton is Professor of History and former Head of the Department of History at the University of the West Indies, St Augustine, Trinidad. She is the author of *Race Relations in Colonial Trinidad 1870–1900* (1979), *A History of Modern Trinidad 1783-1962* (1981), and, most recently, *Law, Justice and Empire: The Colonial Career of John Gorrie, 1829–1892* (1997). She is also a co-editor of *East Indians in the Caribbean: Colonialism and the Struggle for Identity* (1982), and *Engendering History: Caribbean Women in Historical Perspective* (1995). Her major publications also include a number of journal articles and book chapters, including "Social Organisation and Class, Racial and Cultural Conflict in 19th Century Trinidad", in Kevin A. Yelvington (ed.), *Trinidad Ethnicity* (1993).

Kevin A. Yelvington teaches anthropology at the University of South Florida. He is the author of *Producing Power: Ethnicity, Gender, and Class in a Caribbean Workplace* (1995), the editor of *Trinidad Ethnicity* (1993), and the author of several journal articles and book chapters, including, most recently, "Cricket, Colonialism, and the Culture of Caribbean Politics", in Michael A. Malec (ed.), *The Social Roles of Sport in Caribbean Societies* (1995), the chapter on the Caribbean in Alan Barnard and Jonathan Spencer (eds.), *Dictionary of Social and Cultural Anthropology* (1996), and "Patterns of Ethnicity, Class, and Nationalism" in Richard S. Hillman (ed.), *Understanding Contemporary Latin America* (1997).

Carl Campbell is Professor of History at the University of the West Indies, Mona, Jamaica, and has served as Head of the Department of History there. He is the author of *Colony and Nation: A Short History of Education in Trinidad and Tobago, 1834–1986* (1992), *Cedulants and Capitulants: The Politics of the Coloured Opposition in the Slave Society of Trinidad* (1992), *The Young Colonials: A Social History of Education in Trinidad and Tobago, 1834–1939* (1996), and *Endless Education: Main Currents in the Education System of Modern Trinidad and Tobago, 1939–1986* (1997), as well as numerous chapters in books and articles in journals. He is currently editor of the *Jamaican Historical Review* and is a past president of the Jamaican Historical Society and the Association of Caribbean Historians.

Bridget Jones is Senior Research Fellow, Department of Modern Languages at the Roehampton Institute of Education, London. She taught for many years at the University of the West Indies, Mona, Jamaica. She has published extensively on Caribbean writing in both French and English. She is the translator of *Cathedral of the August Heat* (1987) by the Haitian novelist Pierre Clitandre. Most recently, she co-authored the chapter "Society, Culture and Politics in French Guiana", in Richard D.E. Burton and Fred Reno (eds.), *French and West Indian: Martinique, Guadeloupe and French Guiana Today* (1995).

M. Noel Menezes recently retired as Professor of History, University of Guyana, and served as Head of the Department of History for many years. Her books include *British Policy towards the Amerindians in British Guiana, 1803–1873* (1977), *The Amerindians in Guyana 1803–1873: A Documentary History* (1979), *Scenes from the History of the Portuguese in Guyana* (1986), and *The Portuguese of Guyana: A Study in Culture and Conflict* (1994). She has also published widely in edited books and in journals. She recently celebrated fifty years of service as a Sister of Mercy.

James Millette was a founding member of the Department of History of the University of the West Indies, St Augustine, Trinidad, and served as its first Head. He is now Professor of African American Studies at Oberlin College, Ohio. He took his BA in History at the University of the West Indies and his PhD in History from King's College, University of London. He has taught for more than three decades on Caribbean, African, African American and imperial history with specific reference to comparative slavery, colonial government and administration, labour history, and the modern Caribbean and Third World. His many publications include *The Genesis of Crown Colony Government: Trinidad, 1783–1810* (1970; reissued 1985). He is currently completing two books, one comparing the postemancipation process in the Caribbean and the United States, and the other a working class history of Trinidad and Tobago.

Brian L. Moore is Senior Lecturer in the Department of History, University of the West Indies, Mona, Jamaica, and currently serves as its Head. He is the author of the books *Race, Power and Social Segmentation in Colonial Society: Guyana*

After Slavery 1838–1891 (1987) and *Cultural Power, Resistance and Pluralism: Colonial Guyana, 1838–1900* (1995). His articles include "The Settlement of Chinese in Guyana in the Nineteenth Century", in Howard Johnson (ed.), *After the Crossing: Immigrants and Minorities in Caribbean Creole Society* (1988).

Robert J. Moore recently retired as Senior Policy Advisor in Public Engagement at the Canadian International Development Agency (CIDA). Born in Guyana, his teaching career spanned two decades, first at the high school level and then at the University of Guyana, where he served, at various times, as Head of Caribbean Studies and of the Department of History. In the mid 1970s, he became Guyana's High Commissioner to Canada, a posting which lasted over five years and produced a book on developing country diplomats. He then taught at Carleton University's School of International Affairs at Ottawa before joining CIDA. He holds a BA degree from the University of the West Indies, an MA from Cambridge, and his doctorate from the University of Sussex. His research interests include race relations and Caribbean church history.

Brinsley Samaroo is Senior Lecturer in the Department of History, University of the West Indies, St Augustine, Trinidad, and served as its Head for several years. A former government minister, he has published widely on questions of ethnicity and the Indian diaspora in the Caribbean in such journals as *Social and Economic Studies*, the *Journal of Caribbean History*, and *Caribbean Studies*. He is co-editor of the books *India in the Caribbean* (1987), *Across the Dark Waters: Ethnicity and Indian Identity in the Caribbean* (1996), and editor of *Pioneer Presbyterians: Origins of Presbyterian Work in Trinidad* (1996).

Glenroy Taitt is Librarian in charge of Special Collections at the Main Library, University of the West Indies, St Augustine, Trinidad. He recently received his doctorate from the University of Sussex with a thesis on "The Development of the Peasantry in Trinidad and Guadeloupe, with Particular Reference to Domestic Food Production, 1897–1946" (1995). He is co-compiler/editor of *The Dictionary of Caribbean Biography: Volume I, Trinidad and Tobago* (1998).

Mary Turner is Senior Visiting Fellow at the Institute of Commonwealth Studies, University of London. Formerly Professor of History at Dalhousie University, Canada, she is the author of *Slaves and Missionaries: The Disintegration of Jamaican Slave Society 1787–1834* (1982; reissued 1997), and the editor of the recent book *From Chattel Slaves to Wage Slaves: The Dynamics of Labour Bargaining in the Americas* (1995). Two of her recent articles are "Slave Workers Subsistence and Labour Bargaining", in Ira Berlin and Philip Morgan (eds.), *The Slaves' Economy* (1991) and "Religious Beliefs", in Franklin W. Knight (ed.), *UNESCO General History of the Caribbean, Vol. III: The Slave Societies of the Caribbean* (1997).

Abbreviations

AWIL	Afro-West Indian League
CIDA	Caribbean International Development Agency
DOM	Department of France
FLN	Algerian Front de Libération Nationale
GRS	Groupe Révolution Socialiste
IAFA	International African Friends of Abyssinia
IAFE	International African Friends of Ethiopia
ICTA	Imperial College of Tropical Agriculture
LACC	Latin American Caribbean Center
MIM	Movement Indépendantiste Martiniquais
NAACP	National Association for the Advancement of Colored People
NUM	National Unemployed Movement
NWCSA	Negro Welfare Cultural and Social Association
PPM	Parti Progressiste Martiniquais
TCC	Trinidad Citizens' Committee
TCL	Trinidad Citizens' League
TLP	Trinidad Labour Party
TWA	Trinidad Workingmen's Association
UNIA	Universal Negro Improvement Association
UWI	University of the West Indies
WIRC	West India Royal Commission
WIYWL	West Indian Youth Welfare League

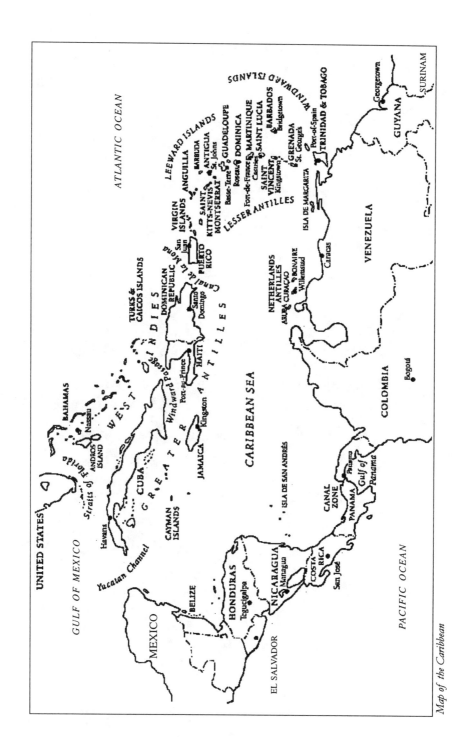

Map of the Caribbean

Introduction: The Promise of Emancipation

*Bridget Brereton and
Kevin A. Yelvington*

The coming of age theme is widely used in the Caribbean novel. In a scene in Joseph Zobel's *La rue cases-nègres*, set in 1930s Martinique, the young José listens, as he always does, to the old storyteller Mr Médouze. Mr Médouze is a canecutter, the son of a slave. He evokes 'Guinea', the 'country' of his father. In Guinea, intones José's narrator's voice, "people were like him and me; but they did not die of tiredness nor of hunger. There was no misery as there was here": "Nothing stranger than to see Mr Médouze evoke Guinea, to hear the voice rising from his entrails when he spoke of slavery and related the horrible story his father told him, of the rape of his family, of the disappearance of his nine uncles and aunts, of his grandfather and his grandfather." Mr Médouze recalls his father's words:

'I was young', my father said, 'when all the blacks fled from the plantations because it had been said that slavery was over'. I, too, danced with joy and went running all over Martinique because, for a long time, I had so wanted to flee, to run away. But when the intoxication of my freedom was spent, I was forced to remark that nothing had changed for me nor for my comrades in chains. I hadn't found my brothers and sisters, nor my father, nor my mother. I remained like all the blacks in this damned country: the *békés* kept the land, all the land in the country, and we continued working for them. The law forbade them from whipping us, but did not force them to pay us our due.

"Yes," he adds, "at any rate, we remained under the *béké*, attached to his land. And he remained our master."[1]

The idea of a coming of age can be seen as metaphorical in one reading: the coming of age of a people, a coming of age, however, stunted by continued economic, social, and cultural oppression. "We remained under the *béké*," says Mr Médouze referring to local whites, "attached to his land. And he remained our master." The emancipation of African slaves was a widely varying process in the Caribbean, in its chronology and its causes. It ranged from a vicious civil war beginning in the 1790s that led to an independent Haiti in 1804, to a slow, prolonged, trickling away of the institution in Cuba by 1886. But everywhere the promise of emancipation was not lived up to. As in the images summoned by Mr Médouze, emancipation brought with it expectations which were ultimately not fulfilled. Postemancipation society can be seen as a struggle on the part of the mass of ex-slaves and their descendants to make emancipation meaningful. At the same time, emancipation unleashed material and cultural forces that transformed the region's social structure and continued to do so for the next century and a half. Colonial power in many cases became *more* entrenched *after* emancipation. At the same time, the dispossessed and disenfranchised masses worked within severe constraints to create structures and situations that would guarantee autonomy, dignity, and advancement, although these were often mutually exclusive in historical practice. Placing subsequent developments in the context of emancipation, Donald Wood writes in his classic study of the aftermath of slavery in Trinidad,

Then as now suspicions existed that the old order was lingering on; the old cries of neo-slavery are reminiscent of the modern cries of neo-colonialism. And just as one can be sure that what is happening now will have a decisive influence on the future, so did the postemancipation years leave their unmistakable imprint on the times that followed.[2]

As a novel set in a Caribbean colony in the 1930s, yet whose main characters are forced, whether consciously or not, to continually assess emancipation's legacy, the themes of *La rue cases-nègres* provide us with the chronological framework for this collection of essays. This is a device that also provides us with a lesson. In Mr Médouze's case, he was resigned to 'returning' to Guinea when he dies: "Yes, when I'm dead, I'll go to Guinea." In his narrative, Médouze's voice slips from quoting his father to Médouze's own words –

indicative of a cultural construction of a communal memory that continues to sustain the descendants of slaves even as it motivates them to find ways to transcend slavery's legacy. Understanding the causes and effects of the complex forces and processes determining the lives of people largely hidden from history depends on an understanding of cultural stances, linguistic modes, and states of mind as much as one of formal politics and economics. Therefore, it seems the postemancipation Caribbean is best understood through social and cultural history. This is the promise of this book.

Emancipations

The ending of African slavery in the Caribbean was a prolonged trauma which lasted for almost a century. A complex interplay of local, regional and metropolitan factors shaped its course, which was neither uniform nor predictable. Enslaved Africans and Creoles, free mixed-race and black persons, planters and merchants, missionaries and officials, European humanitarians and Enlightenment thinkers, all contributed to the process. Long before the first 'metropolitan' emancipations in the 1790s, some enslaved people had emancipated themselves, notably the Maroons of Jamaica and Suriname, who won their freedom and quasi independence in the 1730s and 1760s respectively. There were also smaller pockets of Maroons and permanent runaways in most colonies.

But the first group of enslaved Africans to free themselves en masse were those of French Ste Domingue, the richest European colony in the world in the 1780s. They rose up in terrible rebellion on the great plains of the north in 1791. This was self-emancipation on an heroic scale, involving over a decade of bloody civil war before the achievement of the independent Black Republic of Haiti in 1804. Of course, the conjunction with the upheavals in revolutionary France was also of critical importance to the Haitian epic. Indeed, France was the first European nation to liberate its colonial slaves. In 1793–94, the National Assembly abolished slavery in the colonies and declared the ex-slaves citizens of the republic. In the Lesser Antilles, slavery was ended in Guadeloupe for a few poignant years (1794–1802); British military occupation throughout that period prevented implementation of abolition in Martinique. Napoleon embarked on the restoration of slavery in Ste Domingue and Guadeloupe in 1802. In the former, of course, he failed; Dessalines completed the defeat of the French forces in 1803 and presided over the birth of Haiti in January 1804. In Guadeloupe, after tremendous resistance in which thousands died, he succeeded.

Slavery was re-established in the French Antilles, and survived until 1848. On the whole, the antislavery movement in France was weaker than in Britain; the strong impetus from the Protestant and nonconformist churches there was lacking in France, for one thing. It was not until another revolutionary regime seized power, in 1848, that the efforts of French abolitionists like Victor Schoelcher bore fruit with the metropolitan abolition of slavery in the colonies. The Danish government also ended slavery in its three small island colonies in that year, stimulated by British and French abolition, by a major slave revolt in St Croix, and by the intervention of its liberal governor general, Peter von Scholten. On the other hand, the Dutch government waited until 1863 before it ended slavery in its Caribbean colonies. It was not particularly important in Curaçao, or in the other five small Dutch islands, but Suriname was a major plantation colony depending heavily on slave labour.

Emancipation in the British colonies, as in the French, reflected a complex interplay between local and metropolitan forces. In Britain, a strong antislavery lobby had emerged by the 1790s; by the 1820s, it had considerable influence in government circles. It was largely fed by religious impulses: many British men and women came to believe that slavery was an evil incompatible with Christianity. The Quakers, the nonconformist churches, and the evangelical Anglicans led this transformation of British thought. Though the antislavery leadership was largely middle or even upper class, large sectors of the industrial working class came to share their conviction that slavery was a sin and began to support the movement. British women, moreover, played a key role in mobilizing public indignation against colonial slavery. So did missionaries who went to the Caribbean to convert the slaves, especially in the 1820s and early 1830s. Their eyewitness accounts of the slaves' sufferings – and their own persecution at the hands of planters and local officials – were powerful propaganda for the cause. Moreover, many influential people, not necessarily swayed by religious arguments against slavery, were persuaded by the political economists that the institution was inefficient and outmoded. Adam Smith, articulating a widespread Enlightenment belief, had argued that slave labour was always and necessarily unproductive and that free labour was invariably more efficient. This idea had become almost an article of faith among many British intellectuals by around 1830.

As Eric Williams argued over fifty years ago, the work of the antislavery movement bore fruit when it did largely because of important shifts in the British economy. The slave trade, and the Caribbean sugar trade, were far less important to the overall national economy by the early 1800s than they had been in the 1700s. Liverpool was shifting from importing slaves to importing raw cotton; the industrializing economy was interested in the far vaster markets of India, the US and Latin America; manufacturers wanted raw sugar from wherever it was cheapest. With these changes, the political clout of the West India interest inevitably dwindled, and the antislavery movement, gathering strength in the 1820s, was able to sway government and Parliament. In 1833, the Act of Emancipation legislated the formal end of slavery in the British Empire on 1 August 1834. A transitional 'apprenticeship' was imposed on the ex-slaves, but this was ended in 1838, marking the final end of African slavery in the British Caribbean.

But, to a much greater extent than Williams recognized, the slaves helped to achieve their own freedom; not, indeed, by a great and successful rebellion like that in Haiti, but by the persistent undermining of the planters' interests. 'Day-to-day' opposition helped to chip away the foundations of the slave system and to reduce the profitability of the slave plantations. Everywhere, slaves bargained with their owners and managers for more 'rights', more 'privileges', and resisted, often effectively, when any of these were encroached upon. Alliances with antislavery missionaries, especially after about 1815, boosted the slaves' confidence. And three great rebellions – in Barbados in 1816, Demerara (Guyana) in 1823, and Jamaica in 1831–32 – showed the metropolitan government beyond a shadow of doubt what would happen if emancipation was not speedily enacted. One year after the Jamaican 'Baptist War', as the planters called it, the Act of Emancipation was passed.

African slavery, on the whole, was less important to the social and economic development of the Hispanic Caribbean than it was to that of the French and British colonies.[3] In Santo Domingo (the Dominican Republic) there were relatively few slaves by 1800, and a plantation economy hardly existed. Slavery was, in any case, abolished in 1822, when the colony came under Haitian occupation. As Puerto Rico began to develop its sugar economy in the early 1800s, slaves came to be correspondingly more significant as a source of labour, especially in the sugar zone along the southern coast of the island. But slaves were always a relatively small group in the population as a whole. Unlike the Dominican Republic, Puerto Rico remained a Spanish colony until 1898, and Spain lacked a vibrant antislavery movement in the nineteenth century. It was not until 1873–76 that the government abolished slavery in Puerto Rico; the final end of the institution came in 1876.

In Cuba, by far the largest of the Caribbean territories, massive slave imports from the late 1700s and the explosive growth of the plantation system changed the social and racial configuration and made that island a slave society by around 1850. Though many black and mixed-race Cubans had freed themselves, or had been manumitted, well before 1880, formal abolition came late to Cuba. As we saw, antislavery in Spain was weak; and Cuba was Spain's 'pearl of the Antilles', the loyal (and lucrative) colony she was able to retain until the end of the century. It was not until 1886 that Cuban slavery was finally ended.

The end of formal slavery in the Caribbean, achieved after an agonizing ordeal lasting from the 1790s to the 1880s, left the region's societies deeply divided. Certainly, the effects of its abolition were far from uniform or simple to predict; yet, with few exceptions, Caribbean societies in the post-emancipation era were largely shaped by the legacy of the slave system and its twin, the plantation mode of production. The transition to a 'free society' was, inevitably, a hard road to travel for all the region's people; above all for the formerly enslaved, for Mr Médouze's father and all his counterparts up and down the region.

The Caribbean in Transition

Formal emancipation, of course, did not mean equality for the ex-slaves, nor did it effect a transformation in social and power relations in the region. The white elites continued, by and large, to monopolize ownership of the major economic resources, to exercise political ascendancy (subject to the colonial powers), and to enjoy the greatest social prestige. Yet, although the continuities between the decades before and after emancipation in the different territories are striking, the formal end of slavery was an event of great importance to the people living in the nineteenth century Caribbean. It removed the most horrendous abuses which had been inseparable from enslavement: for instance, the eighteen-hour shifts on the sugar plantations, the ubiquity of physical punishment, the vulnerability of all slave women to sexual abuse. And, for many though not all of the formerly enslaved, it opened up the possibility of carving out new lives, on their own terms, with a chance for independence from the plantation. Not all the freed men and women 'remained under the *béké*'.

The course of postemancipation history in the different islands and colonies was shaped by the clash between the aims of the two main contending groups, the planters (mainly but not invariably white) and the ex-slaves. Especially in the plantation societies, where enslaved Africans had been the only important source of labour since the 1700s, the planters sought to make the freed men and women into semi-serfs tied to the estates by customary tenure arrangements and obliged to labour for them for minimal wages. The ex-slaves, by and large, sought a way of life which would grant some degree of independence from the plantation. Few of them, except in Haiti, wanted to sever all relations with the planters. By 1838 or 1848, most of the ex-slaves were accustomed to a market economy and had cash needs which only estate wages could meet. Few escaped 'into the bush', as the whites claimed to fear; they wanted to be close to the estates, the churches and chapels, the schools (where these existed). Instead, families tried to develop several different income sources: some of the men might work for wages on the plantation, one or two might be a skilled artisan, the family might acquire by purchase, renting or squatting a small piece of land which would be cultivated by the women and children. Most of the freed people tried to move off the estates to live in their own cottages or huts on plots not owned by the planter; they knew only too well that if they remained 'under the *béké*, attached to his land', the planter would, inevitably, remain the 'master'.

The extent to which the freed people were able to achieve these aims depended on a complex cluster of factors. One important variable was the amount of uncultivated or under-cultivated land in each territory at the time of emancipation, and the relative density of the population. Generally, the territories with abundant land outside the plantation sector, and with fairly sparse populations, afforded greater opportunities for the ex-slaves. But even in colonies where land was abundant and population density was low, such as British Honduras (Belize) and the Bahamas, planter control over the land and other resources might cut off or minimize these opportunities. Nevertheless, in nearly all the former slave colonies, significant groups of the freed people did succeed in carving out lives which were not wholly dependent on the planters.

For the planters in many territories, the best long-term 'solution' to the problem of controlling free labourers, and keeping them in a state of semi-serfdom, was to import new ones. By importing significant numbers of immigrant labourers, the planters and colonial governments hoped to achieve two aims. First, competition for estate jobs might be generated between the new imports and the freed people, forcing many of the latter to return to the labour market on the planters' terms. Secondly, if the immigrants were held to binding indenture agreements, they would constitute a core of unfree labour, and the growing numbers of ex-indentured immigrants would also swell the pool of estate workers. As a result, there was large-scale labour immigration into the Caribbean after abolition. Small numbers came from Madeira (these people were called 'Portuguese' in the Caribbean), Africa (the so-called liberated Africans), Europe, Indonesia and China, but most of these contract labourers came from India. Indian immigrants, and their descendants, came to form a major component in the populations of three Caribbean territories, Guyana, Trinidad and Suriname. As early as 1891, Indians (India born and their locally born descendants) comprised about 38 percent of the population of Guyana and 28 percent in Trinidad; in Suriname, Indians comprised 24 percent and Javanese 9 percent of the population by 1915. Hinduism, Islam and many key aspects of the culture of South Asia took firm root in these three societies.

Post-slavery immigration made many Caribbean societies more ethnically and culturally diverse. And lively popular cultures flourished throughout the region in the nineteenth century. Nearly everywhere, the elites tried to impose European cultural forms on the people and to weaken or denigrate forms which derived partly or wholly from African, Amerindian or East Indian elements. Yet the elites had, at best, only partial success. African-Christian religions became fundamentally important to blacks in the French, British and Dutch colonies, in Cuba and in Haiti. Other, more secular cultural institutions – for instance, popular festivals like Jonkonnu in Jamaica, Belize and the Bahamas or the pre-Lenten Carnival in Trinidad, Martinique and elsewhere – also developed and flourished as a creative *mélange* of African, European and uniquely Caribbean influences. Popular music, song, dance, folklore all reflected a similar *mélange*, and continued to develop despite official disapproval or actual persecution. The process of 'creolization' – a blending, but also a confrontation of the region's cultures, the nature of which has been the subject of a huge debate amongst and between local residents and foreign scholars – which arguably began on the slave ships themselves, and continued to affect all aspects of plantation society, was now at its most evident, most public as a form of expression.[4]

One of the most important social developments after the end of slavery was the gradual emergence and growth of a black and mixed-race middle stratum in the Caribbean colonies, led by men and women who had been exposed to formal education and were familiar with European culture. They, too, began to develop their own cultural institutions and to express their world-view. For instance, most of the colonies in the nineteenth century had one or two newspapers owned or edited by educated black or mixed-race men, and these journals (even if their lives were often short and their circulation painfully small) provided an important forum for them to formulate a sense of identity. Many of them began to develop a sense of racial pride and to construct an identity with which to confront white racism. Intellectuals and writers such as Edward Wilmot Blyden, who was a native of the Danish

West Indies, Samuel Prescod of Barbados, Robert Love of the Bahamas and Jamaica, J.J. Thomas of Trinidad, and Hegesippe Legitimus of Guadeloupe were important precursors of the better-known twentieth century ideologues of race awareness and *négritude*.

The emergence of an important black and mixed-race middle stratum meant that Caribbean societies were becoming more complex by the turn of the century; the arrival of new immigrant groups introduced more ethnic and cultural diversity. Class and ethnicity helped to shape the region's social formation. But so did gender. Plantation slavery, in some respects at least, had been 'gender blind', in that enslaved women were expected to perform much the same kind of work as the men. After emancipation, the European nineteenth century gender ideology – men as the breadwinners in the 'public sphere', women as dependent 'housewives' confined to the 'private sphere' of the household – was adopted more or less by the colonial governments, the churches, and the upper and middle strata. But it never reflected the realities of most Caribbean women's lives.

After the end of slavery, most African Caribbean women continued to work in agriculture, either as wage labourers on the sugar, cocoa or banana plantations, or as peasant farmers cultivating family owned lands. They were also fully involved in marketing farm produce. Others moved to the towns and worked as domestics (the key non-agricultural occupation for Caribbean women after slavery), seamstresses, laundresses and petty vendors. Very few could be described as 'housewives' uninvolved in social production. Indo-Caribbean women were indentured along with the men; they laboured on the plantations as indentured and as 'free' workers after their contracts had expired; and after the 1870s, they were increasingly absorbed into peasant production when many Indians moved off the estates into new farming villages. Again, few were truly 'secluded' women confined to a strictly domestic role; this was probably true only for a handful of wives of upper caste, wealthy men or educated professionals. The European gender ideology was only really adhered to by the small white elite – it was rare for white Caribbean women to work outside the home before 1900 – and, perhaps, by the upwardly mobile middle stratum, though many mixed-race or black women could be found running small businesses such as guest-houses, nursing homes or restaurants. Caribbean women outside the upper and middle strata also rejected European notions about marriage and family patterns. They cherished several different family forms, and the evidence suggests that many, if not most, declined to adopt the model of lifelong, monogamous marriage.[5]

Continued Colonialism

By the end of the nineteenth century, if Caribbean peoples were indeed 'free', everywhere they were in chains. Caribbean peoples remained in colonial chains, which continued to bind them through a combination of a hegemony worked by encompassing oppositional elements into its structure and, more often than is supposed, by naked force. While in no way should colonialism be seen as a uniform process or monolithical structure, it must be understood as providing an ideological, political, economic, and, perhaps above all, social and cultural context for the studies in this book that focus as they do on social and cultural history. As Barry W. Higman writes, "social history becomes mere description or trivialization when isolated from its material and ideological environment"; "successful social history always depends on establishing links between particular 'social' groups, institutions and activities, and the broader framework of historical evolution".[6]

Social and cultural responses to the broader framework of colonialism must be understood as part of the heterogeneity of the postemancipation colonial context. By the end of the nineteenth century, sugar continued to loom large in most islands, while other crops, such as tobacco in Cuba and Puerto Rico, coffee in Haiti, Jamaica and Puerto Rico, and bananas in Guadeloupe, Jamaica, and the Windward Islands, were produced by workers and peasant proprietors alike. In many islands, such as Nevis, Dominica and Tobago, the rural folk were "neither 'peasant' nor 'proletarian' ", in Richard Frucht's phrase, but, instead, combined peasant-like means of production with proletarian-like relations of production through share cropping and other kinds of arrangements.[7] Elsewhere, in islands such as Jamaica, plantations were able to consolidate more and more land.[8] Then, a sugar depression gripped the British and French Caribbean from the 1880s brought about by eroded metropolitan protective preferences, increased competition with subsidized European beet sugar producers, and inefficient local production techniques.[9] Many plantations were left abandoned, but this did not always mean that land suddenly became available to the peasantry. Those planters that survived did so by diversifying, by further consolidating land, and by further marginalizing peasants. In Trinidad, Guyana and Suriname, many creoles and Indian ex-indentureds became cane farmers, supplying the plantation factories; many cultivated rice on land marginal to the estates. In Puerto Rico, the mechanization of the sugar industry accelerated after the US takeover in 1898 as American companies bought land and established *centrales*, or sugar factories. By the 1930s these *centrales* controlled 80 percent of the sugar lands, squeezing out the *colonos*, the local sugar cane growers who supplied them. In Cuba, where sugar production was more than the British Caribbean exports, competition from beet sugar and, later, the vagaries of US import tariffs threw the island into boom and bust cycles, even though the trend there was for production to expand until about 1925.

In many places, rural decay and impoverishment hastened processes of urbanization and proletarianization that brought many men and women to the burgeoning towns, which became characterized in the first decades of the twentieth century by uncontrolled growth, poverty, overcrowding and disease. In the towns, however, work was scarce, although there was perhaps more of a chance to eke out a livelihood on the margins of the urban landscape – men and women engaged in casual employment, with women, too, in domestic service – than as a peasant or rural worker. There was also the hope of sending remittances back to the family members who stayed behind. But as one 1879 official report from Jamaica stated, "As a rule such persons are not qualified for skilled labour, and as there is no constant demand for such services as they can render, they pass a considerable part of their time in idleness, and so fail to make adequate provision for the care of their families." The dwelling places of these migrants were, the report continued, "of a most miserable description, many of them being unfit for human habitation. They consist of single rooms opening into a common yard. In these rooms families are herded together under conditions that defy the simplest observances of decency."[10] In other towns, such as Port of Spain, Trinidad, the urban poor lived in 'barrack rooms' located in 'barrack yards'. They were havens for all kinds of social maladies: theft, prostitution, disease and a debased world-view. By 1930, more than twenty-five thousand people, or one-third of Port of Spain's population, lived in barrack yards. One barrack-dweller described them as "like the boxes horses are shipped in. A long line of ten by twelve feet boxes, nailed together with a window and a door allotted to each. The outward appearance is enough to give one a shuddering sense of repulsion."[11] The urban poor survived in part through mutual aid groups and so-called friendly societies. In Cuba, the *sociedades de recreo y ayuda mutua* (recreation and mutual aid societies) were derived from the *cabildos*, the mutual aid organizations that were formed during slavery and maintained by African ethnic groups. The urban proletariat, then, became a large corporate and class group as distinct from the rural proletariat and the 'reconstituted'[12] peasantry. Wages – where they were paid – in all sectors were low, and, to compound matters, work was seasonal in most industries.

The cultural and economic dislocations and contradictions inherent in these processes produced dire living conditions for the urban and rural masses, but also a growing political awareness and class and ethnic consciousness, as well as organizational and leadership skills. With class diversity proceeding apace, intellectuals and working class leaders and their followers increasingly came to view the colonial apparatus – with its attendant cultural imperialism – as their enemy and to identify and vilify the local beneficiaries of such systems: white members of the upper class, 'brown' and, increasingly, black members of the middle class. But organized or even more spontaneous anticolonial activity often provoked harsh responses from the metropole – or, almost as bad, benign indifference, misrepresentations, and betrayals. Residents of the old colonies of Britain responded to the economic dislocations caused by the sugar depression of the late nineteenth century with a number of violent disturbances. Responding to low world market prices, the planters, especially in the small islands most dependent on sugar, had reduced sugar cane acreage, lowered wages, and prevented their labourers and the peasantry from extending subsistence agriculture. The culminating actions of this period, and perhaps the most serious, were riots in St Kitts that began on two estates in early 1896 and quickly spread across the island into a general revolt, and protests by Indian estate labourers in British Guiana later that year. The depression led to the decision to send a Royal Commission to investigate the plight of these islands; it suggested the establishment of more smallholder settlements – as Bonham Richardson writes, no doubt "as a ploy to curb social unrest and a sensible step to reaching some kind of solution for the problems of the region".[13] In Guadeloupe, the creation of a peasantry was encouraged by the local government which issued small plots of land in the first two decades of the twentieth century. Other islands, such as Grenada, Tobago and Dominica, developed sturdy peasantries. Peasants and part-time rural proletarians were involved in complex family and village based systems of mutual aid and reciprocity. There was, for example, the *gayap* in Trinidad, a cooperative labour endeavour found all over the region under several different names. Throughout the Caribbean, the institution known as 'family land' ensured land ownership and use rights for generations without the threat of alienation.[14]

Urban dwellers, as well, revolted against the political order. Sometimes this involved coalitions between the upper and middle classes and the working class, sometimes it involved cooptation *by* the upper and middle classes *of* the working class. In Trinidad, a Crown Colony with no elected members in the Legislative Council, the Ratepayers' Association was formed in 1901 by members of the urban business community, and black and brown professionals. The association seized upon the question of water costs – a concern of the upper and middle classes only because, after all, most of the urban poor hardly had access to pipe-borne water – and succeeded in using the issue to stir the Port of Spain masses against government policy. The result was the 'Water Riots', which occurred in March 1903 when a crowd gathered at the Red House, the major government building, to disrupt council proceedings. The police fired into the crowd, leaving sixteen dead and forty-three wounded; the Red House was destroyed by fire. The water issue was almost incidental; what the association and others were really after was political representation and an end to Crown Colony rule. Opposition to the social order in the *vielles colonies* of France featured a number of strikes and public manifestations of protest – as well as violent repression – in the first decades of the twentieth century. In Martinique in 1900, during '*la grève de 1900*', eight protesting agricultural workers were killed by authorities. In May 1925, in Diamant, Martinique, the masses were prevented from fairly voting in a municipal election by the thugs of a *béké* distillery owner candidate; when the election was repeated three weeks later, at least ten were killed and as many wounded in what became known as '*la guerre du Diamant*' when police and soldiers fired into a crowd. In 1930 at Abymes, in Guadeloupe, three workers were killed and a number wounded in the midst of a strike of sugar workers.[15]

The turn of the century Caribbean saw a new colonial power on the scene, the US. In Cuba, a bloody war for independence from Spain (1895–98) followed the Ten Years' War (1868–78) and a number of smaller skirmishes. Cuba's independence began with the US as an occupying power and the Americans installed military governments from 1899 to 1902 and again from 1906 to 1909, although the latter ended up as a civilian administration. The US forced the Cubans to accept the Platt Amendment (1901–34) to their constitution, which allowed the US to intervene in domestic political affairs, as well as to approve international treaties. Haiti, since independence in 1804, had become mired in a tortuous isolation imposed from without. The national revolution had led to an agricultural one, with small peasant plots largely replacing the plantations. By the mid nineteenth century, political in-fighting had led to the creation of the *caco* armies, bands of peasants organized into private forces to protect landlords and to raid powerful opponents and poor rural dwellers alike. The US intervened in Haiti, sending the US marines to occupy the country from 1915 until 1934, to secure what it defined as US strategic interests. In Haiti's neighbour, the Dominican Republic, the US controlled the government from 1916 until 1924. Puerto Rico went more or less directly from Spanish to US colony after 1898.

It is true that everywhere they went the US occupiers built roads, schools, government buildings, created police forces and improved the health services in these countries, albeit, especially in the case of Haiti, with the use of conscripted *corvée* labour – which was particularly offensive to proud Haitian small holders. In Haiti and the Dominican Republic the American occupiers were met with armed insurgencies. In Haiti, a *caco* army led by Charlemagne Peralte engaged the marines in intense warfare, especially in 1919. In the Dominican Republic, armed guerrillas prevented the marines from controlling the eastern part of the country from 1917 until 1922. But the superior numbers, materiel, and brutal methods of the marines finally succeeded in quelling their opposition. And a new kind of cultural imperialism came to exist, defined especially by its racialism. This variant of racialism even prevented the US from carrying out many of its stated paternalistic goals. Eventually, the US was to cooperate with, if not essentially create, some of the region's most notorious dictators.[16]

The US military occupation laws often both favoured and opposed US investments, at least on paper. However, the overall effect was an expansion of US owned agricultural firms and a concentration of land from small landholders to the large corporations. The US controlled the customs and tariff laws of the occupied territories, and these islands became more and more dependent on the US as they became markets for US exports and the US became the sole destination of their own (mainly agricultural) exports. The Jones Act of 1917 'granted' US citizenship to Puerto Ricans, but their political rights have always been limited.

The presence of US capital and geopolitical interests in the region also encouraged large migrations within the wider Caribbean during the first decades of the century. Jamaicans, Barbadians, Martinicans, Guadeloupeans and others moved to Panama to work on the construction of the canal; many West Indians also ended up in Central America, working for such concerns as the United Fruit Company in Costa Rica, Honduras and Guatemala; 'small islanders' from the eastern Caribbean went to work in the canefields of the Dominican Republic, as did innumerable Haitians; Jamaicans and Haitians migrated to Cuba looking for the same kind of employment; Trinidadians and others migrated to the Netherlands Antilles and Venezuela to work in the growing oil economy. As early as the 1880s, Cuban cigar makers and their families had migrated with their factories to Key West and Tampa, in Florida. These migrants suffered severe hardships but were able to develop functioning enclave communities, where they made their lives, sent money back to relatives in their home islands, and hoped to save enough to take themselves back and build a house there one day too.[17] These transnational communities presaged those that would eventually develop in Amsterdam, London, Miami, New York, Paris and Toronto. But, in 1924, when the US enacted racist laws to exclude certain types of migrants, Caribbean territories found this 'safety valve' largely closed.

Caribbean responses to colonialism were multifaceted; the efforts to make emancipation more complete were conducted along 'cultural' lines as well as political and economic. The early twentieth century saw the flowering of religious, 'racial', literary and artistic and social movements – and most of them tended to combine all these aspects. The most notable were the movements that were self-defined as 'racial' in nature, which is perhaps not surprising given the persistence of a rigid, if slowly transforming, hierarchical social structure that placed 'whites' at the top, 'browns' in the middle, and the 'black' masses on the bottom, as it had been under slavery. These 'racial' movements sought to instil self-pride and self-worth in blacks and browns, and also formulated specific plans for the concrete betterment of the general situation of those that they defined as their brethren and sistren. These efforts coincided with similar efforts by blacks elsewhere in the diaspora. The first Pan-African Congress, held in 1900 in England, featured the participation of many West Indians, including Henry Sylvester Williams of Trinidad and Bénito Sylvain of Haiti. When these movements incorporated the black masses and tended toward separatism, they incurred the wrath of governments which viewed them as threats. Their leaders and followers were hounded and harassed and even massacred as in the case of '*la guerrita de 1912*' in Cuba. In 1907, the basis for the Partido Independiente de Color was formed, based largely among Afro-Cuban officers from the old army of liberation. Comprised of the black petit bourgeoisie as well as farmers and small property owners, they mobilized to fight institutional racism and to gain access to the expanding state bureaucracy in the republic they played a key part in establishing. Led by Pedro Ivonet and Evaristo Esteñoz, their challenge was serious enough for the government of José Miguel Gómez to enact the Morúa Law in 1910 – proposed by the only Afro-Cuban to become president of the Senate – that outlawed the formation of political parties and other organizations along racial lines. In 1912, the *independientes* resorted to armed rebellion. The Gómez government dispatched troops to Oriente, the site of the rebellion, and at least three thousand Afro-Cubans were indiscriminately and ruthlessly slaughtered in the several-month 'war' and subsequent repression.[18]

The movement led by the Jamaican-born Marcus Garvey, from 1914 up until Garvey's death in 1940, was by far the most powerful in its emotional and political appeal for the region's blacks, the most organized in its far-reaching institutional structure, the most ambitious in its leader's plans, and the most popular in numbers of followers it attracted internationally. At its height in the 1920s, the Universal Negro Improvement Association (UNIA) boasted nearly 1,000 branches internationally. In the Caribbean area, there were a number of branches, especially in British West Indian enclaves. There were 52 in Cuba and 47 in Panama, and the Dominican Republic had several chapters; in the British Caribbean, there were 30 branches in Trinidad, 11 in Jamaica, and the small islands such as St Kitts and St Vincent had one or two each. It is hard to minimize the effects of Garveyism on some members of the black middle class, including later nationalist leaders and, especially, those blacks who aspired to middle class status, all the way down to the grassroots level. Garveyites were among the leaders of the effervescing labour and nationalist movements, especially in the British Caribbean.[19]

If Garveyism became like a religion to some, there were many religious movements that incorporated what could be identified as Garveyite themes. At times, these religious leaders were formal members of Garvey's organization. The common themes were positive senses of black identity and a promise of redemption, whether worldly or other-worldly. In Jamaica, Afro-Christianity had always been a vehicle and wellspring of political protest, and it also entailed the expression, certainly creolized, of African world views. The Afro-Christian religious complex – from Kumina, to Myal, to Revival, and all the zones of mutual influence between Myal and mainstream Christianity – threw up several forms of political protest and religious observance during the first third of the twentieth century, all infused with ideas of black deliverance and resistance to white malevolence, through religious ritual, explicit ideological treatises, and, often, medical practices, all of which paralleled and sought to displace European derived ones. Charismatic leaders popped up, such as the Revivalist Alexander Bedward. By 1920, his Jamaica Native Baptist Free Church was the largest Revivalist church in Jamaica. In the 1930s, in Jamaica still, several preachers, including Leonard P. Howell, imbued with Pan-Africanist and Garveyite ideals from his time in the US and Panama, proclaimed that Ethiopian emperor Ras Tafari, crowned Haile Selassie I in 1930, was God on earth. Rastafarianism was seen as a serious challenge to the colonial state; early leaders and adherents were jailed at various times. To a great extent, the 'religious idiom' informed all kinds of popular political protest in Jamaica.[20]

Many of these movements traded on idealized images of Africa. In fact, one theme of these movements, from the more millenarian to Garvey's, was 'repatriation' to Africa. Many popular religions, forms of popular culture, and language maintained significant continuities derived from various African cultures. Most black peasants and perhaps to a lesser extent the urban black working class were in some way involved, as leaders or participants, in the great syncretic religions, such as the Yoruba-derived *santería* or *lukumí*, and the Congo-derived *palo monte-mayombe* in Cuba and the Orisha religion in Trinidad, and *vaudou* in Haiti. At the very least, they believed in the efficacy of the African gods – the *orichas* in *santería* and the *loa* in *vaudou* – and their Christian saint counterparts. They respected these forces, with their abilities to mediate between the supernatural and natural worlds. The intervention of religious specialists, such as the *houngan* in Haitian *vaudou*, the *santero* or *santera* in *santería*, the obeahman and obeahwoman as they were called in the British Caribbean, and the *quimboiseur*, their counterpart in the French islands, was sought for a variety of reasons: to fight off the effects of sorcery, to heal with herbs and ritual practices, to interpret dreams and various signs, and to conduct rituals. Despite the ostricization of their practitioners from middle class society and the official persecution of these religions, this did not prevent individual members of the middle classes and even the white upper classes from clandestinely consulting these religious specialists. Yet, official religious and social persecution involved specific laws aimed not only at overt Africanisms in religion, but also at their manifestations in public celebrations and festivals. Many of the public festivals which featured African influences were not coincidentally seen by the upper classes as rowdy, loud and obscene. At various time, the pre-Lenten festivals such as Carnival in Trinidad, the French islands, and Cuba, and Rara in Haiti, were restricted or suppressed. Along with Christmas celebrations such as Jonkonnu in Jamaica, the Bahamas, and elsewhere, these institutions not only combined what is glossed as 'African', 'European' and, in rare cases, indigenous elements, to create something essentially Caribbean, but they also became media for popular protest as much as showcases of artistic talent. The same could be said for musical traditions such as the calypso in Trinidad, which, too, was censored during the 1930s. Furthermore, the gulf between the masses and the middle and upper classes was cemented through language. A wide variety of rich creole languages had been developing since contact, conquest, and enslavement. Many of these had an identifiable African structure undergirding them. However, these languages were seen as defective by those aspiring to or holding positions of relative privilege: "Language not only [was] correlated with social class differences and generally used as the most widely recognized index of social class but also [had] become associated with backwardness and the lack of 'culture', whereas the use of the standard form of European languages [was] associated with intelligence, enlightenment, and 'culture'."[21]

In the 1920s and 1930s, the intellectuals of the incipient nationalist movement looked to the people for a way of representing 'national' culture. They developed local schools of folklore and ethnology where, for the most part, 'Africanisms' were defined and labelled as such. These included Fernando

Ortíz in Cuba, Antonio Salvador Pedreira in Puerto Rico and Jean Price-Mars in Haiti. Most were from the upper or middle classes but yet dealt with Afro-Caribbean themes, documenting 'folklore' and religious cosmologies. Others' aims were avowedly political. Beginning during the US occupation, Price-Mars urged his fellow elites to accept *vaudou* as a legitimate religion, to celebrate their African along with their European past, and to join with the masses in accepting indigenous, peasant culture as 'Haitian', forming a cultural nationalism-as-resistance. In many ways he set the stage for the *négritude* and *noiriste* political-literary movements. The work of Ortíz inspired the Afro-Cubanism literary, cultural and intellectual movement. In Puerto Rico, the image of the *jíbaro*, the peasant, began to be exalted as the 'true soul' of the island. In Trinidad, Suriname and Guyana, an Indian middle class emerged, as did Indian nationalism, creating images of India that inspired communal feelings. Middle class cultural production was facilitated through the establishment of new newspapers, magazines and journals, such as the *Beacon* in Trinidad, *Bim* in Barbados, *Kyk-Over-Al* in British Guiana, *Les Griots* in Haiti, and *Tropiques*, established by Aimé and Suzanne Césaire in Martinique. There was a literary flowering as writers examined – and sometimes glorified – local social life.[22]

But if the expanding middle classes were a source of anticolonial ferment, their members were also imbued with what they regarded as metropolitan 'high culture'. This both reflected and was reflected in the educational systems of these islands. In general, primary education for the masses was underfunded and, where it existed, woefully inadequate. Secondary education was in effect reserved for the upper and middle classes. Those with middle class aspirations saw in education their main – sometimes only practicable – objective for their children's social mobility and made great sacrifices accordingly. Education, it was held, could partially mitigate racism and classism, and the ultimate aim was to secure a white-collar job or a profession, with a position as a schoolteacher or a government clerk perhaps a more realizable goal.

Middle class and working class met with the formation of fledgling workers' organizations and political parties. The years after World War I, sparked in a large part by the returning soldiers who fought for Britain and France, and by the influence of Garveyism, saw increasing working class pressure on antidemocratic colonial polities. In the British Caribbean, colonial legislation forbade the formation of trade unions. Instead, as in the case of Trinidad, workers' associations were organized as political parties. Once trade unions became legal, the local governments could choose not to register them, and they did not have the legal protection that their counterparts did in Britain. But elsewhere, radical parties and trade unions were beginning to blossom. A

Partido Socialista Puertorriqueño had been formed as a political arm of the labour movement in Puerto Rico in 1915. In Martinique, there was a socialist party from the turn of the century, and the communist Groupe Jean-Jaurès traced its beginnings to 1919 and maintained links with the French Communist Party and the Communist International. In 1936, the socialists and communists reached a *rapprochement*, and the labour protests that had been so prevalent from the 1920s to the mid 1930s actually escalated. In Cuba, the Partido Socialista Cubano was formed in 1899 and the Partido Obrero in 1904. By the 1920s, labour militancy had grown, in part due to the influence of Catalan immigrants. There was a significant anarcho-syndicalist movement. In 1925, the Partido Communista de Cuba was formed immediately after the consolidation of what it claimed to be 200,000 workers into one national labour federation, and communists exercised leadership of a number of important unions. And Caribbean peoples abroad, such as George Padmore and C.L.R. James of Trinidad and Otto Huiswood of Suriname, came to hold important positions within international radical movements. In some countries, however, organized labour and radical left political parties were subjected to state control. In Haiti, the writer Jacques Roumain founded the Parti Communiste d'Haïti in 1934, but it was immediately outlawed and the labour movement there would not gain ground until well into the 1940s. And next door in the Dominican Republic, the dictator Rafael Trujillo effectively controlled organized labour during his reign.[23]

The 1930s were years of popular revolt in the Caribbean. While each incident in each individual island may have had causes and outcomes particular to that locale, there were strong commonalities, linked to the pressures resultant from the 1929 US stock market crash, the consequent fall in the prices of agricultural exports, such as sugar and tobacco, and, at the same time, the (re)ascendence of metropolitan interests in the sugar, banana and oil industries. These industries on the whole remained profitable during the crisis, incurring further resentment.[24] Furthermore, the local social structure seemed even more unyielding. In Martinique, for example, the small number of *béké* families maintained control over the economy by controlling the land and a large part of the commercial sector. In 1935, 3 percent of the total number of landowners owned 61 percent of the cultivable soil, and 5 percent owned 75 percent of the soil. On the other hand, 72 percent of the owners held 7 percent of the farming land.[25] The *békés* were representative in some ways of the elite classes elsewhere.

The protests called for the amelioration of working class and peasant distress. Workers rallied, as well, against institutionalized racism and imperialism. The ultimate success of these movements varied, and all of them incurred an immediate and deadly response by the authorities. In 1929, Haitian student strikes against the US occupation forces and client president Louis Borno culminated in a peasant uprising at Cayes, where US marines fired on a crowd, killing at least twenty-four and wounding twice that many. In 1930, a huge strike in Cuba ended only when the army of strongman president Gerardo Machado moved in. The political and labour crisis continued there, however, and, in 1933, a widespread general strike succeeded in driving Machado from power. A strike in British Honduras in 1934 was the start of a wave of strikes in the British Caribbean: St Kitts in January 1935; St Vincent in October 1935; St Lucia in November 1935; Barbados in 1937; Trinidad in 1937, extraordinary because blacks and Indians cooperated in working class activities; Jamaica in 1938; and British Guiana in 1939. In February 1935, in response to a reduction in wages and worsening conditions, sugar workers in Martinique staged a hunger march on Fort-de-France. In March 1935, in Cuba, another huge, general strike paralysed the country. This time, however, the government of President Carlos Mendieta and army chief Fulgencio Batista brutally suppressed it, outlawed unions and occupied the University of Havana, the site of radical activity and source of leadership. Everywhere, repression followed rebellion. In the British and French islands, local forces were augmented when the metropolitan troops were called in. When labour began to organize in Puerto Rico, the sugar corporations used the time-honoured US strike breaking tactics of scab labour, strike-breakers and closed shops. In the Dominican canefields in 1937, Trujillo ordered the massacre of perhaps twenty-thousand Haitian migrant workers.[26]

Women played a crucial role at almost every level of the popular protests. There was, for example, Elma François of Trinidad, the leader of the Negro Welfare Cultural and Social Association (NWCSA) and a Marxist ideologue. In Cuba, there was an active women's movement, albeit middle class in orientation. As workers, many women were involved in the planning and execution of the strikes. And women were active in other kinds of radical organizations, such as the UNIA. But in the aftermath of the popular protests, most of them saw any gains abrogated. The 1930s proved a turning point in the colonial Caribbean. As a result of the strikes and disturbances, official metropolitan inquiries – the best known of which was the Moyne Commission – investigated the widespread poverty and dreadful living conditions of the working class that had contributed to its desperation.

The Moyne Commission's devastating findings were not published until after World War II, presumably lest they provide a propaganda source for the Axis powers. The commission decried the high number of what anthropologists came to call 'female headed' Afro-Caribbean families (seen in contrast to 'normal' nuclear families) and, among other things, urged that "an organized campaign should be undertaken against the social, moral and economic evils of promiscuity". The comptroller for development and welfare in the West Indies, a post resulting from the Moyne recommendations, echoed these sentiments. One comptroller wrote in 1947 that "the darker side" of the social welfare picture "is the vitally important and historic weakness in the family", pointing to Jamaica's "illegitimacy" rate of about 70 percent, warning that "such statistics show a really serious social disorder". The first Social Welfare Advisor was British sociologist T.S. Simey who lamented the "looseness of family structure" and tied it to prevailing poverty. Lady Molly Huggins, the wife of Jamaica's governor, started the Mass Marriage Movement in 1944. The marriage rate increased slightly, but by 1951 it had reverted to its former level and by 1955 the movement had ended.[27]

The close of the period covered by the essays in this book saw more transitions in the Caribbean. Colonial arrangements almost everywhere were destined to change. The 1930s marked the beginning of the end of British colonialism in the area. In Puerto Rico, dependency on the US and an ambiguous political status was contrasted to the French colonies of Martinique, Guadeloupe and French Guiana becoming *départements d'outre-mer* in 1946 – legally integral parts of France. No matter what the political status of these islands, however, nationalist movements informed everyday life. And such important developments as the expansion of the state sector and the growth of a nascent industrial sector, through such programmes as Operation Bootstrap in Puerto Rico and the 'Industrialization by Invitation' schemes in most of the British islands, the advent of mass tourism, and the continuing and increasing US political and cultural hegemony presented different kinds of challenges for Caribbean people.[28] While their historization must wait for another time and place, these developments, too, were informed by the enduring legacy of emancipation.

The Essays

All but one of the chapters in this book present case studies from the British Caribbean. Rather than an attempt at a representation of the various geographic and linguistic areas of the region, the chapters instead explore themes common to the postemancipation Caribbean as a whole. Such a thematic approach appropriately begins with the slavery period. During slavery, it was the planters' aim to control the labour of their slaves. They did so through various direct and indirect means, although the consequences of these efforts were often not what were intended. As Mary Turner shows, to the Jamaican planters and government agents, Christianity was a volatile and unpredictable entity in the hands of slave religious specialists and dissenting missionaries. The slaves adapted, accommodated and opposed through religious means, merely coping here, and there organizing deadly rebellions with freedom – the definition of which was still to be determined – as the goal. The meeting of the African gods and eighteenth century Christianity produced a radical and inspirational world-view, that not only hastened slavery's end in the British Caribbean through the 1831–32 'Baptist War' in Jamaica, but outlived emancipation and guided its adherents for a century or more afterwards.

If the story of emancipation involves the prior story of Africans and people of African descent as legally defined chattel, and the dramatic social and cultural changes unleashed with the change in that status, what about those who were in many ways on the margin of several statuses? Throughout the experience of plantation slavery there were communities formed by blacks who were able by legal or extralegal means to convert their own status to that of freedmen and women. In a chapter that innovatively uses the wills of free blacks in pre- and postemancipation Trinidad, Carl Campbell seeks to show something about their lifestyles, their personalities and their accomplishments. Both creole blacks and Africans held significant amounts of property, including a few slaves before emancipation. In many of these wills, the testators emancipated their slaves or arranged for the purchase of the freedom of their relatives held as slaves by others.

The transition from slave to wage labour involved not only an economic equation, but social and cultural transformations as well. James Millette shows how, in the immediate aftermath of slavery in Trinidad and Tobago, the ex-slaves were able continuously to leverage planters, obtaining relatively high wages and reasonable working conditions and other concessions. However, these gains were short lived. Trinidad planters were able to make a powerful case for chronic 'shortage' of field labour – a case they continued to make right up to the end of the century and beyond – partly by exaggerating the difficulties involved in managing free and mobile workers, as Donald Wood pointed out in *Trinidad in Transition*. The withdrawal of many women from plantation labour (the subject of the following essay) was also an important part of the argument, which certainly succeeded. In a determined, expensive and far-reaching effort, local planters and imperial power allied to tip the balance in favour of capital, mainly through the importation of Indian indentured workers whose presence tended to drive down wages and lessen the bargaining power of all workers. As Millette neatly shows, the advantages accruing to capital from this process, and the inherent conflict therein, account for the continued battles between capital and labour up to the strikes and protests of the 1930s.

The shift to wage labour also entailed a shift in family strategies for the ex-slaves. During slavery, women worked in the fields alongside men. In slavery's aftermath, when the ex-slaves pursued when and where they could alternatives to paid plantation labour, many women withdrew, or were withdrawn, from the estates. In the first step towards a systematic historization of this phenomenon for the Caribbean, Bridget Brereton focuses on the British Caribbean to argue that various family strategies were at work and can explain this movement. Although planters often exaggerated the extent of female withdrawal from field labour, in order to bolster their case for indentured immigration or other concessions, Brereton shows that this was a reality. Women left the estates to participate in a number of activities, many simultaneously, such as peasant agriculture and the care of their children. The ex-slaves are seen by Brereton as active subjects, self-interested and rational, not just under the sway of European ideologies of gender. These ideologies, however, obviously did have some influence on the ex-slaves, especially the 'respectable', upwardly mobile men, to whom (Brereton speculates) having a 'not-working' wife who could 'sit down' at home became an important index of status.

This kind of 'leisure' – that of a peasant or urban working class 'housewife' not engaged in wage labour – was very different from that consciously enjoyed by the colonial elites. Indeed, 'leisure' was perhaps almost unknown as such to the ex-slaves, even though they participated in activities not considered work, such as religious observances. In his chapter on postemancipation Guyana, Brian L. Moore brings a theoretical perspective into play on the differentiation between leisure and spare time, and shows the difficulties of adopting wholesale theories made to fit other kinds of realities. Moore uses the concept of leisure as a sort of lens with which to analyze the social structure of a dependent plantation colony. He shows how organized leisure was in many ways the preserve of upper class white men in this frontier environment, and how institutions such as sports clubs were organized by them, for them. Moore also shows how the other ethnic and class groups used their spare time to engage in community oriented activities which tended to be determined by the ethnic and cultural community. Creolization meant, in terms of these activities, conformation to the dominant mode.

The culture of ethnicity in Guyana and the rest of the Caribbean was only partially constructed 'on the ground' by subordinate groups such as Afro-Guyanese, Indians, Chinese and Portuguese, but was also informed by a colonial ideology of race that was established by – and tended to justify –

colonial interests. Robert J. Moore shows how ethnic stereotypes were established by colonial powers, and how these stereotypes became part of the cultural landscape, as inescapable as the rising tides lapping at the earthworks that protected the Guyanese plantations from the sea. Ironically, a crucial aspect of their construction was the myth of the 'lazy Negro', Carlyle's indolent lotus-eater happily consuming the tropical bounties which were there for the taking, a myth elaborated and exploited by precisely those elites whose highly organized leisure activities form the subject of the preceding chapter. Those most harshly affected by these stereotypes not only internalized them to a degree, but used the stereotypes created about differing groups to seek the approval of the colonial rulers and their representatives. These colonial stereotypes have been remarkable not only for their transparency by also for their persistence, as Donald Wood had pointed out in his study of postemancipation Trinidad.

But ethnicity is not a monolithic entity, and those deemed to be of a particular ethnic or racial group are often differentiated in significant ways, including along gender lines. M. Noel Menezes nicely shows the burdens on Madeiran Portuguese women in Guyana from the time of their arrival to the 1930s. They were part of a community that was relatively privileged, many of whose members would become prosperous. For the Portuguese in Guyana were not generally burdened with the kind of negative stereotyping described in the preceding chapter. Although not conceptualized by the elite as 'European', their 'whiteness' set them apart from the ex-slaves and the Asian immigrants, and they were encouraged and helped by the elites, partly in order to create a 'buffer' ethnic group. Yet Portuguese women had to bear many hardships. As indentured workers, they worked alongside their men on the plantations. When many families were able to leave the plantations and establish themselves as shop owners, Portuguese women were in many ways the backbone of a family strategy, dividing their time between work and family responsibilities. But, as Menezes shows, Portuguese women in Guyana were not completely defined by their men and their family, as many were active on their own account, as business owners and as teachers, for example.

The connections between livelihood and ethnicity not only defined the 'trading minorities' such as the Portuguese, Syrian/Lebanese or the Chinese, but these connections served to define and divide the masses as well. This was very evident with respect to the colonial arguments regarding the group most appropriate to labour on the sugar plantations, arguments which often repeated many of the stereotypes discussed by Robert Moore. As Glenroy Taitt documents with respect to rice in Trinidad, it became associated with

'Indianness' even though it was first introduced there by blacks, former slaves from the US South who settled there after 1815. Indians introduced wet rice in the 1860s and henceforth became associated in the political and cultural mind with its cultivation. Rice cultivation took on special cultural meanings for Indians. It became tied to a sense of communal solidarity through reciprocity. As such, it interfered with the planters' attempts to secure labour – a familiar theme in the postemancipation era.

The next chapter also deals explicitly with ethnicity. Kevin A. Yelvington looks at the construction of blackness in the context of 1930s Trinidad and the effects of the Italian fascist invasion of Ethiopia. Afro-Trinidadians, as did people of African descent in the US and West Africa, strove to assess the meaning of the war in the context of colonialism and the structure of a world hierarchy of ethnic identities. They also cultivated the symbols associated with a war on the other side of the world in order to address issues of local importance. What seems at first glance to be a straightforward identification along 'racial' lines is anything but that, Yelvington argues. This incident shows ethnicity to be a culturally constructed idiom, with its pillars culled from many unlikely sources.

There is a shift of emphasis in the book's final two chapters, where the authors self-consciously explore alternative histories and historical sources to explain events or explicate mindsets and ideologies. In his chapter, Brinsley Samaroo looks again at the Trinidad labour strikes and disturbances of 1937, employing a novel penned by a liberal French creole 'mixed-race' author and a rare memoir left by the wife of a sympathetic colonial official who was involved in the strikes and mediations with the workers. These alternative sources are not exactly the 'history from below' so familiar and cherished by social and cultural historians, but they are employed with excellent effect and show how there are many sides to history, not just a 'top' and 'bottom', further demonstrating the fallacy of simplistic readings of class.

Bridget Jones' chapter brings us in many ways full circle. Haiti was the first country to achieve independence, in 1804. Jones examines representations of Haiti and the meaning of its bloody war that threw off colonial chains only to be mired in incessant internecine ethnic and class warfare. She does this through an examination of post-*departmentalisation* Martinican drama, created by some of the island's best-known international literary and political figures. Haiti and the giant personages of the revolution come in for varying interpretations. It is through drama that these writers explore depictions of blackness, the weight of history and, ultimately, the meaning and promise of emancipation.

1

The Colonial State, Religion and the Control of Labour: Jamaica 1760–1834

Mary Turner

The orderly extraction of labour requires keeping the workers subordinate. The methods of subordination in late twentieth century industrial democracies have been brilliantly detailed in numerous works by Noam Chomsky. Key to the process is knowledge control: information withheld, 'disinformation' supplied, both by the government's manipulation of the mass media and the media's own simplifications and distortions. The intended end product is a submissive labour force, "diverted with emotionally potent oversimplifications . . . isolated . . . in front of the television screen watching sports, soap operas, or comedies, deprived of organizational structures that permit individuals lacking resources to discover what they think and believe in interaction with others, to formulate their own concerns and programs, and to act to realize them".[1] Only this induced submissiveness, he argues, makes it possible for the system to sustain its current unemployment rates.

It is always difficult, however, for the ruling class to know how workers will interpret the myriad forms of information they are bombarded with. Can there be a revolutionary subtext in soap operas, such as Britain's "Brookside"? Or in "Coronation Street"? The question of understanding and interpretation is particularly acute in relation to religious beliefs. All religion invokes supernatural power: all have heroes and heroines, particular rules and value systems and all encourage and reflect to differing degrees elements of individual autonomy. Religion can both invite escape into the spirit world and fuel determination to change this one.

Religious practices and beliefs are traditionally a terrain the extractors of labour power expect to dominate. This chapter deals with the policies adopted by the colonial state in Jamaica to deal with the slaves' religious beliefs. It shows how the Jamaican planters – in their public capacity in the Jamaica Assembly, on the bench as magistrates, as slave owners, and as attorneys – dealt first with the threat posed by Jamaican traditional religion and, second, with the Christianity imported by dissenting missionaries.

The Jamaican planters, who always comprised a small fraction of the island's population and who commanded few police and limited military resources, considered that the key to slave control was the planters' own unlimited power. To this end they assumed that as owners they had to have total control of their workforce and, as assemblymen, they permitted the colonial state very limited rights to make statute law regulating slave labour.

Religion was not regarded as an assistance to slave control. In the first place it interposed an authority figure with claims to supernatural powers between themselves and the slaves. Christian beliefs in England, moreover, once the Catholic church was destroyed and Protestant sects and churches flourished, had become expressions of intellectual and class conflict rather than instruments of class cohesion, and the English Revolution had affirmed their disruptive potential. At the same time the organizational weakness of the state Anglican church, which scarcely mustered manpower enough to serve the planters' ritual requirements, complemented their reluctance to expose the workers to the uncertain effects of Christian instruction. By the end of the seventeenth century, the heathenness of the Africans was being used to justify their enslavement.

The Jamaica Assembly dealt neatly and consistently with the conversion problem by ruling in its first slave code (1696) that the slave owners were responsible for teaching the slaves Christianity; the question was taken out of the public arena and placed in the hands of estate managers. The statutes that supplemented the slave code were intended to bind the slaves to their villages and sanction their "innocent amusement".[2] The slaves' own religious beliefs and powers, characterized as superstition and witchcraft, were beneath the Assembly's notice until 1760 when they proved instrumental to an islandwide rebellion, precursor of the Haitian Revolution, which aimed to take over the country. Until then, responsibility for the control of slave religion was left to the discretion of the slaves' owners and workplace supervisors, the overseers and bookkeepers.

Access to supernatural powers, however, was crucial to the slaves' survival amid the terrors generated by forced migration and the barbarities of plantation discipline. The beliefs and rituals they formulated, utilizing concepts embedded in the consciousness formed in their African homelands, reordered their universe, regulated their village communities, and empowered their overt and covert resistance to the slave labour system.

The material circumstances which prompted recourse to supernatural power are vividly demonstrated in the oral history of the Saramaka of Suriname.[3] It records how a slave worker, Lanu, and his wife defied a work rule that prohibited cane juice drinking. She offered it and he accepted. Both were punished; she was flogged to death, he was flogged unconscious. When Lanu recovered, his wife's spirit prompted him to run away to the forest. In the wilderness he sought her guidance again, but his invocations were answered instead by Wamba, the spirit of the forest itself, which led him to an Indian settlement where he found refuge.

The bestiality of plantation life forced slave workers to invoke support and guidance from the spirits of dead kinsfolk, spirits representing the forces of nature, and spirits of human destiny personified by a pantheon of gods. The process identified leadership figures in the plantation workforce, some with knowledge and skills learned in Africa, others, like Lanu, self-ordained.

The basic component of slave beliefs (as Lanu's story demonstrates) was in the power of ancestral spirits, an element found throughout sub-Saharan Africa. Ancestor worship allowed each slave worker to rationalize historic reality and acknowledge both their family in Africa and their new kin relationships. The ancestors supplied each individual, household and kin group with a source of spiritual power by nature exclusive to the slave community, marked over time by burial places that served as family shrines. Regulating relations with the spirits of the dead constituted a primary duty acknowledged, as missionaries observed, even by Christian converts, to the end of the slavery period.[4] The ancestral spirits were the slaves' best protection but at the same time were easily offended and punished the living with the worst misfortunes, sickness and death.

The slaves exploited their masters' acute sense of their own mortality and the fact that corpses in a tropical climate required rapid disposal, preferably without cost to the production unit, and claimed the right to bury their own dead. They celebrated the essential worth of their relatives and their workmates, and accorded the dead the respect denied the living.

The development of household worship was paralleled by the establishment in the village community of religious specialists, experts in communication with and regulation of a wider spiritual universe. They included African trained as well as new experts, called into action, like Lanu, by emergencies. It is clear that as long as the slave trade continued knowledge of African spirit hierarchies was continuously refreshed. 'Coromantee' slaves at the end of the eighteenth century, for example, could give an account of the Akan spirit hierarchy. Two broad categories of religious specialists can be dimly discerned on the slave plantations: cult leaders, priests, diviners and mediums who invoked the nature spirits and creatures representing the forces of nature, and the doctors or obeahmen and women who used supernatural power for individual ends.[5]

Cult worship made its mark on local vocabulary throughout the Caribbean: Myal, *vaudou*, Shango, Winti and Confu, and embraced diverse ritual practices which invoked water, forest, air and earth spirits. These spirits communicated the strongest powers known to the slaves and the sacred nature of the shrines established for their worship, in silk cotton trees, and in particular springs (such as Chester Castle in Jamaica), endured generations after slavery was abolished. The possibility that shrines to these gods, village centres of cult worship, the equivalent of *honfours* in contemporary Haiti, existed on some plantations cannot be overlooked.[6] Cult rituals propitiated the spirit world in general, affirmed the community's religious convictions and attempted to resolve specific crises which continued to prompt cult activities in the postemancipation period: drought, epidemics and reverses of political fortune.

Service to the gods was also a motive force for cultural activities and prompted, to the extent circumstances permitted, instrument and artifact making – drums dedicated to the gods, statues, masks and objects to represent them – the establishment of sacred places, rituals, objects, and a panoply of dance and drama. It was the core element in the accretion of folk tales, proverbs, work songs, the popular culture that surfaced at the end of the work week, a vessel for the creative imagination of people living at the margins of subsistence.

The doctors or obeahmen and women were leaders who had learned from the spirits, or were able to devise, in moments of crisis, rituals to deal with problems that could only be resolved by acute judgment heightened by a tendency to prophesy, and with the assistance of specialist knowledge. These inventions reflect the determination, common to all pre-scientific societies, to find definite and practical ways to bridge dangerous gaps in every important pursuit or critical situation. The original revelation takes place in "those passionate experiences which assail [man] in the impasse of his instinctive life and of his practical pursuits".[7] The Jamaicans, like the Saramaka, called these special powers *obias*. *Obias* required the use of sacred objects and substances together with ritual knowledge which was handed down from generation to generation of specialists.[8] They were consulted in relation to the particular fate and destiny of individuals. They interpreted dreams and signs from the spirit world. They conducted rituals to divine the future, to locate enemies and pursue vengeance, using their powers for benevolent or malevolent ends. They were consultants to the whole slave population. No conflict among the slaves, no crisis in slave–master relations relating to punishments, work loads, privileges, or sexual rivalries took place without their knowledge and no action of any significance by individuals or groups took place without their ritual assistance.

Religious specialists as sorcerers could tie up the victim's spirit with string, stab it through the heart when it appeared reflected in a bowl of water, or capture it to put in a miniature coffin. Descriptions of these once-secret rituals recorded by Europeans in the nineteenth century as examples of pagan practices do not convey the power with which they were invested. Churchmen of all denominations, as well as slave owners and managers, were well aware, however, that special signs set near a door, or on a threshold, and even glances from an obeahman or woman, promised death. The deaths so attributed demonstrated the deep-rooted convictions among the slaves that gave these practices their power. Oaths sanctioned by the obeah were, consequently, authoritative instruments which constituted either a form of trial that threatened the guilty with death, or promised commitment to the death in rebellion.

Doctors or obeahs also commanded curative techniques. Central to African medicine was the conviction, typical of twentieth century traditional medicine cultures, that the mystery of ill health reflected the operation of supernatural power, most commonly represented among slave workers as the displeasure of ancestral spirits, or the ill will of relatives, or neighbours. All forms of treatment involved supernatural power invested in special food, objects, charms, rituals such as conjuring objects from the victim's body, as well as in herbal and medicinal remedies, all methods which continue to be used in the twentieth century Caribbean. The equipment associated with Jamaican obeahs, commonly regarded simply as sorcerers, included medicinal ingredients still used in traditional African medicine: herbs, leaves, roots, fruits, barks and grasses together with minerals, dead insects, bones, feathers, powdered shells, eggs and smoke from different objects.

Slave religious beliefs peopled the universe with spirits whose powers reflected the contradictory forces that determined mortal fate. This universe pertained specifically to the slave community; it was the spiritual locale of slave worker power, a force to which the slave population had sole access. The cults and the religious experts built a stockade of beliefs and practices whose *obiahs*, like the ark of the covenant, symbolized the spiritual power particular to the slave population.

Saramaka tradition records the story of Ayako who saw his infant nephew murdered by the overseer. He feared to witness the final destruction of his family and said to himself, " 'Now, when I was in Africa, I wasn't a nobody. I will make a special effort, and see if since I left there what [power] I had has been spoiled.' Then he prepared himself [ritually] until he was completely set. And he escaped. He ran off with his sister and her baby daughter."[9] Religious beliefs and practices sustained the slave workers' belief that they were not 'nobodies', that they could eventually escape white oppression.

The slaves' workplace supervisors, overseers and bookkeepers, as well as some resident planters, acknowledged some aspects of these developments and incorporated them as customary features of plantation life. The slaves were permitted to conduct their own funerals (which became increasingly elaborate) and have their own burial grounds; to indulge as 'innocent amusement' in the drumming and dancing that accompanied cult activities; to wear and hang about their houses charms to protect against evil – a practice that resembled those of rural England and Scotland. The slaves' medical experts even emerged publicly in the plantation hospitals where the cures they effected for sores, ulcers and even yaws (an extremely contagious, long-lasting and disfiguring tropical disease), astonished the official doctors.[10] On occasions the moral authority exercised by religious specialists in trial by oath taking was used to investigate thefts of plantation property. The officiating slave, redesignated "He who acts the Priest", assembled the slaves at the burial ground and opened a grave. He took a little earth and put it in every person's mouth. "They [the slaves] tell, that if any has been guilty, their Belly swells and occasions their Death." One boy's belly did swell and he confessed the theft as he lay dying, a fact the visiting observer could conveniently dismiss ("a Thousand Accidents might have occasioned it"). Resident planters, however, respected these techniques.[11]

To afford the slaves certain customary rights and allow their specialists a degree of credibility was virtually the only control technique available to the slave managers, who were vastly outnumbered by the workforce they commanded, hedged in by Maroon bands and apprehensive that the medicine which cured in the estate hospital might kill in the great house.

The political potential of the slaves' religion, however, was only brought home to them by the uprising of 1760 which, like the subsequent revolution in Ste Domingue, demonstrated that the slaves' religion could become a force in itself. Tacky's Rebellion, or the 'Coromantee War', still awaits in-depth analysis; the accounts to hand largely rely on the planter-historians Edward Long and Bryan Edwards. The outline, however, is clear: at a time when the planters had become accustomed to slave subordination and the garrison had been depleted by the 1756–63 war, rebellion erupted at Easter 1760 in the eastern parish of St Mary. Efforts to contain it by making a military cordon sanitaire across the island failed and by May 1760 the western parishes of St Elizabeth, St James and Clarendon were involved. Kingston and Spanish Town were not entirely trouble-free and the numbers of rebels have been guesstimated at 30,000 in a population of 150,000. It was not until October 1761 that the governor announced the total suppression of the rebellion, and the key military victory in which the rebel leader was killed was achieved only by the timely intervention on the planters' side of the Maroons.

The planters identified Tacky's revolt with their favourite (to that date) Coromantee slaves, imported from what is now Ghana, in much the same way that their heirs and successors identified the 1831 rebellion with the Baptist missionaries – probably with about as much justification. It was essential for the planters to convince themselves that *one* sole identifiable element in the slave population was their enemy. Edward Long perfectly reflected this need when he claimed that the rebellion involved virtually all the Coromantee slaves and *very few others*, although the leader himself was Jamaican. Tacky, however, as political and military leader, surrounded himself with obeahs as advisers and organizers – fulfilling the role customary among the Saramakas. One of them was captured in the first phase of fighting and Long identified him as an old Coromantee and claimed that his death by hanging deterred many disciples from joining their countrymen.[12]

The rebellion, nevertheless, continued and Edwards, writing a generation later, revealed that the barely victorious Jamaican planters, shaken by near defeat at the hands of an inferior race, found it necessary to assert their intellectual and scientific superiority to the rebels' captured obeahs. A magic lantern show was provided and then some 'experiments' – shock torture – were made with electrical machines. One prisoner, after "some very severe shocks" was driven to comment "this master's Obi exceeded his own". His fellows, however, refused to acknowledge any such thing, and one obeahman about to be hanged told his executioner: "It was not in the power of white people to kill him." His statement encapsulated the political significance of the slave workers' religious beliefs.[13]

The rebellion forced the planters to publicly recognize the threat slave religion posed; the Assembly identified obeah as a felony, and made its practitioners punishable by death or transportation. The pouches and huts containing the ingredients which incorporated their powers were burnt. The extent to which this law was applied, however, has yet to be investigated. Certainly in the 1820s such arrests were few and far between and made usually in response to slave informants. Their new-found respect was also marked by planter historians who began to record information about the slaves' 'tutelary saints' and the Akan spirit hierarchy.

At a practical level the rebellion prompted slave owners throughout the West Indies to reconsider their management methods. The process of 'amelioration' traced in J.R. Ward's *British West Indian Slavery, 1750–1834*, was precipitated, arguably, by the 1760 rebellion. It is also in the aftermath of the rebellion that evidence of outright labour bargaining involving slave workers, workplace managers and attorneys on Jamaican sugar estates can be found.[14]

The planters did not, however, attempt in any systematic way to substitute Christian beliefs for the slaves' religion. They were not great churchgoers: the Anglican church was poorly staffed by clergy who were themselves slave owners and, like their English counterparts, ignored their 'home heathen'. The ruling class had neither the will nor the means to increase their control of the workforce by incorporating it in their own religious ideology. Only a few individual planters made a gesture toward this by employing Anglican clergy for mass baptisms which replaced African with Christian names. Slave conversion through Christian instruction was pioneered by outsiders: first by an absentee planter family which from the 1730s employed Moravian missionaries to work on their estate, and subsequently in the 1780s by black American refugees from the independence war who got permission from the magistrates to open a Black Baptist church in Kingston.

The most important and sustained impetus for slave conversion, however, derived from the British antislavery campaign launched in 1784. The attack was formulated in religious terms: slavery was condemned as a sin and the attack on the institution was combined with a demand for the slaves' spiritual instruction. The dissenting churches, already inspired by the religious revival to visions of worldwide conquests for Christianity, took up this challenge. The first representatives of this missionary movement to arrive in Jamaica were the Wesleyan Methodists who opened a chapel in 1790 on Kingston's main square.

From the outset, therefore, slave instruction in Christianity was associated with churches rooted in the tradition of dissent and associated with black freedmen and the antislavery cause. The missionary societies carefully differentiated themselves from the political attack on slavery and declared their position on the issue as neutral. All their recruits were explicitly directed to avoid all civil and political questions and address themselves wholly to saving souls.[15] Nevertheless, missions were an intervention, and they introduced into Jamaican society personnel supported by British funds for purposes considered desirable by the planters' sworn enemies.

The planters, however, were urged by their own parliamentary agent in London and the powerful lobby of West India Planters and Merchants to tolerate the intervention so as to present a humanitarian image in Britain and counter abolitionist propaganda. The Jamaican Assembly went so far as to devise new slave codes and even made nominal provisions for the clergy to baptize and catechize slaves each Sunday. On this basis the Wesleyan mission bridgehead in Kingston was established and the Black Baptists opened a second church.[16]

This politic tolerance gave way to outright hostility in times of political stress: the Maroon uprising in 1796, the threat of French invasion in 1802, and the abolition of the slave trade in 1807 all jeopardized the efforts to convert the slaves and prompted attempts to make instruction by dissenters illegal.

The Assembly found, however, that its constitutional rights did not include the right to choose religious intolerance: the imperial government disallowed the legislation. The ruling was hotly contested and planters as magistrates refused to license preachers. This persecution destroyed the Black Baptist Kingston churches which lacked the resources to wait out the legal impasse, as the Wesleyan missionaries proved able to do. Dissenting Christianity was clearly seen as undermining rather than strengthening control of labour.

In the postwar period, however, the Assembly was forced to rethink its position. Baptist missionaries, invited originally by the Black Baptist Kingston churches, joined the Wesleyans and took over estate based Black Baptist congregations which had survived the legal onslaught. Faced by the prospect of mission expansion, but tied by the principle of religious toleration, the Assembly attempted to contain mission influence by funding Anglican instruction and limiting mission church attendance and participation. The 1816 Jamaica Slave Code made night meetings illegal and prohibited slave converts from undertaking the work of preaching and teaching which was customary for lay persons in dissenting churches.

The missionaries themselves were left without legal rights; their credentials were reviewed by the magistrates in each parish where they worked to decide whether or not they were qualified for a license to preach. The missionaries were placed on perpetual probation to planters acting as magistrates. The

Assembly aimed to make the mission churches conform to ruling class requirements.

The interstices for mission work were in fact provided by planter patrons who, with the exception of a few religious sympathizers, were the '*grand blancs*', the substantial Jamaican squirearchy who saw the need to follow the imperial government's lead on religious toleration and who perceived the potential utility of Christian morality as an element in labour control. Their position was defined by Richard Barrett, custos (chief magistrate) of St James, speaker of the Assembly, and proprietor of the *Jamaica Journal and Kingston Chronicle*, the one liberal newspaper in the island. "I have a bad set of people," he told a Presbyterian missionary. "They steal enormously, run away, get drunk, fight . . . the women take no care of their children. Now, if you can bring them under fear of God, or a judgement to come, or something of that sort, you may be doing both them and me a service."[17]

When the slaves were emancipated there were sixteen Wesleyan and fourteen Baptist stations, many urban based, throughout the island. Eight Moravian stations mostly clustered in the southwest and five Presbyterian were strung along the North Coast. In all, there were forty-seven missionaries, usually assisted by their wives.

The pattern of mission expansion, however, was to a large extent determined by the support of the free coloured and black population. They sold the missionaries land for chapel building, extended interest-free credit and, most importantly, provided them with houses to preach in as well as land for building when they reached out into the rural slave population centres. Rural outstations on the very borders of planter dominated territory owed their existence to free coloured and black mission supporters. This was all the more important since licenses did not entitle missionaries to work on the estates. Estate based missions were, characteristically, established by absentees. Estate visits were rarely authorized by resident planters and were often obstructed by overseers. Free coloured and black church members also provided congregational infrastructure as lay preachers, deacons and advisers. Often they held churches together when death or sickness interrupted regular services. Their support was also politically significant, particularly in the 1820s when they launched a campaign for civil rights and a newspaper, edited by Edward Jordon, pillar of the Wesleyan Kingston church, to support it.

Key to the missions' success, however, was the fact that the slaves were customarily free to leave the estates on Sundays to go to cultivate their provision grounds, or to go to market. While the tradition of Sunday marketing limited the extent of church attendance it facilitated the activity and enabled slaves, like free converts, to contribute to their churches. The tradition of Sunday marketing hampered efforts to keep the slaves away from the missions. By 1834, some 10 percent of the slave population were accredited mission church members.[18]

Attendance at the mission churches gave the slaves access to the supernatural powers of the whites. The needs that generated the slaves' traditional religion were served in part by the mission churches which also provided a new universal framework for supernatural powers which encompassed slave and free, black and white. The slaves' response to mission teaching showed them moving out from the stockade of powers specific to the slave community to either embrace outright a new religion, or to syncretize the traditional and the Christian.

This movement reflected in part the fact that by the 1820s the majority of the slave population was Jamaican born. Africa was the land of their ancestors whose spirits remained powerful; but knowledge of the white man's gods was desirable, even necessary in order to regulate the present and command the future. Staking their claim to new supernatural powers by attending the mission churches, they simultaneously claimed new customary rights within the slave system: the right to public worship, the right to choose Christian salvation, to define themselves as people with religious convictions.

By voting with their feet to attend the mission churches the slaves in effect chose to make the missionaries their leaders, they chose to acknowledge their authority. Their actions collectively established a new network of public figures who necessarily modified the customary authority structure. The mission churches themselves, built with the assistance of slave members' contributions, were monuments to the slaves' collective efforts. Though the chapels owed much to free coloured capital and subscriptions from England, the slaves' contribution allowed them to see the chapel as their own and neighbouring chapels as the work of other slaves. The chapels were the first publicly recognized monument to the slaves' organized opinion.

The ideology the missionaries taught embodied contradictory elements. The good Christian was a good servant: the path to salvation was tightly hedged by duty and obedience. Ideally, the missionaries intended to promote, in the words of one Wesleyan, the "due discharge of the duties of the lower classes and the total destruction of every principle of discontent and insubordination".[19] In other words, to repeat the process that had taken place in England and uplift the moral consciousness of the labouring classes without disturbing the existing power structure.

On the other hand, the fact that the missionaries were there to teach the slaves, the fact that they assumed the slaves capable of choosing Christian roles and acting like free citizens in the mission churches, proclaimed the slaves as "men and brothers". This element in mission teaching was expressed in numerous ways: by schools and classes which affirmed the slaves' intellectual capacities and fed an appetite which astonished the missionaries themselves; by membership tickets which connected them with their counterparts in England; by contributing themselves to missions for Africa, termed "throwing up for Guinea country"; and, most importantly, by the role played by trusted converts in the church hierarchy – as chapel servants, deacons and stewards and as 'leaders' who helped the missionaries conduct and supervise membership classes. The leaders were strictly enjoined to refrain from teaching and preaching, as the law required, but their activities were only partially supervised by the missionaries themselves.

The slave leaders secured the missions' success. Able and pious black class leaders, in the missionaries' own estimation, won more converts in twelve months than they themselves could in three years. "If a missionary preach and pray like an angel the negroes . . . think he has learnt his trade better than some of the church ministers. But . . . hearing other blacks spread the love of God with so much life, and pray with so much liberty and power, they are overcome at once and ignorance and disbelief soon give way."[20] Class leaders also carried the gospel outside the churches into the estates closed to the missions. They worked to a large extent independently and enjoyed great authority. They learned consequently the limitations of freedom within the mission churches: they spoke up freely in leaders' meetings, but could never aspire, as their English equivalents might, to be in charge of the church themselves. The political consequences of the limitations will be discussed below. In general, however, the slaves found in the mission churches, and in relations with the missionaries themselves, as an Anglican clergyman remarked, "the temporary Elements of Liberty and Independence".[21]

The factor that brought into play all the elements in Christian teaching and the mission churches which contradicted the values of slave society, critiqued plantation culture, and condemned its social structure, was the opposition it excited from slave owners and slave managers alike. In 1823 the antislavery movement began its attack on the institution of slavery. It confronted the churchgoing public with the question "Can a Christian condone slavery?" and proposed in Parliament that slavery was "repugnant to the principles of the British Constitution and Christian Religion" and ought to be abolished. Popular support, which included the Wesleyan and Baptist churches, was substantial and the imperial government, in cooperation with the Committee of West Indian Planters and Merchants, concocted a reform package for the slave colonies, expressly intended to prepare the slaves for free legal status. The reforms gave central importance to the religious instruction of slaves; this was defined as an "indispensable necessity . . . the foundation of every beneficial change in [the slaves'] character and future condition".

The Jamaica Assembly treated the imperial government's demands as a constitutional challenge to its authority and formulated its own adjustments to the slave code. These included, significantly, new restrictions on mission work. Mistrust of missions and missionaries was heightened and confirmed by the discovery, in December 1823, of two slave conspiracies, the first for many years – one on the estate where the 1760 rebellion started. The following July there was a small-scale rebellion. One group of alleged conspirators was found "hurrahing for Wilberforce" and the rebels insisted the imperial government had freed them. One declared at the place of execution "the war has only begun".

The popular press perceived the island was "on the brink of a volcano"; the missionaries were categorized as wolves in sheep's clothing and the imperial government was accused of intimidating colonial governments into prostrating themselves at the feet of every agitator who called himself a missionary. Knowledge of the 1823 Demerara slave rebellion, allegedly instigated by missionary John Smith, whose case had become a cause celebre in England, added venom to these attacks.[22] This militant antisectarianism found support among the magistrates and some of the missions' most stalwart patrons were, inevitably, influenced by the turn of events. As a result, missionaries who arrived in the island in 1824 were attacked piecemeal by magistrates who refused to license premises for preaching purposes.

The new wave of Wesleyan and Baptist missionaries, like their predecessors, remained committed by their Societies to neutrality on the slavery issue; but they were recruited from churches which supported abolition. They tended to regard the planters as natural enemies and reacted to obstruction not as men placating their superiors, but as men claiming their rights. One, denied a preaching license, appealed straight to the attorney general and another served ten days in jail rather than pay a fine for preaching in an unlicensed house.

The imperial government assisted their struggle by disallowing the revised Jamaican slave code primarily on account of the clauses "for restraining religious liberty". The Wesleyan mission, emboldened by this support, brought a test case based on the imprisonment of two missionaries at St Ann's Bay for alleged illegal preaching. As a result, the attorney general ruled against the magistrates and for the first time provided the missionaries with a legal framework by finding that the 1711 Toleration Act, which entitled preachers to a license valid throughout the island, was in force.

The conflict between magistrates and missionaries was symptomatic of the conflict between slave converts and workplace supervisors. Slave converts were the readiest sacrifice to the antisectarianism of their managers and the least publicized. Punishment and obstruction were no doubt episodic, consistent with periods of political tension and dependent on individual passions. But efforts were made to keep them from chapel. Free time was cut down; sometimes alternative instruction by an Anglican curate was provided; more often, direct orders were given and punishment inflicted. Slaves who took their Christian duties seriously cut themselves off from the customary compensations of plantation life and necessarily exuded a certain independence the managers feared. The slave activists, however, who exerted themselves to make converts and identified with the mission churches excited peculiar animosity and it is clear that under such pressures the slaves made far greater sacrifices for conscience sake than were ever required of the missionaries. Two such cases were brought to light by the missionaries. In one, whites, determined to punish slaves for preaching and teaching, disrupted an informal Easter prayer meeting in the Savannah-la-Mar Baptist chapel. As a result, a respectable slave tradesman and deacon in the Baptist church was put on trial and sentenced to imprisonment and flogging (although the law specified one or the other) by a magistrate clearly determined to intimidate church members and prevent meetings in the absence of the missionary.[23] The other involved an attempt to intimidate an entire estate workforce whose headman, Henry Williams, was the first slave leader appointed in the St Ann Wesleyan mission. The estate attorney and magistrate, as part of the St Ann campaign against sectarians, told Williams he must give up his religious work or be sent to the workhouse, and told all the slaves not to attend the Wesleyan chapel. Henry Williams' sister, who had been housekeeper to the late proprietor and enjoyed a pension of £10 per year, greeted the order with a "great sigh". The attorney had her flogged and the following Sunday ordered Williams to the Anglican church. When questioned as to the whereabouts of other slaves he said: "The people had said Sunday was theirs, and that some had gone to chapel and some in other directions." Next day he was sent to the workhouse where he was flogged within an inch of his life and escaped Christian martyrdom only because his case was publicized by the missionary in the free coloured newspaper, the *Watchman and Jamaica Free Press*. His sister in the meantime was taken to the rectory and threatened in the presence of two militia men that, if she did not attend the Anglican church, she would be turned off the property. Recently flogged and with a brother in the workhouse, she told the missionary "I am a poor woman and Mr. Betty is a great fish and might swallow me up, but I will not leave my religion."[24]

The slaves claimed for themselves the religious rights enjoyed by other categories of His Majesty's subjects and their efforts were seconded by the missionaries, the free coloured press and the imperial government, which dismissed the offending magistrates in these cases together with the governor who supported them.

The colonial state, denied the totalitarian right to simply prohibit missionary activity, was unable to control its impact on the slave population. The mission churches, despite the best efforts of the missionaries to teach and train, to test and discipline their members, were equally unsuccessful. Christianity gave no credence to the ancestors; provided no protection save prayer against witchcraft; dispensed no medicine; most importantly, perhaps, afforded no equality to the leaders they trained.

The mission churches, consequently, generated syncretic sects under their own leaders, known to contemporaries as Native Methodists, Native Baptists and Spirit Christians. The missionaries condemned these versions of Christianity and called their leaders "Christianized Obeahs"; but many such leaders were mission members and included some of their own confidential class leaders who leapt over the limitations imposed by law and mission church regulations to claim a dual role. The new sect leaders in part competed with the obeahs, introducing new ideas, new skills and new practices. The slaves valued literacy and ability to read the Bible became for some the mark of a true prophet. At the same time their connection with the mission churches enhanced their status and made them part of an islandwide organization. The new sects did not replace traditional religion; obeahs remained into this century significant religious figures. But they introduced a new element into popular religion in much the same way as the missionaries introduced a new element of Christianity.

The slaves' political consciousness came to fruition in the independent sects – a pattern observed in twentieth century Africa. It was sect leaders, some of whom, like the rebel leader Sam Sharpe himself who organized the 1831 rebellion for free status and wage work, were also leaders in the mission churches. In contrast to the rebel leaders in 1760, they characteristically bound their followers with biblical, not obeah oaths.

The rebels invested the missionaries, however, with a special status: they were perceived as direct conduits to the powers in England who promised freedom. There was a very interesting moment on the brink of the 1831 rebellion. The slaves crowded to church for the Christmas services and the missionaries realized not only that they were about to rebel, but expected active support. It is as if they envisioned the missionaries surrounding their leader, Sam Sharpe, as advisers and recruiters, affording him the protection of the spirit world in the way the obeahs who surrounded Tacky had done. When the missionaries in fact preached against rebellion, the slaves were not only disappointed but angry that their religious leaders were failing to fulfil the role expected of them.

The 1831 like the 1760 rebellion demonstrated the power of religious convictions to fuel political action, and the weakness of state control of workforce ideology. Military defeat of the rebels and execution of its leaders were complemented, as in 1760, by an effort to extirpate the religious ideologues the planters perceived as most influential: the Wesleyans and Baptists. The obeahs captured with Tacky in 1760 were an elusive element whose activities could only be declared illegal; the missionaries and their missions were by contrast open targets and planters, magistrates and slave supervisors united in lynch mobs and raiding parties to destroy the chapels and prevent services being held. As a result the missionaries became what the planters had always feared they were, agents both of Christ and Wilberforce. They sent representatives to England who became outstanding propagandists for abolition which they saw as necessary to secure their own future as well as the slaves'.

The colonial state throughout the period under review extended, de facto, a margin of toleration for slave religion and for slave religious instruction. De facto toleration of the slaves' traditional religion reflected the racist contempt articulated by the slave owners, the slave supervisors' grudging respect for and fear of heathen occult practices, combined with a pragmatic sense that elements in slave village life were best left ignored. The power of slave religion revealed by the 1760 rebellion made obeah a felony, but at the same time it confirmed the slave supervisors' sense that heathen practices were best left alone.

The de facto toleration for the missionaries, however, depended from the first on the imperial government's power, exercised indirectly and directly, over the colonial Assembly and magistracy. The struggle over the religious toleration issue reveals a sharp difference in Jamaica between the slave supervisors (the *petit blancs*) with immediate responsibilities for worker discipline and the more substantial planter-magistrate assemblymen (the *grand blancs*). The *petit blancs*, committed by their occupation to maintaining the black–white divide on minimal salaries, feared the missionaries' impact both on slave-worker discipline and on white authority.

From the point of view of the slave workers it is clear that Jamaican traditional religion, the dissenting churches and the sects all fulfilled broadly the same functions. Religious beliefs and practices varied, but in political terms they all created an autonomous area, outside the workplace and the village, under leaders to some degree separate from the existing class structure who claimed access to supernatural power. And all provided an organizational structure which permitted "individuals lacking resources to discover what they thought and believed in interaction with others, to formulate their own concerns and programs, and act to realize them".[25]

2

Black Testators: Fragments of the Lives of Free Africans and Free Creole Blacks in Trinidad 1813–1877

Carl Campbell

This study concerns a little known but important component of the society of nineteenth century Trinidad: free Africans and free creole blacks. It is based on notarial documents, namely wills, which so far have not been used in any systematic manner.[1] These wills executed by blacks are documents of the highest importance. They are capable of bringing the modern researcher into close contact with the free black people of the colony. The free blacks, whether Africans or Creoles, excited little interest among the planters, colonial officials or British government, who have together generated most of the documents which have been preserved in archives. If free blacks are mentioned at all by these elites, it is only in the vaguest terms, and at best intermittently. The few travellers' accounts that exist hardly ever mention the free blacks. Therefore the researcher who attempts to examine this segment of the population on the basis of the standard range of information is bound to be frustrated.

Taken singly each will tells us a little about the individual involved. But when examined in quantity, wills can shed much light on the social and economic history of a colony.[2] In this study the wills of fifty-two testators are examined; of these thirty-five were Africans, and seventeen were black Creoles. I took notice of all the black testators who made wills between 1813 and 1877; but it cannot be said that this number (fifty-two) represents an exhaustive count of all the blacks who made wills during the period. Unfortunately, a few volumes of the Protocol of Wills were missing or misplaced at the time the research was done (August–September 1975); and some wills, for one reason or another, were bound up with the vast number of Protocol of Deeds, some of which were destroyed, or misplaced.[3]

No researcher has yet made a systematic study of the wills and deeds of Trinidad, and there are two good reasons: their inaccessibility and their disarray. The research on which this study is based, although done nearly twenty-five years ago, is still a pioneering effort. (A much larger pioneering effort, with the same limitations, was accomplished in respect to free coloured [mixed-race] testators.)[4] Although I was not able to quantify all the wills or deeds, there are some interesting observations which can be made about the lives of free Africans and free black Creoles without quantitative exactness. Nor is it intended to suggest that all the free blacks considered here formed a single community; they were obviously not all living at the same time. But they certainly represent experiences which several other persons of similar origins probably had in the same generations. Nearly half of them (twenty-four) were alive at some point during the long governorship of Ralph Woodford (1813–28). The rest lived through parts of the postemancipation era (see Appendix 2.1).

The peculiar qualities of a will are that it is personal, intimate, and expressive very often of an honesty which derives from the testator's sense of the inevitability or closeness of death and divine judgment. The will sometimes lays bare the soul of the testator, some hidden hurt, some secret love. A degree of accuracy is imparted to the inventory of property and the identification of relatives by the intervention of a lawyer, solicitor or trusted friend. This combination of circumstances imparts to the will a level of veracity far above several other types of personal documents.

There arises, however, a question: How far might extra-personal factors influence the making of these wills? For one thing they were all dictated by the testator to someone else, and eventually written by some coloured or white person who had some training in these matters. There is only one will that is written in a form and at a level of language which suggests convincingly that it was written down by someone whose hold over the English language was rather tenuous (Will of Nancy Rivers alias Bruce). Then again, most of the wills were probably dictated in French Creole, which possibly was rendered first into French and then translated into English by the official translators attached to the courts and the government. Perhaps something, some intention, or some nuance, was lost in the passage of thoughts from the illiterate testators to the final product.

What is more certain is that the form of the will and the structure of its parts were partly determined by custom and the professional habits of the drafters who were not the testators. Wills in the early nineteenth century tended, for example, to be longer than wills in the postemancipation period. Moreover, wills down to the 1840s almost invariably made a small financial donation to the Roman Catholic church in cases where the testators were Christians; after this period donations were rare. One suspects that in these respects not only the temper of the times, but the professional predilections of the drafters of the wills were of some importance. Obviously the extent to which the black testator dominated the making of his or her will depended on a number of variable factors: literacy or illiteracy, senility or lack of senility, sickness or good health, the presence of friendly or unfriendly relatives. In most cases death followed fairly closely upon the making of these wills.

There are no reliable figures for Trinidad's free black population. The question however arises why there should be more African than creole black testators in the postemancipation group. It might be that after emancipation some black Creoles making wills stopped identifying themselves by colour, while the ethnic feelings of the Africans (who were not postemancipation immigrants) were still powerful enough to make them declare their origins. Some of these Africans were old men and women by then, and had presumably a strong sense of achievement of property ownership. Of course the explanation might be that these African testators, like many African slaves before Emancipation, lived in or near Port of Spain and hence had access to facilities for making wills.

The following are two tables of the distribution of property between free African and free creole black testators. The breakdown into two lists has been adopted to follow the previous suggestion that there might be at least two sets of free blacks under examination: a pre-emancipation set and a postemancipation group.

These tables do not take into account other types of property such as cash and movables, such as furniture and clothes. The most significant examples of property left out of these tables involved 10,000 francs claimed by a free black woman from Martinique, and schooners partly owned by two African men. Two things stand out clearly from the tables: the testators had very few slaves among them, with the Africans from the 1813–32 group having more

TABLE 2.1 DISTRIBUTION OF PROPERTY IN THE 1813–1832 GROUP

Land (quarrées) in countryside	Houses in Port of Spain	Lots in Port of Spain	Slaves
Africans 2.5+	4 ++	4.5	22
(11) (1 unit)	3 units)		(8 units)
Black 47.5+++ Creoles	10.5	–	16
(14) (3 units)	(10 units)		(6 units)

1 quarrée = 3.2 acres
'Units' means number of persons who owned the particular asset.
'Lots' means land without a house.
'Houses' mean house standing on a lot (i.e., house plus lot).
+ = Plus a small estate in Santa Cruz and an estate in Diego Martin.
++ = Plus a shop.
+++ = Plus a 'piece of land', also a coffee estate.

TABLE 2.2 DISTRIBUTION OF PROPERTY IN THE 1836–1877 GROUP

Land (quarrées) in countryside	Houses in Port of Spain	Lots in Port of Spain	Slaves
Africans 34.5+	13 ++	12 +++	3
(24) (12 units)	(10 units)	(9 units)	(2 units)
Black 12 Creoles	2	–	2
(3) (2 units)	(2 units)		(1 unit)

1 quarrée = 3.2 acres
'Units' means numbers of persons who owned the particular asset.
'Lots' means land without a house.
'Houses' means house standing on a lot (i.e., house plus lot).
+ = Plus three lots of land. Also a 'half' property, also 'land'.
++ = Including one house in San Fernando.
+++ = Including one lot in Arima.

than the black Creoles; and the creole blacks from the 1813–32 group had larger pieces of land in the countryside than the Africans. Of course no sensible monetary value can now be put on the property of the testators.

The significant observation is the amount of landed property held by the fifty-two African and black Creole testators before and after emancipation: approximately 50 quarrées before emancipation and 44 quarrées after emancipation, excluding the unspecified acreage involved in the 'small estates'. Even leaving aside the houses in towns, chiefly Port of Spain, and the slaves, the property of the testators is not insignificant in the social history of the colony. The largest landed units were the 25 quarrées (cultivated land) in Santa Cruz owned in 1818 by Juan Francisco Farfan, a creole black who also held 13 quarrées of uncultivated land; and the 12.5 quarrées in Santa Cruz which Charles Polasse (probably a Mandingo) possessed in 1851. His wife had another 12.5 quarrées, so that the size of the estate was really 25 quarrées. The smaller units of land tend to be between one and 2.5 quarrées (between 3.2 and 7 acres, approximately). None of the landholdings was in sugar cane, but in coffee, cocoa and provisions, the typical crops of the small farmers of the colony. A considerable amount of the land, consistent with the general pattern in the island, seemed to have been uncultivated; and there is no way to tell the quality of the land. The testators, in view of the small number of slaves they possessed, could not have been cultivating their lands adequately, assuming that they could probably not pay for wage labour. From what is already known of the economic development of the colony, every racial group – blacks, coloureds, whites – had more land than each could cultivate in the pre-emancipation period and shortly after emancipation.[5]

The houses in Port of Spain before and after emancipation must be regarded as a significant source of income for their black owners. The rapid growth of Port of Spain in the early nineteenth century was largely due to the influx of black and coloured people, many from other islands.[6] Blacks and coloureds on the most casual examination of the Protocol of Deeds owned most of the houses in the town. But there is the question of houses as a source of income: the barrack pattern of housing which was so marked in the later nineteenth century was laid down earlier on. A lot of land or a half lot in Port of Spain could have more than one house on it, a 'Negro yard', and outbuildings; and a house could have many rooms each of which could be rented to different persons, and many of them were. In the disposition of houses in Port of Spain the black testators sometimes arranged matters so that different persons had the use of different parts of the house, just as the Spanish-speaking Creoles of Maracas and Santa Cruz sometimes disposed separately of some of their cocoa trees from the land on which they were planted. A wooden house, susceptible to fire, might from its many rooms be as valuable as a stone house (a 'mason house') which was something to be proud of.

The information on the slaves of the black testators is not as full as is desirable. However it seems that most of them were non-agricultural, falling in the category either of female servants or young children. Black slave owners, no less than coloured or white, formed sexual relationships with some of their female slaves. Usually, these liaisons resulted in the manumission of the women. For example, Juan Francisco Farfan gave Gregoria Marin, one of his female slaves and obviously his lover, her freedom and 4.3 quarrées of uncultivated land. Another of his slaves, Louis Marin, possibly the son of Gregoria (but not Juan's son), got his freedom. John Charles, a creole black man, was having an affair in 1820 with Sally Zabeth, his black slave woman, to whom he gave freedom and his house, in case of the death of his illegitimate son then in Grenada. Most interesting of all was the arrangement made by Azor Brisson, an African. He was a boatman owning his own schooner and having a share in another boat. His black slave lover, Luce (one of the schooners was called *Lucy*), was actually the property of another person (a minor), from whom she was hired. She had five children with him, all of whom were slaves, since the status of the mother determined the status of the children. With such a high proportion of his family in slavery and money owing to him for wages and freight, it was no wonder that Azor could only aspire to free Luce and their eldest son.

Apart from the granting of freedom to lovers and children, the manumission of other categories of slaves was not uncommon. In fact sixteen of the forty-seven slaves held by the black testators got their freedom. But there were occasionally obstructing conditions. For example, Adelaide Bardinette, an African woman resident in Port of Spain, stipulated that one of her slaves, a child, was to be freed twelve years after her death. John Charles, in freeing Sally Zabeth, required her to serve his son, presumably as a non-paid servant. But if there were occasionally nagging conditions attached to manumissions, there was also the willingness in some cases to set up the freed slave (not necessarily a relative) with a little money, or a little piece of land or a wooden house. And this must have been an important start in a new life for children as well as adults.

When the black testators were not freeing their own slaves, they were arranging for the purchase of the freedom of some relatives held in slavery by other persons. The wills remind us of the close social relations between people who were placed into different legal categories of slaves and free persons. The free African or creole black of 1820 was perhaps the slave of 1810, and probably had relatives or friends still enslaved. The case of Jean Baptist Morin, a black Creole man from St Ann, is illustrative. He had received land in 1796 in St. Ann from Chacon, the last Spanish governor. By 1810, he had 7.5 quarrées in his possession. The land was planted in coffee and cocoa, though Jean did not describe himself as a planter. He seemed proud however to describe one of his sons, Pierre Philip, as a planter of Naparima. What had happened was that Jean Baptiste Morin had mated with a slave woman and had two sons. One was said to be a planter (Pierre Philip), possibly with slaves of his own; and the other was a slave. The brothers inherited their father's land in equal shares, thus giving the slave brother property from which arrangements could be made to purchase his freedom. But the point is that in 1818 Jean's family was split into sections with a different legal status: Jean himself was free; his children's mother was a slave; one son was free; the other was a slave.

Freedom was the highest boon that could be afforded to a slave by someone who was not his or her master. In fact, if the free Africans or free creole blacks wished to endow a relative in slavery with property, they first had to purchase his or her freedom. Of course the expression in a will of a desire to free a relative, even the provision of funds to do it, did not guarantee that this actually happened. The slave's master might not wish to sell, especially before the 1820s, or some other obstacle might intervene. But the wills of the fifty-two black testators spoke of the process of freeing slaves (their own or other peoples') as if the testators expected a favourable outcome; and on the whole their expectations seems to be in line with what is already known about the relative facility of manumissions in the island.[7]

What happened when someone who was formerly a slave became a slave owner? Was the personal experience of slavery of no account in the psychology of the new owner? The material conditions of the lives of these black testators – their generally small estates, only partly cultivated; their preoccupation with coffee, cocoa and provisions and not sugar; the small size of their slave holdings – suggest that their slaves, who seemed to be servants anyway, were not under pressure to produce for a competitive overseas market. Would it not be reasonable to add to these material factors making for ameliorative conditions the lessons of humility and suffering which the ex-slave, now master, might have brought to the business of slave management? Or perhaps the experience worked the other way, for a slave, even if he or she enjoyed the intimacy, comfort or discomfort of the household of a black ex-slave master with a quarrée or two of cocoa land, was nevertheless a slave. Freedom could not have been such a desirable boon as it clearly was if the status of slavery under black masters did not carry serious disabilities. But the whites never constructed the same stereotype of the harsh black slave master as they did with respect to the free coloured slave holders. So we can only speculate about the nature of black master–black slave relationships.

It is obvious that the wills tell us that free black persons had extraordinary economic privileges in the colony. In company with free coloureds, free blacks were burdened with serious civil disabilities before 1829. Judges punished them more harshly than whites for the same sort of crimes; they could not be officers in the militia; and they held not even the meanest public office. But there was no law limiting the amount of property they could hold in land, houses, slaves or in any other type. They could also bequeath property freely. The origins of their landowning status goes back to the period when the colony was Spanish. In the later eighteenth century some free blacks bought houses in Port of Spain, and under Chacon's land settlement scheme some got land in the countryside.[8] The uncommon advantages which Trinidad offered free blacks and free coloureds led to a situation in the pre-emancipation period in which they became the majority of the small farmers and the poorer householders in Port of Spain.

The fifty-two free Africans and creole blacks under present examination were not wealthy, in fact most had very little property. About five testators seemed to have had rather more land than their social and political status justified. One might guess that some of them were living comfortably at their accepted level which did not involve any conspicuous consumption. They benefited from the abundance of cheap land, and from the lavish way in which Chacon had shared out land to whites and coloureds. They helped to make, and they benefited from, the pattern of small farming established in some of the valleys of the northern quarters (districts). By dividing their property among their heirs, the black testators helped to multiply small holdings, and to establish communities of small farmers and peasants even before full emancipation in 1838. Their existence attests to the generous people–land relations in Trinidad, to the absence of a monolithic plantation system, and to the difficulties which the local white planters and officials had, under the Spanish land legacy and British Crown Colony government, of excluding non-whites from land ownership and small-scale agricultural enterprises. Their existence is evidence of the remarkable fact that for various reasons the colony had ample room for competing interests and competitive groups to develop, though not from the same starting line or to the same point of achievement and status.

On the more personal side, the wills of the fifty-two black testators reveal something of their emotional experiences at the time the wills were made. In the 1840s and 1850s it was the time to die for a number of old Africans, some Mandingos, men and women who had seen and suffered many indignities as slaves and free persons. Marie Angelique, an old African woman, could express in 1872, to whomever wrote her will, either words of suffering or a countenance of suffering which led the will drafter to write that she was "bred and toil in servitude to an old age".[9] She had arrived in Trinidad as a little girl, she had acquired a piece of land (2.5 quarrées) in Cimaronero. But what was that in recompense? Her relatives were all dead, she had only her godchildren. The loneliness of some of the older African testators comes through their wills to hit the modern researcher right in the face. In old age some had become ill, and without relatives had to rely on the care of acquaintances of varying faithfulness. Almost invariably those who helped them became the inheritors of their little properties and houses.

In old age a 'countryman' could be a blessing or a curse. The wills remind us that even in the immediate postemancipation era and beyond, there was a considerable level of ethnic feeling in the island, reinforced no doubt by newly arrived Africans after emancipation. The six Mandingo testators displayed a particularly high level of consciousness of their fellow Mandingoes, a consciousness strengthened by the existence of a Mandingo association and the priesthood of Jonas Bath, their chief priest.[10] Almost invariably a Mandingo was made the executor or one of the executors of another Mandingo's will. Three of the Mandingo testators had houses in Port of Spain on Mandingo Street, a prolongation of Cumberland Street. This was the centre of the religious activities of this group of Muslim ex-slaves; Jonas Bath had his house on Mandingo Street.

Of the Africans, four were specifically said to have been Ibos. They too had a sense of ethnic loyalty. Juan Victoriano Farfan, an old Ibo, seventy years of age, found that in the 1830s his relatives were dead and he had to rely on Miguel, a fellow Ibo, to take care of his lands in Santa Cruz. Miguel, a younger man, had taken advantage of Juan's old age and infirmity and had not handed over rent from some houses left in his care, although he had an agreed commission. Juan Farfan pleaded with his executors to dispossess Miguel. His heirs were to be the people who had cared for him kindly.

Charles Angeron, alias Sainte Messe, was a black Creole from Guadeloupe with an unusual skill. He was a confectioner. His will gives the impression that he was a respectable black workman. But his marriage had gone on the rocks; his wife had abandoned him shortly after the wedding, and in his will he indignantly asked his executor to institute legal proceedings to get custody of his infant son from the erring wife. He wished the boy to grow up to be an artisan, someone who could earn a honest living. The implication was that the boy could not do this if he remained with his mother who had scandalized the family. But Charles had a skeleton of a different kind in his cupboard of respectability; he had an eighteen-year-old illegitimate 'cabress' (the child of a black and a mulatto) daughter in Martinique.

Charles Angeron left nothing for his wife in 1818 (he had furniture, jewellery and two slaves). James Mangomery, an old soldier of the Third West India Regiment, who still had in 1873 the land given to him in the time of Governor Woodford, decided that his wife deserved only one shilling "according to her conduct". What transgressions the lady had committed were not recorded. His grandchildren were his chosen heirs. In Spanish times, or when Spanish civil law was still in force, husbands did not dare to disinherit wives with such a flourish. It would not be surprising if, even under the freer disposition of property by will allowable under English law, the executors of Mangomery (though not Angeron) found themselves unable to fulfil his punitive intentions.[11]

An interesting aspect of the bequests made by the testators is the frequency with which godchildren were made beneficiaries of wills, especially in the absence of near relatives. A previous examination of the wills of a large number of free coloureds of various means has tended to confirm how widespread was the social practice of having godchildren. There is even a suggestion that on rare occasions the practice could cut across colour lines. And understandably so, because there is a suspicion that in some cases 'godchildren' were really distant relatives in disguise because for some reason it was not politic to acknowledge them in a more direct manner. For instance, the godchildren of Pauline Figereaux, an old Ibo woman, in 1839 had coincidentally or significantly the surname of Figereaux.

On the question of names, in these wills, as in other types of notarial documents of free Africans, free blacks, and free coloureds too, I have seldom seen anything like the taunting or classical names given to some slaves and recorded in the Trinidad Slave Registers.[12] In the collection of wills being examined here a possible exception is Dutchess Jones, an African woman, who had the alias Genevieve Jones. In the fifty-two wills there were only four cases of testators having an alias. But, generally speaking, having an alias was not so uncommon among the ordinary blacks and free coloureds of the island.

An African might, in fact, in his or her lifetime have at least three names (or more if we disarticulate surnames from first names): an African name, a slave name (not necessarily the surname given to satisfy slave registration purposes), and the name assumed for him or herself after emancipation. And after becoming a free person, there might be friends, relatives and acquaintances calling him or her all three names at the same time. Governor Woodford used this confusion of names as his excuse for insisting that non-whites coming before the courts or requiring passports should state their colour as well as their name. At this point, however, what is interesting is the possibility of a 'name revolution' insidiously or triumphantly going on among the black and coloured labouring class as people changed their status or moved to new locations. Had this not been so I should have found more ex-slaves, black and coloured, with the implausible names given to them pejoratively by some slave masters.[13]

By and large the testators before or after emancipation belonged culturally to the mass of black and coloured slaves and ex-slaves who were partly French in their cultural orientation, Roman Catholic in so far as they adhered to any European religion, and linguistically capable of communicating in French Creole. About fourteen of them in the 1813–32 group and eleven in the postemancipation group professed to belong to the Roman Catholic church to which some left small donations. Perhaps the most puzzling thing is that three Africans (Pierre Louis Tombe, Fanny García, Pierre Gourville) said they were 'born' in the bosom of the Roman Catholic church. Could this mean that they were baptized as infants in Africa in the Roman Catholic church? Or was it just a form of language to convey a lengthy or committed association with that church? The six Mandingoes (five men and one woman) were Muslims, and three of them left instructions that they should be buried according to the rites of that religion. Jonas Bath, the chief Mandingo priest, did not leave any instructions with respect to his burial, but his associates hardly needed any. For the testators who were Christians, the most common instruction about burial was that it should be simple, without pomp. Surprisingly there was no instance where the black testator indicated the place where he wished to be buried. Only one testator, Florentine Lompres, a black Creole woman from St Lucia, left any instruction about the wake. She was willing to have one quarrée of her cocoa crop (she had five hundred trees on 7 quarrées) sold to pay for her wake, burial and church donation. Dutchess Jones, a forty-year-old African woman professing the Roman Catholic faith, left no instruction respecting her burial; but she certainly had a fair amount of religious pictures to give her beneficiaries, including prints of Jesus on the cross and one of St John; and a bust of St Francis. She also gave away her rosary and a fowl!

By far the greater number of testators could not sign their names. At least thirty-two of the fifty-two blacks made their mark on the wills. The most significant observation about their record of literacy (or illiteracy) was that the three who could sign their names were a shopkeeper (Pierre Louis Tombe), a confectioner (Charles Angeron) and a priest (Jonas Bath), who signed in Arabic. There were no women among those who could sign their names. Of course there was a vast difference between the ability to scrawl one's signature and the possession of functional literacy. Even among the better situated free coloureds functional literacy was a scarce commodity.

Perhaps this brief examination of fragments of the lives of the fifty-two testators can suitably be concluded by the insertion of a verbatim copy of the will of Nancy Rivers alias Bruce. Nancy herself was unable to write; perhaps the will was written down by a friend or a relative whose language skills were far from adequate. It is the only will of its kind among the fifty-two examined, and it might be of interest to the student of language:

In the name of the holy Trinity aman. I nanse rivers of the Town of Port of Spain in the Island of Trinidad being welke in Bodde but of good under-standing Doth Make this my Will and Testament as follows. I Declair myself to bee a free affrican Baptized in the Catholick faith in wich i Live and I trust to Dy in I Rec [rest of word unclear – page torn – but likely returne] my soule to its Creator and my body to the Urth in a Christan Like manner by my Executers in houme I have put my trust and as follows my frend Mr. Mark francis and thomas Eccless bouth of this Town. I Declair I have one female child named Aliza Dickson and I declair never being maried. I make the following Bequits of the Property I posses to the Catholick Church of this town the sum of one pound Currancy to be paid out my funds. I Declair my property to consist of a Lot n.11 in Sussex Street with a house Bult on Each half and the same no 11. the one half Lot with the house on the South sid of the Lot I Derect to be sold to pay my debts and expensis. the other on the north sid and on a half Lot I leve to my beloved Daughter and at her dispoussal after my Deth and all just debets paid; In faith of which I have maid my mark in the Presence of the witheses and of this furft day of febuary in the town of Port of Spain in the yeair of Our Lord 1832.[14]

3

The Wage Problem in Trinidad and Tobago 1838–1938

James Millette

In 1838, the islands of Trinidad and Tobago, like all the other West Indian territories of the English-speaking Caribbean, save for those where there had been no apprenticeship, abandoned slavery and embarked upon a new socioeconomic order which relied on wage earning workers for the supply of their labour requirements. Where, before abolition and apprenticeship, the labour supply on the plantations and other work places had been largely supplied by slaves who worked without wages, after abolition, and still more after emancipation, wage labour became routine and wage payments the accepted form of rewarding workers for their efforts.

Under slavery, the labour power of the slaves was purchased at the time of their acquisition, the slaves being themselves a commodity; after emancipation the social *persona* of the slaves was transformed in that they who were formerly commodities, now had a commodity to sell, namely, their labour power.

The transformation had been a long time coming. For most of the period in which slavery existed, the slave could alter his or her status as an unfree labourer only by manumission or by desertion. It was only in the period of apprenticeship that a formal change in his status became recognizable under law, a modification that in effect introduced a kind of dual *persona* in the character of the slave. The accustomed status of the slaves as chattel was perpetuated by reason of the fact that they remained the property of their masters, obliged to work for a period of forty-five hours per week without wages.[1] At the same time their new status as persons was recognized in that they could bargain with their masters with respect to the extra hours of work which they were called upon to perform.

How the slaves performed this work was, in the first place, dependent on the contractual situation subsisting between themselves as individuals and the master. For example, it mattered whether an individual slave was dependent on his or her master for housing, provision ground or the like, or whether this relationship was such as to leave the slave free to decide if, in the given situation, he or she could opt to do his or her own work and forego the wage available from the employer for extra employment. And, secondly, it was dependent on whether or not the slave was able to evade the laws established in order to criminalize the so-called breaches of contractual obligations to the master, the object of which was to extract additional labour under the guise of punishment for breaches of the law.[2]

After emancipation this dualism was extinguished. The ex-slaves were free, free to work or not to work, and free to a considerable, though variable, degree to determine the price at which they would offer themselves for employment. From that time on their status as workers was increasingly determined by the general economic and sociopolitical environment, by social policy, politics and the marketplace, rather than by any ascriptive personal quality or obligation. An essential characteristic of the new situation was that they could not be legally required to work, and although they could be induced or obliged by a variety of devices, the initiative largely lay with them to decide whether, when and under what commitments they were going to work.

As important as this metamorphosis was for the slaves, it was of no less importance for the planters. Shorn of his right to coerce the ex-slave to work, the planter found himself, for the first time, in a situation of industrial dependence on the labourer. Under slavery the dependence of the master on the slave was not clearly apparent, even though it was real. Without the slave the back-breaking work of clearing and preparing the fields, of planting, cultivating and tending the crop, of making the sugar, of baling and exporting it, could not be accomplished. But the slave had little option but to provide the required labour. Legality was on the side of the master, and conferred upon him the means of commanding it. After emancipation, however, the law specifically divested the master of the proprietary and legal mechanisms which had for so long been at his disposal. Indeed, the balance of legal authority lay in the other direction, itself the consequence of the fact that in abolishing slavery the British Parliament had asserted, against previous tradition, the superiority of metropolitan law in matters relating to the slave system. The logic of this development was that the British government inherited a responsibility for negating colonial attempts to reintroduce slavery. Not only in the West Indies, but widely throughout the former slave owning territories of the British Empire, legislative attempts aimed at reintroducing a legal obligation for the ex-slave to work for the ex-master were regularly and uniformly disallowed.[3]

In these circumstances the dependence of the planter on the ex-slave was characterized by an entirely new element in the relationship between the two: the unfettered, arbitrary and completely self-interested option of the ex-slaves with respect to whom they would work for, and the conditions on which they would be prepared to work. What this meant was that the planters had to confront two realities alien to their historical experience and upbringing. They had to engage in industrial bargaining with the labourers, unorganized though they were, and they had to have an adequate supply of cash with which to pay for their labour.

Cash flow was important, and was a new and unsettling element in the running of the plantation. To an extent not previously experienced in the British West Indian colonies, planters had to find cash, not on an occasional or off-and-on basis but regularly, day by day, week by week, month by month as the case might be, in order to secure the smooth flow of the plantation's operations and, ultimately, to guarantee its survival. In the final analysis, it was the willingness or ability of the planters to fulfil the obligations of this new situation that shaped the character of the conflicts that ensued everywhere in the region in the postemancipation period.

In Tobago, for example, planters could neither bargain effectively nor pay the wages required to secure the labour of the ex-slaves. By 1838, Tobago had already embarked on that sustained economic decline which was to result in the demise of the plantation system, financial collapse and amalgamation with Trinidad before the turn of the century. The *metayage* system was to provide an opportunity to delay but not to forestall the disaster that was to come.[4] Faced with the refusal of the labourer to work for the pitifully small wages which the plantations could afford, the planters experimented with sharecropping, a device that recommended itself to the ex-slaves because it afforded them opportunities to acquire a lump sum of cash at the end of the crop, did not greatly interfere with their pursuit of their own employments, and allowed them to use their individual and family labour profitably.

But such was the interface between labourer and planter in Trinidad that the former was in the fortunate position of being able, virtually, to dictate the terms and conditions upon which his labour power could be purchased. For nearly all of the seven years that elapsed between emancipation and the beginning of Indian indentureship in 1845, wages were high by comparison with wage levels existing in paid employment prior to emancipation as well as by comparison with wage levels prevailing in other West Indian territories, British Guiana alone excepted.[5] Thereafter wages declined and continued to decline, in real terms as well as nominally. They never recovered until well into the twentieth century, and then only as a result of the social and political consequences of the disturbances of the 1930s which were themselves, in large measure, caused by the depressingly low level of wages paid to workers.

The period immediately succeeding emancipation witnessed rising levels of wages for workers employed in sugar. Among planters this was a cause of great annoyance. W.H. Burnley, a resident for forty years in Trinidad, originally a merchant and subsequently a proprietor of several estates, testified that wages had risen from 15d. to 2s. 2d. between 1838 and 1842, that is to say, by 58 percent.[6] Not only had wages risen, but workers were also determining the terms and conditions on which they worked. They refused to commit themselves to written contracts, and opted for task or job work out of crop, and day work in crop. What this meant was that the worker chose to discharge fixed tasks out of season, and to forego unreasonably long hours in crop time. Gone were the onerous work regimes associated with slavery. Efforts by planters to break the industrial ascendancy of the workers, and particularly to reduce wages, were easily defeated by the latter. Speaking to the Select Committee on the West India Colonies in 1842, Burnley complained bitterly about this development:

In November last a meeting of the agricultural committee took place, and they determined to reduce wages to 1s. 3d. a task; but the labourers having more power than the employers, would not accede to those terms; a struggle ensued, and I find by my last accounts, that on 4th February, a task was precisely the same as before, 2s. 2d., throughout the island generally, and in the district of Tacarigua 2s. 6d., as stated by one of the members of the Council.[7]

In his view, task work was not only expensive, it was also decidedly "not fair".[8] For one thing, a task could be completed in four or four-and-a-half hours by "an industrious active man", so that the day's work could be completed as early as eleven o'clock.[9] Good workers could do two or even three tasks a day, which he clearly felt might be good for the worker, but not for the planter: "They should work from sunrise to sunset, with an intermission of two hours for dinner and an hour for breakfast; but it is impossible, except in very rare cases, to get them to work before seven o'clock in the morning."[10]

In addition, planters were constrained to offer inducements in order to get the workers to engage at what planters regarded as ruinously high wages. Efforts at eliminating or reducing allowances were not any more successful than in the case of wages. Customarily, full-time workers were provided with allowances of rum and half a pound of fish, particularly in the distant districts where markets were not easily available.[11] Part-time workers did not normally get allowances, though it seems that a tot of rum often went with the task. Those who lived on the estates were housed free of rent, and obtained as much provision ground as they chose to cultivate. Medicine, it seems, was generally supplied to them, and in some cases medical attendance.[12] According to Burnley, the planters hoped to reduce wages and take away allowances, with the exception of the house and the provision grounds.[13] But even though a continuing struggle was conducted to effect these changes, the situation seemed to be "entirely hopeless".[14]

Three factors, in particular, added to the despair of the planters. First, there was the absence of legal enactment making it possible for the planter to make the ex-slave work, a deficiency for which the planters held the metropolitan government culpable. After a long period of unsuccessfully attempting to persuade the West Indian colonies to embark upon the path of gradual abolition, the British government had been forced to override the constitutional niceties which had given the islands, with the exception of the Crown Colonies, a monopoly of legislating for the conduct of the slave system, and moved to abolish it. Compensation had been paid to the planters, but their power to coerce slave labour was removed.

Secondly, and more seriously, there was the fact that labour was in short supply, and if the planter wanted the labour of the ex-slave he just had to pay for it. In Trinidad labour had always been in short supply. A late developer in plantation agriculture, the island had never enjoyed an over-abundance of labourers, and entered the period of emancipation with a distinct shortage of available workers. Burnley again described the planters' dilemma:

There were certainly many things which would have answered beneficially to the proprietors if they had possessed the power to effect them, but which were impossible, on account of the demand for labour being so much greater than the supply; the supply was always very short prior to even emancipation in consequence of the law which prevented slaves from being carried from one colony to another.[15]

Thirdly, there was the money self-sufficiency of the labourer. Like the planter, many ex-slaves had been unaccustomed to using cash; but unlike the planters they could get by with or without it. With one or two tasks per day, and not every day either, a part-time labourer could earn enough to satisfy basic needs. Full-time workers on the plantation, given access to allowances, housing and provision grounds were under no pressure to work harder in order to earn more money than an ordinarily industrious routine would yield. The indefatigable Burnley observed that an able-bodied worker, working ten hours a day "could easily earn one dollar . . . at task work; and . . . after feeding but not clothing himself, he could save above £4 sterling a month; and that for about 1s. 3d. sterling, he might supply himself with farinaceous food and with the fish he gets from the estate as part of the allowances, support himself comfortably for a week".[16]

Historical research has largely corroborated Burnley's observations.[17] Although these early efforts at reducing workers' wages and allowances, and altering to their disadvantage the conditions of labour, at first failed, they were soon to succeed.[18] In due course, the conflict between planter and worker was to result in arrangements which were decidedly to the advantage of the former. And in this the imperial government was found to be a very willing ally. In the eyes of the British government, the independence of the ex-slave was not to be tolerated; indeed it was regarded as an unwelcome and unintended consequence of emancipation, a development to be undermined in every way possible.

The imperial government, emancipation notwithstanding, had little hesitation about taking those steps which were necessary to ensure the ascendancy of the plantocracy over all other interests. Lord Harris, governor of the island in the mid 1840s, argued that it was imperative "that the proprietors of European race should be enabled to maintain their present place in the society of the colony, which can only be done by giving them greater command of labour".[19] And even Henry Taylor, one of the staunch supporters of ex-slaves in the period immediately after emancipation, was by 1846 supportive of the proposition that their interests should be subordinated to those of the sugar planting industry.[20]

In addition, the fact that the planters had access to colonial and metropolitan establishments and possessed the means of influencing their decisions was supremely important. A whole host of devices could be invoked to try and alter the balance between planter and labourer, chiefly encouraging schemes of immigration which would have the effect of replacing labour scarcity by labour abundance. The labourers had no such access to political influence.

The strength of their position, such as it was, lay in the fact that history was on their side, and accordingly there were concessions which imperialism would not and could not make to the planters.

Imperialism had its own agenda; slavery would not be reintroduced. The profits of the manufacturing classes would not be sacrificed so that expensive West Indian sugar could be imported into Britain. Food had to be cheap, preferential duties had to go, and sugar duties had to be equalized. Free trade had to be introduced and extended throughout the world. But there was a point at which metropolitan power was willing to make concessions to the planters. That was on the supply of cheap labour, provided that it could be paid for. Loans would not be advanced so that West Indian planters could pay high wage bills to the ex-slaves, thereby fostering their economic independence. But loans would be advanced to support schemes of immigration aimed at recruiting labourers willing to work for lower wages. Both metropolitan and colonial philosophy rationalized the redistribution of labourers within the empire, and regarded immigration and the right to cheap labour as rights which ought to be protected not only for the West Indian planter, but for employers of labour generally. Thus it was that the ascendancy of the labourer over the planter, which was the first fruit of the struggles of the immediate postemancipation period, was broken.

Thus it was, too, that the Indian indentured labourer in due course replaced the ex-slave in order to provide a reliable labour force on the sugar plantations particularly in Trinidad and British Guiana. Indian immigration more than any other scheme of worker migration into Trinidad after emancipation assisted the planters in overturning the ascendancy of the labouring population which had existed in the years immediately after emancipation. In the long run, it also led to the gradual emergence of an unemployment problem for the first time in the colony.

What was more, in later years labourers were graded and were paid according to their assessed ability to do the required work. By 1899, wages were fixed at between twenty-five and sixteen cents per day, or per task, depending on whether the immigrant was deemed to be able-bodied or not.[21] In the period 1 January to 31 December 1894 and 1 January to 31 December 1895 only three and six estates, respectively, out of sixty-nine paid more than an average of six pence per day to adult male indentured immigrants.[22] In 1910, indentured workers were in some cases receiving as little as seventy-two cents per week even though the Immigration Amendment Ordinance of 1872 had long since set their minimum wages at $1.25, the same as that established for free labourers.[23] For compensation, the workers sometimes got rations and, more rarely, clothing from the person to whom they were indentured, as well as a place to live. With respect to the former, suffice it to say that food and clothes were not generously issued; as for the latter, the barrack was the standard.

Barracks at Esperanza Estate

BY COURTESY OF THE PUBLIC RECORD OFFICE

Contract labour into Trinidad in the period after emancipation had three most important consequences. First, the regular supply of Indian labourers saved the sugar plantation system by laying the basis for profitability of many plantations. Secondly, it depressed wages generally by introducing competition and, particularly, by reinforcing as a principle the custom that the low level wages paid to immigrants should be paid to other labourers as well. And, finally, it facilitated the extraction of surplus from the labouring population and maximized the level of profits reaped by the planter class at the expense of labour. Indian indentured labour was the perfect answer to the manifold problems of labour shortage, high wage rates, depression and low income returns experienced by the planter after emancipation, paid for at the expense of the entire community, and not only of those who profited from it. And it was a solution that was, for a long time, destined to make the contest between labour and capital unequal and inequitable.

As Henry Alcazar, mayor of Port of Spain, and an unofficial member of the Legislative Council, put it in his submission to the West India Royal Commission (the Norman Commission) in 1897, "Indian immigration . . . has been but a weapon in the hands of the planter *to enable him to obtain at starvation rates the far more efficient labour of local origin.*"[24] And he continued:

Wages have during the last 30 years risen all over the civilized world. Even in ultra conservative India there has been a marked increase, as Lord Roberts not long ago reminded us. In Trinidad and the West Indies generally wages have, during the same period fallen greatly, in some occupations by fully one half, on an average certainly not less than 25 per cent. No doubt the price of sugar has also fallen considerably, but so has the price of iron, of wheat, and of every staple product of the very countries in which there has been a rise. I am justified therefore in contending that the fall in Trinidad is due, not to unavoidable economic causes, but to the operation of a system which places absolute command of the labour market in the hands of the employers. As far as the workers are concerned, industry is then kept artificially in a constant state of extreme depression.[25]

The indictment of contract labour has hardly ever been better put. What made that indictment even more pertinent was the fact that the Crown Colony system, much touted as the saviour and bulwark of the rights of the unrepresented masses, was more and more glaringly being revealed to be a façade behind which the race and class ascendancy of the sugar planter was made irreversible. By the late nineteenth century, that ascendancy had developed to the point where other interests – cocoa, commercial and professional, not labour or petty huckster – were beginning to feel the frustration born of an unequal struggle against an entrenched race and class elite. Out of that frustration was born the Reform Movement of the 1880s and 1890s, directed against the dictatorship of the plantocracy which was fortified in the Legislative Council by the ceaseless advocacy of a strong and powerful group of Unofficials – a "despotism sweetened by sugar".

In the period of depression that ensued in the later decades of the nineteenth century, wages were often substantially reduced (and tasks increased) on several sugar estates, sometimes by as much as 60 percent, and invariably on the ground that sugar prices had fallen. On sixty-three estates in 1894, an average of 29.5 percent of workers earned less than six pence a day for a one-year period beginning 1 January and ending 31 December. On sixty-six estates, an average of 31.09 percent earned as little as six pence per day for the period 1 January to 31 December 1895.[26] Alcazar described the island's working people as being in a "miserable" condition, a state of things caused by

The pauperising of the masses by the artificial state of things created by Indian immigrants. The labour market of the Colony, especially in the sugar districts, is so overstocked that the earnings of the working classes are miserably low. They are unable to find more employment than is absolutely necessary to keep starvation from their doors.[27]

As a result of this wage exploitation a clear alienation from agricultural work was reinforced among the labouring population. Work, to the extent that it existed, was largely agricultural or labouring, and both were despised. Additionally, it was exploitative. Indeed, as early as the 1870s an idle, unemployed lumpen-proletariat element had clearly made its appearance in the streets of Port of Spain. Charles Kingsley in 1871 remarked:

You are told that there are 8,000 human beings in Port of Spain alone without visible means of subsistence, and you congratulate Port of Spain on being such an Elysium that people can live there – not without eating, for every child and most women you pass are eating something or other all day long – but without working.[28]

This alienation was grounded in the high level of exploitation which had become institutionalized in the society. Even after cocoa became prosperous and attracted to its cultivation many peasants who, for the first time, became engaged in a profitable agricultural enterprise, the plight of workers was not spectacularly improved. It is true that cocoa provided many peasants with opportunities that sugar could not and would not provide, and ensured genuine, profitable employment away from the sugar plantation. But others among the labouring population, who were unable to make the transition to peasant proprietorship in cocoa, or to gain employment as contractors, were much less fortunate.

There was a class of workers, elements of the agro-proletariat, who were sucked into the network of labour supply for the cocoa fields. These were sometimes the indentured workers for whom the bigger cocoa planters successfully petitioned from time to time. Their rates of pay were much less than those paid to other casual labourers, averaging around 25 cents per day. But free labourers did not do very much better. Their rates varied between 25 to 35 cents for women, and 35 to 50 cents for men. Once again, the interrelationship between indentured labour and free labour in the wage market was significant. In the Montserrat hills, it was said in 1897, the introduction of 400 to 500 indentured workers depressed the general wage to the extent where, formerly, "wages . . . ranged from 30 cents to 40 cents for piece work, [they] are now down to 25 cents".[29] Indeed, it was freely acknowledged that the 'small wages' paid immigrant labour helped to provide a cheap, adequate, industrious and amenable labour force, which greatly accelerated the rise of the most lucrative cacao industry.[30]

The question naturally arises: What was happening to all this wealth that was being milked from the workers and peasants by the means which we have so far described? Elementary. It went into creating lives of leisure, status and employment, and more wealth founded on the accumulation of capital and its generally profitable employment in a wide variety of lucrative undertakings.

Marx said that wage labour presupposes capital, and vice versa.[31] In the period at which we are looking, wage labour, legally freed after 1917 with the ending of Indian indentureship, was swiftly becoming ubiquitous. And so, too, was capital. The process of concentration and centralization in the sugar industry, the introduction and the rapid expansion of bank capital, the modernization of factory and field operations in sugar, and the capitalization of the cocoa industry, were supplemented by an ever widening range and scale of activity which swiftly and surely was building up the sinews of the maturing capitalism. By 1897, Trinidad was also clearly well on the way to developing the appurtenances of a modern capitalist state. Nathaniel Nathan, judge of the Supreme Court, in his deposition to the Norman Commission described the island as possessing a government that could be described

As being on a high scale of organisation, the population is considerable, large sums of money are being spent on public works . . . and on education . . . There is a judicial staff as large as in much larger colonies, a highly organised and highly paid medical staff, who ministers practically gratuitously to the bulk of the population.[32]

But there was also what Nathan was pleased to describe as "a gigantic installation of commercial houses, both wholesale and retail . . . [a kind of] commercial over-development".[33] And so, indeed, there was. Relative to its wealth and size of population, Trinidad had witnessed in the second half of the nineteenth century a remarkable growth in commercial enterprises, comprising stores, insurance and commission agents, oilfield and hardware suppliers, shipping agents, ship chandlers, manufacturers representatives, food importers, government contractors, drug importers and such like. Nearly everything that was required by the expanding elite for civilized living could either be acquired locally or be supplied from abroad. Imported furniture, lumber, cutlery, household goods, English, American, Swiss and Austrian boots and shoes, harnesses, saddles, guns and pistols, liquors, fine clothes of all descriptions, chinaware, gramophones, bicycles, prams, and many more items were all available for the asking.

It was a kind of shoppers' emporium run by a sort of aristocracy of shopkeepers, particularly concentrated in Port of Spain but represented as well in San Fernando and in some instances in other parts of the island and in Tobago too. This apparent prosperity had its foundations solidly based on the spectacular development of Trinidad as a commercial outpost whose figures for imports and exports would have done much larger nations proud. Between 1838 and 1916, the value of imports per year increased tenfold, the value of exports by rather more. And most of this development had come in the final forty years. Between 1881 and 1896, the total value of all exports, exclusive of bullion and specie, amounted to £27,892,147; the total value of exports, with bullion and specie included, attained the level of £36,124,292. For the same period imports, again exclusive of bullion and specie, amounted to £28,387,272; with bullion and specie, they totalled £36,673,573. As the figures show total trade for these sixteen years, a crucial period in the development of capitalism in Trinidad, equalled £72,797,865 or $349,429,750.[34] Considering the contemporary strength of sterling, the purchasing power of money in those far-off days, the size of the island's population, the low level of consumption by the masses and the size of the capitalist class, this was an astounding sum of money to pass through the hands of the ruling political and economic elite. But Trinidad, if not Tobago, was an astounding country. Writing in 1901, H. de R. Walker was firmly of the view that Trinidad was "the best field in the West Indies for the investment of British capital".[35] In roughly this period, 1880 to 1900, Trinidad and Tobago's imports stood higher than those of all other Caribbean and Central American countries, save Cuba; with respect to exports, only Cuba and Haiti stood ahead. And Trinidad alone of all these countries had petroleum, a factor that added considerably to the prosperity of the island and to the wealth of its landed and mercantile class.

Already, by the 1880s, some of the firms destined in the course of time to be among the largest local enterprises had been established. Many of them started out as single owner, family enterprises or partnerships and became incorporated as private limited liability companies some years afterwards. Among the earliest of the modern firms was George R. Alston & Company established in 1881 and incorporated in 1920 with authorized share capital of $5,000,000. The firm was, by the latter year, involved in general merchandising, shipping, insurance, and estates. It later spawned a large number of associated or affiliated companies including one of today's biggest local conglomerates, Neal & Massy Company Limited, and represented a wide cross-section of the best known manufacturing companies in the UK, the US and Canada. When air travel became a commercial proposition it was also ticketing agent for Pan American, British Overseas Airways Corporation and British West Indian Airways Limited.[36]

The later nineteenth century was a period of marked British capitalist penetration of the sugar industry and of the economy as a whole. As a consequence a powerful landed and mercantile aristocracy, comprising white capitalists of different national origins but increasingly led and dominated by the British, had been established. Gradually, as well, a manufacturing sector was emerging. For a long time this sector could boast only of sugar and sugar related enterprises, namely rum and molasses. Subsequently, after the imperial government had commissioned a geological survey conducted by Messrs. G.P. Wall and J.G. Sawkins in the late 1850s in Trinidad and some of the other islands,[37] asphalt and then petroleum began to disclose possibilities for mineral diversification. But even so, asphalt, which proved first, remained an extractive industry, though it was undoubtedly remunerative enough to attract a varied metropolitan interest.

There was also bitters, associated with the Siegert family who had founded their enterprise in Angostura, Venezuela, in 1824 and shifted to Trinidad in 1875. By the early 1880s it had become customary to list the making of bitters, even more so than asphalt, as the distinctive non-sugar Trinidadian manufacture.[38] But things were beginning to change. In 1879, for example, the official record listed under manufactures, in addition to sugar and bitters, the Pioneer Soap Works in Port of Spain, two coconut oil factories in Nariva-Mayaro and asphalt at La Brea.[39]

In the late nineteenth and early twentieth centuries the petroleum industry began to develop. The period from 1900 to 1920 witnessed its emergence in the form which was to become classic in later years, that is to say, by way of large-scale foreign investment and substantial inputs of local labour. Within the period 1905 to 1920 the number of workers employed in oil and related occupations grew from insignificance to an average daily number of persons employed amounting to 4,526. In oil in 1920, 4,046 persons were in regular employment, 3,990 men and 56 women; asphalt accounted for 480 employees, 400 men and 80 women.[40]

In the oilfields, Trinidad Leaseholds Limited was already by 1920 established as the largest company, prospecting in a wide variety of locations and conducting operations at Fyzabad, Pointe-à-Pierre, Barrackpore, Siparia, Piparo and Guayaguayare. In 1920 it employed 1,529 persons, more than one-third of all workers employed in the oil business. Fyzabad and Pointe-à-Pierre were its biggest fields with Barrackpore a distant third. Next to it in terms of persons employed were Trinidad Central Oilfields (938 workers) at Tabaquite and United British Oilfields of Trinidad (767 workers) at Point Fortin. These were followed by the United British West Indies Petroleum Syndicate (199 workers) at Siparia, British Controlled Oilfields (116 workers) operating at Brighton, followed in turn by the Petroleum Development Company (86 workers) at Forest Reserve, Apex (Trinidad) Oilfields (80 workers) at Fyzabad, Oropouche Oilfields (78 workers) also at Fyzabad, and UROZ Oilfields (68 workers) at Williamsville; to these would be added another group of smaller companies employing an average of two to thirty-one workers on a daily basis.[41]

By 1917, conflict between labour and capital was giving rise to strike action in the oil belt. In February of that year a strike took place among the oil and asphalt workers at Brighton, Fyzabad and Point Fortin. The issues were higher wages and better working conditions. The employers for their part threatened the workers with eviction from the barrack accommodation provided by the company; the workers in turn set fire to the premises of the asphalt company at Brighton. Other strikes that followed this one were put down with vigour by the authorities; the principal leaders were arrested and two of them were imprisoned for two years with hard labour.[42]

For the next twenty years strikes and other forms of labour unrest were to become endemic in the oil industry, principally because of the appalling conditions of work, the low level of wages and the persistence of low living standards for oil workers and their families. Specifically in the period 1919–20, and again in 1935–37, serious strike movements developed in direct response to hardship affecting the working people in oil, asphalt and associated industries and, as well, in consequence of, or in solidarity with, strike actions elsewhere as, for example, on the docks and in the sugar areas. Here and there, however, non-wage issues verging on the political also gave rise to worker discontent and consequently to strike action. In January 1920 at Point Fortin and again in March 1935 at Fyzabad, workers struck in protest against racism and mismanagement and on the latter occasion against what they conceived to be the indifferent political leadership of Arthur Andrew Cipriani.

Nevertheless, low wages paid in oil constituted the fundamental worker grievance. In the 1920s, several years after the industry was securely established, unskilled labourers worked long hours and in return got starvation wages. For a nine-hour day such workers earned five cents per hour, 45 cents per day, under $3.50 for a six-day week. Drillers earned 12 cents per hour for a twelve-hour shift.[43]

For years prior to the crisis of 1919–20 workers of all categories had been bitterly complaining about the low level of wages. Among agricultural workers wages were very low. In Tobago the average rate in 1920 was 36 cents per day; in the aftermath of the strikes, after increases were received, top wages attained the level of 50 cents per day. But before that men normally earned 36 to 40 cents, women 18 to 20 cents. Officials freely admitted that "the lower rates [were] by far the more usual ones".[44] In Trinidad most agricultural wages ranged between 30 to 50 cents per day for men, 20 to 28 cents per day for women.[45]

In earlier years, wages were not only low; they were not always paid. The attention of the Colonial Office had been drawn to the fact that the truck system, that is to say, the payment of wages in kind instead of in cash, was pervasive. After numerous complaints the Colonial Office had directed that an investigation be undertaken, and, if the system existed, to prohibit it by law. As it turned out, the system was indeed widespread, except for Tobago where it apparently did not exist or on estates employing indentured labourers where it was not allowed. As one planter reported, "The great majority [of planters] living in this island depend entirely on their crops to defray expenses, personal or otherwise . . . I have known planters who on many occasions owing to want of hard cash, have had to postpone their pay to three months, and I can assure you, that this occurrence is not of the rarest."[46]

In other sectors the 1919–20 period was also quite difficult as far as wages were concerned. On the docks where the strikes were to originate in November 1919, stevedores earned $2.00 for a nine-hour day, the top rate for rated workers being $3.00 for an eight-hour stint. But work was irregular, averaging ten to fifteen days per month.[47] Nor was the generalized dissatisfaction and distress confined to the ranks of the lower paid manual workers and labourers. Even members of the rising middle class, clerical personnel in the civil service, complained bitterly of the pittance received in their employments. Salaries of the order of £120 per year, or thereabouts, did not go very far; and governors kept substantial files containing complaints against officials who had allegedly fallen into the clutches of their creditors and stood to lose their jobs as a consequence.[48] As with workers, the war years had witnessed a steady decline in real wages of civil servants, particularly so for those in the 'higher-paid' categories, those in receipt of £150 or more annually who did not receive the bonuses sometimes paid to lower salaried employees.[49]

What made these predicaments worse was the rising level of commodity prices. Increases had been substantial during the war years, and wages had not kept pace. Basic food items had risen on average by more than 50 percent.

Five of the most important items of popular consumption – salted fish, milk, rice, flour and sugar – had increased between 60 and 250 percent.[50] Even so, these increases, registered in respect of price controlled items, were small when compared to those affecting uncontrolled items and medicines. In respect of such items increases ranged between 100 and 450 percent over prewar prices.[51]

The causes of this inordinate inflation of prices were also well known. High profit margins and profiteering, facilitated by wartime conditions, were generally perceived as the real culprits. A case in point was provided by the well-known case of John Smith, owner of the Bonanza store, whose remarkable good fortune it was, as told by Governor Chancellor, to rise from "the brink of bankruptcy when the war broke out in 1914" and die a few years later leaving a fortune of £250,000. As Chancellor observed, this was an illustration of the "scandalous prices charged by dry goods merchants", a factor which added significantly "to the difficulties of the poorer classes in maintaining themselves".[52]

Officials were well seized of the facts. The secretary of state himself reminded the governor by cable, at the height of the 1919–20 crisis, that particulars previously supplied to the Colonial Office had clearly indicated that "wages [had] not kept pace with the increase in the cost of living. It seems probable that this fact is one of the chief causes of the present disturbances."[53]

It also appears that an unusual prosperity owing its origins to the oil industry had stimulated the development of a kind of euphoria in some quarters. In the circumstances prices did not just increase, they jumped. And those on fixed wages and salaries paid the price. The civil servants pinpointed the unusual economic conditions as one of the main sources of their problems. "Prosperity," they argued, "has increased elsewhere but not to the same extent as here . . . Where profiteering prevails, prices are fixed, not by the cost at which the retailer procures the goods, but by the prices he can [w]ring from his customers; and where the bulk of those customers, namely, the commercial and industrial sectors of the community are increasingly prosperous, their ability to pay fixes the price for all concerned including the poor government employees who really cannot afford it."[54]

The crisis of 1919–20 marked the beginning of nearly two decades of agitation against the depressingly low wages and parlous working conditions prevailing in the country. Low wages continued to be the most important worker grievance. It was the issue that stirred the sugar workers in 1934–35, and it was the issue, more than any other, that fueled the crisis of 1937.

Among agricultural workers in the early 1930s, the average wage for a six-day work week was 5s. to 12s. 6d. for men; for women the rate was 4s. 2d. to 8s. 9d. Skilled workers could earn as much as 2s. 11d. per day. Task work was paid for at the rate of 30 cents, and even after the 1937 strikes such work only fetched 35 cents. Among sugar workers retrenchment added to the woes of low wage payments. In July 1934 all these factors coalesced to stimulate a significant strike movement on the sugar estates. Wages, already abysmally low, fell by a reported 64 percent at the Caroni, Esperanza and Brechin Castle estates. Retrenchment, and longer and harder tasks completed the cycle of oppression and exploitation and resulted in prolonged unrest in the period 1934–35.[55]

But the crises of 1919–20 and 1934–35 were, in retrospect, dress rehearsals for what was soon to occur in 1937. Notwithstanding the struggles that had ensued almost unendingly since 1919, not much had changed. The wage problem was still the main problem. In 1937 wage rates in oil varied between 15 to 26 cents per hour for skilled workers to 9 to 14 cents for the unskilled. The work week varied between forty-eight to fifty-six hours for production workers and forty-five hours for all other categories.[56]

Then, as in later years, wages paid in oil reflected in a general sense the maximum level paid to workers in the island. In sugar, for example, the lowest categories of workers, those involved in digging grass, handling and applying manure, weeding and cutting cane, earned 20 to 35 cents per day, but tractor drivers, the best paid category of workers, earned between $1.60 and $1.90 per day. On an overall average in the sugar industry, skilled labour got $1.00 to $1.60, semi-skilled labour 70 to 95 cents and unskilled labour 55 to 65 cents per day. In the public works, in the latter half of 1937 after the strikes had come and gone and wages had been increased, unskilled female labour earned 36 to 50 cents, unskilled male labour between 60 and 90 cents and skilled labour 86 cents to $2.00 per day. At the same time cocoa workers earned a bottom of 40 cents and a top of $1.20 per day. Female domestics worked for wages of between $4.00 and $10.00 per month; chauffeurs earned $5.00 to $8.00 per week and men servants got the princely sum of $10.00 to $20.00 per month.[57]

It was not economic difficulties but greed that explained this appallingly low remuneration paid to labour in the oilfields and elsewhere in the labour market. Between 1935 and 1937, as even the Forster Commission recognized, public income regularly exceeded public expenditure as shown in Table 3.1.[58]

As for profits, there was little doubt that the oil companies were having more than their fair share, as the Forster Commission also recognized. In

TABLE 3.1: INCOME, EXPENDITURE AND SURPLUS, 1935–1937

Year	Income	Expenditure	Surplus
1935	8,692,688.95	8,682,708.48	9,990.47
1936	12,560,314.28	9,170,685.99	3,389,628.29
1937	12,252,784.47	10,365,874.68	1,886,909.79

All figures in dollars, at $4.80 to £1 sterling.

1934–35, Apex declared a profit of £300,468 and in 1935–36 a profit of £369,700. Dividends paid in 1935–36 alone represented a 135 percent return on invested capital. Trinidad Leaseholds declared a profit of £570,431 in 1934–35 and £679,409 in 1935–36. At the end of 1936 the company was able to declare a dividend of 25 percent.[59] It is no exaggeration to say that these large profits represented the fruits derived from the super-exploitation of labour at a time when labour was singularly unorganized, although, as events showed, increasingly militant. In fact, on the eve of the 1937 strikes, workers were receiving in real terms less than they earned in 1919–20 not only because of a reduction in working hours from a norm of ten to twelve hours to one of eight to nine hours, representing a 20 to $33^1/_3$ percent drop in wages, but also because of the rising cost of living.[60] Indeed, in 1937, absolute and real wages for lower paid workers compared very unfavourably with wages paid to the ex-slaves on the sugar plantations after emancipation.

On top of all this the social environment in which oil workers toiled added another provocative element to the generally depressed conditions in which they made their livelihood. Their own very rude style of life, in cramped barrack-yard accommodation, restricted to the barest necessities for themselves and their families, and sometimes deprived of even those, contrasted sharply with the sweet living of the managers who were invariably white, foreign and, too often, South African. The white managers in their white, well-kept houses, 'living the life of Riley' with their motor cars, their club houses and their armies of servants, which, according to popular lore, they were known to be unaccustomed to in their country of origin, stimulated all the natural envy of an exploited people put upon by their social 'superiors' determined to drive home the lesson of their 'superiority'. Add to that the arrows, the kicks and the insults of white racists whose behaviour even stimulated at times the unfavourable comment of their peers, and natural envy soon gave way to black resentment and resistance.

The 'company store' market at Forest Reserve oilfields

The general resistance of two oppressed peoples, African and Indian, to the oppression and exploitation of the capitalist class in Trinidad and Tobago, supported and reinforced by imperialist power, is a story of its own. Suffice it to say here that the early oil industry and the conditions prevailing therein up to 1937 played the most vital role in creating the circumstances within which that epic struggle was to take place, and added considerably to the contradictions between employers and wage earners in the century that followed emancipation.

The purpose of this exercise is not only to demonstrate the persistence of low wages as the main worker grievance in the hundred-year period after emancipation, but also to say something of its significance. It was not chance or negligence or oversight or bad planning, or no planning at all, that explained the unrelieved indigence and misery of the working people. It was no accident that they bore the brunt of economic hardship and impoverishment. Unrepresented in the political system, unrepresented in the economic system, and unorganized until the late nineteenth and early twentieth centuries, the working people subsidized their social betters with their labour, and this is what they were meant to do.

In the same sense that imperialism held it important to guarantee the survival of a privileged plantocracy after emancipation as far as that was humanly possible, so too it assigned an important priority to the creation of a dependent labouring population. Both objectives were crucial to the survival of postemancipation society in its static social form, and they were deliberately pursued. In Trinidad especially, the second half of the nineteenth century into the early decades of the twentieth was an era of modernization, largely of the sugar plantation sector, but also later involving petroleum as well. But it was not only modernization, narrowly and technically and technologically understood, that occupied the minds of policymakers. They were equally concerned with social engineering and socialization. The creation of social classes was as important as technical and technological advancement; and it was a commitment that permeated all the main aspects of social policy. Educators, for example, no less than policymakers and managers had very clear notions of what they were trying to do, the kind of society they were trying to build and the kind of people they were producing for it.

This is not to say that the process was unique. In the nineteenth century, one of the principal goals of the major imperial powers was to proletarianize labour; that is to say, not to create industry so that the labouring population could be made 'industrial', but rather to convert tribesmen, peasants and other rural folk who had no need of 'industry' into wage earners, dependent for their existence on the sale of their labour power to the enterprises engaged in generating profits for metropolitan and colonial capital. What was happening in Trinidad and Tobago was happening, or had already happened, or would in due course happen, in South Africa, South West Africa, in India, Indonesia, Kenya, Malaysia, Zambia, British Guiana, Jamaica, Madagascar, Kenya, Algeria, Indochina or any of a score of other colonies and semi-colonies that one can cite.

J.A. Hobson, the liberal critic of late nineteenth century imperialism, put it as follows:

The entire economic basis of the industrial exploitation of inferior races has shifted with modern conditions of life and industry. The change is a twofold one: the legal status of slaves has given place to that of wage-labourer, and the most profitable use of the hired labour of inferior races is to employ them in developing the resources of their own lands under white control for white men's profit.[61]

In other words, however much the whites might have despised the 'native' as a race, they esteemed the latter as workers and valued their labour power. Laws were invented, restrictions were imposed, customs and traditions were uprooted and, ultimately, even war was invoked in order to accomplish the robbery of native land and native wealth and to convert the native into a docile, tractable labourer. Louis Valery Vignon, a voluminous writer on the French Empire in the late nineteenth and early twentieth centuries, asked the key question: "What will become of a colonist having land to clear or plant, forests or mines to exploit, if he lacks men?"[62] And he answered by asserting the obligation of French colonial administrators to supply labour either from among the inhabitants themselves, or by immigration. The labour must be disciplined and cheap.

In South Africa, the rise of the diamond and gold industries provided the motivation and the means for effecting the subjugation of the indigenous peoples, and thereafter all that remained was to convert them into a reliable, cheap labour force for the mining industry. New land laws, the disarming of the natives, the imposition of taxes on their land, on men's wives, on their huts, on their cattle; the prohibition of native possession of gold and diamonds; the pass laws, the vagrancy acts, the underpayment and the various restrictions which prevented the black labourer, even the most skilful, from being employed in the most remunerative categories of work, ultimately and permanently reduced him to a helot worker at the beck and call of the mining camp. Also, imperialist assault on and devastation of the neighbouring states enlarged the available reservoir of labour and created a permanent surplus, reinforced by the migration of black mining workers.

Nor were low wages the only device of proletarianization. taxation was equally important. One of the most respected economic historians of the British Empire in the early decades of the twentieth century said that "taxation is a necessary corollary of the abolition of slavery". What she regretted was that "in these primitive countries . . . there is so little to tax".[63]

George Padmore would not have agreed. As he put it in one of his major publications:

Every male African between the age of 18 and 65, whether employed or not, is obliged to pay a poll tax of 29/- and a hut tax of 10/- a year. Quite often, young boys tending sheep and receiving a wage of only 5/- per month, are, if they look grown-up enough to be eighteen, obliged to pay the poll tax. This represents almost a 50 per cent income tax, while 'poor whites' are exempt from any form of direct taxation, and before the war, Europeans with incomes of £500 or less paid practically nothing.[64]

For the African the poll tax receipt was in several different places a kind of passport; but it did not suffice as such even though failure to produce it on demand often constituted a penal offence. Other pass laws, apart from being offensive in the extreme, saddled the African worker with an additional series of taxes; failure to pay could mean arrest without warrant, detention or sentencing to a work colony.[65]

In Trinidad in 1897, Walter Mills, the founder of the Trinidad Workingmen's Association, complained that

The very cutlass with which [the labourers] work in the cane field is taxed, whilst the sugar mill is introduced free . . . [Taxation] falls very heavily on the poor man who has to pay 4s. . . . for his hut, 1s. for the acre, 1 dollar for his gun, and one dollar for his dog . . . I think it unfair that the gentlemen who drive about with their carriages and pairs should not contribute something to pay for roads while the poor man's cart and cab are heavily taxed.[66]

The history of modern imperialism is and continues to be much more the chronicle of class formation than of racial extermination. To be exploited a people have, first of all, to exist. Races that cease to exist are no use to the imperialist, and are usually replaced, as the Caribs and Arawaks were replaced by the African slave. But existence is merely the precondition, in so far as subject peoples are concerned, for exploitation, for stratification and for the consolidation of race and class rule by the underpayment and exploitation of the majority and the selective remuneration of the chosen few.

In this process proletarianization was, and is, not left to chance. We are reminded again of Marx's famous dictum: "A negro is a negro. Under certain conditions he is a slave." And under different conditions he is a wage earner. In the imperial scheme of things, race was a given but it was nothing without class. Class was what imperial policymakers sought to create. And all policy, even the most 'enlightened', was geared to that purpose. The iron law of starvation wages and unrelenting taxation, among the most unenlightened of policies, was the cornerstone of the imperial design aimed at providing an oversupply of low paid workers in the service of colonial enterprise.

4

Family Strategies, Gender and the Shift to Wage Labour in the British Caribbean

Bridget Brereton

The women (who in croptime on sugar estates . . . formed two thirds of the Field Gangs) have now withdrawn themselves, to a very great extent, from field labour, to pursue those avocations to which females usually devote themselves in other countries.

–Special Magistrates' Report for St George's Parish, March 1839[1]

Introduction

From Brazil to the Caribbean to the United States, one "meaning of freedom", R.T. Smith has proposed, was "the withdrawal of female labour from plantation work". Contemporary observers – planters and estate managers, officials, missionaries and others – certainly devoted a great deal of comment to this development in the months and years after the final end of slavery in the British Caribbean (August 1838). But Smith is correct to suggest that this "withdrawal of female labour" has been "more remarked upon by historians of the United States than by commentators on the ending of Caribbean slavery". A review of the literature certainly suggests that the development has not been subjected to systematic analysis by historians of the British Caribbean. Both the extent and the significance of the movement seem uncertain. Was it in fact the case, as the American journalist W.G. Sewell commented some twenty years after emancipation, that "the effect of freedom was to abolish almost entirely the labour of women in the cane-fields"? And what lay behind the withdrawal of women, whatever its actual extent? As Smith asks, was it "an attempt by freedmen to establish their control over women, women's own declaration of their primary interest in domesticity, or what?"[2]

The purpose of this essay is to examine, on the basis of still very preliminary research, the withdrawal of women from estate labour in the British Caribbean following the end of formal slavery in 1838. I shall attempt to marshal evidence about the extent and timing of the withdrawal, to examine the use of 'family strategies' by the ex-slaves in their efforts to secure a degree of autonomy and economic security, and to consider the role of gender ideologies in women's removal from the estate labour force. I hope to show that in some colonies, many, probably most, women (and children) were able to leave the estates to pursue other occupations and goals; in others, however, this was possible for only relatively few. I will then argue that different kinds of family strategies lay behind the withdrawal of women and children, where that took place. Some were designed to ensure better care and security for members of the ex-slave household, especially children, and to enable the latter to go to school. Often the development of independent family farms was crucial, or the pursuit of other occupations (often gendered) to secure some independence from the plantation. Finally, while I acknowledge that European derived gender ideas must have influenced the choices of freedmen and freedwomen, I conclude that they were not merely obeying hegemonic ideology when they attempted to keep women, and children, out of full-time plantation work wherever possible.

There is now a scholarly consensus that enslaved women played a key role in the field labour force of Caribbean sugar plantations, outnumbering men in the crucial 'first gangs' during the last decades of slavery. As Marietta Morrissey argues, in the semi-industrial types of plantation agriculture, of which Caribbean sugar was the clearest example, there was relatively little gender differentiation in field work. But as sex ratios among Caribbean slave populations began to even out with the abolition of the slave trade (1806–7), as more and more men were absorbed in non-field occupations, as sugar consolidated its hold on most of the British colonies – women came to be *more* fully exploited in the field labour force than men, and they outnumbered men as field workers nearly everywhere by around 1815, if not earlier (much earlier in the case of Barbados). Significant numbers of male slaves were deployed in the skilled jobs and other non-agrarian occupations, while much smaller proportions of women were utilized in domestic service and other tasks outside the cane pieces. In the fields, women (along with men) performed all the routine tasks of cultivation, including holing and reaping, the two most physically demanding jobs. Not surprisingly, enslaved women paid a heavy price for their involvement in intensive sugar production. Their notoriously low fertility was due, to a large extent, to their punishing labour in the field gangs during their reproductive years (though other factors, including poor diet, disease, and voluntary control of fertility by contraception and abortion, were also significant).[3] But the critical point to establish is that women's labour was absolutely essential to Caribbean sugar plantations, especially in the last twenty years of slavery. Women (as well as men) were also fully engaged in the 'spare-time' cultivation of provision grounds and garden plots, and in the marketing of the produce that was not used for immediate consumption – the so-called provision grounds complex which was well developed in many colonies by the end of slavery.

When the British slave trade was abolished, planters generally attempted to adopt pronatalist policies designed to improve the fertility of their female chattels and to reduce infant and child mortality.[4] These policies failed everywhere in the sugar colonies (except Barbados), since they did not address the real causes of low fertility and high mortality (gang labour by women, poor diet, disease). But they did establish customary 'indulgences' to women slaves which became important during the transition from slavery to freedom. In particular, pregnant slaves were withdrawn from the first gang, generally during the second trimester, and assigned lighter tasks; women were not required to resume work until two or three months after delivery; nursing mothers were allowed shorter working hours and breaks during the day; and mothers of several living children were granted various rewards, including exemption from field labour in rare cases.[5]

Slavery in the British Caribbean was abolished in two stages. In August 1834, formal emancipation came into effect, but all the freed people over the age of six became 'apprentices' obliged by law to labour for their former owners, without wages, for most of the working week. This transitional 'apprenticeship' lasted until August 1838. In his study of the apprenticeship in the British Windward Islands, W.K. Marshall suggests that grievances during that period relating to the 'indulgences' to women probably had a major effect on the withdrawal of many after full freedom was granted in 1838. In the Windwards, planters generally refused to continue the special treatment of pregnant and nursing women after August 1834; the Abolition Acts passed by the various islands were silent on the question, and in the absence of any specific legal requirement, owners convinced themselves that they no longer had any obligations towards the health or even survival of their apprentices' infants. Nursing mothers, midwives and infant nurses, mothers of six or more children (previously enjoying a customary exemption from all field labour), were pressed into first gang labour. Pregnant women lost some of their special concessions. Inevitably, these women were deeply resentful at the reversal of exemptions and concessions which had come to be seen as customary; for them, Marshall notes, "apprenticeship could not have been seen as any mitigation of slavery". He further notes that women were the majority of Windward Islands apprentices purchasing their freedom before August 1838, reflecting, he suggests, "both a direct reaction to the withdrawal of labour exemption allowances and a growing concern for family welfare". Most of these female 'self-purchasers' left both plantation labour and residence.[6]

Marshall's argument is fully corroborated by the evidence, especially the testimony of the special magistrates, the officials appointed under the Emancipation Act to implement its provisions and monitor the transition to freedom. Those in Grenada, for instance, reported that on most estates, concessions to pregnant and nursing women – allowances of sugar and flour, "time in the morning to attend to their Children" – had been stopped. "The exemption of Women from labour during the latter stages of pregnancy," stated one, "is left to be decided by custom . . . and much Injustice is occasioned, and numerous complaints arise, from the defective state of the Law in this respect." Moreover, "those who had bore a certain number of Children, had advantages and indulgences in slavery, which they do not now possess". Planters reacted in similar ways in Jamaica; apprentices in the late stage of pregnancy were sometimes forced to work in the fields, mothers of many children were sent back to the cane-pieces, the services of midwives and infant nurses were withdrawn, and nursing mothers were denied special breaks during the day. In Trinidad, in a belated effort to give legal status to these concessions, the governor issued a proclamation – six weeks before the final end of the apprenticeship! – stating that any "exemptions from labour, allowances, privileges, and indulgencies, which by law or custom" were established for three years before 1834, must be continued to the apprentices. Specifically mentioned were total exemption from all labour for any woman having seven (not six) children "who are praedial Apprentices attached to the estate of her Employer"; the deduction of seven-and-a-half hours from the weekly compulsory labour time of any woman with more than three such children, *except* during harvest time; and two half-hour breaks from work for any woman with an infant under twelve months old. Clearly, the arrangement in force on the Barbadian estates owned by the Anglican Society for the Propagation of the Gospel – by which all "married" female apprentices, the mothers of young children, were given the "indulgence" of remaining at home until 9:00 a.m. – was a very unusual concession.[7]

But the arbitrary reversal of the customary concessions to mothers was not the only grievance which affected women during the apprenticeship and which no doubt helped to alienate them further from plantation labour. The situation of the 'free children' – those under six on 1 August 1834, who were not automatically apprenticed to their mothers' masters – became a significant issue contested between apprentices (especially mothers) and planters. In most colonies, planters generally refused to continue 'allowances' (food rations, clothing, free medical care) to the free children, unless they were *earned*, either by letting them work on the estate, or by the mothers giving additional, unpaid labour in return for these allowances. In Grenada, one magistrate reported, "the majority of Estates withhold, even Medical aid, unless the Mother will give four days of her own time every year when some Employers will consent to the Estate's Surgeon attending to the free Child".

Clause XIII of the Imperial Act of Emancipation gave mothers the option of apprenticing their free children to their masters, which would have secured them the contested allowances. But, throughout the four Windward Islands, parents rejected this option, despite planters' inducements and the magistrates' advice; only six such children were apprenticed in the four years after August 1834. In Grenada, some mothers refused to accept medical care for their free children "lest they should compromise them" or be "trapped" in some way; when a magistrate advised them to apprentice their little ones, they complained "the Special Magistrate wanted them to sell their children for Slaves!" In St Vincent, parents without exception refused to apprentice their children; in Tobago, the women, fearing re-enslavement, hid their young ones and rejected tempting offers from their employers. The children were supported by their parents, other relatives, or godparents; some were probably close to destitution, but mothers would not give in to the planters' crude coercion to get them to "yield up" their young children to the estate.[8]

Jamaican women responded similarly. "A greater insult could not be offered to a mother," reported a magistrate in 1835, "than by asking her free child to work." The Select Committee of the House of Commons on the apprenticeship was told by a Jamaica witness "Negro mothers have been known to say, pressing their child to their bosoms, 'we would rather see them die, than become apprentices'." Virtually no Jamaican child who was under six on 1 August 1834 was either apprenticed, or allowed to do estate work, for the duration of the apprenticeship. In Barbados, where provision grounds were inadequate or nonexistent and apprentices lived mainly on rations from their masters, the situation of the free children was especially difficult. Planters refused to supply the customary allowances to the island's 14,000 free children, despite the governor's appeals. And the mothers refused to apprentice their children; "magnificently adamant", as W.A. Green puts it, they said they would prefer to see them starve than to bind them to the estates. Despite evidence of rising infant and child mortality, it was not until 1837 that the Barbadian free children were guaranteed customary allowances by a local act.[9]

These grievances and issues surrounding the transitional experiment with the "Negro Apprenticeship" between 1834 and 1838, affecting primarily the women as mothers, and their young children, must have further worsened relations between planters and freed people. They must have brought home to the ex-slaves, men and women, the precariousness of family life for people who were fully dependent on the estates for survival, and the fragility of 'customary' privileges extended to them. Certainly, the contests over 'indulgences' to mothers and the situation of the free children during the apprenticeship must have made many women – and, no doubt, many of their male relatives – determined to withdraw from full-time estate labour once 'full free' came on 1 August 1838.

The Withdrawal from the Labour Force

It seems accepted in the literature that most ex-slave women who were married, or had small children, withdrew from the regular labour force of the British Caribbean sugar estates after 1838. For many contemporary commentators – such as the Jamaican special magistrate whose words are quoted at the head of this essay – this was "natural"; it was to be expected that women would take up maternal and domestic duties, their proper "avocation", once they were no longer coerced by law into field labour. And this also seems to be the view of some historians who have considered the development.[10] There can be no doubt that European gender ideologies which promoted this view were powerfully operative in the Caribbean colonies after the end of slavery, and we shall consider their influence later in this essay. Nevertheless, it is important to 'problematize' the women's withdrawal from estate labour, rather than to accept it as natural, granted that they had been the backbone of the field gangs during slavery and apprenticeship; and granted also that it is by no means clear that European gender norms were significantly entrenched among the ex-slaves (or, at least, most of them) during the immediate postemancipation period. To problematize the withdrawal is to seek to explain it, one of the objectives of the essay. It will also encourage us to examine carefully the *extent* of the withdrawal; and we are likely to find that Sewell's sweeping statement already quoted, to the effect that freedom virtually eliminated women's labour on the sugar estates, is wildly exaggerated.

The evidence suggests that many women, including mothers of young children, remained in the estate work force in the months and years after August 1838. Whether this was the result of coercion by managers, the lack of alternative modes of survival, or the women's own wishes, female labour in the field continued to be important to plantation production in most places. Probably this was particularly true in Barbados and the Leeward Islands; small, intensively cultivated sugar colonies where the provision grounds complex was relatively underdeveloped by 1838. A witness to the 1842 Parliamentary Select Committee on the West India Colonies stated that the Barbadian women engaged in field labour as willingly as the men; though there were a few tasks that they avoided, "generally speaking, at the ordinary work of the estate, I think they do as much, and quite as willingly" (as the men). In the middle of 1839, the police magistrates in charge of Barbados' eleven parishes responded to various queries on the working of free labour in the island; the replies certainly do not suggest that the ex-slave women had withdrawn from field labour to any significant extent. As several contemporary writers noted, a large proportion of Barbadian women continued to work full-time on the sugar estates into the 1850s and 1860s, including mothers of small children.[11] Antigua, another densely populated sugar island, opted to proceed straight to complete freedom in August 1834; and four years later, it was reported that women were fully engaged in field labour, though the mothers of small children received various concessions: they started work between 7:00 and 8:00 a.m. instead of at dawn; they could stop at 5:00 p.m. instead of at sunset; on very rainy days they were excused from field labour. Many women were classified as "first class labourers" earning a shilling a day, but mothers of babies tended to fall into the "second class" (nine pence a day), working the reduced hours. A witness to the 1842 Committee stated that the Antiguan women were "considered equally efficient with the male labourers". Throughout the 1840s, many women were still employed on the sugar plantations, and this remained the case in the second half of the century. St Kitts planters, too, considered the female labourers "as effective as the men", even for physically demanding tasks such as "holeing".[12]

There is no doubt that many women left plantation labour in the Windward Islands, which were less intensively cultivated and had well developed provision grounds/marketing complexes. Nevertheless, significant numbers stayed. A St Lucian special magistrate reported early in 1842 that "females claim no exemption from the usual work of an estate, and, indeed, are in many instances the foremost in setting the example of industry". A St Vincent colleague agreed, but he thought that most of the women stayed at work only under compulsion, for fear of losing their rent-free houses and grounds if they quitted the labour gangs. In Tobago, many women were still on the estate payrolls by 1847; in the Leeward District, for instance, there were 1,377 men and 952 women so enrolled in that year. In Grenada, over half of the estate labourers were women, according to the 1851 census; by 1881, there were some 7,000 female agricultural labourers out of a total of around 12,500.[13]

Conflicts over the obligation of married women and mothers to turn out to field labour every day, in return for 'free' houses and grounds, erupted all over Jamaica immediately after 1 August 1838. Though planters complained bitterly of the withdrawal of such women from regular estate work, there is some evidence to suggest that they greatly exaggerated the situation. For instance, though many ex-apprentices of both sexes simply stayed away from work in the weeks and months after 1 August those who did turn out included fair numbers of females: returns from the special magistrates for October 1838 indicate that on many sugar estates more women than men were returned as "resident agricultural labourers" and were actually engaged in field work. Both special magistrates and Baptist clergymen refuted the claim that most Jamaican women had totally withdrawn from field labour. The Trelawney magistrates stated that most of the women turned out at the start of the harvest in February 1839, and the crops were being efficiently reaped:

The result of the combined labour of males and females to the extent required – in fact, the proportion as far as regards the females is now so great as to excite the regrets and awaken the fears of the philanthropist, who regards the civilisation of the people and their moral improvement as the objects of incomparably greater importance than the manufacture of sugar.

The noted Baptist leader in Trelawney, William Knibb, said that in March 1839 his congregations included 1,703 men and 1,485 women at work on the sugar estates; and his colleagues in St James claimed that 2,209 men and 2,004 women belonging to their chapels were actually at work on the plantations.[14]

There is evidence from British Guiana, too, suggesting that many women remained on the estates after August 1838. A special magistrate, reporting on his 'tour' of Berbice towards the end of 1840, quoted a manager's remark that "the number of women at work is not so large as during the apprenticeship, but those who do go to the field labour well and steadily and frequently earn at their favourite employment, cane cutting, a dollar per day each". Another told him that "the women upon this property (Lochaben) work steadily and industriously", though many had withdrawn from field labour since August 1838. Special Magistrate J.A. Allen of Berbice stated that, in his district, about two-thirds of the adult women on the estates during the apprenticeship were still at work by the end of 1840. Allen went on to note:

With reference to the average number of women stated to be at work – it has been found that the labour of a greater proportion, was seldom obtained during the apprenticeship, owing to sickness or other casualties – and it would appear that the number of men and women on the pay lists who now usually turn out for the performance of the daily task on estates, equals and often surpasses the *number* of those who were coerced to work during slavery or apprenticeship.

Allen and his colleagues in Berbice reported that the women worked the same hours as the men, received exactly the same wages for the same type and quantity of work (one guilder a day for "first class" labourers), and performed the same tasks in the fields, except that trenching ("shovel work") was done only by men; women cut canes "better than men". Differential wage rates certainly did exist in some parts of British Guiana; however, in 1844, women were paid less than men for tasks such as feeding canes to the mill, fetching megass, threshing young canes, and weeding, all jobs done by both sexes. But whatever the truth about wage rates in the post 1838 period, it is clear that many African-Guyanese women continued to labour on the sugar estates.[15]

In Trinidad, planters do not seem to have complained of a female exodus from the fields, at least during the first years after 1838. In an interesting newspaper exchange in August 1839, a letter writer claimed that women were the best workers, that much of the labour previously lost "in hospitals, nursings and pregnancies" had now been restored to the estates, that females and boys provided the "most continuous" services to the plantations, and that many women performed two tasks in a day while men rarely did; "this may arise," he speculated, "from a deep-rooted African idea of female inferiority." The newspaper editor commented:

It was generally prophesied, that the women would not work in a state of freedom. [The writer] honestly admits that it is the women who work best, so confessing the error of the former opinion, and there was no opinion, we believe, that was more generally held by those who plumed themselves on an acute knowledge of the negro character.

The anonymous correspondent received some support for his views from experienced Trinidad managers who gave evidence to a local enquiry conducted in 1841. The Philippine manager (himself an ex-slave) testified that many women on his estate performed exceptionally well: "I have two women on the estate who do three tasks per day with ease", though he admitted that this was a rare feat. Richard Darling, 'planting attorney' for seven estates, was asked "Are you supposing that the women are to work as steadily as in a period of slavery, and would you calculate upon this as a probable result?" He replied: "I find in general that the women work much more steadily now than I expected, and I am not disposed to make any material deduction on that account." There seems to be little evidence, at least for the period before the start of indentured Indian immigration (1845), that the Trinidad planters were interested in minimizing female employment in order to secure a "rationalized", predominantly male, labour force, as Kusha Haraksingh has suggested.[16]

Sufficient evidence has been presented here, I hope, to show that many ex-slave women remained in the estate labour force of the British Caribbean in the decade after August 1838, for whatever reason or combination of reasons. Unfortunately, my data do not permit me to say whether most of these women were mothers, or whether they were young rather than older persons; I am simply unable to distinguish between those who stayed and those who withdrew in terms of age, motherhood, or family size. As a generalization, I would suggest (speculate) that women with small children would be more likely than others to withdraw if they had alternatives. There is certainly abundant documentation to show that the female 'withdrawal' was a reality, though far from universal, and naturally more pronounced in some colonies than in others. I now turn to review some of that documentation.

Even in Barbados and the Leeward Islands, where most women probably had fewer alternatives to continued plantation labour, some of them left the full-time estate work force. Frances Lanagan reported from Antigua that, by 1842 (eight years after complete emancipation there), 'many' female ex-slaves had left agricultural labour to settle in St John's, generally as washerwomen, hucksters, or manual labourers. The inspector of police in Barbados thought that some women had abandoned field labour in the nine months after 1 August 1838, to work as domestics, or "petty hucksters"; "others attend to their families and are supported by their husbands, and it is said (and I believe correctly) that many young women have come into the Town [Bridgetown] and Garrison and live by prostitution".[17] Still, the evidence suggests that most ex-slave women in these islands remained locked into their estate labour force.

This was probably not the case in the Windward Islands. W.K. Marshall believes that perhaps one-third of the workforce in Grenada, St Lucia, Tobago and St Vincent had withdrawn from the plantations by 1846, and that "women were probably the largest group" among the "permanent defectors from estate labour". A St Vincent estate manager suggested to the 1842 committee that "many women who used to work, refuse to labour now on the plea of being married" and that "fully two-thirds" of St Vincent females had given up working in the field, though Marshall comments that he probably meant two-thirds no longer worked regularly rather than rejecting all estate employment. In Tobago, the magistrates' returns suggest that while there were 4,305 female apprentices on 31 July 1838, only 2,037 women were on the estate payrolls by July 1842, and Susan Craig agrees that most of the *permanent* withdrawal from estate labour in that island was by women. The withdrawal from estate labour in Tobago was accelerated by the reduction of wages in 1846–48, and by the effects of a disastrous hurricane in 1847, but the figures suggest that far more women than men left the work force in these years. In the Leeward District, for instance, 195 men and 387 women left the estate payrolls during the second half of 1848. By 1852, men greatly outnumbered women on the payrolls of all the Tobago estates.[18]

In British Guiana, significant numbers of women left the estate labour force. The antislavery activist John Scoble told the 1842 Select Committee:

On some estates the same classes of women work as did during the periods of apprenticeship and slavery, but a very large number of the women upon the estates do not do either the same kind of work or the same amount of work as they did . . . Those who are mothers and have families, or have young infants to take care of, are mostly found at home, taking care of their children.

A Berbice special magistrate wrote in December 1840 that "we find the number of women and children occupied in agricultural employment to be considerably, I may add, alarmingly, diminished". One Berbice manager thought that "one half at least" of his women had withdrawn from field labour since August 1838; a magistrate believed that only one-third of the female apprentices turned out on an average day on the sugar estates and about two-thirds on the coffee properties, and even they seldom stayed in the fields for more than four hours, "according to their inclination". Although the evidence for a significant female exodus in Trinidad after August 1838 is very thin, there is some indication that women quit the labour force "to be supported by their husbands" or to work as "washers, hucksters, servants etc".[19]

Labour relations in Jamaica, relatively large and ecologically diverse, were especially volatile during the apprenticeship and after its end; and issues surrounding the right of women, living in houses and farming grounds which were owned by the estates, to refuse to labour for them on a regular basis, were bitterly contested. Partly as a result of these conflicts, large numbers of Jamaican ex-slave women withdrew from regular estate employment. The planters believed (or pretended to) that these women had received positive encouragement from the governor to quit estate labour; in an address to Jamaican "Praedial Apprentices" on the eve of full emancipation, Sir Lionel Smith had appealed to the (male) ex-slaves: "Be kind to your wives and children – spare your wives from heavy field work, as much as you can – make them attend to their duties at home . . ." Planter opinion had it that women all over Jamaica interpreted these words as a positive injunction to 'sit down' and leave estate work entirely. Smith's words generated a protracted controversy, which was reported in the Trinidad newspapers, much agitated in the Jamaican press, and thrashed out in a voluminous Parliamentary Paper.[20] But though all this was useful ammunition in the Jamaican planters' campaign against the 'pro-labour' governor, it is not very likely that the women were significantly influenced by his words when some of them decided to opt out of field labour.

Swithin Wilmot has shown how Jamaican ex-slave women and their families fought to secure the right of wives and mothers not to be obliged to work for the estates on pain of eviction from houses and grounds. He notes, for instance, that on Golden Grove, a large estate in St Thomas which had 137 resident females on 31 July 1838, only 19 of them were back at work by the end of October as compared to 137 men (out of a total 142). All over Jamaica, ex-slaves insisted that mothers of young children and large families should be exempted from regular field labour without facing eviction; and managers were forced to concede the point. On Golden Grove, it was reported, "the females generally have declared they are not again to work in the field, although determined, as they say, to continue on, and be supported by the estate"; management had to agree (in the case of mothers). On Hopewell estate, Hanover, "it is agreed that married women are . . . not required to labour unless they are so disposed to labour. Children also are not to be [required to work] unless it is the wish of their parents and guardians." In the first few months after 1 August significant numbers of women withdrew from full-time labour on the Jamaican sugar estates, especially in those districts where provision grounds were available and profitable.[21]

The planters complained bitterly of the loss of so much female labour, a loss they may well have overstated to make their point. In Hanover, they claimed that before 1 August 1838, there were 4,253 'persons' resident on the estates, by January 1839 there were 2,143; "of the former number, about one-half were females, while of the latter, the proportion is between one-fifth and one-sixth". Similar claims were put forward by planter dominated committees in other parishes. Though magistrates and clergymen felt that these claims were exaggerated (with respect to the numbers abandoning estate labour completely), there was wide agreement that a significant withdrawal by married women and mothers had occurred by the middle of 1839. The special magistrates of St George's parish summed it up:

The women (who in crop time on sugar estates which continues in this parish throughout the whole year formed two thirds of the *Field Gangs*, the men being principally employed about the works and as wainsmen etc) have now withdrawn themselves, to a very great extent, from field labour, to pursue those avocations to which females usually devote themselves in other countries. In addition we may be allowed to mention, that women within a few weeks of their confinement, or with infants a few weeks old at their breasts, – mothers of large young families, – children under 12 years of age, – . . . no longer, as hitherto, form a part of the labouring population of this parish.

They estimated that there were some 900 women who had withdrawn from estate labour in the parish due to pregnancy or maternal duties, plus another 500 "women in general". And it was not only the sugar estates which experienced a loss of female labour; coffee properties reported the same trend, though it seems to a lesser degree. On the cattle estates ("pens"), Verene Shepherd shows that the proportion of female labourers steadily declined after August 1838. On Fort George Pen, as early as 1843, there were only twenty-seven women out of a labour force of one hundred. Pen labour forces became increasingly male by the mid century, the result both of voluntary withdrawal by females and the phasing out of 'women's tasks' by managers.[22]

During slavery and apprenticeship, women had been the backbone of the field gangs on the sugar estates. It is not surprising, therefore, that managers attempted to coerce them into continued labour after 1 August especially by tenancy at will and other arrangements involving the huts and grounds. These efforts reflect the importance of female labour to sugar production. When women, and men, resisted them, they were demonstrating that they were not prepared to subordinate their own and their families' welfare to the needs of the plantation. When their resistance failed, and wives and mothers returned to regular estate labour, this was often the result of the lack of alternative means of survival rather than positive choices. As a Jamaican special magistrate put it, in 1839:

Does a considerable portion of the population, especially of the women, look with dislike on that description of labour to which they were peculiarly devoted as slaves, and which is inseparably associated in their minds with the idea of pain, oppression and degradation? . . . If they have no other subsistence, hunger will soon compel them to take a hoe again into their hands; if they have other sources of support, do not interfere with them.[23]

In the Windward Islands, planters tried to compel the labour of women (and children) by insisting, as a condition of 'free' occupancy of a house and grounds, that every family member of working age should do regular estate work at stipulated wages; wives and children could not enjoy a right of residence in their husbands' and fathers' houses unless they complied. In St Vincent, this issue was submitted to the lieutenant governor for his opinion; he ruled that while the *legal* wife of a resident labourer, who refused to work, would be entitled to claim residence in his house, the *reputed* (common law) wife would not; she could therefore be lawfully evicted. On Penniston Estate, St Vincent, Adam went to the magistrate just after 1 August stating he was willing to work, but claiming "an exemption from labour, and a right of residence on the estate, for his wife". The magistrate, guided by the lieutenant governor's ruling, decided that common law wives could not claim any exemption from labour and enjoy residence on the estate. Did this violate a man's right to receive his wife into his home? Yes, argued the magistrate, but it was "the restraint of *one* right, in consideration of *another*" – the right to insist that he and his wife be employed and housed by the estate, even if the owner did not wish to. This kind of legalized coercion must have driven many families away from the estates forever, but it no doubt succeeded in tying down female labour for a time. A St Vincent magistrate thought that the system forced women to labour continuously to avoid eviction, but it was the general "desire of the peasantry" to release wives and mothers from regular estate work.[24]

Tenancy arrangements were also exploited in St Lucia and Grenada to compel the women (and children) to work for the estates. A St Lucian newspaper insisted that every labourer living on an estate must be forced to give regular labour, nine or ten hours daily, Monday to Friday, in return for cottage and grounds: "The proprietor who allows a single male *or female*, or the husband of a family, to remain on his property, without receiving the continuous work *of the party*, acts unjustly to himself." A Grenadian planter proposed to deduct for rent one-fifth of the weekly wages of every member of a resident family who was old enough to work, that is, every member over the age of six. The deduction would be two-fifths whenever a family member was absent from work without leave. This plan was recommended to Trinidad planters by the *Port-of-Spain Gazette*, though tenancy at will was rarely resorted to in that island. Trinidad planters, like their counterparts in British Guiana, did sometimes bring delinquent female labourers before the magistrates for breach of contract – leaving their employment without notice or leave – but, at least before 1848, they could do little to stem the movement away from their estates in either colony, by both men and women.[25]

It was, however, particularly in Jamaica that planters tried to compel the labour of women (and children), especially during croptime, by manipulating payments for huts and grounds in 1838–39, charging per capita rents for every member of a resident family judged capable of estate work. Wilmot describes the intense struggles which ensued between ex-slaves and managers in the island's sugar parishes, which often resulted in concessions by which wives and mothers were relieved of the obligation to turn out in the fields every day on pain of eviction. The Jamaican special magistrates fully documented these struggles over the coercive manipulation of rents in the months after 1 August 1838. "I have this week been visited," reported a Trelawney magistrate in September 1838,

> by several married, and some aged and decrepit females, from Gibraltar Estate, who have exhibited notices . . . served on them by the overseer, because they had devoted their attention to their husbands and families who are working on the same estate, evidently with the design of compelling them, under the fear of a separation, to relinquish their attention to their domestic duties, and apply themselves unremittingly to the labours of the field. I have apprised them of the impractability of ejecting them from the residences of their husbands, and assured them of legal protection . . . It is most probable that these notices, absurd and unjustifiable as they are, will very much unsettle the feelings of these illiterate persons.[26]

In St Elizabeth parish, a magistrate stated, "It is a fact that two, three, and even four days' labour are demanded from every member of a family; from the husband, from the wife, and from every one of the children, as the rent of the miserable dwellings with which negroes have hitherto been contented, and of an acre or an acre and a half of provision ground." At the average wage of 1s. a day, the rent thus demanded might amount to £40 or £50 a year, an enormous sum. In one typical case, Charles Williams was charged 15s. per week for himself, his wife, and three children, while his elder son (living in the same house) was charged 2s. 6d. for his use of the family grounds – a total of £45 per annum for an "old thatched house, built by the family's own hands and expense, with the provision ground cultivated in like manner". The magistrates recognized that the main object of these iniquitous demands was to compel women back into the fields, and one warned *"the binding down of married women* should be studiously avoided, the people never will be induced to consent to this". Although on many estates managers were forced to make a crucial concession – to agree that mothers of young children or large families could be exempted from field labour without risking ejectment – the magistrates saw that the rent exactions were driving people away from the estates, especially the "respectable, confidential men" who were anxious to get their wives and children out of the planters' control.[27]

The coercive tactics to compel the women and children to give regular labour to the estates generally failed; or at least, they failed in those colonies and districts where ex-slave families could maintain themselves without the wages of wives, mothers and young children. The 'withdrawal' by women was a reality, and on a fairly large scale except in Barbados and the Leeward Islands, though naturally its extent and timing varied considerably. We can now turn to an investigation of the ex-slaves' motives and strategies.

Family Strategies

As Nigel Bolland has suggested, the concept of freedom held by most ex-slaves in the British Caribbean (as elsewhere in the Americas) was not necessarily Western individualism or personal autonomy; family and community goals were frequently given priority over individual advancement, or perhaps the distinction was simply irrelevant. The survival and welfare of the family group were probably paramount for most of the freed people in the unsettled aftermath of 1 August 1838. Moreover, their concerns were probably not limited to the material advancement of the family unit or even the desire to make it independent of the plantation; freed people were also anxious to build up networks of social ties (especially but not exclusively kinship ties) within which they saw family life as properly functioning.[28] Their goals were not always, or even primarily, economic. A communally oriented social life, dignified treatment by employers, time to devote to religious and cultural pursuits, physical and emotional security for the most vulnerable members of the family – these were all important to the ex-slaves.

Women and children were especially vulnerable to abuse of all kinds during slavery and apprenticeship, and it is reasonable to assume that the ex-slaves wanted to assure them a degree of protection and security. One way of doing so was to remove them, wherever possible, from the direct control of estate management, and to locate their lives and productive labour within the household and the family farm rather than the plantation. As R.T. Smith puts it, freedom might mean the opportunity for women to work on behalf of their families "within the protected spheres of household and community". Family welfare, moreover, might dictate that the mothers of young children should devote much of their time to child care. Walter Rodney saw the determination of many women to give priority to their children, rather than labouring for twelve hours a day in the planters' fields, as "an advanced decision" taken in the interest of family continuity (and, indeed, sheer survival).[29]

It is clear that one of the primary motives behind the withdrawal of women from estate labour was to allow them to give more time and attention to child rearing. Clergymen, antislavery activists, magistrates and planters all made the same point, though with varying degrees of approval. "Those who are mothers and have families," John Scoble asserted, "or who have young infants, are mostly found at home, taking care of their children." Knibb of Jamaica said the women were spending more time on their "domestic duties, and the care of their families". A St Vincent planter noted that the ex-slaves were "constantly looking out for land where they can go and live, and allow their wives to sit down, as we call it, and take charge of the children". In 1848, a British Guiana planter told a parliamentary enquiry that since 1838, the better-off ex-slaves "keep their wives at home to take care of their houses, or look after the children, who used all to be reared in the nursery of the estate; and for that reason at least half the female labourers have been taken from the field and from the estate". When a St Vincent manager tried to compel all the resident women to work, on pain of eviction, they complained to the magistrate "that when the mothers are in the field, the children are neglected, because the grandmothers are also compelled to labour". Withdrawal from field labour, a Grenadian magistrate noted, gave "the mother the opportunity of personally attending her child in sickness; during apprenticeship the infant was left under the care of an old person, called a nurse, while the mother was at her compulsory labour". In Jamaica, a magistrate rejoiced that pregnant and nursing women, and mothers of large families, were no longer forced into the fields each day; they were now free to choose "those pursuits best suited to their condition and necessities". And a colleague suggested that one of the greatest "blessings of freedom to the labouring people" was the fact that "no women, suffering from pregnancy or from having numerous children, are now brought before magistrates to be punished for not turning out to work in the fields".[30]

As in the US, Caribbean ex-slaves expected that freedom would mean the chance to consolidate the family unit and reconstitute kin groups separated by slavery. Women seem to have played the leading role in these efforts. Samuel Smith, an Antiguan born in 1877, heard as a child of the heroic efforts of Rachael, his African-born great-great-grandmother, and her daughters, to re-unite the family. In Trinidad, in the weeks after 1 August the freed people were moving around the island, migrating to different areas to resume "family connexions". At Orange Grove Estate, for instance, people were reported to have left and "attached themselves to friends and families elsewhere". Although the evidence of family reconstitution after emancipation in the British Caribbean is rather thin, there is no reason to doubt Marshall's conclusion that many ex-slaves did succeed in this goal.[31]

Of course, there was considerable diversity of family forms among the newly freed people. The demographic historians, especially B.W. Higman, have shown that family units including coresidential husbands and wives were common, at least on fairly large estates, during the last few decades of slavery. In Higman's sample of three Jamaican estates in 1825, about 100 (out of 252) households included a coresidential conjugal couple, and nearly half of the slaves lived in households approximating the nuclear form. His work on Trinidad in 1813 establishes that – of the slaves who did live in a family of some kind – about 44 percent were in mother–children units and roughly the same percentage were in units including a conjugal couple. The consensus seems to be that casual sexual liaisons were common among young slaves, but that relatively stable monogamous (consensual) unions were the norm for other adults. Mother–children units, and units consisting of a conjugal couple with children (hers, theirs, less often his), were the most commonly found family types on the plantations.[32] Although the data do not allow us to discuss the effect of family structure on the departure of women and children from the estate labour force after freedom, we can at least speculate that women in stable coresidential unions might have had greater opportunities to quit plantation work than those solely responsible for child support. These women, too, were more likely to have had husbands anxious to keep them out of the estate labour force, and (probably) to have been the mothers of several children.

It is clear that the withdrawal of many women from gang labour on the sugar estates helped to effect a "demographic transformation" in the British Caribbean. The excess of deaths over births in Jamaica was "completely arrested" by 1844, for instance. As Richard Sheridan notes, the fertility of African-Caribbean women, and the health of themselves and their children, improved significantly after 1838, largely the result of the abandonment of estate labour by so many females in their reproductive years. As a St Lucian special magistrate put it, freedom had produced this "happy change": on several estates, "where the female slaves rarely had children, or if mothers rarely succeeded in rearing their offspring – the free woman is now both fruitful and successful in bringing up her children". Clearly, withdrawal from full-time gang labour by ex-slave women promoted family welfare in the most basic sense: its physical survival and continuity.[33]

The decision taken by men and women to keep mothers out of the estate labour force, if possible, clearly contributed to the stability of family units and the upgrading of domestic comforts (within the constraints of persistent poverty). Many testified to the upsurge in legal and Christian marriages after 1838, the greater harmony in ex-slave households, and the improvement in their housing, clothing, diet and furnishings. We do not need to accept the ideological premises of much of this testimony to recognize that many freed people reaped solid benefits in their domestic lives from the withdrawal of women from field labour.

Numerous witnesses to the 1842 Select Committee testified to the strong sense of family responsibility among ex-slaves, especially where couples had married (as so many did in the immediate aftermath of 1 August). The freed people felt responsible for their children and aged or ill relatives, feelings "alien to a state of slavery", as one put it, and worked hard to support them. Parents tried to send their children to school, and nearly always had them baptized. "The well disposed labourer is now as anxious," wrote a St Lucian magistrate in 1842,

and shews as much solicitude, in rearing his offspring, as he was in times gone by, callous and indifferent to its fate ... While in former times, the mother was burthened with the trouble and expense of her offspring, abandoned as was frequently the case, by its reputed father, the obligation now becomes mutual, and the interest in the welfare and preservation of the child is enhanced in the same ratio.

Respectable married people generally observed their vows, sexual morality had improved (though one British Guiana magistrate tartly observed "the example of the higher classes is not calculated to raise the tone of morality in this respect"), and disputes and violent quarrels in the home were less frequent. Many ex-slave families succeeded in raising their standard of living with respect to their homes, furnishings, meals and dress. These achievements by the freed people were due, at least in part, to their efforts to keep mothers (and children) out of estate labour and to consolidate the family unit.[34]

There is a great deal of evidence to show that children under the age of sixteen or seventeen were not generally allowed by their parents to do field work on the estates in the post 1838 years, especially not on the plantations on which they resided. (In Barbados, it was noted that when "juveniles" worked on sugar estates, "their engagements are not generally assumed on the same properties where their parents are located".) Planters complained loudly that the young people were idle, that they were being kept away from agriculture; but it is clear that they were routinely employed on their parents' grounds or family farms, or were taught a trade in the case of the boys. In Berbice, a magistrate thought that "dire necessity alone would induce parents to allow them to perform field labour". In Trinidad, R.H. Church stated that virtually no children under the age of twelve were put to field labour; many of them were sent away from their parents' estates to live with godparents or relatives in other places. Parents believed it was "degrading" for the children to do field work. A newspaper correspondent in Trinidad claimed that all the "young people" between ten and sixteen or seventeen were kept out of the fields by their parents. A Barbadian planter agreed: "They will not put their children in any respect to learn the labour of the fields." A magistrate from the same island asserted in 1839: "I know of no case where the parents will permit their children to be brought up to agricultural pursuits", despite offers of 'liberal' wages and kind treatment.[35]

Although it is clear that some parents did send children over the age of eleven or twelve to plantation employment, these seem generally to have been the poorest families who needed their small earnings to survive. A St Vincent magistrate thought that it was only the "children of the more ignorant class" who were sent early to the estates, "the parents having in view the benefits of their earnings". But it seems to have been the universal practice to employ the children, boys and girls, on the family grounds, to have the girls help at home in the housework and household production, and to use both to help transport garden produce to market. Clearly, the children were being absorbed into domestic production, working as part of the family unit, only sent out to the estates in times of real need.[36]

Moreover, parents showed extreme anxiety to send their young children to school, especially immediately after 1838. Church stated that Trinidad parents "exult very much in the idea of sending them to school; and it gratifies them very much when one of their children can read"; "whenever they can get to school they will go". In Barbados, a deputation of (male) labourers from St George's Parish told the governor's secretary in 1839 that getting their children to school was very important to them:

On the subject of the children, [the leader] answered that it was true that they did not put them to work on the estates just now, but this was because they wanted them to get some education to learn to read the Bible. It was this feeling and no wish to keep them from work, which urged them to give their children a little schooling.[37]

Keeping young children, as well as their mothers, out of field labour on the estates, sending them to school if possible, and using the older boys and girls in domestic production and housework, as part of a family work unit, were important aspects of the ex-slaves' strategies. Moreover, the remark by the Barbadian spokesman quoted above illustrates the point that *non-economic* purposes were important too: the children should go to school so that they could read the Bible rather than (or as well as?) getting ahead generally. Religious and social goals lay behind the ex-slaves' strategies, as well as economic ones.

We have already seen that many women remained in the full-time plantation workforce, perhaps for lack of alternative means of subsistence, and certainly many older children did too. Another strategy was to organize estate work so that women and children laboured within a family unit, giving them a greater degree of protection, and more flexibility with respect to time, than gang labour could afford. In the US, the shift from slave plantations to sharecropping meant that most ex-slaves worked in family units rather than gangs, with the male heads of families usually allocating tasks and controlling earnings. Something like this may have developed on Caribbean sugar estates here and there after 1838, though gang labour remained the norm in most places. On sugar estates in St George's parish, Jamaica, where work was allocated by 'task', "the father works his family under his own superintendence, his name only appearing for the work done, and getting paid weekly for the work". Such 'jobs' might be large scale, such as a contract to prepare and plant a cane-piece of nearly eight acres; the contractor received £60, and employed only family labour, presumably including women and children. In Antigua, during crop, male cane-cutters worked with female 'tiers', who tied up the bundles of cane; they were usually relatives, and they might also help to cut the canes, but they did not receive any wage directly from the planter. On St Vincent cotton estates worked on the *metayer* (cropping) system, the 'heads of families' entered into *metayer* agreements and used family labour to cultivate the fields. When children laboured for estate wages, it was the norm for them to hand over their earnings to their parents or other relatives; and they all worked on the family provision grounds ("kept as little *slaves* by their relatives", according to a Tobago magistrate).[38] Such strategies, while affording some protection to women and children working for the estates, and relieving them of the full rigours of the gang regime, must have enhanced male authority over the women and generally have reduced their control of their earnings and (perhaps) their status in the family unit.

As many historians have argued, and as contemporary observers were well aware, one of the most important objectives of the ex-slaves in 1838 was to become independent cultivators. The ability to grow crops, for family subsistence and for sale, was crucial in securing a degree of independence from the plantation. The provision grounds complex, already well developed in most colonies long before 1838, was central to the freed people's family strategies. The goal was to combine wage labour (mainly by men, perhaps also by young, single women) with independent farming carried out by all family members, but especially by women and children. Where suitable land could be procured – by purchase, renting or squatting, or estate owned grounds farmed by resident labourers – this was the preferred family strategy. The labour of female and youthful members of the family would, for the most part, be absorbed in domestic agriculture and marketing, while the men worked for wages on the estates, or practiced artisan skills, as well as helping out on the farm. Certainly, the care of children and domesticity provided important motivations for wives and mothers withdrawing from estate labour; but farming and marketing on lands controlled by the family were equally crucial to most of these women.

Strategies such as these were followed by ex-slave families nearly everywhere in the British Caribbean after 1838. I propose to illustrate the point by using the Windward Islands as my example. In St Vincent, H.M. Grant of Calder estate believed that "every industrious family" could earn a hundred dollars per annum from its provision ground, "besides keeping the family"; the men were always "looking out for land on which they can go and live, and allow their wives to sit down". He had been obliged to give his female workers every second Friday off, so that they could have extra time for provision cultivation and marketing. A St Vincent magistrate reported that the men often quit their estates, "leaving their wives and children living on them, by that means reaping the provisions whilst they get higher wages in another quarter". In other words, the men sought wage jobs at the highest rates they could get, while the women and children worked the provision grounds (and presumably gave some labour to the estate to avoid eviction). A similar tactic was reported from St Lucia; on a large estate near Souffrière,

which during 'apprenticeship' had an excellent gang of both sexes – has now [1843] scarcely any but women located upon it, the men have nearly all left, dwell in town and hire themselves as non-located labourers, the women however, slyly enough, remain and keep possession of houses and grounds, knowing well that their sex can easily find excuses for their frequent absences from regular field labour – and the men I have every reason to believe under pretence of helping the women still enjoy all the benefits of ample provision grounds rent free.

Although this family strategy was obviously serviceable, most ex-slaves wanted to establish themselves on lands wholly independent of the plantation, where they could be "completely emancipated from the thraldom of an estate, and beyond the influence of caprice or compulsion, as to the occupation of their dwelling or the appropriation of their labour". On such lands, family farms were established, "abounding with poultry and livestock raised by the industry of the Cottager's family", while the men often gave labour to nearby sugar estates. In Tobago, labourers quitted their old estates to live on lands they bought or rented; if the 'cottager' was married, "his wife acts the part of Domestic, Gardener, and Marketer, whilst he readily earns one shilling a day on an Estate when he likes to work, or he may cultivate Canes on the Metairie [cropping] system". Everywhere, parents used their children's labour to help on the provision grounds and family farms. In Grenada, it was reported in 1839, "parents of families, headmen and tradesmen, hire the dependent negroes to no small extent in cultivating their gardens and preparing the manioc for sale . . . So long as a family by sending one member of it, in routine to the cane field daily, can retain acres of fruitful soil", sugar estates, lamented a Grenadian newspaper, would always be short of hands.[39]

These family strategies, combining wage labour by men with domestic production and marketing by women and children, were pursued in most Caribbean territories, including Jamaica, British Guiana and Trinidad. They were much harder to achieve for the ex-slaves of Barbados and some of the Leewards, where the provision grounds system was not well developed by 1838 and sugar monoculture was the norm. Located labourers in Barbados certainly "evinced an anxious desire to become more independent in their domestic establishments" by erecting cottages on lands away from their estates, but it was difficult to realize that goal. When Barbadians immediately after August 1 asked for four eight-hour days instead of five of nine hours, in order to secure more control over their time, they were threatened with immediate ejectment. With virtually no provision grounds accessible to them, Barbadian labourers had few options but to "come to terms" and accept tenancy at will arrangements. Marshall's assertion that "economic pressures ensured that family labour had to be directed outward rather than toward a family farm" in the years after 1838 is certainly true for most of the Barbadian and Leeward Islands ex-slaves.[40]

Many ex-slave families after 1838, we have argued, tried to employ women and children in domestic production and marketing, while men sought wage jobs as estate labourers or artisans. This was a gendered occupational strategy adopted by the freed people for their own purposes. (It would be interesting to speculate on whether men and women were broadly *agreed* on this strategy, or whether it was primarily supported or imposed by the men; my hunch would be the former.) In general, in the Caribbean as elsewhere, the ex-slaves expected men to work at skilled trades and in occupations requiring long absences from home (fishing, seafaring and forestry, for instance), while women were mostly involved in domestic work and independent farming. The most important exception to this generalization is probably provided by the hucksters, or higglers (Jamaica), or *marchandes* (Trinidad, St Lucia, Dominica). They were nearly always women, and they were highly mobile, routinely travelling relatively long distances as they went to markets and visited rural villages. This tradition predated 1838; women slaves might keep a huckster's shop on the estate, such as 'C', the head cook on A.C. Carmichael's estate in Trinidad in the late 1820s. Charles Day wrote that around 1848, "every third negress" in Trinidad kept a little shop, selling ale and beer, plantains, salt fish and other goods, while female vendors walked the streets selling food and drinks. Others travelled on foot with their baskets or trays deep into the country, over roads impassable by carts, wagons or even horses, "bringing within the reach of the labouring population, necessaries and luxuries".[41]

In St Lucia, too, the *marchandes* travelled from estate to estate, employed by town shops to peddle prints, handkerchiefs, jewelry and assorted 'dry goods' to the rural labourers. On pay day, they turned up "like Vultures, scenting the Carrion", according to an unsympathetic magistrate, successfully extorting their payments since they were "greater adepts than the labourer in the mysteries of Commerce". They made sufficient money to make it worthwhile for the St Lucian government to impose a license fee on them in 1843. Other women kept small village shops. Many Antiguan women were hucksters in and around St John's; Frances Lanagan described them as occupying "every street corner". They specialized in different goods – cloth, thread, lace and so on; or fruits and vegetables; or salt fish, rice, cornmeal; or soap and candles. Some had tiny shops, some sold in the town markets; others walked all over the island with their goods. This was a flexible kind of occupation, allowing mobility and considerable independence even for those employed by storekeepers, and probably some of the hucksters lived reasonably well from their earnings. It was certainly preferable to the dependence of the domestic's life; as a Grenadian magistrate noted, "Girls are mostly employed at needlework or as hucksters, very few like the confinement of Domestic Servants."[42]

Except for seamstressing and laundry work, the skilled, mechanical and artisanal trades were male occupations. Everywhere, parents tried to have their sons learn a trade: the ideal family strategy after 1838 included at least one member who was a skilled worker. Work on the sea and the rivers, and in the forests, was also a male preserve. In St Lucia, men cut timber, made charcoal, fished and made boats. In remote ex-slave settlements up the rivers and creeks of British Guiana, the men fished and transported goods by boat, cut timber and made charcoal, and tapped ('bled') balata; women did some subsistence farming. In British Honduras, virtually all the men were employed in the timber industry (82 percent of the male slaves aged 10 to 59 in 1834) and most of the women were domestics in Belize Town (73 percent in 1834). This employment structure had implications for gender relations after slavery, as Bolland points out: the absence of most men for many months every year when they were at work in the forests must have given the women considerable authority in the household, yet women had little occupational flexibility and few alternatives to domestic service. In British Honduras, where the provision grounds complex had hardly existed before emancipation, the failure of peasant development after was especially limiting for women: they had little chance to earn incomes independent of domestic wages, which were lower than those of the male woodcutters. The result, Bolland speculates, may have been greater dependence on men economically than in the peasant colonies.[43]

British Honduras was one of those Caribbean colonies that were not plantation economies in 1838; here the question of withdrawal of women from estate labour did not arise, since there were virtually no estates. The gendered division of labour there – male timber workers, women domestics – was less a survival strategy as much as sheer necessity. But this mainland territory was the exception. The other non-plantation colonies were very small islands – the Bahamas group, the Grenadines, Anguilla, the British Virgin

Islands, Barbuda, probably Montserrat and Nevis after 1850 – and the ex-slaves here engaged chiefly in subsistence agriculture, with little possibility of wage work for men or women. Peasant farming was combined with exploitation of the sea (fishing and whaling, sponging and wrecking in the Bahamas, boatbuilding and seafaring) and of the forests (timber cutting, charcoal production, hunting and foraging). The men monopolized these occupations while the women practised subsistence agriculture. Moreover, in many of these small islands, male out-migration became the norm after 1838. By this 'emigration adaptation', young men left their impoverished home islands for long spells working abroad, although the intention was always to return and family ties were usually kept up. Postemancipation migration was chiefly, though not entirely, male; the women left behind survived by farming and by remittances. In these small, non-plantation economies, where there could on the whole be no "shift to wage labour" after emancipation for men or women, out-migration was an essential strategy for family survival.[44]

Gender Ideologies

It was, I believe, concern for the welfare of the family unit, the anxiety to secure a degree of independence from the planter and his demands, a desire to offer protection to vulnerable women and children, and a commitment to social and religious pursuits, which lay behind the withdrawal of females from the estate labour force after 1838. But there can be no doubt that the coercive force of hegemonic gender ideologies played a part too, reinforcing the family strategies which were pursued by many ex-slaves after emancipation.

Antislavery activists, clergymen, officials and British policymakers all shared a basic assumption: the ex-slaves should model their domestic lives on the middle class Western family. Husbands should be the head of the family, the main bread-winner, responsible for family support and endowed with authority over wives and children; wives should be dependent and domestic. Of course, lifelong monogamy based on Christian marriage should be the norm. Men must both control and protect their wives (and daughters), something that slavery had made impossible; the sexual abuse of female slaves had been an attack on the 'rights' of their menfolk as well as on the chastity of the women. Wives and mothers must rear their children and provide a decent, comfortable, Christian home. As Catherine Hall puts it: "A new gender order was central to the vision of the abolitionists. In their new Jamaica black men would survey their families with pride, black women would no longer be sexually subjugated to their masters but properly dependent on their husbands."

Missionaries like J.M. Phillippo and William Knibb thought that "the wife's proper release from toil" – plantation labour – was an important, wholly positive result of freedom, allowing her time and energy to create a model home for her family and to secure the comfort of her bread-winner.[45]

This was a consensus shared by antislavery opinion and by most officials in the islands. Charles Buxton, for instance, rejoiced in the end of coerced labour by mothers: "Happily this system went out with slavery. Most mothers now stay at home to look after their homes and house-holds. To us this seems a clear gain." The point was echoed by a visiting abolitionist in a lecture to a Trinidad audience in 1839, who said that the forced labour of mothers had resulted in the "undue and despotic withdrawing of them from many of the attentions which infants need. I thank God that mothers of families can freely now, when they please, nurse their little ones with all the ceaselessness of a mother's love." Governor Light of British Guiana was one of many ranking officials to share this view; he advised the secretary of state just after August 1838 that "many of the women may now be expected to withdraw from field labour, and as their moral ties become more sacred, so perhaps may their inclination to confine themselves to indoor occupations be increased".[46]

There was a general assumption that the male ex-slaves were to assume the responsibilities of heads of families once the apprenticeship came to its end. Governors addressed gendered appeals to the ex-apprentices based on this premise. Light of British Guiana told them "if you did not work for the Estate you could not remain on it – you must take away yourselves, children, wives, and old people dependent on you". They had the obligation to support their aged parents, "but there were few persons so old who could not assist in some degree the industry of their son – and I told you that God had blessed those who have good sons". A few months later, he urged a group of free labourers to work hard to support their families and to cultivate a taste for domestic comforts: "Learn to appreciate the advantages of a comfortable home . . . there is no reason why, having finished your day's work, you should not return to a clean room and a decently served meal."[47]

Announcing the imminent end of apprenticeship, the governor of Barbados urged on the people (in fact, the men) the duty of maintaining "by your own industry, yourselves and your families"; "no employment", he stated, "can be mean or dishonourable, or unworthy of a free man, which is honestly pursued". And Sir Lionel Smith told the "Praedial Apprentices" of Jamaica in July 1838:

Remember that in freedom you will have to depend on your own exertions for your livelihood, and to maintain and bring up your families. – You will work for such wages as you can agree upon with your employers . . . Be honest towards all men – be kind to your wives and children – spare your wives from heavy field work, as much as you can – make them attend to their duties at home, in bringing up your children, and in taking care of your stock – above all, make your children attend divine service and school.[48]

Husbands and fathers were to exercise authority over wives and children; females were to be primarily dependent housewives; independent wage labour away from the home was unsuitable for married women and mothers. And part of this ideological package was contempt for the woman who did engage in hard manual labour; she was defeminized. The point was made by J.B. Colthurst, a St Vincent special magistrate. Lamenting the estates' dependence on female labour in the fields during the apprenticeship, he argued:

This is what has principally made the negro woman so lamentably coarse a creature as she is. How then can we find fault with her! The planter made her so, and exposed her to everything she aught not, to brutality of every description, till the woman has perished within her and left her mind vitiated and her heart as hard as the palm of her horny hand. The weight of labour aught ever to have fallen upon the men, as it no doubt will shortly do.

And much the same idea was expressed by Frances Lanagan of Antigua, in a revealing passage which is worth quoting at some length:

Many of the negro women, particularly those who live in the country, and are employed in agriculture, are so very masculine in their voice, manners and appearance, that it is at times a matter of doubt to say to which sex they belong. This may be attributed to the general system of treatment during slavery: they were required to work the same as the men; and when punishment was thought necessary, no regard was paid to their feelings, but their persons were equally exposed as those of the other sex. Of course, these proceedings in time rendered them callous, and in the end, divested them of all those principles of modesty which are so great an ornament to the feminine character, whether in a high or low condition of life. The manner in which they were accustomed to dress during their ordinary employments tended in great measure to have this effect. A petticoat of coarse linseywoolsey, or blue check, with a short jacket of similar materials, constituted the chief part of their covering; and even this was put on so carelessly, that frequently the upper part of their persons was left quite bare. While employed in their daily avocations, it is customary to tie up their garments almost – if not quite – as high as their knees; and even when walking about the streets of the capital, the same degree of indelicacy is practised. All these causes combined, tend to lessen the woman in the eyes of strangers; although the Creoles appear to see no indecorum in their style of dress, or manners.[49]

Hard labour in the fields was incompatible with nineteenth century Western notions of femininity, notions which, of course, were highly class-specific at home in Britain. Estate labour was also seen as dangerous to female morality, unless it was organized in a family unit. Though the end of slavery also meant an end to the flagrant and routine sexual abuse of females by plantation staff, there can be little doubt that free estate labourers were still vulnerable; and men and women (including teenagers) worked together in gangs and might be housed together in barracks. This situation helps to explain why antislavery activists and clergymen were anxious to remove women from field labour. A Baptist minister at Manchioneal, Jamaica, stated in 1839:

The Negresses that compose [his wife's] 'maternal association' (a society of from 20 to 30 mothers who meet once a week to receive instruction in the best method of training up their offspring) complain much of the ruinous effects of field labour on their Daughters' morals . . . [and] the contagious influence of lewd conversation and indecent conduct in the field.

E.B. Underhill, the prominent British Baptist cleric, wrote that the "careful, respectable men" of the Jamaican sugar parishes did not let "their women" (or children) work on the estates, complaining of the handouts of rum, the night work during croptime, the "promiscuous mixing" of males and females in the barracks. Respectable "mountain people" would only work for owners whom they trusted, and even then, they kept aloof from the "estates people", labouring separately from them in family groups. No decent man, said another observer, would let his family work on those "nurseries of iniquity", the Jamaican sugar estates.[50]

This kind of testimony certainly suggests than many ex-slaves, men and women, had come to accept the hegemonic ideas about female morality and femininity, or at least many of those under missionary influence. Certainly, women wanted to remove themselves and their daughters from the risks of sexual abuse (whether at the hands of estate staff or fellow workers) in the labour gangs even after 1838; and men must have wanted the same for the female members of their families. An important "meaning of freedom" for women and men – but above all for women – must have been the right to control one's own body, the right to be free of violation and abuse. Ex-slaves hardly needed European gender ideology to persuade them of that.

Yet it seems reasonable to think that the hegemonic gender norms did exert influence on some of the freed people, especially men and women who were upwardly mobile and who were strongly influenced by the churches. It was especially in the church dominated villages that the wives and mothers withdrew from estate labour and concentrated on domesticity and household production. No doubt the ability to let their wives 'sit down' and devote their time to home and children became an index of status for many ex-slave men, as well as part of a family strategy to seek the welfare of all its members. A British Guiana magistrate thought that one reason for the decrease of estate labour by 1841 was the men's "general desire of keeping their wives in attendance on their domestic duties", and a St Vincent planter stated that they were anxious to "allow their wives to sit down . . . and take charge of the children". Several Jamaican magistrates pointed out that the attempt to "bind down the wives to labour as heretofore during the apprenticeship" would only provoke the men into quitting the estates permanently:

Many respectable people are now [1839] availing themselves of opportunities of purchasing or leasing small pieces of land where they are preparing to place their wives and children, and where they also will retire when they quit the estates . . . so as to secure themselves and their families from molestation hereafter in their settlements.

Rejecting the *"binding down of married women"* as unacceptable, the (male) ex-slaves of Chester Castle estate in Hanover told the magistrate: "that it was of no use being free, it was only the name 'so-so', that when it was necessary their wives would assist *them* by performing light work, but they could not give their assent, to make them work always, and at all sorts of work".[51]

That some Caribbean freedmen adopted all or part of the British gender ideology of the mid nineteenth century seems highly likely. But, on the whole, the ex-slaves, men and women, declined to buy the package. They did not enthusiastically embrace monogamous Christian marriage, except during the immediate aftermath of August 1838 (and even then, probably, only among a minority); they rejected the notion that confinement to domesticity and economic dependence on a husband were necessary to female respectability. Such ideas were too much a denial of African-Caribbean family forms and gender roles, not to mention those derived from West Africa. In postslavery Caribbean societies, as Sidney Mintz has pointed out, women's right to economic independence was generally acknowledged among the people, who did not see such a right as implying any corresponding loss of status for the women's husbands. The idea of male economic dominance within the family and household was not imbedded nearly so deeply as in the West, except among the (small) middle and upper strata.[52] Few Caribbean women outside those strata became wholly dependent housewives confined to domestic roles, even if many – most in some places – had withdrawn from estate labour.

Caribbean freedwomen did not withdraw from estate labour because they, or their men, had become aspirants to European bourgeois gender norms. They did so in order to exchange hard, dangerous and degrading gang labour – twelve hours of daily manual work in the fields "is not liberation", as Clare Robertson reminds us – for work in the household, on the family farm, in marketing and in child care. One reason for the withdrawal was certainly to escape the risks of sexual and other abuses which were still inseparable from gang labour on the sugar estates, even after slavery had ended; another was to allow mothers to devote more attention to rearing their children. But ex-slave men and women were not blindly obeying hegemonic gender ideologies nor seeking to transform freedwomen into dependent housewives confined to the home. They were pursuing rational family strategies aimed at securing the survival and welfare of their kin groups, in the face of appalling odds.

5

Leisure and Society in Postemancipation Guyana

Brian L. Moore

This chapter is a preliminary enquiry into a relatively complex phenomenon and is limited to postemancipation Guyana. Among those sociologists who have attempted to develop a theory of leisure, there is considerable controversy over even a basic definition. Stanley Parker, for instance, identifies three broad definitions of leisure employed by some sociologists. By the first, all time not spent working, sleeping, eating, attending to physiological needs, and so on, is leisure time. This residual approach, however, is imprecise. It is more a description of 'spare time' than 'leisure time'; and not all 'spare time' activities are necessarily 'leisure'. Unemployed and retired persons, for instance, who have much spare time are not necessarily leisured.

A second definition perceives leisure not in temporal terms but as "a quality of activity or of the person engaging in the activity". Leisure in this sense is not simply spare time activity, but is an attitude of mind which seeks the spiritual or artistic 'upliftment' of the individual. This definition, however, seems very restrictive and would exclude many activities, for example, many sports that do not conform to such exalted notions. The third approach, favoured by Parker himself, combines spare time with the type of activity: hence, "leisure is 'the time which an individual has free from work or other duties and which may be utilized for purposes of relaxation, diversion, social achievement, or personal development' ".[1] The problem with this definition is that it does not indicate the extent to which such activity is voluntarily undertaken by the individual or is determined by the need to fulfil familial or societal obligations.

The French sociologist Joffre Dumazedier, however, attempts to bring some more precision to the concept of leisure and argues that it is related to the type of society and its stage of development. "While spare time . . . must obviously be as old as work itself, leisure has distinct characteristics, specific to the civilizations born of the industrial revolution." Hence, neither in ancient nor in preindustrial societies did leisure exist. Whereas in the first work and play were integrated in feasts through which humans shared in the world of their ancestors, in the latter work followed the natural cycle of seasons and days:

It was intense during the good season, slower during the winter. Its rhythm was natural, interrupted by breaks, by songs, by games and ceremonies. It tended to coincide with the pattern of the day, from sunrise to sunset. There was no clear-cut division between work and rest . . . Natural cycles were punctuated by a sequence of Sundays and holidays. Sundays were devoted to religious cult. Holidays often gave rise to a great expenditure of food and energy; they were the obverse of everyday life or its negation. Feasting was inseparable from ceremonies and generally closer to religious ritual than to leisure.

For Dumazedier, therefore, two principal conditions have to be met for people to have leisure: social activities must be freed from ritual obligations imposed by the community so that individuals are free to decide how to spend their spare time. And, secondly, remunerated work must be clearly differentiated, and not by the forces of nature, from other activities in order to separate it from spare time. Since those two conditions exist only in industrial and postindustrial societies, the concept of leisure is not applicable to ancient or preindustrial ones. "When leisure appears in modern rural communities, it is because work in the countryside tends to pattern itself on industrial work and life on its urban counterparts", and this applies to preindustrial agrarian societies in the Third World as well.[2]

It is against that background that Dumazedier defines leisure as "the time whose content is oriented towards *self-fulfillment* as an ultimate end" (my emphasis). This is spare time granted by society after the individual has completed all social obligations (occupational, familial, sociospiritual and sociopolitical), and is then free to do with that time as he or she thinks fit. Leisure thus has certain vital characteristics. First, it is liberating in that it is "freedom from a certain number and from certain kinds of obligations". Secondly, it has a disinterested character in so far as it serves no lucrative, utilitarian, ideological or proselytizing end. Thirdly, it is hedonistic in the individual's search for a state of satisfaction. Finally, it is highly personal, being geared specifically to satisfying the needs of the individual.[3] This chapter will utilize Dumazedier's conceptualization as a theoretical basis for the discussion of leisure in postemancipation Guyana.

Postemancipation Guyana

Nineteenth century Guyana must be classified as a preindustrial agrarian society. But as a dependent part of the British industrial economy its *raison d'être* was exclusively to produce staples for the British market. Hence its organization and modus operandi were heavily influenced by the demands of an industrial market and this had a major impact on work and life on the plantations. Indeed some contemporaries were struck by the similarity between the work environment of Guyanese plantations and that of British factories.[4] Although agrarian, therefore, the plantations sought to organize labour and mould work attitudes not dissimilar to what obtained in industrial Britain; and in their efforts to maximize profits the planters shared the same motivations and made the same kinds of demands of their workers as British industrial entrepreneurs.

The British West Indian plantation economy found itself in severe crisis during the first decade after emancipation in 1838, and the crisis accentuated the planters' desire to extract as much labour as possible from their workers. This led to a confrontation between employers and labour throughout the region which was no greater than in Guyana where two major colony-wide strikes were staged in 1842 and 1848. Planters not only sought to reduce workers' wages and 'perquisites', but also workers' spare time. Freedom, it was feared, had given the ex-slaves too much latitude as regards plantation work since they either stopped working altogether or their attendance became highly irregular. By 1848, the entire colonial establishment was using its collective power to force the ex-slaves back to work on the plantations for low wages and a ten-hour day.[5]

This period of crisis also witnessed the beginnings of a new policy of immigration to deal with a chronic problem of labour shortage. The planters wasted no time in this regard, importing the first batch of immigrant workers from India in 1838, the very year the slaves won their freedom. Although beset by health and financial problems which caused a temporary stoppage to all immigration for a few years during the 1840s, by 1850 the process had been fully restored and immigrants were imported from various parts of the world including India, Africa, China, Madeira and the Caribbean. The number of immigrants landed by the end of the century far exceeded the native population of 1838.[6]

Most of these immigrants were compelled by contract to work on the plantations for a term of years which in most cases extended to ten.[7] Failure or inability to complete the statutory five tasks per week was treated by law as a *criminal* offence punishable by fine or imprisonment, or both. Although statutory working hours were ten per day, in reality the daily tasks were so onerous that, with the threat of imprisonment hanging over their heads, these indentured workers were normally compelled to work longer hours in the field, and on Saturdays as well; and, during the 'grinding period', work in the sugar factories often required sixteen or more continuous hours. In rare cases it could reach twenty or even twenty-two hours![8] If unindentured plantation workers enjoyed greater freedom in deploying their time, that luxury was rapidly eroded as the number of immigrant workers increased. By 1860, therefore, a contract-free labourer had 'voluntarily' to increase his or her working hours in order to retain his or her job on the estate. Spare time was thus a scarce commodity for all plantation workers in Guyana, free or indentured, during the second half of the nineteenth century.

People who had alternative employment had greater control over their time. But there were other constraints to overcome. Those ex-slaves who continued in the employ of the colonial elites as domestic servants, grooms, carriage drivers, gardeners, handymen, and so on, or who worked as clerks in shops and stores, were largely dependent on their employers' whims and were literally on call at most times. On the other hand, those who acquired land and became small peasant farmers in rural villages, or who established themselves as independent artisans or shopkeepers, had full control over the disposal of their time. The same goes for immigrants who freed themselves of their contractual obligations and moved off the estates. The Portuguese immigrants from Madeira benefited most in this sense since most of them were never placed under labour contracts and were able to establish themselves very soon after arrival, mainly as shopkeepers and independent farmers. Late in the century several ex-indentured Chinese and Indian immigrants joined their ranks.

Of all the ethnic groups in nineteenth century Guyana, the dominant British whites enjoyed the greatest degree of control over their time. Even then, however, one needs to make a distinction between different classes within their ranks. If wealthy planters and merchants, independent lawyers and doctors did to a large extent exercise full control over the disposal of their time, the opposite is true of lowly overseers and bookkeepers on plantations, and clerks in stores and government offices.

The question that needs to be addressed at this stage is whether, contrary to Dumazedier's conceptualization, leisure could exist in a preindustrial agrarian society such as postemancipation Guyana. It is my contention that it did even though the two principal criteria set out by Dumazedier may not have been met in their entirety. Certainly within the dominant plantation work environment, there was a clear distinction between remunerative work and spare time. Efforts were made to minimize the latter in the interest of profits, but the two spheres were clearly delineated one from the other. However, as we have seen above, spare time and leisure are not necessarily synonymous. Dumazedier considers it essential that social activities should be freed from communally determined ritualistic obligations. In Guyana, the extent to which that may have been so was largely dependent on ethnicity and class.

For the most part it was the products of industrialized Britain, the dominant whites, who were least restricted by ritualistic communal obligations. And as more and more coloured (mixed-race) and black ex-slaves acquired Western education and assimilated the dominant culture, so too they became liberated from similar obligations. But even the white elites were not wholly free of communal obligations: for the state of society in postemancipation colonial Guyana, characterized by instability, created in their minds the need, not only to foster a sense of ethnic solidarity ('Britishness') to bolster their insecurity as a minority in a 'sea of blackness', but also to promote a consensus of values among the subordinate population around the notion of the superiority of British imperial culture. For this reason, they found it necessary to adhere to certain communally determined rituals (and even to invent some on the spot where necessary), such as the commemoration of imperial and religious events such as the Queen's birthday and jubilees, other royal births and deaths, Trafalgar Day, the Feast of St Andrew (Scottish), Christmas, and Easter — most of which were marked by street decorations and illuminations, pompous military parades, fireworks displays, formal public dinners or dancing parties, and specially organized cricket matches.[9] Thus some elite spare time activities were not, strictly speaking, 'leisure'.

At the other end of the social hierarchy of *creoledom* were ex-slaves in rural villages and urban ghettos who, while absorbing the dominant value system (the notion of British cultural superiority) largely as a result of missionary proselytization, still adhered to many fundamental Afro-Creole beliefs, practices, and values. But whatever vestiges of communal behaviour survived the rigours of slavery were systematically attacked by the colonial state, the press, church and schools. The cooperative spirit out of which the communal village movement was born just after emancipation, which saw ex-slaves pooling their limited financial resources to purchase whole plantations, rapidly dissipated with the active encouragement of the colonial establishment. Reinforced by missionary exhortations on the virtues of self-reliance, the ex-slaves even in remote rural villages began to pull apart. By 1850, the communal villages were fragmenting and cooperative activity was confined to pockets of Afro-Creole social life, such as lodges, friendly and burial societies, weddings, death wakes, and Cumfo religious gatherings.[10] For the most part, the prevailing ethos of individualism became dominant among Creoles, and communally determined ritualistic activity declined under a barrage of attacks from the colonial establishment and the missionaries. By the later nineteenth century, therefore, most Creoles were uninhibited by communal considerations in deciding how to spend their spare time.

Most of the immigrants introduced in the nineteenth century came from societies where not only was there little distinction between work and spare time, but also where many social activities were ritualistic and largely determined by religion and community. Although initially working and living on plantations where a clear distinction was made between work and free time, most immigrants sought to retain their parent traditions and a distinct sense of ethnic identity in a multiracial environment, and thus continued to be influenced by ethnic communal prescriptions and proscriptions relating to the use of their spare time. In that context, limits were imposed on the freedom of individuals within those ethnic groups to decide how to spend their free time.

On the other hand, it must be noted that since by its very nature migration was an assertive act of individualism, there existed within the several immigrant communities persons who were quite prepared to break communal restrictions if it suited their *individual* purposes. In that context, the existence and enjoyment of leisure depended on a combination of factors: conditions of life in the physical and social environment, the pace at which individuals assimilated aspects of the host culture and in particular the values associated with the dominant ethos of individualism, and the individual determination to satisfy personal interests.

The British Elite

Even though there may have been several persons within each ethnic group who were quite prepared to make individual decisions with a view to enjoying leisure, in practical terms the control which the dominant British elites had over the working hours of certain sections of the subordinate population considerably restricted their ability to do so. In addition, neither the private nor public sectors provided leisure facilities for their workers. Indeed, the dominant whites provided relatively few facilities even for their own pleasure since they considered their sojourn in the colony as temporary. Hence, social life outside of working hours for individuals of *all* ethnic groups in nineteenth century Guyana was quite dull; but the more wealth and power one possessed, the greater was one's ability to create and enjoy leisure activities.

This meant that it was the dominant white elites who were in the best position to indulge in leisure. The wealthy planters and merchants, senior government officials, church leaders, army and police officers, lawyers and doctors formed the aristocracy of colonial society, and their lifestyles reflected their exalted social status. These men and their families (if any) inhabited large, elegant, multiroom mansions with magnificent flowering gardens in relatively exclusive areas in the towns, or in select sections of plantations separated from the other buildings.[11] Their homes were exceedingly well furnished and serviced by an army of servants which included cooks, maids, nannies, butlers, grooms, gardeners, carriage drivers, and, given the scarcity of public facilities, were important centres of elite leisure activities. These elites generally enjoyed a lifestyle of opulence and privilege which set them apart from the rest of society, even other (less favoured) whites such as clerks, overseers and bookkeepers who worked very long hours, often in excess of twelve per day.[12] The few leisure facilities erected in the colony were intended essentially to cater to the small elite class.

This colonial aristocracy came closest to being a leisured class, particularly the women who did not work outside of the home. It is true that the men had to work. Their fortunes depended on that. Most were self-made men who had arrived in the colony with very little by way of assets and so had to earn their way up the social and economic ladder. Those who succeeded either acquired plantations or were successful plantation attorneys and managers, businessmen or professionals. Their accumulated wealth or access to credit, or both, enabled them to support a lavish lifestyle.

This elite class had full control of their time and, *as individuals*, could freely decide how to utilize it. For public officers and professionals the working day was not often more than eight or ten hours, six days a week; merchants and those in charge of plantations might have a longer day especially in the harvest and grinding periods, but they enjoyed a considerable degree of flexibility as well. Although Victorian middle class ideas of gender differences and morality restricted colonial elite women mainly to the home, their domestic roles were largely confined to the supervision of their servants. Even child rearing was left mostly to nannies. They, therefore, generally had a considerable amount of spare time.[13]

As the colonial aristocracy was male dominated both in terms of composition and power (at the end of the century there were still just two women to every three men among the Europeans), social life was male oriented and this was reflected in leisure activities. Far greater emphasis was placed on 'macho' type activities such as drinking, gambling, 'womanizing' and outdoor 'manly' sports than on the more genteel fine arts (music, theatre, dance) and intellectual activities (reading, writing, debating). This was in part also reflective of the social origins of many of these men, their single minded pursuit of a quick fortune, and the relative absence of 'civilizing' or refining influences in the frontier environment of the colony.

The younger more energetic males thus participated in a variety of sports in the afternoons before sundown and on weekends: cricket, football (soccer), rugby, rowing, cycling, athletics and so on. Of these, cricket was considered by far the most important with the Georgetown Cricket Club (one of several devoted to this sport) accredited the status of being the most aristocratic sports club in the colony. By its very time consuming nature (matches were often scheduled to last more than one day), cricket was the quintessential leisure activity for this elite class. Croquet, tennis, golf and horseback riding extended the range of physical activities to women and older men, while rifle shooting and archery not only provided fun and competition, but also sharpened the self-defence skills of both sexes.[14]

When, however, sports clubs were established, they catered almost exclusively to elite men although some permitted restricted 'lady' membership. Women, however, were expressly barred from the elite social clubs such as the Georgetown Club and the British Guiana Club where elite males spent a considerable amount (for some it was most) of their spare time relaxing with their peers: chatting, drinking, eating, reading, playing indoor games (such as billiards, cards and chess) and gambling. In effect, these clubs served as 'home away from home' for elite men.[15] On the other hand, because middle class Victorian morality forbade too much physical or 'unladylike' exertion by 'decent' women, the latter participated mainly in church related activities, charities, fairs, bazaars, tea parties and minimal select *supervised* sporting activities such as tennis. There were no corresponding social clubs catering to female leisure activities save those in the churches.

Hunting, like cricket a time consuming activity, enjoyed high status among elite men both on account of its aristocratic roots in Britain and the expense incurred in putting together a party: trained dogs, handlers, good horses, proper dress and equipment. It also catered to their macho images in the frontier environment. Although women were excluded from the fray, they often were allowed to camp in a safe location nearby and picnic with the children. Indeed, outdoor picnics at the back of plantations were fairly common among elites on weekends and holidays.[16]

Even in a far-off colony such as Guyana, steam power had an impact on elite leisure activity. The advent of steamers on the Demerara River encouraged the organization of day excursions to the sandhills upriver, while the construction of the East Coast railway permitted similar outings to various destinations along that coast of Demerara. But this type of activity was too limited among the small number of elites to permit the establishment of permanent holiday resorts as in Britain.[17]

Another very popular elite outdoor activity in colonial Guyana was horse racing. Again, apart from the fun and excitement it provided, its appeal to the elites was its British aristocratic connection. While there were several irregular small meetings held in different parts of the country featuring horses of indifferent pedigree, there were two red-letter racing days per year (May and November) in Georgetown patronized by no less than the governor. These provided rare opportunities to socialize with fellow elites of both sexes from all parts of the colony and were marked by a great show of opulence. Although not so declared officially, these two race days were practically public holidays as most businesses were closed.[18] The only other annual event that permitted elites from across the whole colony to gather in one place was the levée and ball held by the governor in June each year to celebrate the Queen's birthday. In every respect, an invitation to this event established one's recognized membership of the colonial aristocracy.[19]

Generally speaking, public balls formed an important leisure activity among the elites largely because they served as an important indicator of personal status in colonial society. Moreover, though few (no more than about three or four per year) they broke the boredom of elite social life, particularly for women. Other forms of public entertainment were very rare indeed. Because the elites saw their residence in Guyana as short or impermanent, they expended very little attention or energy on creative arts. Local concerts and theatrical performances were thus very few. Instead there was a tendency to import artistes from Europe, but Guyana was so remote that such visits were rare. Generally speaking, therefore, the Guyanese colonial elites were starved of entertainment.[20]

That does not mean that they did not enjoy leisure. Formal private dinners and informal social visits played a major role in filling in the many empty evenings. The former were pretentious affairs at which the hosts spared no expense to put on lavish multicourse dinners complete with expensive European wines.[21] The latter were very casual after-dinner affairs in which a small group of close friends gathered at one of their homes for an evening of relaxation: music, indoor games, drinking, chatting or even dancing.[22] These, however, were not everyday occurrences and particularly for young (and older) virile bachelors there were still far too many evenings of boredom. This invariably made for the high level of sexual promiscuity so prevalent among them. 'Womanizing' became a major leisure form in colonial Guyana among elite males, married and unmarried alike, and in the macho frontier environment this was considered a critical symbol of manhood.[23]

It is evident from the foregoing that among the colonial elites not only was a clear distinction made between work and spare time, but they (particularly the wealthy males) were able to determine for themselves how to spend their spare time with a view to maximizing their personal satisfaction. Power, wealth and social status were critical in making this possible.

The Creoles

It has already been pointed out that the Afro-Creole population also increasingly freed themselves from communal obligations as they sought to assimilate British culture in the quest for respectability and mobility in the colonial society. But their ability to convert spare time into leisure activity was constrained by the relative absence of wealth, power and status which were in large part determined by their ethnicity in the colonial society. There were those (mainly coloureds) who by virtue of a Western education did assimilate British culture and were in some cases virtually indistinguishable culturally from the white colonial elites. But they were a small minority and many did not acquire wealth to match. Besides, the boundaries of the colonial aristocracy were so zealously guarded that non-whites were hardly admissible.[24] Nevertheless, in so far as money would permit, their leisure activities sought to emulate those of their white models, albeit in different social (colour/class) circles.

The vast majority of working class Creoles (mainly blacks), whether peasants, artisans, unskilled or even white-collar workers, were by and large enmeshed in a syndrome of poverty and disprivilege which imposed severe obstacles to their enjoyment of leisure even though they may have had the spare time. Many were either seasonally employed, underemployed or unemployed, and free time in that context does not mean leisure time. For these disprivileged people, therefore, *liming* (simply standing or sitting about in the yard, on the street corner, or perhaps at a Portuguese rum shop, chatting, 'cussing', drinking) became a major leisure activity. Indeed, heavy drinking was an integral aspect of the poor man's leisure and part of *their* macho ethic. Some quickly dissipated their meager earnings in the rum shop and not only became inebriated and unruly, but also chronically indebted to the Portuguese shopkeeper. The formation of temperance societies, modelled on those in Britain, principally among female church members to instil a sense of sobriety in workingmen, were of little avail,[25] as those arrested and convicted for disorderly conduct in the Police Courts stood testimony.

Liming and drinking went hand in hand with gambling among Creoles. Although generally cash starved, male Creoles always seemed to be able to find a pittance with which to gamble; and while reputedly not as 'addicted' as the Chinese were said to be, they gambled on a variety of things, but most notably cockfights, horse races and dog races. The latter activities were themselves major leisure activities for Creole males, but while cockfighting was outlawed and dog racing deplored by the colonial elites, horse racing was encouraged because it was organized by the elites. Horse racing thus became as much a passion among the Creoles as it was among the elites, and they, too, generally refused to work on the two red-letter race days in George-town.[26]

Apart from horse racing, sports increasingly became important leisure activities among Creoles later in the century. However, they were restricted by limited resources and facilities as they were excluded from membership of the elite sports clubs. They thus had to form their own 'ethnic' clubs if they were to participate in any form of organized sport. Cricket, the principal imperial sport, was by far the most important adopted by the Creoles because it seemed to offer the greatest prospect of social respectability and recognition. But it required expensive equipment which was very often out of their financial reach. Their involvement thus necessitated a high degree of improvisation in this respect (and others as well).[27]

Unlike the situation among the Euro-elites, Creoles' participation in sports was not restricted to men,[28] though among those aspiring to higher social status females were discouraged from such 'vulgar' exhibitions of physical exercise. Generally speaking, however, female leisure activity was more family, community and church oriented. Storytelling, tea meetings, charity bazaars and fairs, family and community celebrations on special occasions or holidays, were among the leisure activities participated in by women.[29]

Dancing was perhaps the most popular leisure activity. A drum and shak-shaks for rhythm and a few other instruments, such as a banjo or flute, or both, for melody, were all that were required at the basic level.[30] More elaborate affairs, however, necessitated a fuller complement: clarinet, trumpet, saxophone, guitar. Dances ranged from Afro-Creole folk forms found mainly in rural villages (some of which were religious) to elaborate European-styled ballroom affairs.[31] But most commonplace were the so-called dignity balls which were held almost nightly in lower class sections of Georgetown much to the annoyance of the elites. Their unlicensed organizers and participants were targeted by the police in order to curtail these so-called orgies.[32]

The Christmas–New Year festive season, however, was the high point of Creole leisure activity. This provided a week of jollity marked by scarcely afforded expenditure on food, drink and dress to the accompaniment of loud music and dance. Of special significance were the 'masquerade bands' composed of brightly costumed and masked street dancers to the accompaniment of music by flutes, drums and other percussion instruments. Some Creoles also made use of the railway to spend a day or two on holiday out of town.[33]

The Easter holiday weekend offered another special major period of leisure to Creoles, and apart from music, dance and drink it was specially marked by kite flying along the sea wall or in any open field. It is probable that kites were introduced by the Chinese immigrants, but certainly by the late nineteenth century kite flying at Easter had become a creole passion. Women, men and children participated with kites of a variety of shapes, sizes and colours producing a virtual kaleidoscope in the skies.[34]

The Portuguese Immigrants

Although there is evidence that the Portuguese immigrants made a clear distinction between remunerative work and spare time, as in their homeland of Madeira much of their free time was taken up with family and ethnic community activities in association with the Roman Catholic church. It is, therefore, moot whether the Portuguese did enjoy much 'leisure' in accordance with Dumazedier's conceptualization. Although for the most part employed outside of the main plantation sector, primarily as traders, farmers and woodcutters, whether self-employed or working for other Portuguese entrepreneurs their keen desire to become wealthy translated itself into long hours of arduous work each day, including Sundays. This did not leave them much spare time to begin with; and its use was largely determined by the Catholic religious calendar.

The principal holidays were Christmas and Boxing Day, Good Friday and Easter, and the feasts of the Virgin Mary and the Holy Ghost (Pentecost). Several 'saint days' were also celebrated but most of these did not require time off work except for religious services. Even social organizations designed to cater to their recreation and relaxation were very often founded in connection with the church.[35] For the most part, therefore, the use of spare time among Portuguese immigrants was largely ritually determined by obligations to the family, ethnic community and church rather than by the personal needs of individuals.

Even so, these ethnic festivities did provide a considerable amount of personal satisfaction. Most Portuguese celebrations were marked by elaborate feasting, loud band music, fireworks and gunfire, and brilliant lantern (and later electric) illuminations and decorations. At Christmas colourful masquerade bands were a feature in Portuguese communities.[36] But, as if to underscore the ethnic communal nature of these celebrations, some (particularly Pentecost and the feast to commemorate the anniversary of the Portuguese Benevolent Society) were marked by the feeding of indigent members of the Portuguese community.[37] These religious festive occasions thus permitted the celebrants to mix religious and social obligation with personal pleasure. Often day excursions were organized by rail from Georgetown to a rural village where outdoor picnics were held after a religious service in church.[38]

Despite the strong community and family determination of the use of their free time, as the Portuguese acquired wealth and gradually integrated into the middle and upper echelons of creole society they had more spare time which could be converted into leisure activities for personal pleasure. Hence, while retaining a strong umbilical connection with Madeira (Portuguese nationality) and ethnic and religious identification with Roman Catholicism, their lifestyles slowly began to mirror that of other colonial whites of similar *class*. The acquisition of large mansions and other trappings of colonial aristocratic life paralleled the adoption of elite social behaviour. Elaborate balls and dinners became a feature of the Portuguese upper class, as did the staging of and attendance at concerts and theatricals. They formed musical bands and small symphonic orchestras, and indeed the *Primeira de Dezembro* brass band, formed in 1876, was reputedly as good as the state owned Militia Band. Small drama societies also occasionally staged dramatic performances.[39]

Wealthy Portuguese males also adopted the penchant of their British 'peers' for social and sports clubs. Denied membership of the aristocratic Georgetown Club, elite Portuguese men joined other whites to found the British Guiana Club in 1871. This club provided the same services for its male members as its counterpart.[40] In this sense, these upper class Portuguese members demonstrated their assimilation of elite social values. Portuguese of all classes, however, adopted creole sports, in particular cricket, tennis, cycling, athletics and horse racing. But initially denied membership of the aristocratic sports clubs, they were obliged to form their own. Creole leisure 'vices' such as gambling and excess drinking were also absorbed by the Portuguese.[41]

The Indian Immigrants

If the distinction between spare time and leisure was blurred among the Portuguese, it was practically nonexistent among the Indian immigrants. They came from a society which hardly differentiated between work and free time, and where religion and community (caste) determined virtually everything in life. Despite the desire of the planters to keep spare time to a minimum, a clear differentiation was made between that and work on the plantations. But partly because the Indians perceived their sojourn in Guyana as temporary, and partly out of ethnic considerations, they sought to preserve as much of their cultural traditions as possible. This had direct impact on their ability to have and enjoy 'leisure'.

As pointed out before, the need to work long, arduous hours in the field and factory, often beyond the ten statutory hours per day, circumscribed the amount of spare time available to indentured workers. If their evenings were free, the immigrants were generally too tired after completing their domestic chores, such as fetching water, cooking meals, and childcare, to engage in too much 'leisure' activity before being aroused at 5:00 a.m. the next day. The only real respite came on weekends (mainly Sunday), and in the days between the end of one grinding season and the start of the next planting season when work was generally lighter and more spare time available. There were, of course, the Christian holidays if the Indians were willing to accept these; but there were very few days off (between three and five per year) allowed for their own religious or ethnic festivals.

Although they did have a small amount of spare time, not much 'leisure' activity was determined exclusively by individuals. *Ganja* (cannabis) smoking was a major means of seeking individual pleasure after a hard day's work for both women and men. A few preferred the superior hallucinating qualities of opium.[42] On weekends, many men achieved added personal satisfaction by adding the imbibition of copious amounts of alcohol to the point of senseless intoxication, either in the form of rum purchased from Portuguese shops or home distilled coconut toddy.[43] Free time was also spent in traditional athletic exercises, dances, or singing and playing music.[44]

More often than not, however, spare time activity was conditioned by communal or religious obligations. If permitted by the estates' management, weekends provided the opportunity for individuals to visit friends or relatives, or to attend community events of a religious or quasi religious nature off the estates, like birth and marriage ceremonies and funerals.[45] Some evenings were spent in groups listening to Hindu and Muslim priests recounting sacred tales. *Ramlila* theatrical performances, which dramatized the deeds of Hindu deities, were also very popular.[46] But undoubtedly the centre of Indian ethnic spare time activities were the great annual Hindu and Muslim religious festivals of Diwali, Mohurrum, Durga Puja (Dasserah) and Holi (Phagwah). These were all communally determined affairs in which all Indians, depending on their religion, were enjoined to participate. Although Diwali, the festival of lights, is the greatest of Hindu festivals, its celebration in Guyana (October-November) was relatively low key until late in the century when self-employed farmers living off the estates could devote time to its proper celebration.[47] The same applies to Holi (Phagwah) which is usually celebrated in February-March.[48]

The Muslim Mohurrum and Hindu Durga Puja were often confused by European contemporaries and simply called *tadja* because of similarities in the way and time they were celebrated. Generally held during the first quarter of the calendar year, the *tadja* was the largest Indian ethnic festival for which the estates permitted between three and five days off work. Although fundamentally religious, the celebrations were marked by massive processions of gaudily costumed participants engaged in a variety of acrobatic, dramatic and magical feats under the influence of liberally consumed alcoholic beverages. Because the colonial authorities considered them a public nuisance and threat to law and order, they were circumscribed later in the century.[49]

Such spare time activities, because they were communally determined, would not be considered leisure within the parameters of Dumazedier's schema. But although the Indian immigrants sought to retain their traditional cultures, a certain amount of acculturation did take place which impacted on the determination of their use of their spare time. Mention has already been made of their excessive consumption of alcohol notwithstanding prohibitions against this in both Hinduism and Islam. Along with this went gaming and gambling mainly in the form of cockfighting and the 'three-card trick'.[50] Gambling was also very much in evidence as they acquired the creole passion for horse racing. Although not many did travel to Georgetown for the two annual red-letter race days, horse racing was held from time to time by the planters on or near estates.[51]

The Indians, particularly those born in the colony, also acquired a deep-seated love for the imperial sport of cricket which, like the Creoles, they played using improvised equipment. By the end of the century a cricket match could be found on most estates involving Indian youths, indicative of a growing amount of time Indians were prepared to spend on leisure activities.[52] Thus as assimilation slowly proceeded, some Indians began to determine for themselves how much of their spare time to devote to leisure for their own intrinsic satisfaction. Nevertheless it would be true to say that for the majority, no distinction was made between communally determined spare time activity and 'leisure' for individual pleasure.

The Chinese

The Chinese immigrants suffered from the same disabilities as regards the availability of spare time as the Indians while indentured on the estates. They, however, came from a society where there were few holidays except those religiously and seasonally determined.[53] As such, they were not very demanding in this regard and rarely even took those public holidays on offer even though several were already converted Christians on arrival in the colony.[54] After leaving the estates many became retail traders, woodcutters or farmers (some remigrated to neighbouring colonies).[55] While that gave them more control over their time, like the Portuguese their desire to acquire wealth in a short time caused them to spend most of their waking hours at work. But the Chinese did have a reputation for 'playing' as hard as they worked, and although they sought to acquire wealth that was not to the exclusion of enjoying the material benefits that it could afford them. They were thus not averse to spending (or even gambling) their money in order to attain individual pleasure.[56]

Like the Indians, many Chinese sought to wind down after an arduous day's work by seeking to attain a higher spiritual level through narcotics; in their case it was opium to which they had become addicted while in China largely through the drug trafficking activities of British traders. The Chinese gathered in a room on the estate specially assigned for this purpose. There they would either smoke or chew the drug until a sufficiently high state of hallucination had been attained before retiring to their individual rooms.[57] Although they also consumed alcohol, it does not appear that rum was as great a favourite among them as with other groups. Alcohol intoxication was thus not a major problem for them.

Their 'club' rooms were also designed to accommodate their penchant for gambling. Whether influenced by opium or not, the Chinese earned a reputation for being inveterate gamblers who would literally chance their lives on a bet. Gambling was perhaps their greatest pleasure, and night after night they would assemble for this purpose. This persisted even after they converted to Christianity (despite the denunciations of missionaries), and after they quit estate employment. Indeed, their move into private business earned them more money with which to gamble; and this penchant was further stimulated by horse racing for which they, like other subordinate groups, developed a passion.[58] Time spent consuming opium and gambling was largely determined by individuals for their own satisfaction.

Chinese spare time activities, however, were not confined to what contemporary elites considered vices. They also organized and staged dramatic, acrobatic and musical performances, although these were not on a regular basis.[59] Far more time, however, was devoted to preparing for and participating in their lunar new year festival. Apart from lavish feasting, there were elaborate street celebrations complete with colourful costumes and lanterns, music and fireworks. For several weeks in advance the Chinese immigrants spent a considerable amount of time after work and on weekends making their costumes and lanterns, cleaning and decorating their humble quarters, and preparing several dishes of food. Many of the lanterns were described even by hostile elites as genuine works of art.[60] Although this festival started out as a partially religious, communally determined activity, it is arguable that after their mass conversion to Christianity their continued participation in it was essentially individually determined and thus constitutes leisure.

Conversion to Christianity was a key indicator of Chinese assimilation of aspects of the host culture. Another important element was their adoption of creole sports. Reference has already been made to their growing passion for horse racing. The same could be said of cricket which they learned and played on a purely voluntary, individualistic basis in their spare time for pleasure. As with other groups, they were required to form teams along ethnic lines because membership of elite clubs was denied them.[61] But that they were prepared to do so demonstrates a willingness to devote a fair amount of time in the pursuit of individual pleasure.

Conclusion

This chapter has shown that, despite the preindustrial character of postemancipation society in Guyana, leisure, as defined by Dumazedier, was possible among individual members of the several ethnic groups. The overarching dominance of the plantation system which imposed its work ethic on the whole society more or less shaped the attitudes of its labour force to leisure. Although it sought to minimize the spare time of the workers, it drew a sharp distinction between that and work which was akin to what obtained in the industrialized metropolis. However, a number of factors determined the extent to which a state of leisure was attainable by individuals. These were principally wealth, power, social status, gender and ethnicity.

Generally, it was the wealthy white elite males who were best placed to enjoy leisure because they occupied a position of economic and social dominance which gave them full control over their time. Elite women, although having an abundance of spare time, found their enjoyment of leisure activities constrained by gender and other social restrictions in the colonial environment. So, too, were middle class whites who were employees of their elite 'masters'. Most of the British whites, however, as products of an industrialized society were culturally predisposed as individuals to enjoy leisure whenever the opportunity presented itself.

That was not quite the case with the subordinate populations who were not only constrained by an absence of control over their time if employed on contract to the plantations, but also by ethnic and communal factors. These restrictions more affected the immigrants than the Creoles (blacks and coloureds) who lost many of their communal 'associations' under the pressure to assimilate to the dominant European ways after emancipation. On the other hand, the immigrants generally sought to retain their ethnic identities which often meant preserving traditional attitudes and customs with respect to the use of their spare time. They were thus more inclined to allow ethnic and communal influences to determine how their spare time was spent rather than to seek 'leisure' as individuals for their own personal satisfaction. Still there were some who did, and their numbers increased as the process of creolization advanced.

6

Colonial Images of Blacks and Indians in Nineteenth Century Guyana

Robert J. Moore

In a multiracial society the differing ethnic groups form strong mental images of one another. These images – usually called stereotypes – are a mixture of 'fact' and imagination; their appeal lies in their lack of complexity, since they do not take account of individual variations. The significant feature of a stereotype is that it is as much an indication of the state of mind of those who form it as a description of those about whom it is formed. Stereotypes tend to become a form of racial orthodoxy, with an extraordinary persistence. Facts which are incompatible with them tend to be ignored or explained away, or even reinterpreted to suit the stereotype. They often have a kernel of truth, but equally often they reflect the state of political or economic relations between one group and another. In this chapter, I discuss the formation and role of stereotypes of blacks, East Indians, and other groups such as the Chinese and Portuguese, in colonial Guyana (British Guiana), the nature of these images, and their function in political control and the continuation of commerce in a colonial society.

The Stereotype of the Black

In Guyana in the thirty-odd years after emancipation, the stereotype of the blacks formed by the white elite was of particular importance. For not only did the whites direct and dominate the political, economic, legal and ecclesiastical institutions of the society, but they were also the exemplars of the civilization to which the blacks were expected to aspire. To many in England the great objective of emancipation was to expedite the 'civilizing' of the blacks. Their 'superstitions' and 'African' practices, where they existed, were to be erased from their minds and on the clean slate were to be inscribed the precepts, postures and practices of those Victorians whose social status lay somewhere between the upper reaches of the working class – the 'industrious poor' – and the lower middle class. Most of the ex-slaves were Creoles in whom survived certain features of West African 'tribal' belief and ritual but from whom 'tribal' consciousness or identity had largely been erased by the institution of slavery. Without this sense of identity to obstruct them, the blacks were expected to become ready imitators of the deferential, assiduously churchgoing, status quo-upholding and work obsessed Victorians of the artisan class. Hence the stereotype the whites formed of them was crucial to their self esteem: it could be a powerful source of approval or dismissal.

In fact blacks were aspirants – both in their own eyes and in those of the white establishment. Emancipation was "the Great Experiment" to prove the capacity of the ex-slaves to shed the "baleful influences" of their African past and the institution of slavery and to ascend the ladder of Anglo-Saxon civilization.[1] If this ascent was slow, fitful and painful, it proved that this race was not inherently equal to the Anglo-Saxon and therefore required white tutelage for the foreseeable future. In any case, to be refashioned in the image and likeness of Victorians who 'knew their place', the blacks needed in their midst a sufficient number of Victorians whose place was firmly in the upper echelons of the society. Hence Lord Grey's insistence that British capital must at all costs be preserved in the West Indies to ensure the presence of the British there.[2] The problem was that the blacks were expected to take their cultural 'Ps and Qs' from a group with whom they often found themselves in collision – the plantocracy, the large majority of colonial officials and those who made their living by plantation society, a group in fact that seemed determined to give them the short end of the stick. Hence the stereotype of the blacks held by these whites was bound to reflect their strained social and economic relationship. This in turn was bound to affect the blacks' self-esteem, who felt both the necessity to imitate the whites to assert their equality, and chagrin at finding their efforts dismissed as counterfeit.

But not only was the white stereotype of blacks important to the latter, so also was the white stereotype of the various groups of immigrants who arrived in Guyana from the 1840s onward. Aware that the planters were looking for allies against them, especially as the 1840s wore on, the ex-slaves were particularly sensitive to the encouragement or commendation bestowed upon the newcomers.

This was particularly true of the Portuguese immigrants from Madeira. The blacks formed their own stereotypes of each of the immigrant groups which varied according to whether the immigrants linked their interests to them or to the planters. Thus, their stereotypes of the Portuguese tended to be both unfavourable and derisive: this was to a great extent a form of self-defence against the 'yellow buckras', and an attempt to counteract the favourable image of them which the planters were prompt to propagate. The blacks, for instance, in order to affirm their familiarity with British norms and to place themselves a cut above the Portuguese, derided the latter for their 'foreign' and 'outlandish' ways.[3] They were reported to be particularly adept at caricaturing the Portuguese attempts to speak English and mimicking their obsequiousness to the Anglo-Saxon whites. Some of the blacks insisted that the newly arrived Portuguese address them as 'Lady' and 'Gentleman' in order to emphasize social distance.[4] Blacks frequently referred to the Portuguese as 'white niggers', which put the Portuguese at the very bottom of society, since the term 'nigger' itself was regarded among them as a term of ultimate degradation.[5] A writer to the *Creole* – the chief mouthpiece of the coloureds and blacks – in 1857 pointed out that while the planters and merchants lauded the Portuguese for their energy and industry, there was no occupation more conducive to sloth than lounging on a pork barrel all day waiting for the coins to come in.[6] Another writer pointed out that although the Portuguese were praised for their thrift, the truth was that they kept their shops and their persons filthy and gave little support to their church. The Creoles on the other hand were clean, took a pride in their apparel and were generous supporters of their churches and schools.[7] Stereotype was counteracting stereotype. But the stereotypes held by the white elite carried the critical weight. After all, they controlled the more enduring of image creating organs of the society. Also, the near monopoly of the retail trade of the colony achieved by the Portuguese around the mid 1850s gave strong credence to the estimate of them held by the plantation and mercantile whites and the colonial officials.

The chief feature of the stereotype of the blacks which prevailed among the governing whites, and for that matter the other races, was 'laziness'. The revealing thing about this feature was that it was also the chief characteristic attributed to the blacks during slavery. When the planters and their allies defended slavery they usually invoked the blacks' alleged "congenital idleness" as the reason for preserving coerced labour. Their common cry was that by physique the black was ideally suited to plantation labour; but by temperament he was said to be fitful in his work. Hence slavery mobilized the physical attributes and kept the temperamental defects at bay.[8]

Predictably, after 1838 the majority of planters explained their labour problems as due to the 'indolence' of the freed blacks. In a revolution as profound as that effected by emancipation, there were bound to be many who turned their backs on plantation labour and sought less physically ruinous ways of making a living. It is not surprising that some of them went up the Guyanese rivers to take to woodcutting and charcoal making. Significantly, this occupation was described as one of the 'lazy' forms of employment which encouraged noxious habits, partly because of its seasonal nature but more importantly because the blacks engaged in it were not working for their 'betters'.[9] The withdrawal of the majority of women and children from the full day's task work on the sugar estates, in the years immediately following emancipation, also contributed to a decline in the labour supply. But the planters seldom dwelt upon these considerations. With heavy mortgages hanging over their heads, largely the legacy of the slave regime, they were exasperated with the ex-slaves for even devoting part of their daylight hours to cultivating their own food crops. A complex labour situation was reduced to one simplistic notion: black laziness, and this was presented as the major cause of their financial predicaments.

Barton Premium was typical of the majority of his fellow planters in his scepticism about the blacks' ability to work without coercion. On arriving at his estate from England in 1838, he was assured by an old black driver that the ex-slaves would not slacken in their labour:

'Aha Massa' cried David . . . 'all free now, never mind work all the same, man must work, no work, not eat.' And these commonplace observations they all had in abundance – they had acquired the words but the meaning was lost in the empty air; at least, if they felt its force they did not perceive the necessity of acting upon it.[10]

He was alarmed when the blacks on his estate greeted his arrival with dancing and drumming – a custom much encouraged in slavery times. This sort of behaviour was permissible when the black was a slave: it acted as a safety valve against rebellious promptings. But in freedom it impaired the will of the black to work. Puritanism in freedom was the proper replacement for permissiveness in slavery. Premium summed up the attitude of many of his class when he said: "No, no, there is too much of the sun in the fiery fluid that circulates within – too much of the African rover of the woods to labour if he can do without it – too little of the European mind to know the advantages of a settled occupation."[11]

Although the presumption of black laziness was almost universally asserted by the whites, their explanations varied, sometimes even in the same writer. Some attributed it to irredeemable racial characteristics; others as due to the inverted relationship between labour and capital in the colony. For instance Sir Henry Barkly, a plantation owner who became governor of Guyana in 1849, was not above remarking that it was useless to subject a black criminal to solitary confinement because "he has African blood enough to sleep 23 out of 24 hours".[12] On the other hand, Barkly elsewhere implied that it was the circumstances under which the blacks became free that were responsible for their "laziness"; since they approached freedom not as a stern and sober reality but rather "like a perpetual jamboree".[13] He was confident, however, that if the institutions of the colony were so ordered as to compel them to work regularly the race itself would soon acquire habits of industry.[14]

Henry Light, Barkly's predecessor, was peeved towards the end of his administration because of his loss of popularity among the blacks whose champion he had been for most of his ten-year governorship. He came round to accepting the planters' imputation of black indolence, but he hesitated to give it a racial explanation. Instead, he saw it as due to the erroneous concepts of freedom which the blacks harboured in slavery and to the over-pampering of their wishes by the "friends of the blacks":

. . . the ease with which life is thus supported, contributes to the indifference of the large portion of the Creoles to aught but ease . . . The emancipated Negro has been so flattered and his vanity so excited that he scarcely understands his position in society. In the efforts to verify emancipation, humility has been forgotten.[15]

The truth was that to men accustomed to seeing the working classes in England and Ireland begging for work, particularly in the 'Hungry Forties', the sight of ex-slaves negotiating the terms on which they would work seemed both unnatural and immoral. One observer, comparing the Guyanese black with the labouring man in Britain, noted that "though this class [the freed black] has not at all advanced in the scale of civilization, it has undoubtedly acquired a rude ease and stubborn independence, in comparison with which the condition of the peasantry in Great Britain is one of endless toil and galling servitude".[16]

The blacks' demand for wages which they thought commensurate with their work was interpreted by most of the whites as a symptom of a lazy psychology: they wanted to work for exorbitant wages on a few days so that they could laze away the rest.[17] Hence the popularity amongst the planter class in the 1840s and 1850s of the theory that dear food and other consumables (rendered so by cunning taxation) meant cheap labour: if the black had to pay dearly for the things he coveted, he would have to work long hours to achieve them.

Nothing better illustrates the tendency of stereotypes to ignore or reinterpret facts hostile to them as the explanation given by the majority of planters for the 'Village Movement'. In the decade between 1838 and 1848, the planters were obviously taken aback by the wholly unexpected initiative of a people who had once been their slaves. J. Brummell summed it up when he wrote that the ex-slaves

present the singular spectacle to be witnessed in no other part of the world, and of which history affords no parallel, of a people just emerged from slavery now enjoying prosperity in houses and lands for which they have probably paid a little less than a million in money. This fact would appear altogether incredible were it not substantiated by official documents.[18]

Initiative of this sort certainly seemed the very antithesis of the easygoing, feckless characteristics which the blacks were supposed to possess. But an explanation was soon found to account for this paradox: in the purchase of his own land the black was acquiring the independence to make a slothful life feasible. The whole phenomenon of the Village Movement was, in other words, a strenuous preparation for decadent inactivity. Premium, a useful index of the planter mind because of the clarity of his views, summed it up thus: "they purchased land so that each man could literally sit down under his own fig tree".[19]

In fact, this explanation of the Village Movement was a psychological stratagem of the planters to obscure their own ambivalence in the matter. Many had sold whole abandoned estates to the ex-slaves in order to realize much needed cash for their working estates. Yet at the same time they would have preferred to keep the blacks from acquiring the independence which the possession of land conferred. As is usual in such circumstances, the planters resorted to the scapegoat device: the blacks bought their land for the basest of reasons. As the editor of the *Creole* remarked, a planter "will pocket their dollars, transfer his lands to them and next day stigmatize them as a parcel of squatters".[20]

In 1851, a commission appointed by the planter influenced legislature to enquire into the economic condition of the colony designated the possession of freeholds by the blacks as "licensed squatting", the word 'squatting' having particularly obnoxious connotations for the Victorian landed ruling class at home and in the empire. Yet some of the men who wrote the report had themselves realized substantial sums by selling land to the blacks.[21] The commissioners, standing no nonsense from this solid fact, interpreted the whole Village Movement as a symptom of the retrograde desire of the blacks to avoid work (only plantation work was the real thing, according to them) and therefore of a refusal to be civilized.[22]

The high hopes of independent prosperity that fired the founders of the black villages on the coastal area in the 1840s had largely curdled into frustrated disappointment by the 1860s. To get at the reasons for this we need to pause a little and consider the daunting characteristics of Guyana's Atlantic coastal region – sometimes dubbed a 'Tropical Holland' – as well as the historical forces that inhibited the development of a thriving village economy.

The flat Atlantic coastal strip of Guyana, about thirty miles at its widest, is among the most difficult stretches of terrain in the world to maintain. Below the sea level at high tide, the sea coast is also pressured from the rear by an accumulation of rainwater on higher ground and both the salt and the fresh water have to be kept at bay by a systems of dams and drainage canals. Expensive to construct and laborious to dig, these dams and canals require constant maintenance. The currents of the ocean and complex geological forces operating on the subsoil cause the sea coast to change its contours in regular cycles, retreating in some areas and advancing in others. Even the best maintained dams have to be heavily reinforced as the coast land starts its retreat and if the retreat is severe they have to be replaced. Conversely, when the land advances beyond the sea dams the drainage canals used to release the fresh water into the sea have to be extended outward to prevent the flooding of the land.

Managing this sort of terrain for cultivation demands a firm centre of control, a high level of labour coordination except where expensive, sophisticated technology is utilized, and considerable engineering skills. In the eighteenth and early nineteenth centuries, when Guyana was two colonies of the Dutch Empire, disciplined slave gangs provided the labour coordination and made up for the lack of technology. The Anglo-Dutch plantocracy (there was a significant element of British owned plantations in Guyana before it passed finally into British hands in 1815) deployed on their estates the considerable Dutch engineering and managerial expertise available from the Netherlands in handling such terrain.

During the 1820s, a process of plantation abandonment got under way compelled by the collapse of Guyanese cotton on the English market and by the economic necessity for the planters to put their land entirely into sugar cane and concentrate its cultivation on estates of proven high fertility and manageable water control problems. This explains the number of abandoned plantations available for purchase by the blacks after 1838 and the eagerness of their owners to be rid of them. It also explains the problems of low fertility and waterlogging with which the blacks saddled themselves by their purchases.

By the end of the 1850s, the Guyanese plantocracy, having become smaller in numbers but sturdier in psychology and financing, had also acquired two distinct advantages for making a go of their industry. The first lay in the controlled labour force made available by immigration from India and secured by the severe system of indenture. The second was the refitting of their estates with the new technology of Victorian capitalism, particularly the highly prized steam drainage engine, a godsend for ridding empoldered land of undesired water.

The coastal villagers had no such blessings. And for four main reasons. First, the kind of disciplined, unified, readily deployable and necessarily unpaid labour force required to maintain the water defences and canal system was beyond the cultural resources of a people who had been denied by slavery of any critical experience of sustained cooperation. Secondly, the fragmentation of individual holdings and the uncertainty of ownership encouraged by the inheritance laws of the prevailing Roman–Dutch legal system rendered all but subsistence farming unfeasible. Thirdly, as the economy of the villages stagnated many of the villagers increasingly existed in a state of 'in-betweenity' – theoretically independent by virtue of their village holdings, actually dependent on the wage labour the sugar estates provided – thus further weakening their will to address village problems. Fourthly, the refusal of the planter controlled legislature to aid the villages from the public revenue meant that the technology and engineering skills necessary to make village lands viable were unavailable to them.

The scale and complexity of the problems faced by the black coastal villages (the village settlements up the rivers on less intractable terrain enjoyed a modest prosperity) did nothing to temper the pejorative attitudes of the planter and proconsular classes in Guyana and of the mandarins at the Colonial

Office towards blacks in general. It was less taxing, and much more in tune with the temper of the 1850s and 1860s, to make moral judgements than to address complex issues. The emancipated black, so the judgement ran, had failed to make a go of the villages because in his moral make up there was a fatal flaw: he was unindustrious. The tribulations of the black villagers looked like a triumphant vindication of the plantocracy's stereotype of the blacks and one that justified the legislature's refusal to give assistance to the villages with public money. After all, Guyana was either a sugar colony or it was nothing and the frailty of the blacks' attempt to prove otherwise only served to reinforce that truth. That was the chief article of the planters' credo and it remained so beyond the nineteenth century.

As the frustrations of the village situation became endemic, some villagers began to show signs of apathy – which, to men with Victorian preconceptions, looked too much like congenital indolence not to be considered identical with it. The villagers who wanted to make a success of their land found themselves hamstrung by their neighbours who did not dig their drains or clear their trenches – because they were labouring in task gangs on the estates or had rented land there. Consequently, the former became disenchanted and neglected their holdings or simply planted just enough to provide a mere subsistence. There are several well authenticated instances of apathy mentioned in the newspapers of the 1860s and 1870s. A typical example was quoted by Edward Jenkins. A village on the east coast of Demerara was completely inundated and when the Anglican rector tried to organize the villagers to repair the dam, they preferred to sit on the dam hopelessly contemplating the broken kokers and saying that they needed wages to drain their own lands.[23]

At the deepest level, the phenomenon of the Village Movement was not easily digested by contemporaries. Neither in Britain nor in Guyana did they have a familiar framework within which to explain it and the revolutionary nature of the movement left the planters in a state of shock. When they recovered their nerve they interpreted it purely from the standpoint of their own vested interest. The amount of land the ex-slaves had acquired by the mid 1850s suggested that the Guyanese blacks had too much money in their pockets for their own good. The economic faltering of their villages, therefore, was something to be expected. But to sympathetic watchers of 'the Great Experiment' in Britain it seemed unwarrantable.

According to their reckoning, the landed independence achieved by the Guyanese blacks in the decade and a half after emancipation ought to have led to outstanding economic achievement; the fact that it did not was taken as confirmation of Henry Taylor's (an influential Colonial Office mandarin) characterization of the blacks as "fickle and shallow". Armed with a moralistic interpretation of their Industrial Revolution, the liberal Victorians assumed that people acquired economic know-how by will power plus trial and error. They overlooked the importance of cultural and historical resources as well as political and economic traps. Or if they did glance at them they assumed that these could be easily counteracted by the force of their own example. One can agree with their assuming that freedom from slavery was a prerequisite for the blacks' economic growth. Where they went wrong was in assuming that freedom *ipso facto* ensured their economic growth. When it obviously did not among a non-Anglo-Saxon people, they invoked either the concept of racial inferiority or the climatic assumption about tropical peoples being able to survive without exertion – or both notions.[24]

While Anthony Trollope and others painted pictures of blacks lying in the sun, eating yams, and contributing nothing to the sugar fortunes of the colony,[25] there were a few lonely voices that attempted to dispel this idea as being a gross oversimplification. For instance, ex-Chief Justice Joseph Beaumont in 1871 compared the work of the labourer digging ditches in England with that of a black digging trenches in Guyana and pointed to the vastly more arduous and extensive work performed by the latter for smaller pay. The passage is worth quoting:

But in truth we have no excavating work so heavy as trench digging in Demerara, and if the reader were to see a stalwart Negro at work digging new navigable trenches – sweltering under the blazing sun throughout the day, stripped downwards to the waist and upwards to the thighs standing commonly up to his knees and often up to his hips in water, not only lifting or more properly wrenching 4,000 to 5,000 spits of dense clay (each some eight pounds in weight) and throwing these 12 or 16 feet on either side – not thrown with a pleasant hammer throwing swing but delivered straight from the loins at the end of a 7-foot shovel stick I venture to think he would not only wonder at but admire, and gain some new idea of, the 'lazy nigger,' In truth this is work which none but such giant workers, as these 'idlers' really are, could accomplish, which even they can only do during the years of their prime and which, I believe, wears out prematurely many a one among them.[26]

Beaumont's testimony was dismissed as the deliberately misleading outpourings of an official who fell foul of the plantocracy. But confirmation of this came from a source that can hardly be described as partial to the labourers – William Russell, the champion of the plantocracy in the 1880s. In 1880, while lamenting the increasing withdrawal of the blacks from estate labour, he pointed out that in the 1840s and 1850s a local labourer "in ten hours digged and pitched 32 tons of earth a distance of 15 feet", whereas the best English navvy at the time could only manage twenty tons of earth at a distance of six feet.[27]

Understandably, blacks who did this sort of work felt justified in demanding wages which were commensurate with the labour involved. When they could not get such wages they preferred, as they put it, not to "waste their strong" but to live on the proceeds on their provision grounds. They were not unaware that the planters valued their labour as worth three or four times that of the East Indians, yet they complained that this vast difference in worth was not adequately reflected in wages. They wanted recognition and encouragement, both of which seemed to them to go more to the Indian than to the native labourer. The editor of the *Royal Gazette* was unusually perceptive when he observed that if the black was treated like a machine he reacted with indolence; if encouraged he gave valuable service.[28]

The second unfavourable feature in the stereotype of the black was the lack of thrift. Thrift was to the Victorians the greatest of the economic virtues since it indicated the presence of a critical moral quality – the foregoing of present pleasures for future security – and it was assumed to be one of the cardinal bases of Britain's greatness. In the races they considered themselves to be civilizing, the Victorians looked for thrift as an index of progress. And to most nineteenth century observers, local and visiting, the black in Guyana seemed sadly devoid of this virtue. The amount of money amassed to purchase the village lands – which ought to have given pause to those who claimed blacks had no ability to save – was quietly forgotten. Blacks were generally portrayed as improvident and spendthrift,[29] making ridiculous claims to a status which ill-befitted their station.[30]

In particular, the lack of thrift was held to be exemplified by the black partiality for lavish clothes and fancy weddings. In Victorian society variations of clothing were symptoms of social distance: the working classes were sternly discouraged from dressing above their station. But in Guyana the situation seemed absurdly different. If anything, the blacks by their attire appeared to negate those social conventions which emphasized the social hierarchy. This provoked considerable irritation among the whites who saw in it the shallowness of a race which had got its priorities wrong. In a discussion on education in the Anglican Synod in 1874, Josiah Booker roundly condemned the kind of education offered to the Creoles since it seemed to teach them only to parade on Sundays "decked up in a style far above their station in life". He wanted education to be given a practical turn so as to teach the blacks not to aim at becoming "fine gentlemen and ladies and aping the manners of their betters".[31]

Booker had little sympathy for the blacks. But H.V.P. Bronkhurst, a Methodist minister who regarded himself as very much their friend, had substantially the same comment to make on Creole dress habits. Describing the Creole as basically careless about rising in the world, he added that

if at times he does exert himself a little, it is only for the purpose of earning a little money to deck himself in broadcloth, gaudy coloured necktie, and patent leather boots, wherewith to strut about to his own manifest satisfaction and pleasure, and the admiration of his female friends, and the envy of his less fortunate brethren.[32]

The black wedding was an institution much condemned as a proof of improvidence and vain social pretensions. Clergymen inveighed against it throughout the nineteenth century to no avail. The Revd R.T. Veness, a careful observer of the social customs of "the coloured races" in the colony, denounced the ludicrous expense involved in a black wedding which, he said, never cost less than $200. This kind of display indicated that the black was still a barbarian under the skin, incapable of husbanding resources for future contingencies. The highest ambition of "Quashie" was to "have a grand wedding; to strut to church in frankish garments, looking big like Guvna self; to give a day's jollification to his countrymen collected from all the country around".[33] Bronkhurst had much the same to report. He lamented the "stupidity" of having a trousseau, a dinner for twenty or thirty persons and broughams to convey the bridal party, especially among a people whom he described as "vain, ostentatious, poor, improvident and not systematically industrious".[34]

None of those who denounced these practices realized that perhaps the most powerful survival of West African culture among the Creoles was the significance attached to *rites de passage* of which marriage, burial and christening were the most important. They were rites of status change, deeply communal in their nature, necessarily involving assemblages of people. But even if the white critics of the black wedding had realized its indebtedness to West African culture, the blacks would still have got it in the neck: they would have been accused of a tenacious preference for barbaric practices. The imperial culture was too arrogant not to condemn what it did not understand. And by the 1870s, the winds of change throughout the empire were blowing in directions not favourable to the blacks. What had been suggestions of black inferiority in the 1840s and 1850s were hardening into convictions by the 1870s. The black wedding and the culture that supported it served merely to bolster those convictions.

To the mid Victorians, if saving money was evidence of a sturdy moral fibre, making money was proof of moral dynamism. And the Guyanese black was deemed to be as incapable of the one as the other. It was an assumption, common particularly among Anglo-Saxon whites and the Portuguese, that the black could not run a shop – for spending would always be greater than earnings.[35] Blacks were usually contrasted with Portuguese who ran them out of business, it was said, precisely because the latter knew how to handle money.[36] A writer to one of the newspapers summed up the common stereotype: "Only the Negro is poor: the Portuguese as well as the Chinese enjoy the good things of life; the East Indians send back to India large sums of money."[37]

Bronkhurst, whose contradictory opinions reflected much of the stereotyping of the 1870s and 1880s, underlined this assumption when he wrote:

We place a Portuguese and a black together on a sugar estate and furnish them with the same description of work. We take them both at the same age, say eighteen years. At the expiration of twelve years we look them up, but where do we find them? Look among the plantain farmers, shopkeepers or house and land proprietors for the Portuguese; for the other look amongst the occupants of the common gaol or Massareni [the Penal Settlement].[38]

Nations and ethnic groups inevitably admire those qualities that they consider have made them dynamic. The Victorians prized themselves on making a mix of Christianity and commerce the foundation of their national and imperial greatness. Consequently, they desired to instil that fusion in the races they deemed themselves to be civilizing, particularly the African peoples. In Guyana, the blacks appeared to have undone the magic mix of Christianity and commerce. Christians they had certainly become. But, compared to the Portuguese and later the Chinese and East Indians, they were not a commercial people. The planters, the colonial officials and the clergy of all but the Congregational churches felt compelled to contrast the lax, 'Latin' attitude of the blacks to money with the tougher, would-be 'Teutonic' attitude of the immigrants, to the discredit of the blacks.[39] Trollope spoke for the colonial whites when he said that although Europeans taught their children that the love of money was the root of all evil, this was slightly ingenuous: "The love of money is a good and useful love ... show me ten men without it and I will show you nine who lack the zeal for improvement."[40] But there was something more. The stereotypes of the moneymaking immigrants and the uncommercial blacks were not-too-subtle propaganda devices for East Indian immigration supported from the revenues of the colony.

"Laziness" and "lack of thrift" were enough to earn the blacks disapprobation in Victorian eyes. But to these was added "improper" sexual behaviour. Among the village and urban working class blacks, unstable sexual liaisons as well as stable common law marriages survived the end of slavery and continued to be the social norm throughout the nineteenth century. Meanwhile, the lax sexual ethics of the Regency period in England had hardened into the middle class Victorian moral code in which permissive sex was sternly frowned upon. The non-white races of the empire were adjudged to have "advanced in civilization" as much by their attitude to sex as to work. Besides, the abolitionists had urged that slavery was responsible for "immorality" and that its demise would lead to pure sexual ethics. Yet the blacks, despite their obvious enthusiasm for church membership, showed little signs of abandoning the "immoral practices" of slavery. Nor did the clergy understand or condone common law marriages which they regarded as 'living in sin'. They continued to complain throughout the century that almost half the children brought for baptism were illegitimate. This was seen as evidence of considerable debasement. It appeared that "the curse of Ham still rested on his hapless children".[41]

But there was a double standard at work here. Although the colonial whites condemned the blacks for this moral 'defect', many whites continued to practise concubinage long after the end of slavery. The 'outside family' of the respectable white man was a normal institution in Guyanese life in the nineteenth century. But they appear to have projected their own guilt complexes onto the black whose own less covert sexual practices became the scapegoat for ambiguous sexual ethics of a whole society. Bronkhurst pointed this out when he wrote: "There seems to be great deal more immorality practised by the Europeans who come out to the colony than by the natives themselves. The results of such a life are to be seen everywhere; and yet they are the very persons who cry down the people and make them worse than they are; and speak of them as the most immoral set of beings in the world."[42]

The stereotype of the blacks that emerged after emancipation is fundamentally a reflection of the peculiar relationship between them and the whites. As elsewhere in the nineteenth century where whites and blacks met, the former were expected to civilize the latter and this relationship produced ambivalent attitudes in both. The white elite wanted the blacks to develop a respect for order and habits of deference, as well as a taste for the amenities of 'civilized life' strong enough to make them regular workers but not so strong as to make them socially or politically ambitious. They wanted them educated in school to internalize an acceptance of white and planter supremacy in the society; they wished them to accept the idea of "an indefinitely delayed equality" and leave the crucial functions and positions of influence in both church and state to the whites.[43]

The quiet revolution of emancipation seemed to awaken in the blacks attitudes threatening to the old social order. For instance, it amazed Schomburgk, the German explorer who observed the aftermath of emancipation in Guyana, to find that the black workman performed his job for the white man as if he were conferring a favour – what was really an assertion of human dignity for the ex-slave struck the German as presumption.[44] Other observers found it absurd that the ex-slave should insist on having his wife or his reputed wife addressed as 'his lady', an almost aristocratic pretension in a man recently freed from servitude. The blacks' attempt to emphasize equality with their former masters was labelled "self conceit" and he was contemptuously stereotyped as acknowledging no superior and insisting "that he could easily equal the white man in every respect".[45]

Later in the period many of the whites criticized the blacks' desire to "rise in the scale of civilization" by taking white-collar jobs, jobs which the small white elite felt ought to be left to themselves or, at worst, given to coloureds. One critic put his views thus:

It is certain that a Creole youth with a smattering of scholastic lore, the thinnest veneer of so called learning . . . regards even skilled manual labour with contempt, considers it beneath him and aims at something more 'genteel'. He wants to be a clerk, a teacher, a minister (save the mark), a shopkeeper, an agent, a hedge lawyer . . . anything but an honest workman, the noblest occupation in the calendar if he but rightly understands it.[46]

What the Creoles regarded as an index of their desire to rise in the scale of civilization many of the whites saw as a subversion of it.

William Russell was particularly critical of black ambitions in the 1880s when educated blacks began to raise their voices in favour of a more inclusive electoral and representational political system. He saw them as wanting too much prestige and as too eager to take the place of the whites. He advised the blacks that they "could not all be peace officers and clerks because they can stick a pen behind their ear", and if they banished all the whites out of the colony and the circulation of money which their presence ensured, their education would be severely circumscribed. He preferred the old sort of black whose ambitions were more modest and who, he claimed, would endorse his criticisms and say "true for you Massa".[47] It was not uncommon for Russell and the editors of the *Colonist* and the *Royal Gazette* to refer to blacks with high educational attainments as "good shovelmen spoilt".[48]

It is not surprising that by the end of the nineteenth century the stereotype of the Guyanese black, held by the white elite and the immigrants, was that of an immature creature with the conviviality, humour and even comic characteristics of children. In a collection of humorous satirical drawings entitled *West Indian Illustrations of Shakespeare*, published in Georgetown in 1885, every illustration pokes fun at the black in his various moods. No other race is made fun of. Even as liberal an observer as Sir Everard Im Thurn wrote:

It is all very well to say that a man is a man whether his skin is white or black; but it is certain that the vast majority of West Indian blacks – all but a very few – are not men but children; quiet, strong, generally good tempered children, but always fickle and essentially, though from mere thoughtlessness, cruel. It seems possible to educate individuals of this class to the grown up stage; but this does not alter the fact the great mass of them remain children in all but physique.[49]

Though many would have claimed that Im Thurn overstated his case, the general white view of the black was not far from his own. When in 1888 they celebrated the fiftieth anniversary of the end of apprenticeship, the *Argosy* newspaper in a cartoon summed up what many whites thought of the occasion. It asked what had the blacks done since 1838 and the answer was simply "celebrated a jubilee".[50]

The Stereotype of the Indian

The stereotype which the whites developed of the Indians was radically different from that which they formed of the blacks. The basic reason is not far to seek. From 1851 onwards the Indian became increasingly the prop of the sugar industry which was held by most nineteenth century whites to be the sine qua non of the existence of the colony. The blacks on the other hand, although the statistics do not support this view until the 1880s, were seen as increasingly peripheral to the industry except in the highly skilled sections. Hence the 'East Indian' was considered by most of the whites as more relevant to the country's needs than the black. If things had been left to the blacks, they claimed, Guyana would simply have become another enclave of barbarous Africa in the Caribbean.

The planters consistently asserted that 'coolie labour' had saved the country, and that continued Indian immigration would bolster its prosperity. This was stated quite early, in the difficult days of the 1840s. In 1848 the Court of Policy put on record its views that "had it not been for the services of coolies and Madeirans one half of the cultivation must of necessity long ere this been abandoned".[51]

Sir Henry Barkly consistently reiterated the same point,[52] and so did each of his successors at Government House. The pro-planter newspapers harped constantly on the theme, and in the 1870s and 1880s, whenever there was a suggestion to put a stop to immigration, the Indian as the saviour of the colony was always mentioned.[53] In 1880, Henry Davson, whose prestige in the colony and in England was immense, stated that the time was far distant when immigration from India could cease;[54] and William Russell put it even more emphatically when he wrote: "If they (the planters) were shut out from India they might as well make arrangements to abandon the plantations."[55] The Indians themselves appeared to have taken this view of the matter. When taunted by the Creoles for being cheap labour they were reported to reply: "Yes, you rascal neeghaa man, me come from India dis 40 sikus year; s'posing me and me matty no come dis side fo' work, you rascal neeghaa man been a starve one time."[56]

The chief feature in the stereotype of the Indian was his 'docility' – a quality which recommended him to the planters and the whites especially as, by contrast, they found the attitude of the blacks overweening. Docility was also a quality which, both in Victorian England and in the tropical colonies, capitalist employers required their workers to possess. In the production of sugar it was considered the paramount virtue: for, after the 1840s West Indian sugar had to compete with Cuban slave-grown sugar and docility in workers who had a measure of freedom was a counterpoise to slaves who could be manipulated at will. The docility of the Indians was lauded as their cardinal virtue. In a minute to the Colonial Office the Court of Policy in 1848 appealed for the reopening of East Indian immigration on the grounds that "the Calcutta coolies and the better class of Madras coolies are very little inferior to the African labourers, and in many respects we believe them to be preferable, for they are docile, tractable, intelligent and industrious".[57]

After the great strike of the black estate labourers in 1848 the docility of the Indians was frequently quoted as the best argument for importing them.

In many instances intelligence was added to docility in describing their character, an estimate which was clearly based on the association of their interests with that of the planters. For instance, on one estate it was recorded that the Indians offered to go on working for credit after the blacks had ceased to work and even offered to lend the manager their savings if that would keep the estate in cultivation.[58]

It is not surprising that the Indians were described as a much more valuable class of labourers than the blacks, because, although seen to be generally physically less strong than the latter, they were easier to work with.[59] A writer to the *Royal Gazette* in 1849 emphatically stated that in periods of danger, accident or sudden emergency, most planters turned for assistance not to the "pampered Creole Labourer born and bred on the estate, but to the stranger, the quiet willing coolie".[60] Barkly himself referred to the Indians as of "a naturally quiet and inoffensive disposition and if heathen, as little given to violate the precepts of the moral law as those whose profession of Christianity is most ostentatious".[61]

The docility of the Indians was never as pervasive as the stereotype made out. In fact, there were periods when they gave enough trouble to their employers to destroy the image of an easily manipulated worker. The large number of summonses issued by managers against Indians for breaches of the labour laws, mainly to intimidate them, suggests that there was a great deal more undemonstrative protest against the management of estates than the planters cared to admit. The beating of overseers and drivers, as well as the attacks on black task gang labourers in the late 1860s, when they sometimes manhandled Europeans on their way, should have given those who claimed that the Indian was docile second thoughts. Equally damaging to the stereotype of docility was the "mendacity" of the Indians. The whites often pointed to their tendency to go to court and, with a group of their countrymen, concoct stories of harsh treatment by managers which the latter usually claimed were totally unfounded; and often due to the rather "mysterious animosities" against estate whites which the Indians developed.

The reaction of the white inhabitants along the Essequibo Coast to the Devonshire Castle riot of 1872 suggests that two contradictory attitudes to the Indian existed side by side in their minds. They were both docile and capable of organized murder and rapine.[62] Yet in the stereotype of the Indian the 'revengeful' feature was usually cast in a minor key. There are two reasons for this. The first reason is the propaganda value of the stereotype. The planters were so concerned that immigration from India should continue in an uninterrupted flow that it was considered unwise to dwell on the "turbulent side" of the Indian character. To import troublemakers into Guyana would have been bad imperial policy. On the other hand, to import a people who quietly did the expected, and so preserved the supremacy of the sugar interest, justified the whole imperial policy of immigration. The Government of India was keenly interested in the condition of the Indian in the Caribbean. If it could be shown that in Guyana Indians improved their worldly position, while they lost none of the qualities that made them good labourers, then the imperial conscience would be satisfied. Hence to consistently harp on the idea of docility was the correct strategy. And people who constantly harp on an idea usually come to believe it themselves. The Indians' alleged docility then not only served the purpose of advertisement; it acquired the status of truth.

But an explanation had to be found for the outbursts of Indian fury, especially during the period between 1869 and 1872. The typical answer was given by the governor, Sir John Scott: The Indian was both docile and excitable. When Indians' credulity was played upon by unscrupulous troublemakers, they exploded into violence. When they were properly managed by Europeans they kept quiet. This explanation fitted in with the increasingly invoked imperial concept of 'native races' in the later nineteenth century: that under their own leaders – people with axes to grind – they tended to ignore their own best interests. When led by Europeans, who understood their interests better than they did themselves, they pursued an equable course. The same governor who described the Indians as "easily excited and demonstrative" had no hesitation in saying "they are in reality a people not difficult to govern if proper judgment were exercised in dealing with them".[63] He added that "there are, I have no doubt, amongst them many clever fellows who will be found more disposed to foment discontent than to follow the steady labour required from them by their indentures", but he saw no possibility of real trouble from the East Indians.[64]

The second reason for the formation of the stereotype of the docile Indian is more fundamental. Although the immigrant had official protection against the employers in the immigration agent general, the system of indenture gave the planters an extraordinary degree of control over the life of the indentured immigrant. In imperial relations where one group exercises a tight control over another, the ruling group usually attributes docility to those they control. It is a psychological technique of self-justification.[65] The kind of control over the Indian was well summed up by Jenkins when he wrote:

This great community which lives by itself, is shut in within itself, must find its news and its amusement, as well as its tasks, out of itself. Take a large factory in Manchester, or Birmingham, or Belfast, build a wall around it, shut in its work people from all intercourse, save at rare intervals, with the outside world, keep them in absolute heathen ignorance, and get all the work you can out of them, treat them not unkindly, leave their social habits and relations to themselves, as matters not concerning you who make money from their labour and you would have constituted in no small degree a sugar estate village in British Guiana.[66]

It was not merely the economic and legal control of labour that made the indenture system attractive to Europeans. It was the social control of hundreds of human beings and a sense of power emanating from this control that appears to have attracted so many young men from Scotland to come out to Guyana as overseers in the hope of eventually becoming managers.[67] The life of an overseer throughout this period was an arduous one. The 1870 royal commissioners pointed out that "they have to work very hard, to lead a life of considerable exposure in an unhealthy climate, with few appliances of comfort, no society and small pay . . . In point of house accommodation, physical comfort generally, and above all human sympathy, the young overseer on a remote plantation is often badly off."[68] These conditions, coupled with the risk of dying of malaria or typhoid, and enduring the flat coastal terrain in Guyana, ought to have acted as a strong deterrent to young men of fair education and middle class ancestry. Nor was the job of manager an easy one. It demanded considerable energy, a wide ranging knowledge of soils and manufacturing processes, as well as the state of the market and an intense and unremitting vigilance of the workers. What may have made the overseer's job bearable and the manager's job rewarding was the social system created by indenture. To control, direct and manipulate the lives of large numbers of human beings was a vocation which Europeans found increasingly congenial as the century proceeded.

The overseer and manager in Guyana had something of the feeling of the district officer and the district commissioner in Africa and India. The 1870 royal commissioners described the job of manager as "the task of controlling, humouring and acting earthly providence to some hundreds of labourers of different races, of different kinds and degrees of civilization",[69] a job that carried immense prestige in the colony, "the gentlemen in charge of estates" coming even before stipendiary magistrates in the social hierarchy.[70] It is significant that by 1870 the practice of employing coloured overseers had died out. Only young Englishmen or Scotsmen were employed. The rationalization for this was that white overseers were more trustworthy and vigorous than the Creoles. The truth was that as the indenture system became a settled way of life it developed a mystique which was better personified by a white man than by a coloured one.[71]

The other side of the coin of control was paternalism, which was a strong enough justification for the system of indenture in the nineteenth century.[72] The exercise of paternalism could be seen in such institutions as the estate hospital, where sick Indians were lodged free of charge and treated by the estate doctors and sick-nurses. As an institution the estate hospital emphasized the planter's control over the inmates, since they became heavily dependent on the estate hierarchy when they were ill. In fact, the estate hospital turned out to be a means of conditioning newly arrived Indians to their dependent role because they were usually subject to bouts of 'colony fever', that is malaria, chigoes and dysentery.

On some estates before 1870, newly arrived Indians, even if in good health, were quartered in the hospital for a few days before being located in their separate barracks. On others the hospital was used as a lock-up for those guilty of riotous or disorderly conduct. Many hospitals before the arrival of the 1870 Commission kept stocks to punish "recalcitrant" immigrants.[73] In all this the discipline, regimentation and control of the estate system were symbolized. The fact that up to 1873 doctors were employees of the estates and not public servants, and, therefore, took care not to fall foul of the managers, meant that the latter's power was made to seem paramount in the lives of the Indians.

Another institution that emphasized the self-sufficiency of the estate and the authority of the manager was the Manager's Court. The Indians were encouraged to settle their less serious disputes before the manager and breaches of the by-laws of the estate were dealt with at that court. Settlement of disputes not only prevented the loss of valuable working hours, it also gave the manager an insight into what was going on outside of the sphere of labour. Even more, it underscored the paternalistic nature of the manager's power, since he appeared to be more than just concerned with the Indians as labour machines.[74]

The Indians were made more dependent on the manager's control by the concessions made for the use of estate land. Quite early in the history of immigration, it became evident to the planters that the Indians wanted to keep cows. Some managers were not slow in realizing that permission to use estate lands free, or at a nominal rental, for this purpose was an indirect way of ensuring that the owners of cows worked steadily and gave no trouble. William Russell stated before the 1870 Commission that he granted the privilege of renting lands for pasturage to Indians who had worked specially hard and did not go before the courts.[75] The *Royal Gazette,* soon after the Leonora riot in 1869 encouraged all managers to grant their immigrants land for pasturage. It not only ensured contentment, the editor maintained, but encouraged them to remain on the estate after their indentures had expired.[76] Jenkins, on his tour through the colony, found that a large number of estates allowed the immigrants to pasture their cattle rent free.[77] There was a thin dividing line between paternalism and techniques of control.

The fact that for at least five years the Indians were subject to direct European control ensured that the stereotype of them was less pejorative than that of the black. It certainly imputed grave defects: the Indian was cunning, mendacious and wife murdering. Some said that he was indolent also. But these characteristics were signs that the Indians came from a different and inferior civilization with its "oriental complexities"; they did not seriously affect the working of the estate system. The Indian's 'mendacity' was generally recognized in the courts and his evidence little trusted. Indian men's wife-murdering propensities were due to the disruption of the Indian system of gender relations in Guyana where women were freer and in short supply. And if Indians were indolent by nature, the firm and regular discipline of the system of indenture soon counteracted this and turned them into steady and industrious workers. Even when Indians were not under indenture, the fact that they often remained on the estate meant that they were still amenable to European control, which gave them enhanced value in the eyes of the whites. Of the Indians who left the estates and worked in task gangs in the 1860s and 1870s, the planters had nothing good to say. It was claimed that they had become as "lazy as the Negroes".[78]

But European control had not only schooled the Indian in the value of hard work, it had also, it was maintained, provided a context in which the Indian's love of money could assert itself. It was argued, probably with some truth, that for a large number of Indians, indenture in Guyana had provided the first opportunity to work for a regular wage. The Indian's response had been not to squander money, but to hoard it. In fact the Indian had, it was claimed, reacted to the new conditions of life by practising the virtue of thrift. Where Creole spending provoked contempt from the whites, Indian thrift evoked admiration. The Indians under indenture on the estate had proved themselves Victorian-like. They had the instincts of "economic man". Trollope expressed his admiration. "Both the coolies and the Chinese have an aptitude in putting money together," he wrote, "and when a man has this aptitude he will work as long as good wages are to be earned."[79] Some observers pointed out that Indians saved money in many instances by almost starving themselves.[80] Others attributed this thrift to having fewer personal wants than other races.[81] Whatever the reason for the practice of thrift, the white elite had their own reason for lauding it: it proved excellent propaganda for the system of indenture. At an official level, statements showing how much money Indians had in the savings bank, or how much they took back to India with them, not only in cash but in jewellery, could not fail to have the desired effect – to impress the Indian government and the Colonial Office that the system of indenture in Guyana was a boon to the Indians. At a lower level, those who returned to India with savings and jewellery could convince other Indians that the Guyanese indenture was not a form of slavery. Besides these statements proved something else: although it was dangerous to cushion and coddle some races, like the blacks, because it made them irresponsible and improvident, with the Indians it was the reverse. Even when the Indians wished to assert their status, the men did so by decking their wives with jewellery made from melted gold and silver coins – the jewellery was in itself a form of savings.[82]

Not much of the recorded savings of Indians was accumulated purely from wages. But to the shrewder members of the white elite this was no blot on the system. It proved that Indians in Guyana were not only hoarding money, they were finding ways of making it. If Indians made money by shopkeeping and cow minding this was all to the good.

By 1880, serious thought was being given by the government to the prospect of settling Indians on the land. In that year a leading article in the *Colonist* maintained that the great need of the colony was a 'middle class' and that the Indian population would provide just that.[83] What the writer meant was a class of prosperous peasant farmers with shopkeeping connections. Definitely, he ruled out the Creoles as failures in this field. Again, in 1881, the *Colonist* urged the government to hasten the settlement of Indians on the land since they were the only people in the West Indies that showed any signs of becoming a successful peasantry. "In the present state of affairs it is evident that on the manual labour of the coolie race must the progress or decline of the colony depend."[84] A few years earlier the same paper had praised the parsimony of the Indians as contributing to the real wealth of the colony and had predicted that they were destined not only to become four-fifths of the population but a very flourishing four-fifths as well.[85]

By the 1880s, the prospect of filling Guyana with Indians did not seem to the planters and most of the officials as an unreasonable one. For the planters, immigration had to go on. And as the Indians began to demonstrate their traditional skills in rice farming from the late 1870s onwards, the prospects of large numbers of them settling on the land became not merely tolerable but attractive. Necessity had become the mother of appreciation. As large numbers of Indians demanded return passages to India in 1880 and 1881 – they were entitled to such passages if they remained in the colony for ten years – the plantocracy and colonial officials grew alarmed and decided it would be far cheaper to settle them.[86] All the arguments against granting them land began to turn into arguments for it. And the stereotype of the free Indian, so pejorative in the early and mid 1870s, suddenly acquired a respectable hue. The editor of the *Colonist* echoed the views of many when he wrote apropos the setting up of a settlement for Indians at Huis't Darien on the Essequibo Coast: "There is no reason why British Guiana should not become almost a second India."[87]

There was no fear among the whites of filling Guyana with Indians for two reasons. One was that the presence of other races ensured a certain security in times of disturbance. The second was that the Indians showed few tendencies to bridge the social and political distance between themselves and the whites. This was precisely what the educated Creoles were condemned for trying to do. Whatever money they acquired, the Indians remained sufficiently 'oriental', sufficiently different from the whites, so as not to challenge them in their own sphere. The Indian long resident in the colony, it was said, had stopped "cringing", the habit imposed by the caste system in India. But they did not lose their deference to the whites. They did not have ambitions above their station. Up to the end of the nineteenth century, the Indians showed few signs of producing a Westernized intelligentsia to challenge the white elite in their assumptions of superiority although there were people among them of learning in the Hindu and Muslim traditions. If Guyana was indeed going to be another India, as the apologists for large scale Indian settlement assumed, they were convinced it would be one without the 'examination-wallahs'. Hence there seemed little possibility of Indians challenging white political control. On the other hand educated, professional, articulate blacks, along with coloureds and Portuguese of similar ilk, frequently challenged the narrowly based oligarchic constitution and planter and merchant control.

The attitude of the leading whites to the differing aspirations of the two races was given overt expression in 1905 when the immigration agent general wrote thus about the Indians:

This attachment to the soil and their confidence in the sircar [that is, the colonial government] renders them disinclined to take part in politics – content, so long as they are not overburdened with direct taxation or perplexed with regulations, to plod on in their rice fields and bring up their children in their footsteps . . . Under these circumstances it is not a matter of surprise that but few East Indians have recorded their names as voters: and as a consequence the political power has passed into the hands of a section of the community, alien to themselves in race, religion, habits and interests, and moreover not superior to them in numbers, wealth, industry and thrift.[88]

The reference in the last part of the sentence is, of course, to the blacks.

Significantly, in this connection Edward Davson, the son of Henry Davson who was one of the most powerful sugar barons of Guyana, showed much the same attitude when he argued that the blacks who had the franchise were factious, colour conscious, and self-seeking, while those without it were contented and sensible. He objected to the white element in Guyana being subject to the non-white Creoles, a development that had been initiated by the reform in the constitution in 1891. He recommended an increase in the official element in the Combined Court to counteract the growing power of the blacks.[89]

The white stereotype of the Indian, although it had all the prestige of the hegemonic group in the society, was not often shared by the Creoles. They resented the constant cry of the whites that but for the Indians there would be no colony. In defence they developed a stereotype of the Indian which was largely unfavourable. It is, of course, not easy to arrive at a precise conception of the creole stereotype of the Indian. Some ideas can be gleaned from statements on the subject made by Europeans who observed the two races. However, besides the *Creole,* which was the established organ of the mixed-race group with moderate and liberal views, there existed between 1866 and 1876 smaller newspapers edited by blacks or reflecting black views that gave a much less restrained expression of their opinions and prejudices than the *Creole* did. These were the *People,* the *Working Man,* the *Weekly Penny,* and the *Watchman.*

The most common feature in the creole stereotype of the Indian that emerges from all these newspapers was that of a physically inferior race. The 1870 commissioners had observed that "the Negro . . . despises the coolie because he is so immensely inferior to him in physical strength".[90] The planters themselves generally held this view: they usually asserted that a black could do (if working regularly) three times the amount of work that an Indian could perform in a week. To some extent this was the black labourers' answer to the unfavourable stereotype of them as a lazy creatures. They pointed to their physical strength and said that there was no need for them to work as doggedly as the Indian who had to do longer hours because he could do so much less. When the editor of the *Working Man* asked indignantly "Are the terms fair to give a robust, hardy Creole, the same price as a puny, tiny-handed coolie?", he was both stereotyping the Indian as well as voicing one of the black's main complaints.[91] An oft-repeated epithet used to describe Indian men was "effeminate", a word with strong overtones of contempt among the Victorians and one which was used by the *Creole* as well as by smaller newspapers and on occasion even by Governor Scott.[92]

A corollary to the image of physical inferiority was the stereotype of the Indian as being a constant inmate of the estate and public hospitals. The editor of the *Watchman* gave expression to the popular view when he declared that Indians spent most of their time either in hospital or in jail. Even the ex-indentureds, he claimed, flocked to the public hospitals. The reason was that "they are accustomed to it and they are lazy owing to bad diet; and their begging habits get them a ready admittance; besides they grudge to spend to buy medicine because they get it free at our cost".[93] This stereotype of the Indian as too mean to eat a proper diet and too prepared to go to the public hospital for free treatment lasted right down to the 1930s.

In fact, the most unfavourable feature in the black stereotype of the Indian was precisely the one which the white planters and officials generally commended – his thrift. To the blacks it was not thrift but avarice.[94] In a colony where import duties, they felt, fell heavily on the labouring classes, the blacks complained that the Indians by 'hoarding' their money were forcing them to bear more than their fair share of the taxes. In the columns of the *Watchman* and the *Working Man*, Indians were almost invariably referred to as "unconsuming". They were contemptuously described as "a people who can live on our wild weeds boiled without salt".[95] By 'hoarding' money or even depositing it in the savings bank, the Indian was said to bring stagnation to the economic life of the colony. One correspondent to the *Watchman* severely criticized Governor Scott for his supposed partiality to the Indians because it was said he ordered 4 percent interest to be given on the savings accounts in the post office where the majority of the deposits were made by 'Hindus'. This was merely appropriating 'Christian revenue' for encouraging hoarding by Indians, and the consequence was commercial depression.[96]

The planters and officials constantly asserted that Indian immigration was a benefit to all classes. The *Watchman* replied with a hypothetical analysis of Indian spending to disprove this. The passage is a typical piece of stereotyping and fairly innocent of English grammar:

100 East Indians get 100 shillings a day; or $144 a week; they forfeit $24 for alleged bad work. Their clothing, as a rule, costs them 6 cents a week – $6 average for all.

Their food and rice and green fruit, say $30. Their rum averages, say $12. Extras, say $12. Travelling, say $6. In all about $90. There remain $50 to be strung or melted. They lose 25% on that. In all $37.50 a week left amongst all. Some to be buried and lost while drunk. The remainder is banked at the colonial cost of $4 on every $100 – about the duties on the little imports they have consumed . . . Hence that way the colony does not derive any appreciable benefit of the cultivation of the sugar cane.[97]

The Creoles appeared to have objected to the Indian habit of melting down coins to make jewellery.[98] They also objected to the vast sums of money which the returning Indians allegedly took to India with them.[99] Both by their presence and their departure the Indians were held to impoverish the colony. Only the planter and the Indian benefited. One correspondent to the *Watchman* summed it up: "as things are king sugar is a naked unconsuming Hindu and colonial progress is being retarded".[100]

But the blacks were not alone in their hostility to Indian saving. The merchants and shopkeepers in Georgetown usually traced the dullness of trade to this source. In 1874 when Water Street, the commercial centre of Georgetown, was passing through a depression, the *Creole* lamented:

It is beyond doubt that the tradesmen of Georgetown are beginning to feel the consequences of the importation of such large numbers of East Indians, and whilst the depression in the sugar market may to some extent account for the depression of trade, it does not fully explain it and it can only be fully explained when the influence of the coolie upon the retail trade of the city is taken into account . . . every coolie who lands in the colony is a direct loss to the trading portion of the community, since while the Creole circulates the money he earns, the coolie jealously hoards it to take it away with him to Calcutta or Bombay.[101]

In 1874, a petition signed by some twenty-two leading merchants was submitted to the Combined Court praying for an increase in Chinese and a decrease in Indian immigration. The petitioners urged that Chinese immigrants, being good consumers as well as hard workers, would benefit everyone, whilst the East Indians were of little use to anyone except the planters.[102]

But the Indian was, in the blacks' eyes, not only a financial liability, but a social one as well. Indians kept themselves isolated and remained eternally foreigners. In 1849, an observer commented that while the African immigrant (brought by the British Navy from the coastal area of Africa between Sierra Leone and Liberia to work on the estates) soon amalgamated with the creole population and became one with them in sympathies and attitudes, the creole population tended to look upon the Indian as a foreigner to the day of his death.[103] In 1849, Indians were a relatively new element in the society. By the 1870s, however, they had become a staple part of the population. Yet they were still regarded as foreigners.

Georgetown's Market Square, c. *1880*

BY COURTESY OF THE SYNDICS OF CAMBRIDGE UNIVERSITY LIBRARY

The *Creole,* contrasting the alleged increasing attachment of the Indians in Trinidad to that colony with their countrymen's attitude in Guyana, said: "The men brought here from the East are intensely clannish, they keep to themselves and mix with no other race. Some learn English but never cease to speak their native language. A coolie may be here for ten or fifteen years and at the end of the period know little more of the colony than when he landed."[104]

The Indians were usually contrasted unfavorably with the Chinese, who were said to adapt a civilized life and all its attendant results with considerable ease, because they were not "hedged about with the impassable barriers of caste".[105] Despite the shortage of women among Indians, observers noted that sexual connections between them and blacks were exceedingly rare. The editor of the *Watchman* felt that this was unfortunate. Not only were the children of such unions fine specimens, but marriage with Creoles would have brought the Indians into the mainstream of the country's life.[106]

The often self-contradictory nature of stereotypes is well illustrated by the articulate blacks' view of the Indians as both the planters' allies against them and as the enemies of the whites and their way of life. The blacks prided themselves on their loyalty to the Queen and their willingness to work for the whites, if only the latter would be fair in their dealings with them. In contrast, they formed a picture of the "disloyal coolie" harbouring sullen resentment and only dissuaded from creating serious disturbances in the colony by the presence of the "loyal blacks". The editor of the *Working Man* gave voice to the view that the Indian immigrant had no sympathy with his European masters:

The yoke of England is borne by the Indian from sheer inability to throw it off, and he comes here from circumstances which force him to leave his native land, and he brings that prejudice with him which is always in the minds of the conquered against the conqueror. And we are of the opinion that it is this very feeling which has given rise to those many outbreaks which we deplore, as well as those lamentable murders which are forever darkening the pages of this species of labour and which even now are filling our minds with dread and horror. As long, therefore, as these things are strong in his mind, forming an impenetrable wall of prejudice, Indian immigration will never be more successful than it is.[107]

When the Indians took to rioting in 1869 and 1870, writers in the pro-black newspapers took the opportunity to contrast the peace loving blacks who used legitimate means to correct injustices done to them with the mutinous, disloyal East Indians. Obviously they had forgotten the anti-Portuguese riots of 1856 when the blacks ransacked and looted Portuguese shops throughout the coastal areas. One writer claimed that all the capital invested in the colony was safe only because the Creoles protected it from the Indians, whom the planters treated as their 'darlings'.[108] Correspondents to the *Working Man* asserted at the time of the Devonshire Castle riot in 1872 that the Indians were known to be purchasing guns with which to reenact the Indian Mutiny in Guyana. Although the editor of this paper was uneasy about the police shooting of five Indian rioters, with pointed ambivalence he could not suppress the hope that if it meant the stoppage of Indian immigration this would be no bad thing. Using language that would have sat comfortably with the troops taking revenge on the stragglers of the Indian Mutiny he declared "we have a dislike for Hindu murderers in our midst".[109]

The creole stereotype of the Indian was perhaps best summed up by the editor of the *Working Man*:

They proved dogged, sullen, obstinate, alike pernicious to themselves, planters and the community at large. To mention a few defects: idleness and theft, a liking to be, if allowed, always in hospital; vindictiveness which is hydraheaded and exhibits itself in these [sic]: manager and overseer murder aback of estate, should their money be stopped for work badly done; wife and other murders and often suicide on the most frivolous pretenses. No matter what people may bring forward as an opposite argument in their favour, I affirm these people are dissatisfied at heart with their position here; hence this wilful trouble and consequent expense to the colony and their desire to return home whence they came.[110]

Two things are interesting about this passage. In the first place, it is noteworthy that characteristics which the planters frequently attributed to the Creoles – obstinacy, doggedness, idleness and theft – were attributed by the editor of the *Working Man* newspaper to the Indians. Secondly, behind the passage is the assumption that the Indian was an uncivilized alien outside the society with no desire to become part of it. That aspect of the stereotype remained in existence long after the Indians had given every indication that they wished to make Guyana their home.

The image of the Indians as being foreign and alien, even of those who opted to remain in the colony, was in the educated creole mind frequently associated with their being 'infidels'. Their ascribed miserliness and refusal to spend were also traced to the same source. As was mentioned above, in the contemporary Victorian ideology the twin paths to civilization in Africa were commerce and Christianity. In Guyana, the articulate blacks were urging that Christianity and public spirited consumption went hand in hand. They were evidence that the black was a civilized being notwithstanding the prevailing stereotype of him as improvident. If the Indians were Christianized they could soon oil the wheels of commerce by a liberal spending of money. If they were civilized they would learn that "the strength of the nation which protects his life and liberties was not acquired nor is truly sustained by a rude, unconsuming manner of living, melting down Her Majesty's coins and hating the tenets of the Prince of Progress material as well as spiritual".[111] This statement, written by a black, could not be more typically Victorian even to the designation of Jesus Christ as the Prince not of Peace but of Progress.

Lower down the scale, however, some of the blacks did not even appear to feel that the Christianization of the Indians would make much difference to their social worth, as the following reported conversation suggests:

Christian sisters. First sister: Have you heard of the accident? Six persons in a bateau and all drowned? Second sister: Oh dear, how sad, and so quick; but perhaps they found a home in heaven at least with their Maker. First sister: Yes perhaps so, six of them and all coolies. Second sister: Coolies, only coolies! Tshups! I thought you were speaking of people.[112]

The Aftermath

At the end of the nineteenth century the stereotypes sketched above were robustly alive in Guyana. With slight variations they had become ingrained in the minds of members of the various ethnic groups. They were the normal lens through which they perceived one another and they were symptoms of a deeply divided colonial society characterized by a pathological emphasis on race and colour. That emphasis on race was neurotically clung to by the Anglo-Saxon whites who saw it as the psychological underpinning of their preeminence and privilege in the society, since their political monopoly of the levers of power was being tempered by educated blacks, coloureds and Portuguese. In this they had the tacit support of the Colonial Office which took it as axiomatic that non Anglo-Saxon political figures were ethnically partisan, self-seeking and corrupt in a colony that needed the racially impartial whites to guarantee its social stability.

The first four decades of the twentieth century witnessed a settling of the blacks and Indians into recognizably different roles in the society even as they increased their contact with each other. A significant minority of Indians took up residence in the coastal black villages and lived in reasonable harmony with their black neighbours. Black educators in the elementary schools, particularly since the first decade of the twentieth century, had been leading Indian youth into the Anglo-Saxon world, thereby laying the foundation for a cadre of professionals, particularly barristers, who achieved notability in the 1930s and 1940s. These contacts did not annihilate the stereotypes but they became more euphemized.

The stereotypes now tended to reflect the differing roles of the two races. Blacks saw Indians as classic sugar workers, alternating between a stoic endurance of estate indignities and rigours and outbursts of violence against estate authorities. They also saw them as entrepreneurs capable of spartan self-denial in pursuit of capital accumulation in order to purchase land or start a business; clever in manipulating loopholes and adroit at the practice of law; energetically litigious and disputatious; prone to drunkenness; determinedly endogamous; enjoying the conspicuous display of wealth when economically secure; hospitable, generous and neighbourly; tending to racial solidarity in matters of politics; and with a romantic attachment to the Indian subcontinent and considering themselves Indians even when Westernized.

The Indian stereotype of the blacks likewise reflected both their role in colonial society and some of the features ascribed to them in the nineteenth century. Blacks were seen by Indians as better at trades than at agriculture; essentially non-entrepreneurial and without business tenacity; given to conspicuous consumption without an economic base; didactic and rhetorical therefore making good teachers, preachers and journalists; sexually irresponsible; overzealous collaborators with and imitators of the British; addicted to constitutional forms for their own sake; determinedly convivial; much given to the outward practice of religion; generous, open handed and hospitable to an extreme.

In the early 1960s, as Guyana approached independence, Indians and blacks came into conflict over who would inherit the British mantle of government. The conflict in some parts of the country became intense and brutal. What was very significant was how the old, distinctly derogatory, stereotypes given a twentieth century veneer were brought forth to justify each side's hostility to the other. Indians based their right to succeed the British on their electoral majority but they also argued that the blacks were as incapable of running a country as they were a shop; that they possessed no capacity for fiscal restraint and big spending would be the rule; that they would be more concerned with the ceremonial pageantry of state than with the rigorous realities of statehood; that being imitators they would mimic American ways rather than base the culture of government on the culture of the Guyanese; that their sexual irresponsibility would lead to assaults on Indian family values; that a black government would inevitably be a corrupt one; and that they would be intolerant of the Indian's desire to preserve their culture. The blacks matched their opponents in the zeal for damnatory stereotyping. They characterized the Indians as so racially exclusive that Guyana would be in their grip for the foreseeable future as South Africa was in the grip of the whites. They envisaged the upper reaches of all public institutions reserved for Indians with blacks occupying only the lower levels. The saw themselves being subservient to a race whom their grandparents had educated out of their benighted ways. They gravely suspected that after independence Guyana would be Indianized and that all other cultures would be denigrated. As the violence between the two races escalated, blacks reminded Indians of their capacity for violence and murder on the estates but also cited the partition massacres of the subcontinent in 1947. Blacks claimed that their human rights would be abused and that all the cunning of which they accused Indians would be deployed to give that abuse the air of legality. Finally, the blacks predicted that an Indian government would deny them the assistance to strengthen their cooperatives in favour of support for Indian small-scale enterprises.

Observing the behaviour of stereotypes is very instructive in the study of race relations. As we have discovered in Eastern Europe and elsewhere, they can surface in times of uncertainty with a virulence that surprises us and revive attitudes and assumptions that appear to have given way to enlightenment.

7

The Madeiran Portuguese Woman in Guyanese Society 1830–1930

M. Noel Menezes

The men all so good for nothing, and hardly any women at all, it is very tiresome.
—Jane Austen, *Northanger Abbey*

These words of the heroine Catherine Morland in *Northanger Abbey* can well be the prologue of many, if not all, histories of the nineteenth century. In the history of nineteenth century British Guiana, the profile of women in society, regardless of their ethnic group or class, was minimal almost to the point of nonexistence. But this was not a phenomenon unique to that British colony in South America struggling to bolster and maintain the sugar industry with a spate of indentured immigrants, first from Madeira and later from India and China. It merely mirrored the prevailing attitude of the times towards women. It was not until the latter part of the nineteenth century that women began to agitate for their place in the sun; not until 1918 in Great Britain and 1920 in the United States, two leading democratic countries, were some women given the vote, albeit reluctantly. In British Guiana, this step forward did not take place until 1928.

In the Caribbean and Guyana, emerging from slave society through immigrant society, the woman was considered, by the established colonial (and religious) hierarchy, a mere breeder of children as well as plantation labourer with no rights whatsoever. The proportion of women to men among the indentured labourers who poured into the country after 1835 was always overbalanced in favour of the male until near the end of the century. Madeiran immigration to Guyana presented no exception to this pattern. In May 1835, when the first group of forty immigrants arrived from Madeira to work on the sugar plantations, there was no woman among them. In the first wave of immigration this is not surprising as a new venture into the unknown necessitated – for these immigrants – that the men would reconnoitre the situation and send later for the women and children.

And send for them they did – very early! With the economic situation in Madeira in a precarious state, the men were desperately seeking employment overseas. The postemancipation labour hunger in Guyana seemed an answer to their needs. It would only have been desperation that would have led those first immigrants to set sail for a distant land without their wives and children, for the Portuguese were noted for their strong family ties; children were extremely close to their parents. So in subsequent arrivals between 1835 and 1841 some women and children were among the Portuguese immigrants from Madeira. Unfortunately, poor accommodation and depression brought on by sickness and high mortality among their fellows led to "despondency and death".[1] Yet, despite the strong objections raised by the Madeiran authorities to the drain on the island population, the 1841 official returns noted a very high number of immigrants – 3,893. But sickness and death, especially among the women and children, continued to occur. Many, it was true, had brought with them their endemic diseases stemming from poor nutrition, consumption, elephantiasis and pneumonia. The Report of the Commission of Inquiry in 1841, besides noting measles, yellow fever and dysentery as causes of death, also listed "nostalgia" as a cause, particularly among the women.[2] Nostalgia resulted in their refusal to eat or take the correct nourishment. Above all, the women missed the consolations of their Catholic faith as well as the expressions of their faith in the processions and *novenas* (nine days of prayer in honour of Christ, the Mother of God, or special saints in the church's calendar) and their close family relationships in their community, the village in their small island home.

As all immigrants brought with them their deeply ingrained culture, let us look briefly at the attitude of Portuguese men towards their women and the role of the women in their society. As Charles Boxer observed: "Portuguese women were notoriously the most secluded in Europe and it was the boast of a seventeenth century Portuguese writer that a virtuous Portuguese woman left her home only for her christening, her marriage, and her funeral."[3] This attitude both Boxer and Sarah Bradford attributed to the Moorish heritage of the Portuguese which placed an ideological insistence on the seclusion of women.[4] This seclusion did not fully apply to the peasant class of women, as men and women worked closely together on their small farms. Nevertheless, the men were rather protective of 'their' women. Although the Madeiran society was supposed to be patriarchal, the mother ran the household. She was *dona de casa*, 'lady of the house'.[5] Her days were filled with the bearing of and caring for her children, doing the cooking and household chores as well as manual work on their small piece of land, and looking after the animals. After the 1860s, a large number of women were employed in the embroidery industry which was introduced by a British resident, Elizabeth Phelps, to Madeira during the 1850s and 1860s. The 'odium' disease had devastated the vineyards where the women shared with men the task of crushing grapes.[6] Separated from the social life of the men, the women in the town found their relaxation in sitting at the window watching life go by. The Portuguese verb *janelar* (to 'window')[7] expresses this aspect of social life in Madeira which later became a feature of life in Guyana when the Portuguese were settled in their own homes.

Portuguese Women and Family Life

So protective were the men of 'their' women that it was a mammoth step to bring the women across the seas. On the other hand, given their close knit family life it was natural for them to do so. The Return of Immigrants in March 1842 noted 655 women and 882 children to 863 men. Of the 863 men, 624 worked on the plantations, as did 427 of the 655 women and 370 of the 882 children.[8] By 1842, official immigration from Madeira was stopped due to the devastating reports on the immigrants' mortality. Although official immigration was not resumed until 1846, large numbers of immigrants, both men and women, continued to arrive in the colony. The 1841 census listed the Portuguese in the city of Georgetown as 1.88 percent of the total population; ten years later the percentage had increased to 6.98.[9]

The rapid rise of the Portuguese immigrant from canefield to commerce was somewhat phenomenal. Walter Rodney, M.J. Wagner and Brian L. Moore attributed this phenomenon to the fact that the planters very early freed the Portuguese from their contractual obligations on the plantations or waived them altogether, thus giving the edge to the 'whites' over the 'blacks'.[10] It must be noted, however, that throughout the 1830s contracts were flexible.

The length of contracts varied between seven years in 1836 to five years in 1837. In 1838, under an Order-in-Council one could received a monthly verbal or a one-year written contract.[11] This flexibility, coupled with the usually ignored element, that of Portuguese familiarity with commercial enterprises on their island, put them in a position to move off the plantations into the huckstering and later the shopkeeping trades.[12] By 1841, thirty of the original immigrants had paid their own passage of $30 back to Madeira to encourage their relatives and friends to come to Demerara as British Guiana was known to them. By 1843, the Portuguese were chartering their own vessels to bring in from Madeira shipments of wine, onions, potatoes, garlic, fish and other goods, as well as labourers (*colonos*), and women were among the passengers. Moreover, their easy access to goods from Madeira helped them to move quite easily into huckstering and shopkeeping. By 1852, the Portuguese held 312 of the 423 shop licenses; in Georgetown 171 out of 296, the Creoles and Europeans owning the balance of 125,[13] and this ratio would increase throughout the century. From 1853 onwards the *Registo de Passaportes* of Madeira listed not only wives and children but also servant girls (*criados*) among the *passageiros*. The wives were mostly in their thirties; the servant girls in their twenties.[14]

Among the many reasons for the success of the Portuguese shop was the fact that it was a family business. Together with her husband, the Portuguese wife helped behind the counter.[15] Shop and house were on the same premises. Thus it was an easy task to keep an eye on both business and domestic arrangements. As early as 1844, Manuel Pereira, who had emigrated in 1841 and completed a three-year indenture, managed a shop in Leguan with his wife. Later he opened a shop in Alberttown in 1845. The success of the Portuguese in the retail trade aroused the jealousy of the Creoles to such an extent that they attacked the Portuguese shops. In one such attack in 1846 on Pereira's shop, his wife, escaping with their child, received a violent blow and had to be hospitalized.[16] During attacks on Portuguese shops in 1856 and 1889, the women also suffered physical violence. While in the early years of immigration, women laboured beside their men on the plantations, later on the Portuguese woman took up her role as both housekeeper and shopkeeper which, in many cases, was similar to her life in Madeira.

The shop served also as the family centre. Family life, buttressed and bolstered by deeply religious roots, was extremely important among the Portuguese. There was a strong network of family relationships – brothers, sisters, uncles, aunts, cousins. Members of the family were very close and helped each other. In that environment the woman played an important role; she was, above all, the mother who devoted her life to the upbringing of her children, a trait that did not disappear en route from Madeira to Guyana. The children were brought up to respect Church and home. The children were taught to ask a blessing (*bensão*) of both mother and father before leaving the home or going to bed at night.[17] Grandmothers and godmothers were key figures in the Portuguese family structure. Godmothers took their responsibility for their godchildren very seriously; in some cases children were sent during the early years of their life to live with their godmother.

Portuguese woman with her godmother

Portuguese en famille

The Portuguese newspaper, the *Watchman*, noted that the women "made good wives and generally prevent their husbands from going astray from religion and order".[18] However, they could not always prevent the men from going astray with other women. Concubinage was quite prevalent. Although the woman was *dona de casa* and the man the *pater familias*, both having a sincere love for their children, the Portuguese wives suffered in silence the roaming propensities of their husbands who, especially as their wealth increased, kept a mistress or two on the side. In most cases the Portuguese wife not only closed her eyes to those affairs, but also, in some instances, accepted the illegitimate children of her husband into the household. This propensity of the Portuguese men astounded the English priests in Guyana who considered it hypocrisy to see those same men devoutly attending Mass on Sundays with wife and children and lighting candles to their favourite saints.[19]

Both custom and civil laws of the eighteenth and nineteenth century in Britain indicated that the husband was the master of his own household and head of the family; he prescribed the 'laws'; his wife was bound to live with him and follow him wherever he wished to reside.[20] Thus, the woman was in no position to take action against his infidelity; in this, as in other instances, she had no rights, much less the right to upbraid him or criticize his actions, domestic, business or otherwise. In most instances, the Portuguese woman made no overt decisions nor did she state her views. A popular saying about Portuguese women in Brazil could well have been applied to their counterparts in Guyana: "A woman's place is in the home with a broken leg."[21] With or without the "broken leg" it was she who prepared the meals for her family. It is to the Portuguese woman that we owe the Portuguese foods which became part of the Guyanese diet: the *bol de mel* (molasses cake), the garlic pork, the *sonhos* and *malassados* (pancakes), *bacelhau* (salt fish), *cus-cus, milho* (cornmeal cakes) – no small contribution to the Guyanese cuisine. The families were large, the pots were large, the cooking was endless. It was no mean feat for the woman to serve in the shop and prepare the meals. In the latter half of the nineteenth century the young girls who came as servants helped in the household chores. It was often with these young girls that the master of the household slept when his wife was too tired to offer him conjugal satisfaction.

Portuguese girls married young both in Madeira and in Guyana. In general, it was the custom for the parents to choose the partner who was sometimes an older man and closely connected with the family. With few exceptions, Portuguese women in Guyana married within their own ethnic group. Large families were the norm. Among the wealthy middle class, weddings were grandiose and lavish affairs which were reported in detailed and flowery language in the *Daily Chronicle* and other publications from the early 1900s through the 1930s. Not only was the dress of the bridal party and of the guests minutely described, but also lists of the gifts given, those from bridegroom to bride and vice versa, mostly gold and diamond jewelry indicating the wealth of the couple. The poorer classes married simply; no guest list nor gifts were recorded. Divorce was not subscribed to because of the Portuguese adherence to Catholic teaching which forbade it.

Portuguese in Education

All education begins in the home. In educating her children, the Portuguese woman took the lead. It was at their mother's knee that the children first learned their prayers which, throughout the country, were taught in Portuguese. Because language was such a bonding force among people out of their home country, Portuguese was spoken in the home. As the number of children increased, the majority being born in Guyana, the need to maintain the language was a vital one. Even though by the end of the century the Portuguese had lived and worked in an English-speaking country for six de-

cades, many never became naturalized British subjects nor did they Anglicize
their language. Their desire to retain their language resulted in some Portuguese women branching out in the field of education. In 1862, a Portuguese
Female School was opened in Brickdam by a Miss C. D'Oliviera.[22] Later she
served as mistress of a girls' school established in Water Street.[23] Mrs Clothilde
Reis De Souza of 48 Regent Street was a well-known school mistress who
taught her pupils not only Portuguese, but also English, reading, writing,
arithmetic, piano and dancing. The *Watchman* gave great praise to Mrs De
Souza's school which produced "fancy needlework, bead work, crochet and
embroidery fit for a London exhibition".[24]

By the 1870s, the Portuguese woman in Guyana had come a long way
from the plantation and the shop, though many still not only worked in the
shops but owned them. They were becoming literate and educated women in
their own language. In 1888, the nuns at the Ursuline Convent established a
Portuguese school which won much praise from the local press. The *Daily
Chronicle*, wishing the school "every success", observed:

We are very pleased to hear that the Nuns have completed their arrangement for
the establishment of a Portuguese School for young children of which Lady
Gormanston has kindly consented to become special patroness. The Portuguese
are very fond of their own language and all who wish them well would be grieved to
see it fall into disuse; for it is the strongest link between their present and their past;
it keeps alive among them the love of their ancient faith and memory of glorious
achievements of their noble people; it is in a word the most effective means of
presenting intact all the best qualities of their race.[25]

The school flourished and the girls held their own and outshone the boys
who were attending a Portuguese College founded in 1890 to turn out
"intelligent businessmen".[26] The Portuguese founded their own schools
because they were reluctant to send their children to schools supported by
government grants and lacking the Catholic atmosphere. Literacy was good,
yes, but religious instruction was a sine qua non. It was therefore providential
that a Madeiran woman, Sister Pauline De Freitas, one of the founders of the
Sisters of Mercy in Guyana in 1894, was asked to take charge of the newly
opened girls' school in the Sacred Heart Parish in 1895. Fluent in Portuguese,
she was able to teach the students, communicate with the parents and provide
the Catholic atmosphere so much desired by them.[27] The dedicated work of
the Sisters of Mercy in the field of education inspired many young Portuguese
women to enter the community and serve as teachers in the various elementary
schools and a secondary school in the early decades of the twentieth century.

In 1920, Sister M. Gabriel Fernandes became the first Portuguese principal of a secondary school, St Joseph's High School, a post she was to hold with distinction for thirty-six years.[28]

While some young women were branching out in the profession of teaching, others continued not only to run both provision and spirit shops but also to own them, both in the city and in rural areas.[29] Legal documents attest to the fact that women also owned land and property. One unique case was that of Mrs Francisca Dias, who claimed compensation from the government for land and property which had been included in the Award of the Arbitration Commission to Venezuela. On that land were three cottages, two logies, or the barracks formerly occupied by slaves and then indentured immigrants, thousands of cocoa trees, as well as coffee and coconut trees, among others.[30]

Portuguese Women – Backbone of their Church

By and large, one could safely deduce that the majority of Portuguese women lived a routine life as housewife, mother and shopkeeper. Their outlet from what was a seemingly unexciting and bland life was their involvement in the devotional life of their church. This was a natural for Portuguese women. In Madeira, their life was bound up with the celebration of their religious *festas* (feasts) and their attendance, with much and sincere devotion, at the many *novenas* which preceded the special feasts throughout the year. A much-loved and one of the greatest feasts in Madeira was that of *Nossa Senhora de Monte* (Our Lady of the Mount). On the day of that festival, 15 August, the women walked with bare feet in the processions and climbed up to the Church of the Mount on their knees.[31] This love of their faith was brought with them to their new home in Guyana and was one of the bonds which held their families together. If the men were lax in church attendance, and many were, the women compensated fully for their negligence by their involvement in the sodalities which abounded – the Children of Mary, the Blessed Virgin Society and the Society of St Philomena, who was a favourite saint among them. At the inauguration ceremony of the new chapel of St Philomena at the Sacred Heart Church in July 1901 there were four hundred ladies of that society present dressed in white, with wreaths, veils and scarlet ribbons.[32]

Throughout the country, especially along the East Coast where Catholic churches mushroomed between the 1850s and 1870s, Portuguese women cared for the church in cleaning, polishing, sweeping, dusting and washing of the altar linens. For all the church festivities the women were responsible for the floral arrangements, the drapery and the bunting which decorated the church. In later years they served as organists and sang in the choir. It was noted in church annals that many donors of altars and statues in the various churches were women. The women, too, were in the forefront of those attending the famous Christmas Novena which was held nine days before Christmas. It was primarily the women who set out early at dawn, as early as

Portuguese woman pianist

4:30 a.m., wrapped in shawls to be present in church for the singing of the *Bemdita Sejaes*, the Christmas Novena hymn still sung in the churches, each morning before the Novena Mass.

It seems a mark of deeply religious people that they are also very superstitious and the women were especially so. On the Feast of St John the Baptist they broke eggs in glasses of water to find out their future: the shape of the egg would determine their fate – a church, marriage or death; a ship, travel; a star, success among other portents.[33] During Christmas, young women would visit the crib and place their hands in the straw with a prayer that a husband would soon appear on the horizon. The Portuguese woman moved between home and church with the greatest ease, content in the realization that she was doing her duty to her God and family.

Portuguese Women on the Sociocultural Scene

In Madeira, a vibrant folk culture coexisted with a fully developed high culture. Both men and women loved to sing and dance while they laboured on the sugar plantations and while they crushed the grapes in the vineyards. They brought with them their inherent love of music, as well as their musical instruments. Less than twenty years after the arrival of the Portuguese in Guyana, a group of Portuguese Amateurs was founded in 1854. By the 1860s, when a number of cultural societies, both musical and dramatic, mushroomed, "the Portuguese also entered the cultural stream of music and drama in the Georgetown society".[34] The Portuguese women played a very prominent role in music. The two de Vasconcellos sisters, Mary Christina and Mary Amalia, were noted singers who not only performed with élan but also organized innumerable concerts. Mary Christina de Vasconcellos was considered "the leading artiste in British Guiana, the prima donna of her day".[35]

Piano lessons were given both privately and in the schools, and it was de rigueur for the young ladies of the middle and upper classes to become accomplished pianists, playing at both family celebrations and public concerts. Music was very much in the air when on 1 December 1876 the *Primeiro de Dezembro* Band was founded in honour of the anniversary of Portugal's liberation from Spain on 1 December 1640. Other bands were subsequently established by the end of the nineteenth century. Not to be outdone or outshone in this musical field, the ladies organized a string band of bandolins, violins and piano in early 1900. At a vocal and instrumental concert held in the Town Hall on 1 June 1900, the young bandolinistes, Mrs L. Da Costa, Miss E. Serrao, Miss V. Teixeira, Miss G. Henriques, Miss M.C. Serrao, Miss

L. De Souza, with M.P. Gonsalves at the piano, stole the show. This group became an integral part of the musical scenario, contributing much to the social entertainment of a wide cross section of the population.[36]

The Portuguese women had a strong flair for drama. Mid nineteenth century Madeira boasted its *Teatro Esperanca* (1859), which produced its own plays and hosted as well drama companies from Portugal and Italy. By the end of the century, other theatres evolved in which were produced a spate of dramas and musical comedies. One significant play, *"A Familia do Demerarista, A Drama de Um Acto"*, produced by a well-known Madeiran dramatist, A. d'Azevedo, immortalized the Demerarista, the one who returned from Demerara, *muito rico* (very rich).[37] Significantly, the play, while depicting the sufferings of the poor in Madeira, highlighted the dignity and integrity of the Portuguese woman who, though deprived, was not depraved.

Two decades after the Portuguese landed in Guyana their penchant for drama surfaced and found expression on the stage. Formal Portuguese drama can be said to have begun in April 1854 when the Portuguese Amateurs presented a dramatic performance in aid of the Girls' Orphanage in Georgetown. By the end of the nineteenth century, the Portuguese Amateur Dramatic Club was in the forefront of dramatic societies in the colony. These dramatic recitals and plays, mostly comedies, were executed in Portuguese. The few schools that taught the Portuguese language were the training grounds for potential artistes both in drama and music. Reports of these performances in the local press noted that the 'lasses' as well as the 'lads' were the principal characters.[38] By the end of the century, Portuguese women were among the well-known and leading artistes performing at the Philharmonic Hall and the Assembly Rooms. They featured in many productions, operas and plays.[39] Costume making and designing were mainly the women's job. In general, the standard of acting among the actresses was of a high quality. As in music so in drama, these women played an important role in the cultural life of the colony. Nevertheless, it must be noted that these women artistes were drawn from the educated classes. The majority of the Portuguese women stayed within their four walls of home and shop (home and shop were usually one compound). Laundry work and sewing were done in the home more often than outside of it in another's home. They spent their time caring for their families or working as domestics, seamstresses or laundresses. One could safely say that only the minority were educated in the colony. Later, the daughters of wealthy businessmen and professionals were sent to school in Portugal or England. Generally speaking, young women were expected to become housewives and mothers.

Portuguese Women in Sports

In the early years of Portuguese immigration the women were engaged mainly in supporting the men in making a livelihood in the provision and spirit shops; there was not much time for leisure pursuits. The men had moved earlier into the field of sport and by the turn of the century were distinguishing themselves in the major sports of cricket, football, boxing and, above all, cycling. The women appeared later on the scene. But even before the early twentieth century, when the women entered formally established sports, some Portuguese women, following the tradition of their Madeiran counterparts, joined their men in hunting and horseback riding in the rural areas. The founding of the Portuguese Club in 1924,[40] as well as that of the Ladies Hockey Club in 1927, gave the women an entrée into tennis and hockey. It was noted in the membership book of the Portuguese Club in 1925 that twenty-eight women joined the club as members or 'Lady Subscribers' to eighteen men, and their membership continued at a high percentage through the years. The Portuguese woman ventured onto the tennis court and hockey field with vigour and soon became proficient in those sports. Again, they were drawn from the upper middle class; some had been educated overseas

Out hunting – a favourite sport

and were already well versed in sport. By the 1930s, Portuguese women became leaders on the tennis courts; some excelled. The *Christmas Annual* of 1934 observed: "Of all the girls who have indulged in sport in this country it cannot be denied that Phil D'Aguiar is the best all-round sportswoman that British Guiana has known." She was classed as a brilliant hockey player, a hard-hitting tennis opponent, oarswoman and horseback rider, a walker and a cyclist, while her sister, Monica D'Aguiar, was ranked as the country's tennis champion.[41] By the turn of the century, a few women, chiefly from the upper middle class, had begun to assert themselves and no longer meekly accepted a home-bound existence. However, the majority of the middle class and lower class women were still very much *dona de casa*.

Conclusion

Although it has been shown that women were prominent in the cultural social life of the colony in music, drama, dance and sports, it must be emphasized that these women came from the upper echelons of society, the wives and daughters of prominent businessmen and professionals. The majority of women presided, seemingly quite contentedly, over 'hearth and home'. Few Portuguese women worked outside the ubiquitous Portuguese shop or outside the home where they raised their children, taught them by word and example the rudiments of their faith, and inculcated in the girls the characteristics of a good and patient housewife. There were, as among all peoples and classes, the exceptions. Although mothers guarded their girls with tenacious vigilance, this did not preclude the young woman from stepping 'out of bounds' and eloping with either a Portuguese or a black man. There were, of course, examples of intermarriage of Portuguese women with men of other ethnic groups, but this was more the exception than the rule.

Within the home, another occupation for which the Portuguese were well known was that of seamstress. The women produced exquisite pieces of Madeira embroidery for many a church bazaar and wedding and also taught the skill to others. Charitable works comprised much of their day to day life – feeding the poor and visiting the sick among the most popular. Many joined the Ladies of Charity, a Catholic group of women established in 1926 which devoted its time, energy and funds in assisting the aged, widows and mothers with young children from among the poorer classes. There were few Portuguese beggars seen around the streets.

No mention has been made of Portuguese women in political life because not until 1928 was a limited franchise granted to women, restricted to those who could "read and write some language" and in addition had some property and income qualifications. Thus, literacy and property requirements disenfranchised the majority of Guyanese women, not only the Portuguese. Women were not permitted to enter the Legislature until after World War II. It was only in the first decade of the twentieth century that Portuguese men, despite planter objection, distrust, and downright dislike, inched their way into the formal political arena. It would also have been a political phenomenon, apart from the naturalization obstacle,[42] for Portuguese women to have even evinced an interest in politics; theirs was a background role of supporting their husbands in their campaigns. Even when the first women's political organization was founded in 1946, no Portuguese ranked among the founding members.[43] Not until 1960 with the establishment of the United Force party did the first Portuguese woman, Eleanor D'Aguiar-Da Silva, enter politics.

In conclusion, it must be stated that this is a pioneering article on the role of the Portuguese woman in the Guyanese society. Much of the material rests on evidence given by Portuguese families who recalled the day to day life of their relatives – mothers, grandmothers, aunts, cousins and godmothers. For Portuguese life in the nineteenth century, the newspapers of the times provided a wealth of information, but only a glimpse of the women. This is indeed an under-investigated topic and much more research needs to be done in exploring the heights and the depths, the lights and the shadows that would bring into sharper focus the picture of the Portuguese woman throughout that hundred-year period, from 1830 to 1930. Yet, despite the paucity of material, it must be conceded that, though living during a period of colonial history when all women were relegated to the side lines, the Portuguese woman in Guyana did make a contribution to the society. She was seen and heard on stage, vibrantly present in and involved with her church, and an anchor in the home – a *dona de casa*.

8

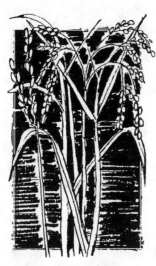

Rice, Culture and Government in Trinidad 1897–1939

Glenroy Taitt

Rice was a crop with unique cultural resonances among the East Indians of Trinidad. It possessed powerful religious and symbolic overtones, as several writers have indicated.[1] Morton Klass, who spent a year in the Indian village of Amity in central Trinidad in 1958, noted an extensive use of Hindi terms in discussions of rice and rice cultivation. Rice alone had several common names: *dhan,* unmilled rice; *caura,* milled rice; *bhuja caura,* rice that had been boiled before milling; *bhath,* rice cooked and ready to eat; and *mahaparsad,* rice cooked in great quantities for weddings. The only other aspects of Indian life where Hindi expressions were more common were ceremony, ritual and kinship. Klass also witnessed a regular thanksgiving ritual to the *Di* of the rice field. The *Di* was the spirit of the first owner of the property, even though no one knew who the original landowner was. After the rice had been cut, and before it was beaten, the male head of the family made an offering of cigarettes, biscuits and either *ghee* (butterfat) or rum in a corner of the rice field. Since the grower always performed this rite, in the case of rented land it was the tenant, rather than the owner, who made the offering. Everyone in Amity followed this practice.

Klass found that, in Amity, the peasants were not interested in making money from rice cultivation. From his calculations, a good acre of rice land would produce up to twenty barrels in a good year, each of three hundred pounds weight, with a barrel of unmilled rice then selling for between $8 to $10. But the East Indian peasants refused to plant more rice, passing up the extra income. They preferred to grow cane since, in their view, rice cultivation was more difficult. Cane was also easier to dispose of, being carried directly to the factories, which paid them cash in one or two lump sums, whereas they would have had to sell the extra rice either through individuals for small amounts of money, which would disappear rapidly, or through unknown dealers in Port of Spain who might cheat them. In the few cases where a family had enough rice land to contemplate feasibly a large crop, that well-off household still felt obliged to rent most of its land to its less fortunate neighbours. As a landowning family explained, "To deprive them of their riceland . . . would be a cruel and unneighbourly act."[2] Klass therefore concluded that: "While having a surplus to sell makes for a pleasant addition to the family income, the rice is raised primarily for subsistence, not for sale."[3] The Niehoffs, who conducted their research in the 1950s as well, observed that the East Indians were willing to continue planting rice, even when they knew it was uneconomic to do so.[4] Rice was also popular among the Indians because it gave them something to fall back on. Klass described the robust spirit of the Amity peasant:

He feels that a man without a piece of riceland has nothing to fall back upon, and must always be at someone else's mercy. The East Indian who can supply his family's rice needs has a basic sense of security and independence: let any employer mistreat him, he insists proudly, and 'I go live on salt and rice!'[5]

Given the significance of rice to Indians, it is noteworthy that it was blacks who introduced this crop to Trinidad. Former American slaves who were resettled in Trinidad from 1815, after fighting alongside the British in the War of 1812, brought with them the art which they had learned in the southern US. They grew dry rice on the hills. In the West Indies in the nineteenth century, dry rice cultivation, following the same methods as in West Africa, was everywhere associated with the black peasantry. Around the late 1860s, the appearance of irrigated rice fields in the Caroni Swamp and Oropouche Lagoon signalled the emergence of East Indian rice cultivators. These were former indentured immigrants living in the new villages who enthusiastically began raising wet rice.[6] In the 1880s, according to Louis de Verteuil, Trinidad's leading French Creole spokesman, Indian peasants could be seen broadcasting rice seeds in June and harvesting in September.[7] By the close of the century they were hand-transplanting from pre-flooded nurseries, and the rice season was extended from June to December, perhaps due to the introduction of different strains of rice.[8] By 1897, if not before, the Indians had taken over rice cultivation in Trinidad. G.T. Fenwick, a member of the Joint Committee of the Agricultural Society and the Chamber of Commerce, told the West India Royal Commission (WIRC) of 1897 that "Rice is grown to a certain extent in the lagoon land in the direction of Oropuche [sic] and in Chaguanas and two or three other places where they have low-lying and lagoon lands, and it is principally grown by free Indian immigrants."[9]

Rice in the 1890s

In 1897, Trinidad had approximately 6,000 acres under rice.[10] This figure would have included a small amount of dry rice since, from time to time, there was the odd, bland statement confirming that the two kinds grew in the island. For instance, the warden of Oropouche and La Brea, in his report for 1902–3, said that both wet and dry rice were grown in his ward (administrative district).[11] Similarly, four years later, the Revd K.J. Grant, a Presbyterian missionary, stated that the two varieties were to be found in Naparima.[12]

The quality of Trinidad's rice was apparently very high, although here and there it left much to be desired. Testifying at the London hearings of the WIRC, J.R. Greig, of Gregor Turnbull and Company, spoke of "a glutinous, beautiful rice".[13] At the Commission's sitting in Trinidad, J.H. Hart, the superintendent of the Botanical Gardens, said that this rice had won "premiums in preference to any rice imported, and it has been pronounced better than imported rice".[14] But five years later, the peasants of Oropouche were singled out for their poor quality rice, which was dismissed as inferior to the imported product. Because of the obsolete, post-harvest preparation, the warden suggested the introduction of a proper husking and hulling machine to replace "the crude and antiquated 'dekhi' ".[15] An article in the *Port-of-Spain Gazette* echoed his unfavourable opinion.[16]

One issue that would later be crucial to the peasants caught the attention of the warden of Naparima. In 1897, he wrote enthusiastically of the prospects for rice in his ward:

There is one industry, however, which might be developed to an unlimited extent, and that is rice cultivation. It is easily grown and easily reaped, and I see no reason why, if facilities were given to get at all the low and swampy lands and savannahs in the Island, in a short time the Island should not grow sufficient rice for its own consumption.

In the Oropouche Lagoon, for instance, there are hundreds of acres of magnificent land suitable for this cultivation, but they are never likely to be occupied, or made use of, unless they are drained and made accessible.[17]

Water management, a constant theme in his reports over the next seven years, would surface as the major handicap facing the peasants in Naparima, and indeed throughout Trinidad, during the twentieth century.

In the 1890s rice growing was extremely profitable. Hart told the WIRC of 1897: "I have heard coolies say that it is a highly remunerative crop."[18] It was a medium of exchange too, making it a rather versatile crop. As the warden of Oropouche and La Brea observed in 1901: "Rice in the form of 'paddy' is largely used by these East Indian settlers as an article of barter, and all through the year men and women may be seen travelling up and down the districts and settlements with their parcels and bags of 'paddy'."[19] The following year, he noted that it was used for bartering between the Indians of his ward and those of Naparima, with the surplus being sold in San Fernando.[20] Rice was also a useful, first crop, to judge by the Revd Grant's observation in Naparima:

No doubt the tendency is to grow cocoa, and they plant rice first because it can be gathered in four or five months. That gives them a good start, and sometimes they get enough to run the family on for two or three years. That is a great inducement to start with rice, and to end up by cocoa.[21]

Sugar in Rice Season

In 1906, J.J. Macleod, a sugar and cocoa planter, identified the peasants who grew rice as small cultivators renting rice lands from their fellow Indians.[22] The latter, he said, would buy between 10 and 20 acres of land, which they in turn rented out in small lots. It is not clear who organized the initial drainage. Macleod's statement is supported by the returns of rice grown in the island in 1904-5 (see Table 8.1). Most peasants grew rice on plots varying in size from under 1 acre to 5 acres. In Tacarigua, the leading ward in rice production both in terms of total acreage and total yield, out of a total of approximately 2,000 acres, only 94 acres were in lots of over 5 acres. The returns also show that the yields varied considerably, from 300 to almost 3,000 pounds per acre. There is no evidence to account for this variation. Curiously, St. Ann's

TABLE 8.1 SUMMARY OF RETURNS OF RICE, TRINIDAD, 1904–1905

Ward Union (WU) (i.e., several wards grouped together)	Acreage in Lots of -1 Acre	Acreage in Lots of 1–5 Acres	Acreage in Lots of Over 5 Acres	Total Acreage by Ward Unions	Total Yield by WUs in lb. Paddy (a)	Total Yield in lb. Cleaned Rice (b)	Yield per Acre*
Arima	3.5	53.5	36	93	94,860		1,020
Cedros	100	20	–	120	240,000		2,000
Chaguanas	–	321	771	1,092	1,638,000		1,500
Couva	–	–	–	–	–		–
Manzanilla	11	519	105	635	800,000		1,260
Mayaro	70	70	77	217	457,304		2,107
Montserrat	57	42	12	111	58,166		524
Naparima	–	–	–	–	187,040		–
Oropouche	5	583	49	637	1,490,580		2,340
La Brea & Guapo	1	45	11	57	133,029		2,334
Savannah Grande	1,200	350	100	1,650	495,000		300
St Ann's & D/M	12	70.5	–	82.5	231,000		2,800
Tacarigua	1,700.5	356.5	94.5	2,151.5	4,475,460		2,080
Toco	4	12	–	16	10,500		656
Tobago	0.5	–	–	0.5	437		872
Total	3,164.5	2,442.5	1,255.5	6,862.5	10,311,436	6,186,861	

Source: C.O. 298/79, Labour Question in Trinidad, Appendix F, p. 159. C.P. No. 13 of 1906.
(a) 100 lb. paddy = 60 lb. handcleaned rice; 140 lb. paddy = 1 barrel or bag of paddy.
(b) 160 lb. cleaned rice = 1 barrel or bag cleaned rice; total yield 73,653 bags paddy or 38,668 bags cleaned rice.

* Based on this author's calculations.

and Diego Martin, two wards far removed from the major rice growing areas, had the highest yield per acre. Macleod was a witness before a committee investigating an alleged labour problem in the early twentieth century. Sugar planters had complained that peasants were abandoning estate work in order to cultivate rice; this accusation led to two investigations in successive years. Interestingly, planters in British Guiana also regarded rice as "a competitor for labor",[23] and, in 1907, one sugar planter wrote that, "planters find themselves faced with a greatly reduced supply of labour".[24] As a result, they made a major adjustment to avoid this clash between the two crops. They rearranged their times of grinding.[25] In 1905, sugar planters in Trinidad established a committee to investigate this labour shortage.[26] Using the government estimate of 12,000 acres of rice lands in the colony, this committee estimated the annual crop to be worth at least $360,000 from which, it said, government revenues derived no benefit. The report also stated that the planting operation employed three people per acre. Taking Chaguanas as an example, the report claimed that 6,000 Indians were temporarily alienated from the neighbouring estates and surrounding districts. Moreover, the report added that rice growing was unhealthy as many rice growers suffered from fever and anaemia, and often had to leave work penniless to become a burden on their friends and eventually on the ward. The committee therefore recommended that rice pay its way:

The employer of indentured immigrants not unnaturally views with disfavour an industry which at a critical season of the year diminishes his labour supply. He contends that beyond the land tax of 1/- per acre, rice growing, which finds occupation for so many thousands of people, should contribute its share to the Immigration fund.[27]

The recommended share was a tax at the rate of six pence per bag of paddy.

In April 1905, the government set up its own independent committee to examine the planters' accusations and to consider whether rice, which paid no export tax, should contribute towards the cost of immigration. This committee reported in 1906. A witness, S. Henderson, a sugar planter, repeated the charge against rice:

In the district of Chaguanas, however, rice planting takes away more labour than anything else. It also affects Couva to a very great extent; where large droves of rice planters yearly go down to the savannah. At the beginning of the rice-planting season it is impossible to get any outside labour. It is a class of work they like, and very many of these rice cultivators give breakfast and day wages, and, in some cases, pay cash daily for the work at the end of each day. It is impossible also, in the district of Chaguanas, to get free labour from the time the rice is planted. This difficulty also becomes acute again when the rice is being reaped, which extends for about three weeks.[28]

This government committee admitted that there was some dislocation of the labour supply:

There is almost unanimous evidence that the shortage is very serious during the earlier months of the rainy season, when a great proportion of the labourers leave the estates to work on rice plots and vegetable gardens.[29]

Nevertheless, it also highlighted the benefits of rice: the crop helped the East Indians tide over slack periods when work was scarce, and attracted peasants to those districts. In the opinion of its members, rice was beneficial to the estate owners and should be encouraged by them. The chief cause of the existing labour shortage was, according to the committee, the rapid alienation and development of Crown lands, brought on by the expansion of cocoa. The government committee also rejected the planters' recommendation that rice be made to contribute to the Immigration Fund. In rejecting the proposed tax, this government committee displayed a rare sense of concern for the peasantry and the masses in general. It felt that the attendant administrative difficulties made a tax on rice inappropriate. But it also felt that such a tax would necessarily rebound on to the consumer.

As early as the 1870s, reports had indicated that the estates' labour supply dried up during the rice planting season.[30] Later, in 1909, an extract from the diary of the Canadian Missionary Revd John Morton made a similar assertion:

At the moment of writing the rice fields have swept away every spare labourer . . . sugar, cocoa and the gardens must wait when it is the hour for rice. Transplanting and reaping are the most urgent seasons, but much time is taken up in preparing the land and dealing with the harvest after it is cut, so that the rice fields draw away a large amount of labour from the staple productions.[31]

At a glance rice and sugar seemed to go hand in hand quite comfortably, sugar occupied the first half of the year, rice the second. In July–August, depending on the onset of the rains, the peasants prepared the fields, sowed the rice in the nurseries, and transplanted the seedlings, then enjoyed a slack period until the reaping and threshing of the rice in November–December. In Trinidad, there was only one rice crop a year (in Guyana there were two).

But during these months there was a limited, though still significant, amount of work to be done on the sugar estates: planting, weeding, draining and moulding the earth around the canes. While rice cultivation took place during the industry's off-season, it unfortunately coincided with some important work on the estates.

The uneasy relationship between planters and peasants simmered down over the next few years. There were no more complaints nor investigations, an indication, perhaps, that the planters grudgingly accepted that at certain times of the year their labourers would disappear to the rice fields.

A Quantitative Assessment

In 1907, rice acreage hovered around 10,000 acres, a sizeable increase over the 6,000 acres of 1897, and it reached approximately 12,000 acres by 1911.[32] On the other hand, production, somewhat erratic from year to year, fell by almost a half between 1907 and 1913.[33] Admittedly, these statistics do not reveal the full extent of rice cultivation in Trinidad, since the peasants were apparently withholding information for fear of taxation.[34] In addition, the sources do not indicate how much dry rice was grown in Trinidad, confirmation, perhaps, that the amount was insignificant. The declining yields, which no one either noticed or took seriously, hinted that all was not well with rice.

Trinidad was never self-sufficient in rice. In 1911–12, a typical year, the island imported 26,882,595 pounds of rice, three times more than the peasants had harvested.[35] Yet, though customs records showed rice to be relatively insignificant, it was still of considerable importance to the island's Indian peasantry. On the eve of World War I, the protector of immigrants wrote that rice was of particular benefit to the ex-indentured Indians since "it affords them on leaving the estate a means of livelihood".[36]

Rice in World War I

Information on rice during the war is very thin, as the available material covers mainly the last two years of the war. A few references to grants of rice lands to the peasants appear from 1917. The warden of Naparima, in his report for 1917, noted that a portion of the Oropouche lagoon had been thrown open for rice cultivation. In his opinion, this scheme, though somewhat late, was a success, as no less than 442 lots were taken from the 562 laid out.[37] The following year, the governor announced that the peasants would soon be able to rent further portions of the lagoon.[38] In 1918, too, the warden of Manzanilla said that the Nariva swamp on Trinidad's east coast, until then not recognized as a rice growing centre, had been surveyed in half-acre blocks, almost all of which had been taken.[39] Despite the government's offers of land in the Oropouche and Nariva lagoons, which the peasants apparently took up, the wardens' reports showed that, curiously, although Trinidad began the war with 12,328 acres under rice, it had only 6,921 by 1918, a loss of approximately 5,500 acres.[40] On the other hand rice production remained fairly stable throughout the war, increasing only marginally from 5,455,811 pounds to 5,584,800 pounds over the same period.[41]

It is difficult to understand how the peasants managed to retain their level of output while using some 5,500 acres less. If one is to judge by their hostility to the idea a few years later, they did not switch to two rice crops a year, an obvious way of maintaining their usual production while cutting back their land to almost one half. Perhaps they had begun using a new strain of rice, but the sources say nothing of this. Equally puzzling is the peasantry's willingness to take extra land from the government while simultaneously abandoning even more land, unless perhaps they were exchanging new and better lands for old, which may explain the spectacular increase in productivity.

Rice Lands and Irrigation

In these war years, the problems that confronted the peasants had little to do with the war itself. In January 1918, in response to a motion raised by the Naparima District Agricultural Society, the governor announced that rice lands would be rented on similar terms to those under which lands had been let for domestic food crops for the past two years, namely at two shillings per acre. The society had sought a reduction in the rent of these lands. The governor also pointed out that the period of rental of rice lands would be limited to two years or the duration of the war. The reason was that "these lands were held by the oil companies which had a right to exploit for oil, and the Government had not a free hand in the matter".[42] Pollution was another problem caused by the oil industry. An article in the *Trinidad Guardian* in September 1918 pointed out that overflowing crude oil was damaging agricultural lands in several areas. It cited as an example the rice lands of Débé and Penal, which were near to the Barrackpore oil fields.[43]

In the same month, the newspaper reported an altogether different problem. In an editorial entitled "Rice Lands and Irrigation", the paper stated that while Port of Spain and the villages nestling beneath the western end of the northern range had received a great deal of rainfall within the past month, the central portion of Trinidad had been experiencing a considerable drought. This scarcity of rainfall was causing anxiety in the rice growing districts of Oropouche, and more so in the Caroni area, which included Chaguanas and Bejucal. The paper said that although the government had thrown open Crown lands for rice cultivation: "The question of irrigation still remains untouched. Doubtless the cost of the scheme is the main consideration . . . it is abundantly clear that without a system of irrigation there can be no healthy expansion of the rice industry."[44]

The benefit of irrigation was emphasized, in the same year, by one Gransaull, in a talk to members of the Naparima District Agricultural Society. Pointing out that the average yield of an acre of rice land, according to a report by the warden of Tacarigua, was four bags, Gransaull said that an acre could in fact produce ninety-two bags, "a difference of 88 bags per acre or a dead loss through lack of proper cultivation".[45] The peasants were indeed losing out since yields per acre fell in most wards between 1904 and 1918.[46] Only Manzanilla and Naparima showed an increase in productivity. Most likely, this declining productivity was due to the lack of irrigation, which made rice cultivation unpredictable.

Irrigation, unlike oil pollution, was by no means a new problem. Obviously, wet rice cultivation needed water, but a good crop demanded rain in adequate amounts and at the proper time. Already at the turn of the century the warden of Naparima had written year after year of the advantages to be gained by draining the Oropouche lagoon, but his was a lonely voice. As the *Trinidad Guardian* editorial appreciated, a widespread programme of irrigation was costly. Rice cultivation was not an industry, and the humble peasants were clearly unable to afford such grand but necessary infrastructure. They could only have wished for an enlightened governor, like A.H. Gordon or William Robinson in the nineteenth century, who would be willing to irrigate the rice fields and damn the consequences. This persistent problem of water would wear away at the peasants' nerves until their desperate actions would force a quick, though temporary, response from the government.

Fighting for Survival

Rice enjoyed a belated, postwar stimulus thanks to a steep fall in imports in both 1918 and 1919. From 1914 to 1917, imports averaged 25,000,000 pounds annually; however, in 1918 and 1919 overseas supplies were only 18,399,723 and 16,504,182 pounds, respectively.[47] The curtailment of trade with India, brought on by the war, caused this reduction. Foreign supplies of rice only began returning to normal levels in 1921. Reversing the wartime decline in acreages, the peasants expanded rice cultivation from 6,921 acres in 1918 to 9,608 acres in 1920, then cut back to 7,650 acres by 1923, by which time imports were rising once more.[48] Rice production followed a similar pattern, growing from 5,584,800 pounds in 1918 to 6,839,365 pounds in 1920, and dropping to 5,604,055 pounds by 1923.[49] It is noticeable though that while acreage climbed speedily, output crawled upwards, again a symptom of the weakening productivity of the previous two decades. This intriguing inter-play between local rice production and rice imports shows that the peasants were obviously taking advantage of an unexpected opportunity.

In 1934, the *Trinidad Guardian* estimated how much money a peasant could make from rice. Taking Bejucal as an example, the paper said that each peasant normally rented either one or two *Jimmies* of rice land at an annual cost of $1.00 a *Jimmi*.[50] (Five *Jimmies* were equal to one acre, but a *Jimmi* was also known as a 'quarter-quarter', as four of them made up what the peasants referred to as a quarter of land.) From this parcel costing a dollar, a peasant could reap about five barrels of rice in a good year. In season, the price averaged $1.50 a barrel, although the out of season market price was sometimes as high as $3.00 a barrel. As the newspaper reckoned, the peasant made a gross return of $7.50 a year from a *Jimmi* of land rented for $1.00.

This calculation, done in quick, back-of-the-envelope fashion, ignored labour costs. Admittedly, those Bejucal peasants received assistance from their families, as the article indeed revealed: "Everywhere there are scenes of activity, as father, mother, brothers, and sisters all lend a hand at the hoeing and forking, or planting out of young rice."[51]

Yet most peasants drew their labour from a wider pool. For many years they had hired labourers, a practice which, in the early 1900s, had infuriated planters who lost out in the competition. Nearly three decades later, C.Y. Shephard also observed that the peasants took on extra hands, often attracting them by paying higher wages than the estates.[52] C.C. Parasinos, another researcher from the Imperial College of Tropical Agriculture, in his study conducted in the early 1940s of the Indian village with the Spanish name of Las Lomas, found that "Holdings that do not employ outside labour are few and far between."[53] He found that rice had the highest demand for hired labour, even more than sugar. He explained that most of the operations had to be performed in a very short space of time and, because few peasants had a team of oxen and a plough, ploughing had to be done by outside labour. These labourers assisted the family members. In Amity in the 1950s, peasants hired labourers as well, at $2.00 a day.[54] But it was the fortunate few, mainly those who owned their rice fields, who spent money on extra help. The less well-off peasants in Amity were unable to pay. Instead they did the ploughing for themselves, hard work if they did not own a bull, and for planting, these "poorer people, who rent their land, form a cooperative work group called a *hur*".[55]

Most peasants rented land for planting rice, just as we saw in the early 1900s. In Las Lomas, the largest portion of the rice lands belonged to a handful of peasants who rented it to others. In Amity, "most people rent riceland from the few farmers almost entirely of the high castes – who own relatively large holdings".[56] Since rice growing had remained almost identical over the years, the division of labour that Klass observed in Amity in the 1950s might well have been similar two decades earlier. Men prepared the nursery, a task which entailed hoeing and forking the land, and also performed the sowing. Yet the demarcation of responsibility here was not rigid, for women assisted in these tasks if the need arose. The back-breaking task of ploughing the main fields fell to the men. Planting, a much less arduous job, involved two operations: "Pulling the seedlings from the nursery, which is considered man's work, and planting them in the *kolas* [plots] where they will grow to maturity, which is considered women's work, for, 'Ladies go very fast'."[57] Cutting and beating the rice was normally a male responsibility, though women too sometimes cut. The latter also carried and piled the cut rice for the beaters.

Rice cultivation was carried out in extremely poor conditions. In 1929, Shephard noted that most peasants who worked in the rice fields suffered from malaria.[58] Three years later, Eric de Verteuil, the assistant medical inspector of health, condemned the notorious conditions under which the peasants grew rice in "our unhealthy rice fields which now come from dead rivers – caused by persistent blocking over a large number of years".[59] There was, he said, strong evidence that rice cultivation in the colony was dangerous, as the rice fields were breeding grounds for the anopheles mosquito. De Verteuil therefore recommended that rice growing be restricted to those places where water was abundant, and the adoption of irrigation methods which ensured regular flooding and flushing of the fields.

The peasants themselves were well aware of the need for irrigation, which apart from solving the health problem would also put rice cultivation on a more secure footing. In 1934, they raised the issue at a meeting of the Débé East Indian Association, at which Wortley, the director of agriculture, was in attendance. Gunness, a member of the association, read a petition calling for the installation of two sluice gates to control flooding in the Débé lagoon areas, and making out a good case for government assistance:

Some are doubtful of its success. We can assure you that it will prove a success of which you will be proud. But suppose for the sake of argument, we admit that such a thing could happen, the Government will lose little because we are asking that it should be done piecemeal.

Furthermore, the Government has helped our brethren in the sugar, cocoa and oil industries. In some instances they have failed and experienced the loss of thousands of pounds. Do we, not deserve even a few hundred dollars?

... We predict that the Government will be compelled to attend to these lands at some time as a means out of depression, and perhaps, at a time, when it can ill afford to stand the expense. Why not begin now?

Take up the cheap sluice-gate scheme in small portions annually, so that when the necessity arises, Trinidad will find itself in readiness to meet it.[60]

In response, Wortley explained that a large-scale irrigation project would be difficult and costly because of the nature of the lagoon. To this the peasants countered that they were not asking for a dam, but merely sluice-gates. Interestingly, they also said that they had no desire for two rice crops a year, preferring to keep their dry season crop of vegetables. This might have signalled a desire on their part to spread risks. The following September, Gunness complained that the government still had not done anything to provide irrigation for the Débé-Penal district.[61]

Water, though this time the lack of it, was also a problem facing peasants in north Trinidad. Prolonged drought, which in 1934 led to a drastic curtailment of work on sugar estates in St George and Caroni at the end of the harvest, also seriously affected rice growers. With ponds and wells having dried up, they were said to be experiencing their greatest hardship in years, with some peasants abandoning hope of preparing their nurseries.[62] After the 1934 hunger march and disturbances, the government at last initiated several irrigation schemes. Early September saw the start of a temporary irrigation scheme in Bejucal, which was bounded on the west by the Caroni swamp and on the east by Caroni Sugar Estate. The sponsors of the scheme were the government and Caroni Sugar Estates (Trinidad) Ltd.[63] This was an altruistic gesture on the part of Caroni Ltd, which did not own any of the lands being irrigated. The land belonged to peasants and other small proprietors in the district, neither of whom had to bear any of the costs of the irrigation scheme. An irrigation scheme was also put in place in Cunupia and at Streatham Lodge. At Streatham Lodge, rice cultivation had been extremely uncertain as peasants had relied solely on the overflowing of the Caroni and Tacarigua rivers. Much of the land which had been flooded had, in fact, been idle for years because of the precarious water situation.[64] Through these schemes in Bejucal, Streatham Lodge, and some other districts of central Trinidad, some 2,000 extra acres of rice lands were planted in 1934.[65] A *Trinidad Guardian* editorial, appropriately entitled "The Water Way to Prosperity", bluntly assessed the situation: "The need for irrigation has been felt by a few people in the past, but it has taken this year's severe and prolonged drought to drive home its benefits to a wider circle."[66]

These impressive results led the government, in true bureaucratic fashion, to establish an Irrigation Committee, to assess the possibility of installing permanent irrigation schemes in various parts of the country. The fruit of this deliberation was a permanent scheme, in 1937, for the irrigation of 300 acres in the ward of Caroni, with the possibility of extending it over a wider area in the event of an emergency.[67] By the decade's end the authorities had, characteristically, done nothing further.

Two reports at the end of the decade indicated that rice was in a poor condition. The Presbyterian Church told the Moyne Commission of 1938–39 that, because of the lack of irrigation systems in the swamps to compensate for irregular rainfall and oil pollution in some districts, the peasants could no longer count on a satisfactory rice crop.[68] The East Indian Advisory Board cited the same factors, along with attacks by blight. Urging the government to provide a liberal system of irrigation in the rice areas and to reclaim swamp lands for rice cultivation, the board's statement ended on a depressing note: "Thus rice, which is the main article in the dietary of our East Indian people, ceased to yield of late years a dependable annual crop."[69]

It may well be that declining productivity, hidden in the statistics from 1904 to 1918, was now becoming visible. Yet the pessimistic statements by the representatives of Trinidad's Indian community are at odds with the statistics on acreage and yield for the 1930s. In 1923, there were 7,650 acres under rice, and this figure increased to 9,300 acres in 1929 and 10,000 acres by the late 1930s.[70] By 1938, the output had risen to 13,440,000 pounds, an increase of more than 100 percent since 1923.[71] Such an enormous growth is inconsistent with the sad tales about the crop. Clearly there is an unexplained discrepancy in the statistics presented to the Moyne Commission.

Conclusion

These depressing remarks about rice in the 1930s are in sharp contrast to the enthusiastic statements made in the 1890s. One would hardly have expected Trinidad's rice to win any prize for quality in the thirties. There is no doubt that the poor state of this crop was due to government indifference. At the turn of the century, the warden of Naparima called, year after year, for irrigation to improve rice production. In World War I, the economic benefits of irrigation were also demonstrated. In the 1930s, the peasants themselves were clamouring for irrigation, with only limited success. The question of irrigation was all the more important because the peasants' health depended on it. Throughout the decades, people had spoken just as consistently of how prone the peasants were to catching diseases in the rice fields.

Irrigation would have taken the capriciousness out of rice cultivation, and the purifying waters would also have cleansed the rice fields of their diseases. But the government remained aloof until the labour unrest of 1934 dramatized the peasants' distress. Then relief came to the rice growing communities, but only in a piecemeal and temporary fashion.

The government's disregard for rice production is in sharp contrast to its support for sugar and cocoa. While it withheld assistance from the humble peasants who grew rice, it generously spent money propping up French Creole planters who faced bankruptcy when cocoa prices plunged in the 1920s. The Mortgages Extension Ordinance and the Agricultural Relief Ordinance of 1921, the Agricultural Bank Ordinance of 1924, the Cocoa Relief Ordinance of 1930 and the Cocoa Subsidy Scheme of 1936 demonstrate clearly the colonial government's commitment to this export staple. Only in the dark days of World War II would the government, for the first time in Trinidad's history, give priority to food production at the expense of export agriculture.

9

The War in Ethiopia and Trinidad 1935–1936

Kevin A. Yelvington

The title of this essay is intentionally ambiguous. Italian and Italian-led military forces invaded Ethiopia in October 1935. Thus there was no military action per se in Trinidad. In a sense, the title should be "The War in Ethiopia, and Trinidad, 1935–1936". But the placement of the comma after 'Ethiopia' would belie the fact that there was a 'war' of sorts in Trinidad beginning in 1935, that black Trinidadians saw themselves caught up in the military, economic, moral, and cultural conflict that occupied the world's stage almost until World War II, and that Trinidadians cultivated the symbols associated with a war on the other side of the world in order to address burning issues of local importance.

For the most part, the few, brief treatments of the Trinidadian reaction to the war conceive of it as a sort of prelude to the labour agitation and riots of the mid 1930s, themselves culminating in the violent strikes and repression of 1937. In discussions of the role of ethnicity in the labour movement, the war is often conceived of as having 'awakened' or 'stirred' black consciousness, as if 'blackness' was some essential and fixed entity, ready to be awakened and stirred. Instead, the local experience of, and reaction to, the war in Ethiopia (re)created, helped define, and transform who was 'black', never an unproblematic definition anywhere in the African diaspora; it determined what symbols correctly represented such varied experiences and identities and tended to conflate them, putting forth claims about what it meant to be black *in that particular time*, in particular social, cultural, economic and historical conditions. Blackness in Trinidad, and elsewhere, is not nor was not an essential, fixed entity, but a culturally constructed identity – and therefore amenable to change.

Similarly, with reference to the labour strikes and riots of the period, it is often assumed that this 'race consciousness', as it is sometimes termed, so awakened and stirred by the events in Ethiopia, guided the working class as it negotiated its way through the extreme poverty, slum living, hunger marches, riots, strikes and imprisonment that were characteristic of the epoch, and not the reverse: that is, it is argued or assumed, that ethnicity is, again, an unchanging entity that could affect, but could not be affected by, the material and cultural conditions of social-economic class position.

This case study demonstrates how ethnicity and class are mutually constituted. Here, I mean 'ethnicity' as an ideology, a people's conception of 'peoplehood' based on a sense of their putative links to some ancestral group or community. Ethnicity at the same time entails a theory of origins. Sometimes these links are constructed by the people in question as 'racial', that is, an essentialized, fixed identity, a framework for dividing the world's population into a small number of discrete, ranked categories based on physiognomic, bodily, moral and intellectual attributes assumed to be inherited and inheritable;[1] sometimes they are reckoned as 'cultural', defined loosely as a characteristic pattern of behaviour and thought; and sometimes they are deemed to be other-worldly, sacred, or spiritual. At the same time, ethnicity is characterized by a theory of cause–effect relationships between these phenomena, their relative 'fixedness', on the one hand, and 'transformability', on the other. Their specific combination varies from case to case, with emphasis on 'race', 'culture', or some sacred point of origin being stronger here or there. This is an empirical historical and cultural question rather than some either-or, universal a priori proposition. The kind of behaviour and consciousness explored below show how ethnicity is a culturally constructed phenomenon precisely when people act as though it is not constructed at all.

Ethnicity is constructed in a whole class experience – with its material, emotional, and cultural components and consequences. Indeed, in the context of 1930s Trinidad, one cannot conceive of ethnicity as unrelated to class because ethnic identity, among other factors, facilitated class position and identity. Attached to this material base, ethnicity becomes an ideological field proper. In a dialectical process, class constitutes and constructs ethnicity, giving it form and function while, in another historical moment (and thus existing as a dialectical process), ethnicity helps to determine class position, class consciousness and class ideology. Class, then, becomes something more than mere economic relations and a cultural understanding or mediation of those relations, but the experience *in toto* of multiple determinations occurring at many levels of social reality. Ethnicity, then, becomes something more than a metaphor for material situations and relations of dominance and subordination, but a culturally constructed awareness of a connection to mythical or mythologized ancestors and to a similarly construed past.

Advancing these points, this chapter builds on recent historical research that focuses on 1930s Trinidad and attempts an explanation of the war's effects on local culture, social structure, economic relations, and politics. As Rhoda Reddock writes, "The importance of the Abyssinian War agitation to the political consciousness of colonial Trinidad and Tobago is yet to be adequately analysed."[2] The one exception is the late Brian L. Friday's little-known, unpublished, 1986 master's thesis.[3] Here, I attempt to build on Friday's work and the work of others who have written on the social conflicts of the 1930s[4] in order to place the Trinidadian reaction to the war in the historiography of the wider Caribbean.

Ethnicity, Class and Colonialism in 1930s Trinidad

Ethnic and class conflicts and challenges to the colonial cultural and governing apparatus became overt during the 1930s. The period saw the consolidation of protest movements with the establishment of a number of organizations whose general goals were self-government and social justice. These organizations included those whose avowed aims were to advance the interests of subjugated ethnic groups, to advocate for the rights of workers, and those that called for the end of colonial rule. In practice, each of these organizations, many of them with international links, had manifold goals and represented several interest groups at once. These organizations' stated constituencies and objectives often overlapped while, at other times, these organizations were in competition with each other while ostensibly promoting similar causes.

In the midst of the worldwide economic depression, grinding rural and urban poverty were evidenced in the living conditions of black and East Indian workers. In the context of a colonial ethnic division of labour, the descendants of chattel slaves and indentured workers comprised Trinidad's proletariat, although, for the most part, the working class was segmented along ethnic, geographic and occupational lines. Blacks tended to be urban labourers, many of them in skilled occupations, and skilled workers in the oilfields tended to be blacks. Most East Indians were either sugar estate labourers or cane farmers supplying cane to the estates. The black middle class, which included a number of professionals, was well established even if small, and an East Indian middle class had just emerged.

If colonialism was, above all, a cultural system, then it is not surprising that the notion of 'race' was invented and used as a tool in the repertoire of domination. In the Trinidadian culture of ethnicity, individuals and groups were racialized, and the idiom of 'race' – "variously represented in terms of ancestral lands, colour, and phylogeny"[5] – permeated social discourse and activity. 'Races' were presumed to have existed as 'pure', fixed, inherited and inheritable biogenetic entities prior to the arrival of specific 'races' in the New World, and certain cultural dispositions and supposed innate 'racial' characteristics were attributed to each 'race', including 'mixed' ones, in the island. This discourse tended to justify the system of ethnic stratification, at least partially. In colonial discourse, European 'races' and culture were seen as superior. East Indians were seen to possess an ancient culture, albeit an inferior one to the Europeans. Those deemed of African descent, on the other hand, were seen as possessing no ancestral culture, a void to be filled with European teachings. While perhaps 'scientific racism' was generally in retreat between the world wars in the Anglo-American scientific community, it surfaced in Trinidad from time to time, showing both colonial dependence on metropolitan ideas and *colonialism's* dependence on certain ideas – 'race' being one of them. A debate on 'race' raged in the pages of the *Beacon*, an anti-establishment journal, critical of the Catholic church and capitalism alike, started in 1931 by the Portuguese Creole Albert Gomes. It also became a forum for frank discussions of ethnicity, a place where black and Indian identity was debated and defined. Blacks were exhorted to take pride in 'the race' and in African ancestry and to shrug off feelings of inferiority and helplessness originating in slavery and racism. In an article entitled "Black Man", Gomes himself urged blacks to "Bare your fangs as the white man does. Cast off your docility. You have to be savage like a white man to escape the white man's savagery. *But the white man won't spare your neck!*"[6] One poem entitled "An African's Exhortation to His Country" by Percival C. Maynard urged

> Raise thy head, O my land, raise it
>   proudly!
> Shake off thy sadness, look up, smile apace!
> Care not that others decry thee quite loudly,
> Wronging thy children, despising thy race.[7]

And while championing "the negro mother" who "is admittedly one of the finest mothers in the world", Ernest A. Carr criticized black mothers for instilling "a sense of inferiority" in their children and for perpetuating a positive aesthetic evaluation of whiteness. He blamed the legacy of slavery, women's lack of educational opportunities, and questioned whether it was due to "the instinctive religious nature of the negro mother", which "has undoubtedly always had a firm hold on the vivid and undisciplined imagination of the negro mother . . . A white god surrounded by his all-white host of angels with long, golden hair and shining robes of white . . ." Whatever the cause of this self-contempt, he wrote,

she continues to implant an archaic ideal of another race into her children's consciousness, and thus handicaps them to an extent she little dreams. Her children, meeting a ruthless hostility without and an unwitting treachery within, are foredoomed to be crushed by the weight of realities.[8]

The *Beacon's* pages were the site of a revealing controversy on 'race'. Dr Sidney C. Harland, an English scientist stationed at the Imperial College of Tropical Agriculture, wrote a (by definition) contradictory article on 'race', beginning by arguing that humans are "sub-divided into a number of different races" characterized by "a large number of physical differences" where "most of these differences are due to differences in hereditary make-up": "The white Barbadian has lived in Barbados for three hundred years and his children are white, and if the negro lived in an equivalent time in the temperate zone, he would still be black. We can broadly say then, that the bodily differences that we see between the white, brown, black and yellow races are due to differences in heredity endowment."

These physical differences, he claimed, were apparent: "When, however, we come to mental and moral differences we have less to go upon," but "as they are of very great sociological importance, it is necessary to discuss what is known about them in some detail." What was "known", of course, turns out to be based on the kind of studies that were fairly commonplace in Europe and the United States in the period from the end of the nineteenth century until the 1930s – the period that saw the rise of the eugenics movement – that purported to gauge 'race' and intelligence: "Our conclusion is, therefore, that while it is not apparent to what extent the negro is inferior in intelligence to the white man, there is little doubt that on the average he is inferior. Professor Thorndike, the eminent Psychologist, puts the difference at from five to ten percent." Contradicting these ideas were statements such as "there is no pure race in the world" and the claim that "all races show a vast mental and physical diversity". Citing his own experience of teaching blacks in schools, Harland supported Francis Galton's idea of "hereditary genius" on the one hand. But on the other, he admitted that culture played a role (and thus he undermined his own position on 'race'):

Emotional and temperamental differences are more largely the result of race tradition and custom than is usually imagined. It is surprising, even in the West Indies, how the negro takes on the emotional background of the island he lives in. The Barbadian negro is quite different from the Trinidad negro; and both are widely different from the coloured race in Martinique, who in their psychological attitude towards life are virtually French.

He concluded by pointing to the future of 'race mixing', saying (hoping?) that blacks would disappear: "Certainly the destiny of the West Indies lies with a hybrid population, which will, in a few generations be a complex mixture of Negro, white, East Indian and Chinese. It is probable that the distaste for marriage and parental responsibility which exists among many of the negroes will result in their virtual submergence in the other races."[9]

C.L.R. James' reply in the pages of the *Beacon* was quick. It took issue with every piece of 'evidence' Harland offered, chiding Harland for holding antiquated views, pointing to his focus on 'the negro', and expressing in a characteristic way a passionate and reasoned disapprobation of inequality:

The Doctor put forward his antiquated opinions with a confidence and self-sufficiency which betoken his total, his teetotal abstention from recent views on the subject . . . Surely quite casual observation would be enough to tell him that in no field of human enterprise where the competition is open can the negro's intelligence be considered inferior. In the open professions, law and medicine, in the sphere of higher education, in the Civil Service, in politics, in journalism, the negro's record, especially when one considers his immense initial disadvantages, shows intelligence second to that of no other race . . . I do not make excessive claims for West Indian negroes. I know only too well the shortcomings of my own people. But in one thing they are not inferior. And that thing is intelligence. Let Dr. Harland leave his books for a while and take notice. Wherever the negro is given a chance, he establishes himself. And this from a people barely three generations away from the physical and moral degradation of slavery.[10]

This exchange prompted several opinions on the subject. In his letter to the editor, the writer Alfred H. Mendes denied biological blacks' inferiority, but questioned "What contribution towards Art and Science has the negro race made? None that I can think of for the moment . . . In short, Africa has no indigenous culture to show the world, and if culture is not the only standard for judgment among races, I know of not of any other." While maintaining he was talking about innate biological stratification, Harland seconded this notion.[11] Harland's views were also supported by Dr W.V. Tothill, a former British Army physician who had served in East Africa and was attached to the British West India Regiment during World War I and who was at the time of the controversy living in Trinidad. Tothill often contributed works of fiction and poems to the *Beacon*. In his contribution to the controversy, Tothill reproduced measures of cranial capacity and brain weight from the *British Medical Journal* that purported to show black inferiority in mental capacity.[12]

The debate urged Ralph Mentor to contribute three articles pointing to African scientific and cultural achievements from antiquity up to the present. Citing the likes of W.E.B. DuBois, Leo Frobenius, and the *Journal of the Royal Anthropological Institute*, he argued that it was the Egyptians, "a branch of the black race",[13] who brought civilization to the Greeks, deemed to be the source of European civilization. He then endeavoured to "establish above every possibility of doubt" that Egyptian civilization, in turn, "had originally come from Ethiopia".[14] The lesson was that

To-day prosperity and pride have conspired to make the sons of Europe forget that they were rescued from barbarism by a Negro colony of civilized men. And in their forgetfulness they ungratefully ask what has Africa contributed to the world's progress. Coming from a Doctor of Science this question is surprising. It is not evidence of profound scholarship or even of a mind well informed outside of his immediate calling, that Dr. Harland should ask this question, and speak of European culture as something which had spontaneously sprung up out of the superior intelligence of the white race. Any well informed scholar should know that European culture is not an indigenous but an exotic plant which came from Africa where it has its spontaneous genesis.[15]

The debate in the *Beacon* indicates the extent to which nineteenth century ideas of 'race' permeated the learned establishment. However, by the 1930s, Caribbean blacks, especially the educated middle class, were ready to engage their detractors with ideologies of their own that tended to assume that 'race' existed and was significant but that blacks were in no way inferior, only the victims of a brutal European colonialism. Furthermore, that what this middle class apparently regarded of value in what they saw as European civilization was even the result of it being ultimately built upon sub-Saharan, black cultures. And they were willing to upbraid their fellow blacks for indulging in self-hate.

The War in Trinidad

In this context it is hard to underestimate the effects of the 1935 Italian invasion of Ethiopia on the ethnic consciousness of black Trinidadians. Many immediately interpreted their situation with reference to the situation of Ethiopia. But besides the immediate social and economic context of the 1930s, the effects of the Italo-Ethiopian war on Trinidad also must be seen in light of a African diaspora-wide religious and political phenomenon known as 'Ethiopianism', a social and religious movement that sought to identify personages and events in the Christian Bible as 'African'. References to 'Ethiopia' in the Bible were interpreted by New World blacks as referring to the continent of Africa as a whole. Ethiopianism in some times and places also entailed an expectation of an actual migration to the continent, conceived of as a 'repatriation' or a 'return'.[16] In many ways Christianity played an important part in forging a common sense of 'Africanness' and 'blackness' out of the ethnic and linguistic differences between slaves and ex-slaves. African-derived cultural practices, especially originating in West Africa, have been documented for Trinidad.[17] Ethiopianism was part of a process of what I call a 'self-referential Africanism', a discourse that constructed, defined, and validated what are taken to be Africanistic cultural practices and continuities. This is a discourse that labels them of African origin, and accounts for an awareness, a belief, and a sense of them being present and worthy of recognition.

In the twentieth century, Caribbean blacks cultivated the symbol of Ethiopia for political projects and for religious expression. Given anticolonial sentiment and activities, Ethiopia was important as it was essentially the only independent African nation. And the 1930 coronation of Ras Tafari Makonnen, who became known as Haile Selassie I, was followed with much interest in the Caribbean and was seen by many as proof of the veracity of biblical prophesy. Selassie – the "King of Kings, Lord of Lords, Conquering Lion of the Tribe of Judah" – traced his own lineage to the David, Solomon, and Queen Sheba of the Bible. The coronation, seen against the backdrop of Ethiopianism, led to the creation of the Rastafarian religion in Jamaica.

Ethiopia was also a prominent theme in the movement led by Marcus Garvey. One catechism used by the Universal Negro Improvement Association (UNIA) drew upon the best known of the biblical passages that proved Ethiopia's sacred place and Selassie's divinity:

Q: What prediction made in the 68th Psalm and the 31st verse is now being fulfilled?
A: 'Princes shall come out of Egypt, Ethiopia shall soon stretch out her hands unto God.'

Q: What does this verse prove?
A: That Black Men will set up their own government in Africa, with rulers of their own race.[18]

Garvey himself wrote that

We, as Negroes, have found a new ideal. Whilst our God has no color, yet it is human to see everything through one's spectacles, and since the white people see their God through white spectacles, we have only now started out (late though it be) to see our God through our own spectacles. The God of Issac and the God of Jacob let Him exist for the race that believes in the God of Issac and the God of Jacob. We Negroes believe in the God of Ethiopia, the everlasting God – God the Father, God the Son and God the Holy Ghost, the One God of all ages. That is the God in whom we believe, but we shall worship Him through the spectacles of Ethiopia.[19]

And there was the UNIA's Universal Ethiopian Anthem, adopted by the UNIA at the 1920 First International Convention of the Negro Peoples of the World in New York, which began "Ethiopia, thou land of our fathers, Thou land where the gods loved to be".[20]

Blacks in Trinidad and elsewhere sought to equate 'Ethiopian' with 'African' or 'black' as the latter identities were understood as 'racial' in the New World. These images were furthered in Trinidad by organizations like the UNIA,[21] the Negro Welfare Cultural and Social Association (NWCSA), a Marxist-oriented working class advocacy group, and by the working class newspapers. In the middle of the struggle to define class and ethnic consciousness during the 1930s were the 'little newspapers' which became the mouthpieces of an increasingly radical, urban black and 'brown' (mixed race) lower middle class. The successor to the *Labour Leader*, the organ of the Trinidad Labour Party (TLP), itself the successor of the Trinidad Workingmen's Association (TWA), was the *People*, edited and published by Leonard Fitzgerald Walcott, a former New York Garveyite who had returned to Trinidad in 1933 and who patterned his paper after Garvey's *Negro World*, often reprinting stories from his publications. It reprinted stories on blacks in the US, such as reports of speeches made by officials of the National Association for the Advancement of Colored People (NAACP), of lynchings in the US South, of rough justice for blacks in US courts of law. There was the occasional story of West Indian immigrants in Liberia. The *People* regularly printed letters to the editor which urged positive ethnic consciousness among blacks. These views influenced the founders of the West Indian Youth Welfare League (WIYWL), established in May 1935 by a group of mainly black tradesmen and petty merchants, many of whom were Garveyites. Claiming it was non-political, the WIYWL aimed to foster a self-help movement among poor urban blacks; in practice it sought to promote black consciousness and unity. It became known as the "Back to the Land Movement" because it advocated the development of a strong black economic base through agriculture.[22] These were schemes, said the league, which boasted 600 members, "for demonstrating the practical benefits of Industry and Commerce to our people".[23]

The *People* and other Trinidadian publications, including the establishment newspapers the *Trinidad Guardian* and the *Port-of-Spain Gazette*, prominently reported the buildup to the war, beginning with Italian aggression and incursions into Ethiopian territory in late 1934. As war became imminent in mid–1935, the headlines of the little newspapers in Trinidad, as elsewhere in the Caribbean, screamed such phrases as "Members of the Black Race Show Your Sympathy with Abyssinia", referring to Ethiopia's ancient name, "A Section of the White World Gone Mad", and "Race Consciousness is not Race Hatred: Ethiopians Our Kith and Kin". As the Italian forces massed for invasion, and the refusal of the European powers to intervene on Ethiopia's behalf was exposed during 1935, it seemed that there was no other news for these publications. Prayers for Ethiopia were published. Several Trinidadians were moved to write poetry on Ethiopian themes. Some extolled Ethiopia's virtues in lyrical tones, such as one entitled "Ethiopia Around thy Free Banner" by Hilton A. Phillips:

> Oh land that saw the Pharoahs
> pass,
> That saw Carthage fall and decay,
> Whose heroes were of bravest
> caste,
> Down thru the years from bygone
> day.
> Oh land that braved the fierce
> crusades
> Of hostile principalities, powers
> We pray that thy millions shall
> ne'er
> Beneath the yoke of conquerors
> cower.
> Ethiopia – oh that thy free
> banner –

Green, yellow, red – long may it
　　shine,
From Ogaden to Gall to
　　Amharra –
Triumphantly – for Africa's free
　　sun is thine.[24]

Others were more combative and inspired action, such as "Africa Speaks"
by Carlton Eastwick:

To arms ye Africa's
　　stalwart sons,
And march to face the
　　foe.
Heed not the belching,
　　fiery guns
Nor the cries of pain and
　　woe,
March! March with firm
　　and steady tread
Towards the battle
　　heights,
Fear not the living or
　　the dead,
When fighting for your
　　rights.
March to the battle
　　heights!
Fight like negro knights
Think of your children's
　　right
And fight! fight! fight![25]

There were letters to the editor signed by "A Full-Blooded Ethiopian" or
"Son of Ham" or "Yours in Racial Uplift". One letter-writer, Louis R. Sherry,
referred to himself as the president of "The National Association of the
African Progeny". Several articles and editorials spoke directly to the ethnic
question raised by the war, some discussing the possibility of a worldwide
'race war'. A regular column was entitled "The Ethiopian Bugle".

In an August 1935 article "Race Consciousness of the 'Negro' " by
"Narcissus", the author wrote:

During the last two months, Trinidad has been most deeply stired [*sic*]. At street corners, and in the public squares, men – and women, too – are to be seen in excited groups, at all hours of the day, discussing the possible developments of the Italo-Abyssinian question.

At night, local preachers take the Abyssinian question in place of their biblical texts, and offer prayers for Abyssinia; every one with whom you come in contact seems to be able to deal with the history and past greatness of Abyssinia with wonderful facility. Last Saturday, every copy of 'The People,' the paper which treats most fully of the Abyssinian question, was sold out three hours after leaving the press.

This apparent confusion is a happy augury; all of the people who are so deeply stirred are Negroes, and their actions, their anxiety for the safety of members of their own race, point to one momentous fact – the Negro has become conscious of his worth; no longer will he readily submit to oppression and semi-slavery. The humble worm, down trodden for so long, has at last turned and risen against his cruel masters, and will demand its rights.[26]

The Italian-Ethiopian question was the subject of sermons by ministers and church leaders.[27] While many members of the cloth preached that love would conquer the hate evidenced in the incident, more secular opinion leaders advocated a moral and political stance. In an article entitled "West Indian Blacks Rally to the Fatherland!", Philip Lewis, who had a regular column in the *People*, asked rhetorically:

. . . What do the Negroes of the West Indies think of the pending oppression of their brothers and sisters in the Fatherland? Is it that all the children of Africa now residents of the West Indian islands will sit with their arms folded – in other words, stand pat – and allow the brutal people of Rome to dominate their Fatherland? Is it impossible, because of the mixture of colour of skin, for all West Indians to rally to the defense of the Fatherland, the kingdom of Ethiopia? Is'nt [*sic*] it true that all West Indians bear within their nature the true characteristics of the black man and the impetus which impels them to fight for self-possession? Did not West Indians lay their body and blood on the battle fields of Europe to safeguard the imperial powers? What compensation have they got?[28]

Later, in his regular "Through the Looking Glass" column, Lewis complained that the "Hybrid African" was a hinderance to black unity, that "he says he is a Trinidadian, not an Ethiopian and therefore, he has nothing to do with Ethiopia . . . What a pity!", and that this was ironic because "the hybrid Afro West Indian with the yellow skin feels he is aloft of his black African brethren, yet he lacks the quality and standard to cope with his brother on the other side of the line, therefore, he has to play the part of the hypocrite as he goes along".[29] In these articles, Lewis was chiding those West Indians who sought to emphasize their European heritage – including those who came to be socially regarded as whites but who were not really according to Lewis, and he argued that 'real' West Indians were of African heritage (or of predominantly African heritage) and that they could now take pride in that identity. As Godfrey A. Philip, the WIYWL's general secretary and field organizer, wrote in an article:

At last the people of this colony have awakened to the realisation that the term Afro West Indian must be used in describing the racial status of our coloured natives instead of the term West Indian under which many prominent persons take refuge for the pursuit of their aims.

. . . I trust the issue is decided once and for all, that we are Afro West Indians, if the blood that courses in our veins can trace its origin to the home of our fore fathers – Africa.[30]

From the start, the Trinidadian discourse on the war and the ideological fields represented by it was heterodox. However, one area of confluence was the idea that the war could and should be explained at least partially in 'racial' terms. Even the anti-imperialist deputy mayor of Port of Spain, Tito Achong, a Chinese Creole, emphasized this aspect of the war:

In a recent contribution to a local newspaper, a resident European came out flat-footedly for the conquest of Ethiopia by Italy on grounds of the old European concept of morality that the Negro (or, in fact, any non-European race) has no rights which the white man must feel bound to respect. Let Signor Mussolini and his allies cloak their thought in whatever excuses or theories appropriate to themselves, the issue remains, to disinterested men, fundamentally a racial dispute.[31]

Local newspapers ran wire stories on Ethiopia from international news agencies, reprinted pieces from North American and European newspapers, and republished articles dealing with Ethiopia's history and culture. When the film *Wings Over Ethiopia* came to Trinidad, it opened in three cinemas. And Trinidadians read of the opinions and activities in support of Ethiopia by blacks elsewhere in the Caribbean.[32] Trinidadians also read of white reactions to such efforts and attempts, using the idiom of 'race' to undermine such solidarity by emphasizing that Ethiopians were not only not 'racially' related to New World blacks, but, they argued, the Ethiopians in fact disdained them.[33] Like blacks everywhere in the New World, Trinidadians followed with fervent interest their American boxing idol, Joe Louis, who knocked out the Italian former heavyweight champion Primo Carnera in June 1935. Afterwards, black youths reportedly ran through Harlem shouting "Let's get Mussolini next."[34]

The individuals and groups in Trinidad that took the overt 'racial' angle were associated with the *People*. In July 1935, the Afro-West Indian League (AWIL) was established by Hugo Mentor, the brother of Ralph Mentor. Hugo Mentor had previously worked as an assistant editor on the *People*. The AWIL, which included a cross-section of the black and brown petit bourgeois and middle class, including lawyers, municipal councilors, representatives of the NWCSA, the WIYWL, and the TLP, as well as Achong and Walcott, held its first public meeting on 31 July 1935. Mentor was quoted as saying:

It may be asked, why should we be so concerned about Abyssinia? What interest have we, as British subjects, in the entanglements of European policy? What right have we to voice any opinion on the question at all?

Some persons have become suddenly interested, in the African races, are hinting that there is Arab blood in Abyssinia, and that our zeal in her behalf is half wasted.

To these persons, ladies and gentlemen, I have one plain answer: Our ancestors came from all parts of tropical Africa, including Abyssinia, and whether such terms as Bantus, Eastern Hamites, Negroes, Berber mulattoes, are used to describe the various peoples of tropical Africa the clear, indisputable fact remains that we are the descendant of one and all of them. Our conception of race, therefore, is purely geographical.

Mentor continued:

[W]hen we refer to ourselves as a group racially we call ourselves Afro-West Indians, that is, West Indian-born Africans, pure and mixed or West Indians of African blood. Loosely we speak of ourselves as creoles, the African before creoles having been drpped [*sic*] since abolition of slavery as there was no need to distinguish African born from locally born and among us it is assumed that everybody has African blood.

So that, Ladies and Gentlemen, we are in part of direct Nubian and Ethiopian descent.[35]

The idea of being *"in part* of *direct* Nubian and Ethiopian descent" may seem contradictory but it connects with the discourse of 'race mixing' in Trinidad. In the colonial period, "the 'mixing' of disparate 'races' was identified as being emblematic of both Trinidad and, more generally, the West Indies".[36] The local category of 'coloured' or 'brown' included all persons seen as a mixture of 'white' and 'black' ancestors and particular colour terms indicated a person's relative proportion of 'black' and 'white': " 'Colour' was a finely graded continuum ordered hierarchically by the valorisation of the 'European' ('white') over the 'African' ('black')," writes Segal.[37] Hugo Mentor and the other correspondents quoted above assume 'pure races' – hence their concern with 'mixed' individuals and groups – but avowedly seek to challenge and replace racial designations, first by urging those in the 'mixed' category to identify with their 'black' ancestry and, second, by challenging the colonial value put on whiteness and supposedly European cultural accomplishments. For them, race was significant; it determined one's overall attitude, one's political stance, and one's culture. The origins of such differences were revealed in the Bible and their manifestations were evident. A change in racial designation, from 'mixed' to 'black' or 'Negro', would mean a corresponding change in worldview. This is indeed what the AWIL was urging, seeing the racial alignment of 'white' versus 'black' nations as a metaphor for local black-white relations.

Jim Barrette

Elma François

Another strain in the discourse surrounding the war was associated with the NWCSA's insistence on linking ethnicity with class, and placing the local circumstances in the context of imperialism and international capitalist exploitation. The NWCSA arose out of the National Unemployed Movement (NUM), which was founded in 1934 by Jim Barrette, Elma François, and James Headley, who had recently returned from the United States where he was a colleague of George Padmore (born Malcolm Nurse in Trinidad) and a member of communist organizations. The NUM staged various labour demonstrations, hunger marches, and registered the unemployed during the mid 1930s. In late 1934, the NUM became the NWCSA. This was on the advice of Rupert Gittens, recently deported from Marseilles for his involvement with the French Communist Party, and in an attempt to go beyond unemployment as a political issue. Founding members were Barrette and François, Gittens, Christina King, Bertie Percival and Dudley Mahon. Headley, victimized, returned to his job as a seaman and left Trinidad at this time. The NWCSA was Port of Spain-based, black nationalist in orientation, as well as socialist, and promoted gender equality.[38] The NWCSA, Reddock writes, affirmed "racial pride" but that this did not "preclude joint action with anti-colonial, anti-imperialist people of other races and ethnic groups".[39]

Captain A.A. Cipriani

They were extremely critical of Captain A.A. Cipriani's leadership of the established labour movement. Cipriani, a French Creole of Corsican descent who began to profess an adherence to socialist ideals, was the head of the TWA by 1923. By the mid 1930s, he had converted the TWA into a political party, the TLP, and the charismatic leader had seen his popularity with the masses wane precipitously. His leadership style became more reformist and at the same time more authoritarian. He dismissed complaints about the failure

BY COURTESY OF THE *TRINIDAD GUARDIAN* AND THE EXTRA-MURAL STUDIES UNIT, UWI

Tubal Uriah 'Buzz' Butler

of the TWA/TLP to bring about improvement in the lot of the working class by responding with an affirmation of his faith in 'British justice' towards the colonies. He became the mayor of Port of Spain and was seen to side more and more with the French Creole, Catholic planter and merchant classes. The NWCSA became an important alternative to Cipriani and his leadership of the labour movement, establishing links with labour leaders, including Tubal Uriah 'Buzz' Butler, a major leader of the oilfield strikes of 1937.

Citing an interview with NWCSA leader Jim Barrette, Friday writes that "The conflict was analysed and discussed in a manner intended to link the struggle of the oppressed at home against colonial capitalism with the impending struggle of the Ethiopian peasants and workers against fascism."[40] The NWCSA, then, emphasized that the conflict was more than one of black versus white in racial terms, but, of course, they took West Indian blacks' racial identification with the Ethiopians as given. In their ideological stance, they maintained that British colonial exploitation of West Indian blacks was no different than that which the Ethiopians would encounter under Italy. One NWCSA resolution passed at a meeting of more than 500 people in mid July stated: "It is clear to us, here, negroes, and other sympathisers, that the Fascist vote of wanting to civilize Abyssinia is nothing but an imperialist effort to further enslave the Abyssinian negro peoples, as those of your other African colonies."[41] The NWCSA also maintained contact with international organizations which were mobilizing to support Ethiopia. They distributed copies of the *New Times and Ethiopia News*, edited by the British socialist feminist Sylvia Pankhurst. The *New Times* was a London-based newspaper which presented stories from the Ethiopian battlefront and also reported on the activities of London's West Indian community on Ethiopia's behalf.

The Italo-Ethiopian crisis seriously challenged Trinidadian attitudes to Britain. It was not only Cipriani and the TLP who retained confidence in British justice and fair play. Leaders of the AWIL, as educated members of the middle class, thought that it was racism that prevented their advancement in the public service and denied them self-government. Therefore, they tended to concentrate their Ethiopian war-related efforts on raising the 'race consciousness' of Trinidadians, and alerting the Colonial Office to the opinions of its black colonial subjects. In a letter forwarding resolutions from the 31 July meeting, A.E. James, the AWIL's secretary, reminded the governor to point out to the Colonial Office that

coloured feeling on the subject is deeply stirred, that the dispute is being followed with the keenest interest, and that West Indians are anxious not merely for a peaceful but for a just settlement, and expect Great Britain, having regard to the state of feeling in the West Indies, to resist to the utmost any schemes or designs to bring pressure to bear upon His Majesty Emperor Haile Selassie to yield to the unjust demands of Italy.[42]

In one resolution, the WIYWL "pledge[d] its loyalty to His Majesty's Government in enforcing economic sanctions against Italy, and pray[ed] that the League of Nations will succeed in its effort to maintain the national integrity of Ethiopia – the only independent nation in Africa".[43] The WIYWL, like the AWIL, thought that British military power would be used to intervene on Ethiopia's behalf and to prevent war. "This approach," writes Friday, "assumed an identity of interest between colonial subjects and their British rulers, an assumption which the NWCSA did not share."[44] The NWCSA saw Britain as bearing part of the blame and refused to protest to London, choosing instead to petition the League of Nations and to decry imperialism. Indeed, as Padmore himself had recently recalled, Italy and Great Britain had previously agreed in secret to assist one another in carving up Ethiopia.[45] This ideological rift was evidenced at the 31 July meeting of the AWIL, when the NWCSA presented an anti-imperialist resolution. While the resolution was passed, Philip of the WIYWL and other members of the middle class expressed opposition to the resolution.

The *People* chastised the TLP, "comprised of 99% Negroes", for taking no action on Ethiopia.[46] Since 1918, many members of the TWA were at the same time UNIA members and as a consequence the UNIA and the TWA operated in close association. Often, individuals were officers in both organizations. Their aims and activities became, in many senses, formally linked. William Howard-Bishop, Jr, editor of the *Labour Leader*, the TWA's newspaper, was a former TWA president and a UNIA member. However, under Cipriani's leadership, during the Italo-Ethiopia crisis the TLP followed the Second International's resolution against fascism which called for the working class to "do everything in its power to save peace". In its resolution the TLP expressed "grave concern" about the possibility of war and urged the British Labour Party and the Socialist International to work to avert such a "catastrophe". But Cipriani did not sign the TLP's resolution. He said that he had "too much faith in the British nation" to think that "she will allow such an atrocity to be perpetuated". "I cannot believe it," he said, "and feel almost sure that the war clouds will be dispelled."[47]

Organizing for War

The storm of rhetoric was not simply idle talk. As it became apparent that Ethiopia's time was running out, when one after another of the diplomatic attempts to prevent war failed, as half-hearted and self-interested as these might have been, Trinidadians translated their words into deeds. They formed organizations to collect money for ambulances, held mass rallies where they passed resolutions to be sent to the League of Nations and the Colonial Office, called for a boycott of Italian goods, and they volunteered to go to Ethiopia and fight for the emperor.

Some organizations sought to capitalize on Trinidadians' discontent and concern and convert these feelings into class consciousness and class mobilization. At the beginning of August 1935, the NWCSA organized a protest march on behalf of the unemployed and protestors marched to Government House. When told that the governor would not be granting any relief, the crowd rioted, went marching around Port of Spain, looting and causing mayhem. The governor issued a proclamation prohibiting ten or more people armed with sticks or other weapons from gathering, and the proclaimation prohibited any marches or assemblies, other than those of a religious nature, for a month for most areas in the colony. This proclamation was renewed repeatedly through September 1936 – the rest of Governor Sir Claud Hollis' term.

In a general context of working class agitation and foment, the AWIL sought to expand its influence when it held a meeting on 2 September to which it invited several prominent Trinidadians. Hugo Mentor suggested to the multi-ethnic gathering that a Friends of Ethiopia committee be formed to coordinate the various activities on Ethiopia's behalf in Trinidad and to link up with other such organizations in the West Indies. The group accepted the suggestion and made Cipriani its chair.[48] At the same time, WIYWL promoted their own solutions to the crisis: a boycott of Italian goods and businesses in the event of war. They announced it at a ceremonial unveiling of Haile Selassie's portrait, which was unveiled by a member dressed in full UNIA regalia to the strains of the Universal Ethiopian Anthem.[49]

Support came from blacks representing the middle as well as the working classes. The Wilberforce Football League announced that it would hold a football match on 7 September, stating that the proceeds would be given to the fund started in England for sending financial help to Ethiopia.[50] Some middle class black and brown boys at the elite Queens Royal College formed the Pan-African Order of the Shebisti, so-named after the Queen of Sheba. They started a small publication and posted anonymous notices of protest on the chalk boards. One former student, Lloyd Braithwaite, recalled that an English master objected to the notices and forced a confession from the guilty parties.[51]

Some organizations in Trinidad, as elsewhere in the Caribbean, called for blacks to volunteer for the Ethiopian military. In July, the NWCSA sought permission from the British government for the transportation of "thousands of negroes of the West Indies who are prepared to die in the defense of Ethiopia".[52] Trinidadians also heard news of blacks elsewhere in the Caribbean volunteering to fight on Ethiopia's behalf, such as the 500 blacks in British Guiana who sent a petition to King George to seek permission to fight on Ethiopia's behalf. T.A. Wright, president of one of the many black organizations there, said: "Twenty years ago Negroes fought to save white civilisation. Surely they cannot now be refused permission to fight for what they regard as a symbol of their own civilisation."[53] The Colonial Office was forced to publicize the fact that Section 4 of the Foreign Enlistment Act of 1870 and Article 25 of the Ethiopia Order in Council, 1934, made it an offence for any British subject to join the military of any foreign state at war with another state at peace with Britain, punishable by up to two years in prison and up to a £500 fine.[54] Cipriani was sceptical: "Until the British Empire was at war with Italy," he said, "we in a British colony are not at war with Italy."[55]

When the news of Italy's actual invasion of Ethiopia reached Trinidad by radio late on 6 October 1935, there were several spontaneous demonstrations. A large crowd described by the *Gazette* as consisting of the 'street elements' demonstrated in front of the business and residence of Theodore Laurenco at 17 Nelson Street in Port of Spain. Apparently mistaking the two Portuguese Republic red and green flags Laurenco had flying to celebrate the twenty-fifth anniversary of the Republic, for those of Italy, which are red, white and green, the flags were taken down and destroyed. A contingent of police arrived and dispersed the crowd, making a few arrests.[56] The NWCSA took advantage of the ending of the ban on assembly and worked to organize the protest movement. They called for a mass meeting in Marine Square on 10 October, and distributed 10,000 leaflets saying:

SAVE ABYSSINIA
Negroes of Trinidad . . . All out to-day . . . at 2:30 p.m. Join a protest meeting . . . Thousands of Abyssinian peasants – women and children are being slaughtered by the bombing of the Fascist butcher Mussolini . . . Only the united action of all Negroes and oppressed people can stop this horrible mass murder; can stop world Imperialism from the pillage and plunder on the Abyssinian peoples. Voice your Protest . . . Down with Mussolini. Down with the enemies of the Negro Peoples.[57]

The meeting was attended by more than 2,000 people, some with placards saying "Down with Mussolini", "Away with Fascism", and "Down with the Enemies of the Negro". The speakers denounced France for its failure to intervene and denounced England for refusing to sell arms to Ethiopia. They called on all blacks to boycott French and Italian goods and for stevedores to refuse to unload Italian ships. The meeting unanimously passed two resolutions – the first condemning the shooting and bombing of defenceless men, women and children for the purpose of glorifying "Italian Fascist Imperialism", and the second "criticised the prohibition of meetings and marches as a direct attack upon the political rights of the working class by a government incompetent to solve the unemployment crisis".[58] A demonstration from the meeting marched to the Italian consul's office, shouting "Down with Mussolini!" When they arrived there they were met by the police. At their insistence, Bertie Percival met with the consul and presented the NWCSA resolutions. The demonstrators then went to the Roman Catholic Cathedral and shouted abuse at members of the clergy, and marched on to Woodford Square chanting "We want to fight for Abyssinia".[59] These events led to the reintroduction of the so-called Peace Proclamation for two months to prevent further demonstrations. The *Gazette* and the *Guardian* supported the ban, warning the 'street elements' to show restraint.

The few Italians in Trinidad were the subject of face to face derision and organized protests. The 1931 census reported only twenty-one Italian nationals out of the colony's total population of 412,783.[60] As such, the threats and harassment directed against them were figurative – it was what they represented that the activists opposed. Some of them expressed fears for their safety. An open letter to the governor in the *People* by "Junius" urged him to get rid of any public servants with "strong Italian leanings". "Junius" pointed out Bridget Ristori, the matron at the San Fernando Colonial Hospital who, he claimed, was having poor relations with her 'coloured nurses' because of her supposed "Anti-Ethiopianism" and that she took deep offence when the nurses wore Ethiopian Flag Day emblems before the flags went on sale in the streets.[61] There were reports that a local druggist refused to compound a prescription signed by an Italian doctor.[62] Salvatori, Scott and Co., Ltd, the agents for an Italian shipping line, removed their agency sign because it became bad for business.[63] Italian agents were even said to be lurking. Trinidadians read that a rumour that Italian spies had distributed poisoned sweets to schoolchildren led to a panic in Georgetown, British Guiana, with several schools being closed as frantic parents rushed to the schools for their children.[64] A rumour in Trinidad about a doctor – possibly an Italian – making children ill at school produced stick- and cutlass-wielding parents wanting their children.[65] And when it was discovered that Italian-born engineer Giovanni Battista Guisto was working in the Department of Public Works as a temporary draftsman, the TLP organized a protest that resulted in his dismissal.[66]

The anti-Catholic feelings should be seen in proper context. According to the 1931 census, Catholicism was the dominant religion. Of the population, 34.6 percent were Roman Catholics, followed by Anglican, 24.6 percent, and Hindu, 22.8 percent. Roman Catholics were 48.2 percent of those accounted as Christians.[67] These feelings should also be seen in the context of ethnic and class conflict. In Trinidad, the Catholic church was associated with the powerful French Creole elite.[68] The church hierarchy and the priesthood were dominated by foreign whites. Many black members of Trinidad's large Catholic population were indignant because Pope Pius XI was seen as at least tacitly approving of Italy's "civilizing mission". For some Trinidadians, the Rome of Mussolini became the persecuting Rome of the Bible. According to a *People* editorial entitled "Peter Denies Christ", "That coloured Catholics in Trinidad are deeply disappointed and in most cases bitterly resentful at His Holiness' apparent lukewarmness on the side of right and justice in this war is well known. And this circumstance is none too pleasing to a body whose local priesthood is largely of non-African race." The *People* believed that the pope had "failed to put the full weight of the moral influence of the Catholic Church on the side of Ethiopia against Italy".[69]

The *People* reported that at St Joseph's Convent in Port of Spain the students were asked to contribute to a fund to assist Italy. At another Catholic school the children were made to pray for an Italian victory. And at a third, two teachers were said to be victimized because of their displeasure at the school's supposed pro-Italian sympathies. One teacher was reported as being expelled but later recalled and disciplined by the white principal while the other was reported as being debarred from further promotion in Catholic schools.[70]

Such expressions and rumours aroused the defenders of the Catholic Church. The *Catholic News* chided Trinidadians for their criticism of the pope and said that they were forgetting that he held neither economic nor political power.[71] The *Port-of-Spain Gazette*, a newspaper representing the powerful French Creole planter class, played up an address by the vicar general who was given time on the platform of a Friends of Ethiopia meeting to "explain the position of Catholics and denounce those who were trying to sow seeds of anti-Catholicism among the labouring and lower classes because of the present Italo-Ethiopian crisis". He said that in Italy he saw "an unjust invader trying to take possession of another's country and massacring its people; it is sheer murder", while in Ethiopia he saw "an ancient but backward land, primitive and crude in its administration of justice and it is the only land on the map of the world where slavery is allowed". He said, "I plead with you to stretch the hand of mercy to the land of Emperor Selassie in his great struggle against a powerful enemy." He then turned to the anti-Catholic agitation: "The Rome we love as Catholics is the Rome of Peter . . . but to the Italian Rome, to him we owe no allegiance." In his closing remarks to the meeting, Cipriani sought to downplay the ethnic conflict associated with the war. "I am as white as anybody in Trinidad and there is nobody that has more real interest in this Ethiopian question than myself." He also said that, as a Roman Catholic, "I denounce all of Italy's aggression, all that it stands for and all that it means; and I have no doubt that every right thinking Roman Catholic believes the same thing."[72] The Catholic archbishop of Port of Spain sought to explain that the pope's "thoughts are for peace, his prayers are for peace", he explained, "irrespective of colour, race or country".[73] And in an editorial, the *Gazette* claimed that priests had been "subjected to jibes from ignorant persons who mistake them for Italians", while in fact there was not a single Italian priest in Trinidad. Making an veiled reference to the *People* and its readers, the editorial continued: "For a long time it has been known that propaganda of a most pernicious type has been allowed to spread here; literature, which is absolutely insulting not only to Catholics, but also to every other denomination, is being printed and spread among persons who are sufficiently credulous to believe anything and everything which they might be told", and urged the populace to "see clearly that there is no one who is working more wholeheartedly towards bringing about peace than His Holiness the Pope".[74] Even the Anglican bishop, A.H. Anstey, was rebuked by fellow Anglicans when, attempting to ameliorate the situation, he defended the pope.[75]

Anti-Italian activity was also undertaken by working class organizations. The Stevedores and Longshore Workers Union, which was affiliated with the

TLP and a stronghold of NWCSA members, resolved to follow international dockworker unions in their ban on loading or unloading Italian shipping. It was announced that on 19 October the League of Nations agreed to impose economic sanctions on Italy. On 12 November, the stevedores refused to unload the Italian ship *Virgilio* which had arrived from Genoa. A strike was averted when local merchants hired scab workers to unload the ship under police protection.[76] A week later, however, when one of the men who unloaded the *Virgilio* was spotted by other union members in their crew, they refused to unload another ship until he was dismissed.[77] With the League of Nations sanctions taking effect, the local government issued proclamations barring exports to Italy.[78]

Trinidadians also rallied to provide tangible material aid to Ethiopia, but in these efforts, too, they differed along ethnic, class, and ideological lines. Immediately after the ban on further mass assemblies, Cipriani initiated the TLP's Ambulance Fund to raise money to purchase an ambulance for the Ethiopian government. A subscription list which ran daily was opened in the *Trinidad Guardian*. At the same time, the multi-ethnic Friends of Ethiopia was officially constituted with Cipriani as chair and with the following members: A.E. James and Hugo Mentor of the AWIL, Councillor Leo A. Pujadas, who was Indian, George McD. Chambers, who was white, Alfred Richards, the Afro-Chinese druggist and former TWA leader, Alderman Murchison Rigsby, who was white, Audrey Jeffers, MBE, a black social worker, Beatrice Greig, a white social worker, and Paul Louis.[79] Friends launched the Ethiopian Assistance Fund for which a subscriptions list was published in the *Port-of-Spain Gazette*. Friends also established a network of committees and representatives throughout Trinidad and held public meetings and special fund-raising events.

In these efforts, women's initiatives were instrumental. Friends' most successful fund-raising event was an Ethiopian Flag Day:

Women of Trinidad buy a flag on Saturday to help the cause of the women of Ethiopia!
  You know that the Empress has said she will ride to battle with the Emperor, her husband, and thousands of the women of her country will follow their men with courage and determination.[80]

Flag Day was organized by Jeffers and Grieg who appealed to merchants for donations of cloth and pins and recruited schoolchildren as volunteers. These women inspired others. Louisa Wiltshire, president of the South Philanthropic Workers, based in San Fernando, also initiated a Flag Day there to assist the ambulance cause.[81] And the war revived the local Garvey movement. The Daughters of Ethiopia group was formed by Garveyite women who concentrated on fund-raising for Ethiopia's war effort. They held a flag day of their own – with the red, black and green UNIA flag. These women became instrumental in a mini-revival of the Garvey movement between 1935 and 1937, when Garvey himself visited Trinidad.[82]

In the midst of an economic crisis and the Great Depression, the outpouring of funds from a working class population who could scarcely afford to donate them was truly impressive. As Cipriani said, "No one realizes more than I do how empty the pocket of the workingman is, but I take my hat off to him and to my barefooted friend for the manner in which he has so far subscribed."[83] Indeed, with a number of small donations here and there, most of them less than $1.00, by 22 December 1935, the total collected was $2,162.78 for the Ambulance Fund and $1,607.03 for the Assistance Fund, or $3,769.81 total.[84] The Ambulance Fund even had a volunteer driver, a chauffeur from Chaguanas, S. Napoleon Fabian Cuffy.

Enjoying the positive attention associated with his public pro-Ethiopia stance, Cipriani was emboldened to chastise the AWIL and other black nationalist leaders – his ostensible allies in Friends and in the TLP – who questioned his legitimacy as a leader and Britain's role in the crisis. He decried "enterprising would-be politicians" for trying to make the war "a question of colour and creed", dismissing their concerns by asking what "is the question of colour that arises when you find the powerful European nations, England and France, on the side of the Ethiopians?"[85] Cipriani reiterated his faith in British justice and military might, predicting that Britain would shortly intervene on Ethiopia's behalf.

Mentor, who maintained that black consciousness and pride did not imply racism nor preclude cooperation with other races, nevertheless felt that "the leadership of the coloured race should come from the coloured race".[86] Feeling rebuffed by Cipriani, he started the AWIL's Selassie Fund, appealing to black nationalists and to the Afro-Christian churches such as the Spiritual Baptists, the African Orthodox Church and even Hindu and Muslim religious organizations. As part of the revival of the UNIA sparked by the reaction to the war, money was collected, often through the sales of red, black, and green UNIA flags. Through these efforts, Trinidadians were in concert with poor blacks throughout the diaspora, donating their hard-earned money for the cause. Besides the collection of money and materiel, the various organizations in Trinidad continued to hold mass meetings to encourage support and solidarity. The fifth anniversary of Selassie's coronation on 2 November

1935 provided a symbolic opportunity for apparent defiance of the ban on assemblies. At one organized by the TLP, more than 2,500 gathered to commemorate the coronation in Port of Spain. There were lifesized photos of the emperor and empress, and the Union Jack and Ethiopian flag were flown.

These manifestations seriously worried the colonial authorities. They saw their potential to undermine the colonial capitalist system and the system of ethnic relations by which it was buttressed. There were violent disturbances in St Vincent, which prompted restrictions on assembly and on the press there. Trinidadians became aware of

BY COURTESY OF THE *TRINIDAD GUARDIAN* AND THE EXTRA-MURAL STUDIES UNIT, UWI

Adrian Cola Rienzi

such establishment responses and severely criticized them. Adrian Cola Rienzi, a young Indian, Marxist lawyer and former TLP member – he quit when Cipriani denounced him as a communist – was instrumental in setting up the Trinidad Citizens' Committee (TCC) in South Trinidad. A police report described a meeting of the TCC on 28 October in San Fernando as consisting of "95% [. . .] negroes of which about 20 or 30% were artisans i.e. Carpenters, Masons and painters; the remainder were composed of the unskilled labouring class amongst whom were about 30 or 40 women".[87] The TCC, like the NWCSA, analysed the Italian invasion of Ethiopia in terms of international imperialism, but also asked that the governor "take the necessary steps to obtain the facilities to those desirous of mobilising in the defence of Abyssinia" and called for the British government to "induce the League of Nations not merely to impose economic and financial sanctions, but to carry out armed military intervention".[88] The TCC was unable to command the mass following of the NWCSA and by the end of 1935 it began to collapse. Rienzi and Butler then formed the Trinidad Citizens' League (TCL) in an effort to unite black and Indian workers. Ultimately, Rienzi and the TCL were able to mount a serious challenge to Cipriani's leadership and, even though the TCL did not last long either, Rienzi and Butler were instrumental in the mass labour rebellion of 1937.

Trinidadian links with other labour organizations engaged in pro-Ethiopia as well as prolabour agitation extended through the Caribbean and beyond. In December 1935, T. Albert Marryshow, president of the Grenada Workers' Association, was in Trinidad for a meeting of the TLP. He and the Revd Farquhar addressed a meeting where the Ethiopia question dominated.[89] In January 1936, the TLP also sponsored the visit of Susan Lawrence of the British Labour Party. Lawrence underlined the British people's sympathy for Ethiopia, saying that this proved that the war was not one of black versus white but about "the ambitions of Mussolini".[90] This no doubt bolstered Cipriani in his ideological battle with the black nationalists. In London, the Grenadian Marryshow along with Trinidadians Padmore, James, and Sam Manning, and a number of other West Indians, including Amy Ashwood Garvey, Marcus Garvey's first wife, as well as a number of Africans resident there, formed the International African Friends of Abyssinia (IAFA – later

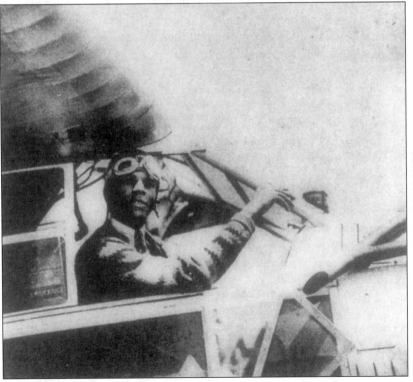

Hubert Fauntleroy Julian, the 'Black Eagle', c. 1935

UPI PHOTOGRAPH, REPRODUCED BY COURTESY OF CORBIS

the IAFE for Ethiopia) in July 1935, as a direct result of the crisis. Indeed, for Padmore and James the links and the ideas they developed during this time turned out to be pivotal in their own careers as political activists and ideologues.[91]

And then there was Colonel Hubert Fauntleroy Julian, the 'Black Eagle'. Born in Trinidad in 1897, Julian moved to London in 1912 and then to Canada in 1914 in the care of relatives. He made his way to Harlem in 1921 where he joined the thriving West Indian community. He met Garvey and by 1922 had joined the UNIA and become a member of the African Legion. He pursued his interest in flying, later developing a reputation for his daredevil parachute jumps and, given his flamboyant sartorial grace, as a Harlem dandy. Julian read of ancient Ethiopia when personally exposed by Garvey to books on Africa's past glories. His reputation also earned him the attention of Ras Tafari who invited him to perform at his coronation in 1930. He trained Ethiopian pilots there and became a favourite of Tafari. But he also became overbearing, defied Tafari's orders, and crashed the soon-to-be-emperor's new airplane. Julian slunk home to Harlem. In early 1935, with the outbreak of war on the horizon, he sailed to Ethiopia, uninvited, to offer his services and to redeem himself in the eyes of the emperor. After three months he finally got an audience with Selassie who forgave Julian, made him an Ethiopian citizen, and commissioned him as an officer in the armed forces. Trinidadians read of his every move.

However, after a public fistfight with the African American aviator John C. Robinson, the 'Brown Condor', he soon fell out of favour again. Instead of flying airplanes he was assigned as a civil administrator in a remote town while Robinson became head of the tiny air force. A month after the outbreak of hostilities Julian left Ethiopia and several critical statements were attributed to him. Among them, he claimed that "Ethiopians do not care for the American Negro and do not want his help", claiming that "They do not consider themselves Negroes".[92] Of course, Tafari's overtures to Julian in the first place belie this claim, as do the experiences of the several Ethiopian emissaries to black Americans.[93] Julian was regarded as a traitor in Ethiopia and by black Americans.[94] In early June 1936, after the Italian occupation of Addis Ababa, he announced that he automatically had become an Italian citizen and would be sailing to Rome to take up a commission in the Italian air force. He even claimed a new name, Huberto Fauntleroyana Juliano.[95] This action further outraged African Americans who suspected that he had been in Italy's pay from early on. Years later, he claimed his Italian jaunt was an elaborate plan, known only to Dr Malaku Bayen, the emperor's cousin and his emissary to black America. Julian said he was to assassinate Mussolini – a daring scheme which was barely foiled at the last minute.[96] However, Bayen, his supposed co-conspirator, bitterly denounced Julian a few years after this fiasco when he wrote: "Another such rascal was in Ethiopia on wings for no other purpose than to gain information which he could sell to the Italian aggressors."[97]

For the black nationalists, the war had an important cultural and religious dimension. Working class Afro-Christian churches became points of identification with and information about Ethiopia. On 2 November 1935, there was a large open-air Spiritual Baptist "Divine Service" to commemorate the fifth anniversary of Selassie's coronation and to pray for his victory in war. More than 2,000 attended. In the African Methodist Episcopal Church, Revd Mahew reminded his parishioners that Ethiopians were a dynasty of emperors who traced their 'pedigree' back to King Solomon and the Queen of Sheba – it was from this lineage that "the immortal Selassie" descended.[98] And worshipers of the Orisha religion, which combines Yoruba and Catholic traditions, staged elaborate public ceremonies to invoke sacred and powerful entities and entreat them to intervene on Ethiopia's behalf. In early December 1935, about 200 members of the African Association of Trinidad participated in a day-long rite in Barataria where a number of animals, including goats, fowls, sheep and a cow, were sacrificed. As the *Guardian* reported, "The slaying began at sunrise on Wednesday when two goats were beheaded at one swoop of a gleaming machet each, amidst the incantation of prayer, chants and the beating of a tom tom orchestra", indicating that the service was to extend to Saturday when, at the climax, a bull would be sacrificed.[99] Such ceremonies were in open defiance of colonial laws, such as the Shouters Prohibition Ordinance, 1917, and the Summary Conviction Offences Ordinance, 1921, which made it illegal to work *'obeah'*, play drums, and so on.[100] In flouting these laws, Trinidadians were indicating just how important the Ethiopian cause was for them, and indicating the spiritual avenue through which the conflict could be resolved in their favour, for they were also expressing an identification with Ethiopia, as well as opposing colonial oppression. The identification with Ethiopia did, however, reach farcical levels at times. Frederick Williams, a clerk in a haberdashery on Mucurapo Street, pounded his chest and proclaimed "When I talk no dog bark. I am Abyssinian." A police constable thought that this behaviour of striking his chest and telling dogs in a loud tone that they could not bark after he had spoken was disorderly. Williams was arrested and claimed that he had been drinking. "God love Great Britain," he declared when questioned by magistrate O.T. Cazabon. "I love Great Britain. Abyssinia must go through." He was fined ten shillings or fourteen days. The fine was cancelled and he was ordered home. Upon leaving the witness box he said "God bless the Inspector."[101]

Sustained and quite serious cultural opposition was also manifested through calypso and Carnival, traditional vehicles for anti-establishment political commentary. As a result, calypsoes were censored beginning in 1935.[102] Hubert Raphael, the Roaring Lion, was arrested as a 'ringleader' of the October 1935 anti-Italian demonstration, found guilty of disorderly behaviour and fined.[103] Houdini recorded his defiant "Ethiopian War Drums" as early as 14 October in New York:

> Black men the bugle call
> Come one, come all
> The Drums are beating and the bugle call
> Come one, come all
> Don't mind what Mussolini say
> Let us march in battle array
> And take a gun in your hand to defend the Ethiopian
> War declare.[104]

Calypsonians staged a drama at the Prince's Building to raise money for Ethiopia's cause. The cast was announced as follows, and Lord Bone Eye and Tune Master introduced the latest songs:

> The Growler . . . Haile Selassie
> Lady Trinidad . . . Empress of Abyssinia
> Lord Beginner . . . Anthony Eden
> Lord Executor . . . M. Laval
> Lion from the East . . . Japan
> The Tiger . . . Benito Mussolini.[105]

The 1936 Carnival season and throughout 1936 saw calypsonians record songs about Ethiopia. Tiger's "The Gold in Africa", which was recorded in New York on 2 April 1936, wailed:

> Gold, the gold
> The gold, the gold
> The gold in Africa
> Mussolini want from the emperor
>
> Abyssinia appeal to the League for peace
> Mussolini actions were like a beast

A villain, a thief, a highway robber
And a shameless dog for a dictator . . .
We have diamond, ruby, and pearl
Platinum, silver, and even gold
I don't know why the man making so much strife
I now believe he want Haile Selassie wife

If he want gold as a dictator
Try in Demerara
Venezuela or Canada
Austro-Hungar' or else in America.[106]

The Roaring Lion recorded "Advantage Mussolini" in 1936, with the chorus: "Advantage can never done/Mussolini, you know you wrong". Radio sang "Abyssinian Lament" and the normally apolitical Caresser recorded "Selassie Held by the Police" in early 1937. Lord Inveigler changed his stage name to Ras Kassa – the name of an actual Ethiopian commander – after the invasion.[107] Several bands and individual masquers at the 1936 Carnival displayed Ethiopian themes. In Arima, the winners for the children's King and Queen competition were the portrayals of Haile Selassie and the Empress. In Chaguanas, the winners of the Kings of the Bands competition were the "Ethiopian Warriors", and in Port of Spain two of the most popular bands were "The Ethiopians" and "Heroes of the Dark Continent".[108] Harry Laughlin was awarded a prize at the Queen's Park Savannah for his costume of Haile Selassie,[109] and the image of Emperor Haile Selassie was crowned King of Carnival in Chaguanas.[110]

Although the Ethiopians fought bravely, the Italian war machine rolled on, finally capturing the capital, Addis Ababa, in May 1936, forcing Selassie to take refuge in England. News of the war and of Italian atrocities, such as the use of mustard gas, the bombing of hospitals, the summary executions of prisoners and civilians, continued to pour into Trinidad. Hugo Mentor of the AWIL reminded the colonial secretary that

Great Britain's prestige among her coloured subjects had been lauded by British West Indians as the expression of the spirit of justice in human affairs.

This belief has been written in blood on many a field of battle. In the Ashanti War of 1874 under Sir Garnet Wolsey, in the Zulu Campaign of 1879, in the terrible campaign against Von Lettow-Vorbeck in Tanganyika in the late war, West Indians fought under the British flag against their own kith and kin in Africa.

They did so willingly because of the conception of British Imperialism which has been preached to them and the coloured people of Trinidad would be sadly disappointed if an Italian victory were followed by a partition of the last remaining independent kingdom in Africa. They appeal to His Majesty's Government to prevent so unwelcome a consummation.[111]

But the black nationalists of the AWIL soon became frustrated with this line of action. They argued that the League had failed because the war was indeed 'racial' in nature. It had taught them, in the words of Ralph Mentor, "at least one salutary lesson . . . the necessity of sticking together".[112]

The Friends of Ethiopia Committee, with Cipriani as the chair, passed a resolution on 7 May 1936 asking the British government to adopt a more "energetic policy in keeping with the League Covenant, to protect the sovereignty, independence, and territorial integrity of Ethiopia".[113] This was followed by a large Friends of Ethiopia meeting on 9 May where a plea was issued to Britain to aid Ethiopia. And the NWCSA held a huge meeting on 29 May at which François addressed the crowd, denouncing the barbaric methods used by Italy against "an innocent and defenseless Black people", speaking of the "Rape of Africa", which had exposed capitalism in its crudest form.[114] By mid 1936, the TLP's Ambulance Fund was able to send £463 to the Ethiopian ambassador in London, while the AWIL's Selassie Fund sent $160 to the exiled monarch, and the UNIA only managed to raise $40.[115]

The Aftermath of the Crisis

The labour strikes and riots of June–July 1937 followed the Italo-Ethiopia crisis. Contemporary commentators confirm that the effects of the war contributed to the 1937 events. Arthur Calder-Marshall, the British socialist writer who went to Trinidad shortly after the turmoil, said that "The psychological effect of British foreign policy on the subjects of the Empire has been to break any bond that existed before. Britain's betrayal of Abyssinia is nearly as much to blame for the riots in Trinidad and Jamaica as the high cost of living."[116] Even the gov-

Sir Murchison Fletcher

ernor, Sir Murchison Fletcher, stated in 1937 that the Butler-led labour disturbances in Trinidad were at least partially due to the consciousness raising effects of the Italian invasion. While admitting that "a considerable number of young white men have been taken on in the higher posts to the exclusion of senior coloured men", he went on to state that "Another aspect of this racial question is the agitation which has been fostered here, and, I am afraid, is still being fostered in certain quarters, regarding the attack by Italy on Abyssinia."[117] In a confidential despatch, he wrote that "racial antipathy was definitely an outstanding factor" in the labour unrest and that the attack on Ethiopia had aroused "an intense anti-white feeling among the Negro population" that was still being fuelled by Butler and by the *People*.[118]

Calder-Marshall chronicled two calypsoes from early 1938. "When the majority of European papers had relegated Ethiopian news to the wastepaper basket," he reported, "the Abyssinian war is still being followed in Trinidad with fervent interest."[119] In one, "Mussolini de Bully", the situation was analysed, at least in part, in Ethiopianist terms, equating Mussolini with Judas:

> Dere is no difference in any way
> Wit' Judas and Mussolini, I'll say.
> Judas betrayed Christ and was fatigue
> Jus' as Mussolini betrayed de League.
> But de Bible made us to understan'
> dat Ethiopia will stretch its han'.
> But I only hope when it's stretching out
> dat it will grip Mussolini's mout'.
>
> On Judgement morning when de Holy Master
> Should call on Mussolini to stand and deliver.
> He shall be perished and cast to hell
> wid de devil and the imps he will have to dwell.
> For those horrible crimes and disasters
> that he have permitted in Africa.
> And in Paradise will be Selassie
> smilin' down at barbarous Mussolini.[120]

Another, "De Whole World in Confusion", commented on the state of the world in crisis and flux and asked "Who must be blamed for dat confusion?" The answer: "Hitler. Mussolini. And de Holy Vatican."[121] As Gorden Rohlehr comments: "International politics was in the eyes of many Trinidadians, no more than the outward and visible sign of the movement of history towards the grand Apocalypse predicted in the Bible. The re-emergence of Italy as an imperial power, was the re-emergence of an unholy Roman Empire which would precede the coming of the Anti-Christ, whose agent was Mussolini as surely as Haile Selassie was, if not divine himself, a blessed emissary of God."[122] The Herskovitses reported that in the village of Toco in 1939 members of the persecuted 'Shouters' group, or Spiritual Baptists, intertwined their religious views with explanations "of the objectives of the Garvey movement or of the struggle of Haile Selassie against the European powers, thus effecting a transfer to the broader, world-wide inter-racial situation".[123] And Trinidadians continued contact with the *New Times and Ethiopia News*. One letter writer complained about low wages and high food prices, requesting "Please, in your paper, let us know something about the war with our Motherland."[124]

It is tempting to see the consciousness raising of the war as a determining influence on the labour rebellions of the period. However, as the above evidence suggests, there were several at times contradictory ideological strains, none of which automatically led to class formation. Further, by claiming that 'racial' feelings were behind the strikes, colonial authorities could not only avoid a discussion of the economic condition of the masses, they could also paint such labour activists as out and out racists. In fact, the complexities of ethnicity and class and Trinidadians' reactions to the war, and the role of these reactions in the labour strikes of 1937, require further explication.

Cultural Constructions of Ethnicity and Class

One might pause here to ask what is so mysterious about this reaction, which seems to be the awakening of real, actual primordial ties to real, actual ancestors. But this view would be to deny, on a theoretical *and* empirical level, that ethnicity is a socially, culturally and historically constructed phenomenon and not a 'given', and it would also be to ignore certain historical occurrences in the case at hand. According to Garvey, resident in London at the time, Selassie ignored a delegation of prominent blacks gathered at Waterloo Station to receive him in June 1936. These included Garvey, who up to that point had been supportive of the emperor.[125] Contemporary British press reports dispute this claim.[126] Soon after, Garvey began criticizing Selassie with such venom through the *Black Man* that he lost considerable respect in the West Indies and elsewhere. He blamed Selassie for Ethiopia's ill-preparedness for war and its general state of backwardness. He also accused Selassie of an "anti-Negro" bias, questioning whether the emperor, as a member of the Amharic ethnic group, was really a "Negro".[127]

Garvey's position *vis-à-vis* Selassie may have helped to dispose Trinidadians against the UNIA leader, now in his years of decline. In 1937, he announced that he would visit Trinidad. Prior to his arrival in October of that year, the *Sunday Guardian* reported that Garvey maintained that the strikers were being used by communists based in London and associated with the International African Service Bureau – a reference to James and others. These 'agitators' had taken advantage of Cipriani's absence from Trinidad and were "being used as pawns in the political game".[128] According to Reddock, this brought angry responses, "and local UNIA leaders were forced to repudiate these statements".[129] He had the support of Cipriani, a long-time ally. However, Cipriani's relations with the working masses were at best distant at this point. Garvey spoke in Port of Spain, San Fernando and visited other parts of the island, and was received at a civic reception organized by the Port of Spain City Council.[130] But in an article evaluating his visit, the *People* concluded that "Garvey appears to have little sympathy for the poor".[131] Garvey later repudiated his remarks on the Trinidad strikes while on a visit to St Lucia.[132] But Garvey's diatribes against Selassie apparently did little to dampen admiration for the latter while damaging the reputation of the former. The Herskovitses reported that Selassie had become "a symbol of similar, if not greater import" than Garvey: "For though by 1939 the Italo-Ethiopian war was over, and Selassie had suffered defeat and was in exile, all this was either unknown or overlooked. The point was made again and again that he was 'fighting the battle for black people against the whites for the control of Africa' ".[133] In a way, Garveyism proceeded without Garvey.

Marcus Garvey

In his analysis of the role played by Jamaican Ethiopianism in the 1938 labour riots there, Ken Post dismisses Ethiopianism "as an ideology, a form of false consciousness, ultimately founded on material reality but mediated in such a way as to be 'pure' or 'mere' thought" and "as a form of social and, by implication at least, political protest, but one which was not able to lead to effective action, so that action, when it came in the form of the riots and strikes of 1938, was a product not of ideology but of economic necessity asserting itself".[134] Yet, it is incorrect to assert that Ethiopianism totally debilitated Trinidadians and precluded their concerted political activities, unless one takes a very narrow view of Ethiopianism and ignores the ways in which ethnicity and class are mutually constructed.

Explaining the Trinidadian reaction to the war necessitates a final abandonment of simplistic models: ethnicity as a reified, essentialized phenomenon, and the familiar 'base-superstructure' model of class with a simplistic, unidirectional conception of causation, with base determining superstructure. As Talal Asad remarks in another connection, practices of economic and political power are articulated through representations, including, I take it, representations such as ethnicity:

The binary separation between economic base and cultural superstructure is untenable – as critics of classic Marxism have long insisted – because it grows out of a misunderstanding of 'material effectivity,' not because a binary mode of analysis is always invalid. Thus, it is not possible to have a serious understanding of modern capitalist production without systematic reference to . . . signifying practices. And of course it is not only in production narrowly defined that representations are 'materially effective.' However, if cultural representations have practical effects, they are *within* the material world, not reflections of it.[135]

Not only are these antimonies not useful, but they actually inhibit research and analysis into phenomena as complex as the conjunction of ethnicity and class. The 'material' versus the 'ideational' perspective, where the material is judged simplistically to be determinant, is the staple perspective of social history, and limiting as well.[136] However, to analyse the 'material effectivity' of ethnicity – that is, the interaction between ethnicity and class – we can take clues from the participants themselves. As we have seen, opinions and recipes for involvement in the war were diverse. Overt Ethiopianist positions, associated with the AWIL and other groups and individuals, took colonialist and dominant class representations figured as 'race' and challenged not the validity of these designations but the negative depictions of those deemed to be of 'the black race'. Indeed, when colonialist practice was to destabilize these categories by casting doubt on New World blacks' links with the Ethiopians of 1935, blacks stressed their identification with the ancient Ethiopia of the Bible. Even Garvey, who had done so much to fan the flames of Ethiopianism, came to repudiate Ethiopia's living symbol in Selassie – repudiating him on the grounds that he was not 'racially' akin to New World blacks. In all of this, ethnicity was 'accomplished' via contestation and cultural construction.

Trinidadian activists were not likely to analyse how ethnicity was invented, but they understood its use in colonialist practice, of which Cipriani ultimately was a part. They developed an acute political understanding of how ethnicity affected class position and issues of political sovereignty, in Trinidad as well as in Ethiopia. Theirs was not simply some sort of gut-level reaction to the pull of ethnic identity, but, rather, these groups and individuals came to see class as constituted by ethnicity and ethnicity by class. This analysis also gave rise to concerted political action aimed at an unfettering of relations of domination and subordination, at the local and international levels. These efforts were made on behalf of oppressed blacks who, like colonial peoples everywhere, were defined by the context of continued colonialism with its attendant racism, paternalism, and the denial of political and human rights.

10

Non-Traditional Sources for the Study of the Trinidad Disturbances of the 1930s

Brinsley Samaroo

The period from the 1920s to the early 1930s was one during which the pot of Caribbean discontent had reached boiling point. The rigours imposed by World War I had hardly subsided when the Great Depression visited with the fury of a hurricane. In Trinidad, unrest started on the sugar estates in 1934. During 1935 and 1936 the unrest continued in the sugar belt and soon engulfed the oil industry. The years 1937 and 1938 were particularly bad for the whole region, with disturbances in St Kitts, British Guiana, Jamaica, St Lucia and Barbados. At the end of 1938, after British troops had suppressed this unrest, at least forty-six people had been killed and 429 injured, thousands of others had been detained and prosecuted.[1] Such a disturbance to the peace of the supposedly tranquil Caribbean had, of course, to be a matter of parliamentary enquiry. The secretary of state for the colonies relied heavily on official sources for his information: Colonial Office records, newspapers and journals, pamphlets and printed texts, themselves dependent on official documentation. Not surprisingly, he expressed total amazement at what was happening in the Caribbean. "The surprising thing," he told his parliamentary colleagues, "was the sudden and widespread outbreak of these disturbances."[2] Shortly afterwards, he despatched a Royal Commission under Lord Moyne to investigate the causes of the discontent and to recommend possible solutions to this West Indian unrest.

This chapter seeks to examine some of these official sources of information and to compare them with non-official accounts of the events of the thirties. The two main non-official sources chosen for this study are a collection of relevant documents left by Florence Nankivell, wife of Howard Nankivell, who was the acting colonial secretary during the period of greatest turbulence, and a novel by a coloured French Creole Trinidadian, Ralph de Boissière. Florence Nankivell lived in Trinidad at a time when her husband was a sympathizer with the cause of the workers. She presented a memorandum to the Moyne Commission in 1938 and left copies of a number of her speeches (to British audiences) on the Caribbean situation during the Depression years. The novelist de Boissière was born in 1907 into a well-established French Creole family whose ancestors had settled in the colony during the eighteenth century. Upon graduation from secondary school in Port of Spain, he had worked as a salesman for a large bakery in the city. This job took him to many parts of the island, including Fyzabad, the scene of the 1937 oil belt riots. As a young man he had also participated in political activities during the 1930s.[3] He was, therefore, a close witness to the turmoil. His novel *Crown Jewel*, recreating the events of 1937, was published in 1981.[4] Both these authors were supporters of the radical left and both stood firmly on the side of the complainants against British rule.

Along with the misery that prompted unrest on the sugar estates beginning in 1934, Port of Spain's working poor lived in horrible conditions in the slums. In her submission to the Moyne Commission, Florence Nankivell gave a graphic description of these habitations:

The slums in Port of Spain are a disgrace. The rents to be paid for rooms, not only in the slums, are out of all proportion to their accommodation and to the wages earned by almost any woman. Under nutrition and malnutrition are the result, with very little stamina to combat colds and diseases.[5]

Ralph de Boissière, who lived in an upper class area of the city, could not fail to see the same poverty being experienced by the seamstress, Aurelia (a character in *Crown Jewel*), out of work but in serious default of her monthly rent for the shack in which she lived with a young daughter. At two in the morning she is unable to sleep, restlessly waiting on the bailiff who would visit, like a thief in the night, to seize her sewing machine, her only means of livelihood, in lieu of the rent:

'God forgive me! God have mercy on me, a sinner!' She prayed rapidly, terrified now, her eyes roving in the darkness as if expecting to see it – the end. Remembering the bailiff and all her troubles, past and present, she felt she no longer had strength or desire to fight it. She went into Elena's room, saw her peacefully sleeping, hugging her pillow, one brown leg stretched out, the other, drawn up. 'As the earth is far from the sun, so am I,' she thought, 'from her life and dreams.' Tears ran down her cheeks. 'Let death take me. It's time, it's time!' (*Crown Jewel*, p. 22)

Florence Nankivell in Trinidad

Florence Nankivell (1901–93) was born Florence Muysken in the Dutch town of Bleinhoover on the Rhine. Her father was an engineer who owned the Werkspoor Steelworks which specialized in the manufacture of sugar refining machinery. As a teenager, Florence was sent to Woodbrooke (Quaker) College situated to the south of Birmingham. Founded in 1903, with funding from the Cadbury and Rowntree families, Woodbrooke appears to have had a profound influence on the life of young Florence. The school's curriculum reflected a philosophy which emphasized social development and the elimination of poverty and greater egalitarianism by means of state intervention in the economic system. According to this philosophy, the existing degrading poverty was due to rampant laissez-faire liberalism which must now be controlled.[6] Social courses were particularly relevant at a time when there was increasing interest in such areas as the emancipation of women, the education and care of children and the increasing threat to world peace. There was always a substantial body of overseas students at Woodbrooke: Dutch, Norwegian, Danish, Indian and Chinese. In her formative years, therefore, Florence had been exposed to a multiracial environment fortified by the historic Quaker concern for the dignity of the person. It was this reputation of openness and concern for the oppressed which attracted Gandhi to the place in 1932 where he slept on the floor. Jomo Kenyatta also visited. As we shall presently see, these Quaker concerns constantly informed Florence's later endeavours. They remained with her throughout her life.

After her secondary education, Florence Muysken returned to Holland from whence she journeyed to the East Indies where her father conducted most of his business. At the time of World War I she was in Europe to witness its tremendous horror. In 1932, she visited Trinidad as a tourist; here she met the acting colonial secretary, Howard Nankivell, whom she married in May of that year. She was with her husband in Trinidad from that time until mid 1938 when he was demoted and transferred to Cyprus. Howard Nankivell's demotion came as a result of his belief that the colony's workers had just cause for revolting against low wages and degrading living conditions in a colony where high production and good prices were making millionaires of British, American and South African investors and managers. In *Crown Jewel*, de Boissière described the condition of workers in the oil-rich southern part of the colony:

In order to be ready for the truck when it call for us at five-thirty we have to get up at four and cook for ourself. At the present time, as you all know, we doing a big job at Erin. No shop's near there. You in the bush. It take us more than an hour to get on the job. We starts at seven. We suppose to stop at eight for food and again at twelve. We leave the job at five. By the time we get back here shop shut . . . If we don't cook what we going' to eat? Bread an' sausage and bread and saltfish three times a day? We could be more undernourish than now. (p. 232)

Howard Nankivell, for his part, felt that he could no longer sit idly by, as a member of the establishment, and condone such inequality. At a tense debate in the Legislature on Friday 9 July 1937, he candidly stated his views:

In the past we have had to salve our consciences with humbug and we have had to satisfy labour with platitudes. Those days have gone by: we can no longer say to labour we recognize your hardships but we cannot afford to remedy them. We have got to look at the matter from a different aspect. To-day Government is collecting large revenues and the oil companies are paying big dividends. Even sugar is now to a considerable extent more than paying its way. As an instance of the confidence which the outside public has in the sugar industry we are all aware that Messrs. Tate and Lyle have now invested in two of our sugar companies and I am sure they would not have done so unless they had confidence in the future of that industry.[7]

The Forster Commission, despatched from London to investigate the Trinidad disturbances, found this open expression of opinion from a senior public officer "not only unfortunate in their substance but most untimely".[8] For this 'indiscretion' Nankivell was transferred to Cyprus as colonial treasurer in mid 1938.

Howard Nankivell had gone off to Cyprus ahead of Florence and their two children who were left in England. In the winter of 1938, he took a train from Milan to London, a destination which he never reached. His body was found on the tracks near the San Florentin station in France.[9] Interestingly, Florence Nankivell visited Trinidad in February 1966. At one of the many parties which she attended in the island she met someone who clearly remembered her late husband whom she had always called 'Peter':

Met a young man who, then a schoolboy of 15, remembered Peter. He told me that among them there was a belief that Peter had been pushed out of the train, because of the role he had played and sympathy he had shown for the people! This gave me quite a shock, for he insisted: they all firmly believed that was the truth![10]

At the time of Howard Nankivell's death, Florence was in England with their two children, hoping to join him after he had been properly settled. During her months in England just prior to his death, and afterwards, she was actively involved in smuggling Jewish children out of Eastern Europe as the Holocaust cast its grim shadow over Europe. She moved in and out of Holland regularly, even venturing into Berlin to fetch refugees. After the war, she returned to an active civilian life working for the Admiralty, raising the plight of Caribbean women and children before British audiences, assisting in 'meals on wheels' programmes and participating in archaeological expeditions on Britain's West Coast. In 1966, she visited Jamaica where her husband was born and where he had worked before going to Trinidad. In 1971, when I interviewed her, she vividly remembered her years in Trinidad and sent greetings to a number of people whom she had known in the island. During her years in Trinidad (1932–38), Florence Nankivell did considerable social welfare work focusing on women and children. She was pained to see the enormous suffering around her and angered by the indifference of the officials' wives to the socioeconomic situation. She informed the Moyne Commission that "in Trinidad very few officials' wives took any interest in Social Work whatever. The 'bird of passage' feeling prevents most of them from taking the trouble to become acquainted with their Colony."[11] De Boissière, unrestricted by the need to be precisely analytical, describes the official's wife in a manner which causes us to picture clearly this bird of passage:

A heavy rapid step was heard. Mrs. Osbourne came in, large-boned, fleshy red bosomed, perspiring. Her head on one side, she was smiling that insincere smile common to society women who entertain a great deal and head various committees. Aurelia was struck by something coarse and insensitive about her man-like head. She felt that the judge's wife was looking not only at her but through her. Aurelia bristled. At the same time she felt uneasy, so that she smiled awkwardly as she inclined her head in greeting. (p. 12)

Unlike the judge's wife, Florence Nankivell took time to visit women's groups, sometimes travelling outside of Port of Spain to empathize with women who were the most oppressed of the underclass. From interaction with women she was convinced that if the Europeans in the colony had adopted a less contemptuous attitude to the non-white population, the disturbances of the 1930s could have been averted. Recalling a conversation with a Trinidadian nurse who had returned after a long stint in New York and was now "president of the feminine section of the oldest Trade Union in Trinidad (in San Juan)", Nankivell reported that this labour leader "based the whole present discontent and lack of feeling between employer and employee on this principle":

If the Manager's wife would only come down to our houses and barracks and show an interest in us and our children we wives would dissuade our men from going on strike against the boss as madam had just been so kind and taken a personal interest.[12]

Because of a public perception that Nankivell was genuinely concerned about the problems of women and children, she was regularly invited to speak to women's groups. Her addresses were brief, unlike most official speeches, simple and easily comprehensible:

And why celebrate – why set apart a special day for mothers? It is a recognition that to be a mother, to be a good mother is a tremendous task. We are here tonight about the duties and responsibilities of Motherhood. These are many and onerous. They don't start at 9 o'clock in the morning and you can't lock your door on them at 4 in the afternoon. They are carried on day and night and they demand one's whole person. The care of the health of your child, its food, clothing, sleep, cleanliness, – all its daily routine – are just as important as the guidance of its mental development. And this last side makes a heavy demand on the Mother herself. The task of teaching your child to be honest, truthful and moral, to have strength of character – to be a good citizen – mostly falls on the mother as she is so much with the child. Education should mean largely self-education. I am a great believer in the strength of example. Acts are of so much more value than words – for a child very quickly imitates what it sees happening around it.[13]

The Trinidad years constituted a time of much activity for Florence Nankivell. Her family's treasure trove of Caribbean photographs indicate extensive travel over Trinidad's Northern Range to the cool waters of the north coast, through the Valencia forests to the yellow beaches at Manzanilla and Mayaro, and to the Nariva Swamp. The Nankivells took the coastal steamer athwart the western coast and visited the settlements along the southwest peninsula from whence they sighted Venezuela. There are pictures too of their visit to Suriname and their stay of four days at a 'Bush Negro' village in the interior. In the city they attended chic parties organized by the elite in pretty suburban gardens and privately they befriended trade unionists and aspiring politicians. At the time of her husband's persecution this latter 'indiscretion' was effectively used against him. In addition to these activities, which she shared with her husband, Nankivell became deeply involved in the social welfare movement, as we have seen. But her active mind pushed her much further. She became an ardent reader of West Indian history, hoping thereby to more fully understand the society of which she had become so fond. She attended sittings of the Legislative Council and in her wide travels she was able to acutely observe people, picking up nuances of behaviour which would have escaped a less perspicacious mind.

This judgement is based not so much on her Trinidad speeches, where she was constrained to be 'politically correct', but rather on the many speeches which she gave to English audiences and in her memorandum to the Moyne Commission. This woman, who has remained carefully hidden from history, waged a one-person campaign on behalf of the Caribbean in a very non-traditional manner, that is, by presenting the region nakedly to British audiences, indicating the considerable damage which Europeans had done:

In observing the actions and life of the present day Negro we must keep in mind that he is only 100 years – that is 3 generations – a 'free' man. When we compelled the Negroes to live as slaves we deprived them of their tribal customs and moral code and we did not give them new values instead. Barrack life on an estate, behavior of white masters around him certainly did not help them to build a new and better life. And nothing was done in an educational way to prepare the Negro for the difficulties with which he had to cope when 'freedom' was received.[14]

On the question of colour prejudice Florence Nankivell was, in the eyes of the British establishment, uncomfortably frank in her description of the subtle manner in which discrimination took place:

I can say that legally and officially there is no colour bar in the West Indies, that is to say black and white people freely mix in trams, shops, cinemas, committees and schools – but we do not as the expression is 'dine and wine' with each other. One meets coloured people at government house – at official dinners – except for the outstanding cases where cultured white women have black husbands one never socially meets them in private houses.[15]

Unknown to Mrs Nankivell, and out of earshot of the British public, the existence of strong racial prejudice had been reported to the Colonial Office by the captain of the Royal Marines sent to suppress Trinidad rioters in July 1937:

I gathered the impression that the attitude of the white staff generally, towards the coloured employees was not as satisfactory as it might have been. The expression 'damned niggers' was used in conversation in the hearing of coloured servants, and I consider that this does a great deal towards the cultivation of racial hatred. It appeared that 'fear of the white man' was being encouraged instead of 'respect for the white man'.[16]

Writing of precisely the same social situation, de Boissière authenticates the ethnic division so accurately described by Nankivell. When the popular black leader Le Maitre seeks to encourage more and more workers to join his union, many of them are sceptical because Le Maitre is not white. One worker taunts another "What Le Maitre could do for you? He ehn't white, he have no influence, he ehn't working nowhere" (p. 90). But Le Maitre's influence was not totally negative. He was a black man who gave his people hope:

And Boisson's men begun going to Diamond Hall to hear what remedies Le Maitre held out – this negro who talked with assurance but who, after all, had less power than the most insignificant of white men on the field. What could he do?

'I can do nothing,' he told them. 'Boisson can do nothing. It's what you can do!'

They chuckled, some of them. They liked to hear him. What he said made sense, voiced their heart's yearning. And he spoke with authority. A negro with authority who was not afraid and who knew the way out. He gave them pride. (p. 229)

But it was to the theme of the condition of women and children that Nankivell kept returning in her various presentations in London. The improper use of women by employers was hardly a matter which caught the attention of the governor or the local politician or trade union leader. This was a delicate matter which the tribe of men kept under cover. Nankivell and de Boissière both kept repeating this subject because both appeared to consider the abuse of women too rampant; in her submission to Moyne, Nankivell pointed out that:

When I left Trinidad the Shop Wages Committee was still sitting, but wages of these girls in the shops are very low, in the Syrian shops often with 'necessities' attached to them. No wonder these girls have to find an additional way of earning money.[17]

To an English middle class audience she sought to explain the causes of illegitimacy in the Caribbean and the burden this placed on women. When the Europeans enslaved Africans, the Europeans destroyed African family life and put nothing stable in its place. During the 1930s it was almost impossible to maintain family life under the terrible housing conditions all over the West Indies, especially in the towns where large families had to live in one room. "Women's wages are low and in most cases they have to provide the rent of their own room, the food and care and clothes for the children. One must admire them how they do it."[18] De Boissière describes the situation on the sugar estate:

On the sugar estate the white overseer – and how well they knew the Indians, riding among them all day long, not shy of enjoying the comforts some black-eyed daughters could provide – yes, they knew, they were convinced the peasants were content with a half-days' work. (p. 308)

It is to these non-official sources that one must go to see how the society really operated. Here is a world of feeling and emotion, devoid of the necessary statistical data with which the writer has to prove his arguments, but full of the stuff of which real life is made. Of considerable use for looking at how the society viewed women is another unofficial source for interpreting the 1930s. A British journalist on an extended visit to Trinidad in 1938 gives an interesting, if humorous, view of how two expatriate women view a chicken-seller:

Meanwhile, old Sarah who has been walking down Charlotte Street with a wooden platter on her head, stops and puts down the platter on the pavement. Old Sarah is tired and angry. She has sold nothing all day. She sits down in the gutter, gets a bit of old rag, out of her bosom and binds her feet. The soles are coming off her shoes. Two women in white dresses and sun glasses stop by her. 'If that isn't the darndest thing' one says. Old Sarah looks up. There is the click of a camera, and the two women laugh and turn away.

The old woman curses them in patois. But they've already moved off, searching for another cute snap.[19]

The Novelist's Account

The second major focus of our study is Ralph de Boissière. Born in 1907, he left Trinidad in 1947 for Chicago where he did a six-month auto mechanic course. In 1948, he migrated to Australia where he still resides. In 1994, he gave a most enlightening interview to Ken Ramchand; this conversation enables us to answer the question, namely, why did de Boissière break ranks with the coloured elite to which, in the colonial context, he naturally belonged? Like Florence Nankivell he was appalled by the acute ethnic demarcations of the society. As a child, for example, he was fascinated by the trams which ran throughout the capital city. After a tram ride he would hold on to brass rod atop his four-poster bed and pedal back with his heels replicating the sound of the train. On such occasions his father would reprimand him: "Goodness gracious! You're going to be a tram driver!". In this way he learned that people of his class and race were not meant to be tram drivers: "I already sensed, without being quite aware of it that I could not become a tram driver because I wasn't black. I couldn't afford to be black. So you see from those memories this conflict was in me at a very early age."[20]

During the four decades he lived in Trinidad, de Boissière lived a hand to mouth existence, moving from job to job, supported by friends when unemployed. Most of his Australian years were lived in the same day to day manner. In Trinidad, his work as a driver for an American salesman took him nearly everywhere: to Princes Town, Point Fortin, Icacos and the oil belt. He worked as an "adding machine" for a commercial company which gave him privileged access to the sugar plantations and to their account books. He had to clear goods at the Custom House regularly. This familiarity with the workers' world is well reflected in *Crown Jewel*. He took careful note, but he was turned off by this reality.

But you look back and think what a barbarous age that was – how if you were black you were at the bottom. There was just a chance that as an individual you could be a doctor, you could be a lawyer, but there was no use trying to be anything else because the whites as a group were at the top in business and in all the important positions and I could see that very early in life. You see, my mother died when I was three weeks old – my English mother, and my black nurse brought me up.[21]

These early Trinidad influences, his fascination with the Bolshevik Revolution of 1917, together with his absorption of the writing of Leo Tolstoy, were the major causes of his joining the Australian Communist Party in 1951. *Crown Jewel* was finally completed in this intense period of de Boissière's radicalism. The book had actually been started in 1937, the year of Trinidad's greatest anticolonial activity. During the Second Word War, de Boissière continued to write the novel, but the final rewriting was done in Australia. This Australian rewriting included new insights. Australia, he said, opened his eyes to a great deal of what was happening in Trinidad:

If you want to know your own people – it's good to go and live and work, that's the operative word, work, in another country. In learning something about that other country, those other people, you learn a great deal about your own.[22]

The book, when it was finally published, did very well. This potpourri of influences, namely the Trinidad eruptions, the communist influence, the longing for home in distant Down Under, and the author's own tenuous, peripatetic existence with a wife and two children, combined to produce a rare novel full of laughter and of sadness, interspersed with the authentic Trinidad dialect and reflective of a reality which formal records can hardly capture. In 1952, the (Melbourne) Australasian Book Society printed 3,000 copies which soon sold out. De Boissière recalled that there was a lot of enthusiasm for the book and "very, very good reviews. I find it is not the public that is afraid it is the publishers who are afraid".[23] In 1956, an East German publisher, Paul List, published the book in Leipzig under the Panther banner and in 1981 Allison and Busby (London) published a hardback edition whilst Picador did the paperback in that same year. It came out in eight foreign languages.[24]

What is it that makes the novel so attractive? The 1930s was a period of considerable colonial unrest. It was a time of political buoyancy after the carnage of the Great War and the gloom of the Depression. It became a period of renewal which had been promised prior to the war. This was as much for West Indians as it was for West Africans who had served as the King's Rifles or for Indians who had fought in Mesopotamia. De Boissière was able to capture that widely shared vision of the enlightenment caused by the war and the aspiration for change:

The people had long been inarticulate, blind in revolt, without a leader, without a party – a body without a head. But they had marched into the first world war with rolling drums and streaming flags, and when they returned in their thousands they no longer regarded submission as their fate. They had seen white men sweating and slaving. They had seen them combining against the white boss and winning: black men could do the same. But life, it seemed, had little use for them though they had fought off death in the trenches, and, on their return, had been counted heroes. Jobs were scarce, bellies empty. And out of their own experiences and those of English workers now was born their Worker's Party. (*Crown Jewel*, p. 85)

De Boissière needs to be read because he highlighted a South African connection in the Trinidad disturbances, a dangerous factor but never publicly acknowledged. An important cause of the disturbances was the racial arrogance of a number of South Africans who had been employed in senior positions in the oil industry. In one instance a delegation of trade unionists approached a South African construction manager at six in the morning to plead for overtime payment and for tarpaulins to protect their workplaces from sun and rain. He "dismissed them with a few rough words, and jabbing his pipe in a corner of his mouth, returned to some reports that he was checking". Out of earshot, the men cursed him loudly, even calling him "South African bastard". They wanted to get their hands on him but were "held at bay by the authority life taught them not to defy" (p. 241). Unknown to de Boissière, Colonel Beaumont, labour relations officer in the island's largest oil company, had hastened to London in July 1937 to counsel the Colonial Office regarding the treatment of black workers. He was experienced, he assured, with black workers since he was born in Natal. Trinidad labourers, he complained, had refused, like South Africans, to live in the 'lines' (barracks) which he had provided for them; they were spendthrifts and womanizers and had to be kept under firm control. The real cause of the unrest was leadership provided by some East Indians of doubtful character "including a particularly notorious East Indian agitator called Rienzi".[25] It was perhaps this same Beaumont whom de Boissière translated into the inspector of police who ordered his men to fire on an unarmed group of strikers, injuring dozens and killing their leader Clem Payne. Just before the shooting this Inspector Bullen had expressed his Beaumont-like view to a white colleague:

Looking somewhere into the distance Bullen replied: 'I've seen this sort of thing in South Africa. You've got to deal with them very firmly.'

'Pretty bad there,' Lorimer agreed. 'So few white people!'

'We're a handful. But we hold our own.'

Lorimer thought he detected a note of pride. 'Yes, that's right! Terrible in the States too.'

'They're savages, of course,' Bullen said without malice. 'A lot of people are only now beginning to realize that fact. You see,' he added after a pause, 'you may educate a lot of them but they revert. What traditions have they got behind them?'

'That's right!' Lorimer agreed. (*Crown Jewel*, pp. 330–31)[26]

From these various sources it seems clear that ethnic considerations played a major role in causing friction between the white and non-white population. The Forster Commission acknowledged that among the many matters upon which they had complaints "were alleged unfair discrimination between white and colored employees" and that "rightly or wrongly, there exists among the workers a strong feeling against the employment of South African staff, and this found marked expression during the course of our enquiry".[27] However, the commissioners found themselves "unable to obtain clear evidence whether the attitude of these members of the staff of Trinidad Leaseholds Limited is in truth such as has been represented by the workers". What they did find was that the colony was "singularly free from religious or racial animosities".[28] The evidence which they received was that "racial feeling when, and to the extent to which, it arises is a secondary symptom of some primary form of discontent".[29]

Being a woman and possessing a revolutionary consciousness one would have expected Florence Nankivell to speak about women's issues. De Boissière is positively non-traditional in the manner in which he highlights the role of women in the disturbances of the 1930s. Rhoda Reddock has amply demonstrated the major role that women played in the uprising, their considerable private and public involvement and the persecution they suffered. However, she does not fail to point out that neglect of this by historians has perpetuated "the myths of women's natural docility, acquiescence in their subordination and reactionary character".[30]

Workers' barracks at Fyzabad

BY COURTESY OF THE PUBLIC RECORD OFFICE

There are many men in *Crown Jewel*, far more than the women characters. Most of the men appear and disappear after having played their roles in the many subplots of the story. There is, however, one dominant female character who towers over everyone else: Cassandra Walcott, Cassie to her friends. Cassie starts off as a shy girl from the 'nigger yard' and, by the end of the story, she is a fearless revolutionary leader leading the mass of workers in a fight to the death. Cassie had grown up in the world of servants, scavengers and dockworkers who lived in Belmont on the outskirts of Port of Spain where "the street lamps seemed dim and sparse. Low houses, aged, propped up one another. Small cake shops, a shoemaker's, a coal merchant's cubby hole, were interspersed among them" (p. 38). She had grown up quickly, becoming a servant with the judge's family in her early teens. By nineteen she was able to reflect on an already eventful life.

The circumstances of her earlier life had not been such as to coarsen Cassie into the usual servant pattern. She had known both father and mother; she had had a home; both parents had been employed even in the hardest times. Six years before, when she was thirteen, her father had died of a fall from an oilrig. There was no workmen's compensation then. The burden of carrying the family grew too heavy for Cassie's mother. Broken by work and poor food, worn out before her time, she was reduced to pushing a little box from door to door, buying or begging empty bottles and selling them to drug stores till death claimed her. Cassie had to live. Who could do so on eight dollars a month? Along came a policeman who had been a playmate of hers. Soon he was keeping her, providing her with furniture on the installment plan. But he had begun to tire of Cassie; not she alone had charms. And one night when he could not have his way he beat her. She seized the pot of urine and threw it over him. So it ended. (p. 119)

Shortly after this incident the bailiff visited and cleared her tenement of her furniture, including bed and mattress, because she had defaulted on her payments. Desperate and destitute, she was forced to accept financial assistance from a much older man, Popito Luna, who was forty-one. In her nineteenth year she married this man-of-all-trades who hustled a living in the city. The first few years of their marriage were all bliss. She persuaded Popito to abandon his lucrative job of enabling opium to enter the island. Too many poor people were being ensnared in this dangerous habit, she insisted. Instead they both became involved in the nascent trade union movement under the black leader Le Maitre who gave them hope as they had never had before. They were both successful in organizing workers in manual areas of trade. But this success was their undoing; in the eyes of the establishment, people who spoke of militant trade unionism had to be stopped! In this way they were both inadvertently drawn into confrontation which changed Cassie for ever more. On the pretext that he was raiding a gambling house, Sergeant Duke arrested Cassie and beat her mercilessly. Her husband Popito sought to intervene on his wife's behalf but she prevented him. She was now in charge:

Popito gazed at her horrified. From her swollen, battered lip blood oozed; her entire personality was altered by the expression of hate, cunning, desperate resolve in her eyes. The blood sang in his head; but a look from her made him pull in the reins, a look not of fear – there was none in her now but of warning. (p. 150)

Immediately after the beating she lost her unborn child. Duke, the police hound dog, came next for Popito. But he had no unborn child to sacrifice, so he had to pay with his life. Worse, Cassie could hear the assassins as she hid in dung-covered grass:

'O God have mercy! Ogoun! Dada Mazookoo!'
'You son . . . bitch! Got a knife? Look out, Carr, he like a mad dog!'
She heard a terrible thud. And again. And then a third, less resonant, so that she knew it for a body blow.
'Don't hit him again,' said the unfamiliar voice.
She knew the dim light of a torch and heard the unfamiliar voice say: 'You hit him too hard, man,' and heavy breathing.
'Take him to the standpipe,' Duke said.
There was a sound of something heavy being dragged through the grass.
Cassie began to crawl behind the bushes. Never afterwards did she forget their pungent smell.
'He had a knife, you know, he had a knife . . .' (p. 205)

During the period following her husband's death Cassie became a fearless, liberated woman. After his funeral she decided to move south to Fyzabad where there was more action in the oil belt. As she took the bus "Sweet Violet" bound for Fyzabad, she faced Duke. But now the policeman saw a different person. "He gave her a searching sly sidelong look. But there was no fear in her now. The terrible glow in her eyes showed him she was a very different girl from the one he had beaten up in the station. He turned his head aside and continued on his way" (p. 213).

In the oil belt Cassie became one of the leaders of the oilworkers. When the men became caught in petty squabbling she scolded them to order; when enthusiasm flagged she mounted the platform to urge the workers to continue: "I see what happen in the baker's strike in Port of Spain. It's true they lose but the hate that mount up in you' heart through that would make you fight like a tiger nex' time" (p. 239). When the Indian/African conflict threatened to weaken the struggle she was there to bridge the gap:

Some of you afraid to join the Worker's Welfare, others feel it have no sense in that, you believe Indian and Negro kcan't help one another to make life better. I say ladies and gentlemen, put that foolish idea out of you mind. (p. 249)

Neglected women and children became her wards as she devised ways and means of assisting them in their misery. She was one of the leaders in the workers march from Fyzabad to Port of Spain. By the time the marchers had reached central Trinidad, Cassie was exhausted. But she bandaged her bleeding foot and urged the others on, refusing to board the truck which was there to pick up tired stragglers on this Long March. By July 1937 confrontation was inevitable. As de Boissière put it, "The calaloo that had long been cooking had came to a boil" (p. 321). Cassie was in the forefront of the demonstrators when the irrepressible Duke whom she knew so well was sent to arrest the leader Le Maitre. Sadly, Duke misread the scene. He saw "only the same people against whom he was accustomed to wreak his spite" (p. 322). Cassie led an onslaught of angry people against him. He sought to escape by jumping through a window and fell below, breaking his leg. Cassie now confronted Yankee the Chinese shopkeeper and demanded pitch oil. Yankee could not refuse: "He scarcely recognized Cassie in this young woman with the wild look of invincible resolution" (p. 322). But even as Cassie stood over the helplessly wriggling hulk of Duke whilst the crowd shouted "T'row it, T'row it", she could not bring herself to do so. Pity seized her – something she had not thought possible. Someone else seized the can with the kerosene from her and poured it on the begging policeman; someone threw a lighted match on Duke and that was his end. Now the real war had started; the oil belt became a virtual killing field with Cassie now a warrior, leading her fighters into battle. The leader Le Maitre had gone into hiding to escape arrest and possibly death. The beleaguered government was forced to call in British ships and troops in order to finally restore order. But Cassie had embarked on a path of resistance from which she could not desist. The novel ends with Cassie's decision to go back to Port of Spain where she felt that the workers needed proper organization in order to continue their struggle for a better life.

Who was this Cassandra Walcott? Do the traditional records speak of someone like her? Indeed they do. In his interview with Ramchand, de Boissière modestly claims that Cassie was modelled after a fellow worker at Staubles Bakery in Port of Spain.

Cassie, the girl in *Crown Jewel*, sprang out of a very unlikely girl that I worked with when I was working for Staubles Bakery. She and another girl called Gladys used to come in at seven o'clock in the morning and the three of us were packing cakes in a great big box to send to another outlet, and this girl, I've forgotten her name because she is so closely identified in my mind now with Cassie's in the book, she was a very attractive black girl, very lively – a lovely personality and I needed a character I could put through certain situations and I was thinking of her, see? But when you put a character through all these evolutions and all these situations, the person you were thinking about initially disappears and the character takes on a life of its own! See?[31]

Charlie King fell from this open window

This photograph shows burnt wood on the spot where Charlie King was set afire. The circle in the bottom left part of the photograph is in the original photograph in the Public Record Office.

In 1988, Rhoda Reddock wrote a biography of the leading woman activist during the revolt of the 1930s. Her study indicates a remarkable similarity between the activist period of Cassie's life and that of Elma François, "the first woman in the history of Trinidad and Tobago to be tried for sedition".[32] In Reddock's biography, a former activist with François states that she was strong on things African.[33] In *Crown Jewel*, Cassie is a devotee of Shango, a very active participant in its throbbing ceremonies (p. 200). In the biography, we read of a woman who had a good voice and was an explicit speaker, speaking "around the town".[34] In the novel, she is called upon to speak everywhere and the crowds hang on to her every word. We have already looked at Cassie in the march from south to north, tired but persisting. The biography of Elma François details this "Hunger March" with Tubal Uriah 'Buzz' Butler.[35] The policeman Duke, the nemesis of Cassie in *Crown Jewel*, was in real life Charlie King who harassed François and fellow activists in Port of Spain and then pursued them to Fyzabad where he was finally cornered, doused with kerosene, and burnt to death. In the novel, Cassie and her colleagues wage constant battle against Boisson, a white Creole trade unionist and politician, quite clearly modeled on Captain Cipriani, the Corsican Creole who, upon his return from serving in World War I, became actively involved in struggle. In the biography, Elma François and her fellows clearly regarded Cipriani as enemy number one. At one meeting she referred to Cipriani as "Britain's best policeman in the colonies".[36] In the novel, there is that same contemptuous reference to Cipriani: "Boisson, on his way back from the coronation, was sending telegrams expressing regret that the workers had permitted themselves to be led into violence by certain hooligan elements" (p. 328).

In looking at the many similarities between Elma François and Cassandra Walcott, finally there is the former's brave and totally fearless defence of her cause at her trial in Port of Spain in February 1938: "Jail sentences and executions do not solve our problems. It is only by organised unity can we better conditions."[37] At a public meeting in Port of Spain she shouted defiance at those who arrested strikers: "In the West Indies, the moment you say strike you get jail sentences because you are Negro and East Indian Workers, but in England and all over the world, the strike is a common thing."[38] Cassie, the heroine of *Crown Jewel*, encouraged the strikers in the South to seize the guns which were being sent from Port of Spain:

'Yes!' Cassie made a violent sweeping gesture with her arm. 'If you could get them to take them – yes. If you don't take them they will give them to the white people to shoot us down. They come quite from England to take what is ours and treat us like dogs'. (p. 338)

As de Boissière indicated in the interview already cited, Cassie is a composite character, beginning with a person with whom he worked. In reading his novel, however, it seems clear that he knew about Elma François and used her as part of his creation of Cassie. The more one reads the novel and Reddock's biography, the more striking are the similarities for the activist period of both lives.

As a sequel to the study of two non-official sources for the 1930s, we could look at the results, if any, of Florence Nankivell's campaign for the betterment of the condition of women and children. We could also glance at the manner in which de Boissière continued to portray Trinidad society from his radical perspective. In the case of Nankivell, the colony's largest and most functional social welfare group, the Coterie of Social Workers, presented her with a handsome, handwritten scroll on the eve of her departure from Trinidad. The list of grateful signatories was headed by Audrey Jeffers who had served in the United Kingdom during the Great War and had returned to pioneer social welfare work. The scroll thanked Howard Nankivell for the interest which he had taken in the Coterie, "for his many acts of kindness, and for the advice which he always gave so willingly". The Coterie then wished him speedy promotion in his new Cyprus appointment. There was even more praise for the acting colonial secretary's wife:

You were not very long in the Colony before you acquainted yourself with its social needs, and at once helped and encouraged those associated in such work by your presence, advice and practical talks whenever the occasion arose.

You have been an example to the women of Iere, many of whom are trying to raise aloft the torch of sacrifice, purpose, duty and service, in their endeavour to illuminate those lives with joy and happiness.[39]

For the longer term, what was even more important than the local praise was the manner in which the major social concerns of Nankivell were reflected in Lord Moyne's final report. Chapter 11 of the report, for example, deals at length with social needs and services in the region. The tenor of the report as well as the recommendations suggest that there were many other people and institutions in the Caribbean with shared feelings on these issues. On the question of the domestic servant, for example, the commission reported:

The normal working day of the domestic servant is from 6 am to 9 pm. She depends on the goodwill of her employer for any sick-leave, annual holiday or other time of release from duty. Workmen's compensation legislation, where it exists, does not apply to her . . . It is not surprising that some of them are helped by men, who make a small contribution to the weekly budget and share the room as 'visitors'. For those who, growing old, get no such assistance, undernourishment amounting to starvation is inevitable.[40]

The report then proceeds to make many of the very recommendations which Nankivell had been continuously making in her public speeches as well as in her memorandum to the commission. These included the establishment of creches and child welfare centres for the desperate poor, the training of girls in various crafts so that their independence could be enhanced, and improvement of housing and living conditions for women and children. The beginning of the introduction of these social services is a feature of the post-Moyne period; Florence Nankivell was one of the creators of this change of attitude of the British government.

Conclusion

Whereas Nankivell was an activist, talking about the colony's problems in the hope of reaching the proper ears and thereby effecting change, Ralph de Boissière vented his anger about the inequalities of the society by writing novels which are excellent social commentaries. In de Boissière's novels, history becomes animated as the author enters the mind of real and lively people using his authentic understanding of the times to energize the whole work. His second Trinidad novel, *Rum and Coca-Cola*, was first published in Australia in 1956, then revised and republished in 1984.[41] The story generally continues from where *Crown Jewel* ends, but here the author focuses on the coming of the Americans in the 1940s. The book is a good documentary of the changes which take place as a consequence of the Americans' leasing of bases in the Caribbean:

By 1942 thousand of West Indians were flocking to Trinidad, flocking in haste as barnyard fowls who rush for the corn that is scattered by a lavish hand at sunrise. They squeezed into the homes that would seek them shelter. No one gave any more, one sold, the times had changed. On the bases the white men were free with blows, but in the street they abandoned racial discrimination for the charms of black women and embraced them for all to see, for they bore no responsibility for Trinidad's past or Trinidad's future. Who the real masters of the island were became clearer day by day. (*Rum and Coca-Cola*, p. 121)[42]

This second novel gives us a good idea of the damage to the fragile society perpetrated by brash, young Americans to whom local men are no more than 'niggers' and the women playthings whose feelings are of no account. As the contemporary calypso (whose title de Boissière used for his novel) aptly pointed out, both mother and daughter were now "working for the Yankee dollar". De Boissière gives the human side of this tragedy; he describes the early struggle for and the debate about opening up the franchise: "They want to give the vote to the nigger in the street . . . They wouldn't know what to do with it" (p. 144).

In her Elsa Goveia Memorial Lecture at Mona, Jamaica, in 1992, Elizabeth Fox-Genovese argues that creative writing, in this case the novel, can be as valid a source for history writing as the clinical documentation and reliance on traditional sources which historians normally use. In her examination of Toni Morrison's *Beloved,* she argues that the profound emotional dimensions of the slave woman's experience can hardly be explained in the cold, analytical style of the traditional historian. In his 1996 Elsa Goveia Memorial lecture at Cave Hill, Barbados, Ken Ramchand reiterated the argument of Fox-Genovese regarding the relevance of creative writing as a tool for the historian's craft. Ramchand adds that the historian should take an imaginative look beyond the facts and should be free from the documentation/unification frame. In this way, Vic Reid's *New Day* can be of assistance to the historian's examination of Morant Bay. In the same way, Naipaul's *The Loss of El Dorado* (though not a work of fiction) and *A House for Mr. Biswas* can shed light on the historical periods covered by those books. The argument of this chapter is similar, namely, that the novels of Ralph de Boissière shed considerable light on the 1930s and 1940s in ways which are difficult to recapture through the use of traditional official sources. Similarly, the writings left by Florence Nankivell form part of another type of unofficial source. Being a woman, of Dutch parentage, and the widow of a discredited public officer, were, in the eyes of the men who ran the Colonial Office, obvious disqualifications. Consequently, the Moyne Commission was deprived of further oral evidence which she could have usefully given, and historians, relying on official sources only, are deprived of her memorandum to the commission because of these same prejudices. To be sure, the researcher needs to allocate considerable additional time for reading through lengthy novels or for detecting and travelling to family archives, not to speak of the sensitivity that has to be exercised in the use of the latter resources. But such efforts are very worthwhile for broadening the historian's outlook and adding to the richness of historical writings.

11

"We Were Going to Found a Nation...": Dramatic Representations of Haitian History by Three Martinican Writers

Bridget Jones

Foutre! / Nous allions fonder un pays / tous entre soi!
Hell! We were going to found a nation all of us together!
                                        - Aimé Césaire

The scrupulous historian, like the scholar honoured in these pages, constructs narratives of the past based on evidence, and where he or she makes guesses, says so. The dramatist enjoys more freedom to use the past to generate passions, settle scores, share visions, preach, frighten and inspire; justified in making a partial selection, which is truer to feelings than to chapter and verse. However, like the historian, the writer of historical plays hopes to make the past live for new generations and to instruct as well as please. Particularly in a postcolonial society, historical drama aims at reaching out to the collective consciousness, and in a region like the Caribbean, it lies close to the strong creative impulses of nation building.[1] As John Conteh-Morgan has observed in the French African context, colonial education gave a privileged place to the drama of Louis XIV's *Grand siècle*, so that the creation of a "counter-hegemonic historical discourse"[2] had a significant role to play in psychological liberation.

The plays to be considered here deal with Haitian history during the revolutionary period, the events which ended white colonial rule and instituted the first black republic. However, they were composed not by Haitian nationalists or European radicals,[3] but by writers from Martinique, a smaller Caribbean island which has remained tied to the apron-strings of *"la mère-patrie"*[4] as an Overseas Department of France (DOM). *Monsieur Toussaint* (1961) by Edouard Glissant, Aimé Césaire's *La Tragédie du roi Christophe* (1963), and *Dessalines* (1983) by Vincent Placoly, all focus on outstanding protagonists in the revolutionary narrative. Though based ostensibly on Haitian history, the plays inevitably also reflect feelings and frustrations in another French sugar colony which has known slave rebellions, revolts and riots, but was sheltered from the impact of the revolution, and enjoys a paradoxical order and prosperity through dependence on France. A contrast is inescapable with Haiti's turbulent history and endemic poverty.

Each play responds to a complex of more or less fully realized imperatives: it is enacting a triumphant chapter of black history, which contests the insidious emphasis of the French schoolbooks. In 1962, for example, a school history text for Martinique and Guadeloupe mentions only Napoleon Bonaparte's reactionary policy which "provoked the despairing Saint-Domingue uprising and resulted in the definitive loss for France of that magnificent colony".[5] The preface states that "Their [i.e. the Antillean] heroes and martyrs are the heroes and martyrs of France", but the only individual hero mentioned is the French abolitionist, Victor Schoelcher. As well as enlightening a local public, Césaire in particular, as a figurehead of *négritude*, central to the networks of black writers fostered by Présence Africaine in its publications and international congresses, addressed himself to African opinion. Within the Caribbean, writers as diverse as C.L.R. James, Alejo Carpentier, Kamau Brathwaite and Derek Walcott, have responded to a heroic chapter in the region's history, but for Martinicans to express their solidarity rewrites a century and a half of largely inglorious survival. The central dialogue of all three plays, variously figured, is between resistance, the maroon option, and acquiescence, the gun or the hoe. To politicians and intellectuals in Martinique, grappling with a disappointed DOM electorate in the years of the Algerian War and the Cuban Revolution, these plays explored problematic models of direct action or compromise. All three writers, though most especially Césaire, have themselves participated in party politics, so we are bound to discern also some underlying dimension of personal feeling.

I

Une vision prophétique du passé
A prophetic vision of the past
— Edouard Glissant, *Monsieur Toussaint*

The first play deals with the man C.L.R. James hailed as "the first and greatest of West Indians" – Toussaint Louverture. Glissant's play, *Monsieur Toussaint,* is the only published dramatic work by an author better known for his essays exploring *antillanité* and the nature of Caribbean discourse, for his compelling but arduous novels, and a substantial body of poetry. Such distinctions of genre are in any event somewhat artificial for what Michael Dash has called Glissant's "uninterrupted internal debate which erupts as it were into conscious articulation",[6] expressed in diverse textual forms, but often seeming to shift seamlessly between cultural and psychological perspectives on Martinique's political stalemate.

Glissant's career as a political activist began with youthful enthusiasm under the influence of his teacher at the Lycée Schoelcher, Aimé Césaire. The excitement of the election in September 1945 is unmistakably present in Glissant's first novel *La Lézarde*, published in 1958 and translated as *The Ripening.* A jubilant torchlight procession celebrates the triumph of "The Representative", "champion of the downtrodden" (Communist Party candidate Césaire). This was a moment of hope, when close union with France seemed the way forward to social equality, a unity demonstrated in the novel by a group of disparate youngsters acting together to liquidate a traitor. But disillusionment was to follow. In the postwar years Glissant established himself in Paris as writer and anticolonial commentator. He was a signatory to the 1960 "Manifeste des 121" which endorsed the right of French conscripts to refuse to fight the Algerian Front de Libération Nationale (FLN). A year later he joined with others to found a Front Antillo-Guyanais pour l'Indépendance. However, the group was dissolved almost immediately by Gaullist decree and Glissant was restricted to residence in mainland France. By the time he was allowed to return to work in Martinique, he chose to direct his energies into education, founding the Institut Martiniquais d'Etudes, a private secondary college with syllabuses featuring Caribbean studies, and an active 'outreach' programme including a journal, *Acoma,* summer schools and conferences. He has spent long periods lecturing in North America and has taken no visible role subsequently in local party politics. The will to influence and liberate Martinican minds informs all his activities, but his later writing often treats island politics with irony if not cynical scorn, as in the bravura pages on how to falsify elections and tamper with ballot boxes in *Malemort* (1975).

What this rapid chronology suggests is that *Monsieur Toussaint* is located at a crucial watershed, when Glissant is questioning participation in the political process. In a short preface to the play he calls it, in a much-quoted phrase, "a prophetic vision of the past". The characteristically opaque paradox stakes out a favourite terrain: the history of the French Caribbean with its real location between the Americas obscured by a mental web of contradictory ties to France and Africa, if not India, China, the Levant . . . A past that is both essential to '*récupérer*', to repossess in all its complexity, and necessary to transcend for a truly independent minded and specifically Caribbean future. It is unlikely that a simple play will follow.

Glissant sets Toussaint in his icy cell in the Fort de Joux in the Jura Mountains. The stiff uniformed figure is at the point of convergence of past and present, he passes from life to death, visited by figures who represent the range of actors in the drama of Haiti's liberation struggle and reenact the pressures, both personal and political, which assaulted his mind and will. It is a sombre wake, chilled to the core by Glissant's fidelity to a project of lucid exhaustivity, a poetic postmortem. As in novels such as *Le Quatrième siècle* (1964), Glissant demands that we lend ourselves to the process of elucidation, its deliberate rhythms and apparent meanders.

In contrast to the consecrated name of Toussaint Louverture, with its religious resonances, both Christian and voodoo, its homage to the precurser role, Glissant's title reduces the general to his common humanity. Indeed, in a poignant late scene, he is shown humiliatingly stripped of his iconic tricorne hat and uniform to be garbed in smock and sabots like the humblest French peasant (the irony savagely pointed by the Maroon leader/sorcerer, Mackandal, reading aloud the proclamations which had progressively promoted Toussaint to the rank of general-in-chief of the French Republic). This condensation of time (Mackandal was burnt alive in 1758, he lives again in Toussaint's doomed consciousness) and space (simultaneously cell and island) is typical of Glissant's method, concentrating on the hero an extraordinarily thorough and flexible interrogation. Some twenty-four speaking characters, both contemporaneous and historical individuals such as Granville, Caffarelli, and prestigious shades of the dead like Mackandal, or a voodoo priestess, Maman Dio, will take the stage around the hero.

The dominant tone of the first act, "The Gods", is triumphal, showing Toussaint's stature as leader, though it opens with harshly racist banter between jailer and captain and establishes the bitter physical and spiritual chill. Toussaint is hailed by Maman Dio and Mackandal who perpetuate Africa in the New World, while his wife urges the demands of home and family. In fast-moving snatches of action and dialogue, Glissant seeks to recreate the interplay of external powers, Spain and England struggling for ascendancy and competing for alliances with the rebels, while the French factions betray the divisions between settlers and metropole, and the interplay with revolutionary politics in France. Internally, the shifting loyalties of the free coloureds, the animosities of plantation society cannot be oversimplified. After establishing Toussaint's authority and wisdom, in a crucial soliloquy the leader pledges his faith in universal values, resisting *"un domaine partout fermé"*, a territory enclosed and cut off by its claim for specificity. Equally, in pointing a contrast with the heroic suicidal end of Delgrès in Guadeloupe, Glissant suggests in Toussaint the stoical valour of living out contradictions.

A later phase in his struggle is suggested in the second act "The Dead"; already he is envisaging the future, anxious for reconstruction, striving to unify, to unite Rigaud the coloured and vengeful Dessalines, while England exploits the factions and in France the First Consul Bonaparte is beginning his ascension. Sombre figures of the dead throng Toussaint's cell. Glissant possesses, to an almost morbid extent, a feeling for the inextricable web of causes and effects, of the continuance into the present of past wrongs. The figure of Mackandal, the Maroon leader, is reinforced visually by another rebel, Macaïa. As poisoner, Mackandal infiltrated indelibly into white consciousness, an intimate daily threat: for black consciousness he is a popular hero, the unslayable sorcerer, amputee,[7] emblem of African survival. Toussaint's troubled strategies of compromise are set against the intransigence of the Maroon tradition, the men of the forest, Dessalines' brutal courage, just as Césaire had to face down the challenge of Fanon, Boukman[8] and other younger militants calling for 'action' to gain independence.

In the third act, "The People", Toussaint briefly presides, striving to deploy his power to reconstruct, but Macaïa bitterly taunts him with betrayal, and Moyse, the "workers' general", is executed for insubordination. Already Dessalines raises the question of the succession, posing the issue central to every revolution, but which Haitian history illustrates with particular clarity: What constitutes legitimacy to rule? What are its conditions and limits? The lights dim again on the Haitian re-enactment, and Toussaint is assailed by the selfish demands of his gaolers, then we are back in Haiti when Napoleon sends his forces to restore slavery. His generals report Dessalines growing more savagely intransigent in the face of white duplicity. While Toussaint accepts to negotiate, the strains of the long struggle foreshadow the division between the surviving leaders.

In a final stage, "The Heroes", we relive Toussaint's ambiguous arrest, tricked into trusting Bonaparte's emissary despite his wife's warnings, fatalistically accepting to complete the crossing (Legba-Louverture), his destiny a willed self-sacrifice. We see Dessalines already repressive, executing Bélair and his pregnant wife. When Toussaint finally succumbs in France, Dessalines is waging the last combat, aided by the wet season and its fevers to vanquish the French, black and coloured fighting together. Future peace seems ill-assured, but in a lyrical celebration of 'Toussaint général' he is called to rejoin the shades of the departed. Glissant brings more African allusions into the final stages, yet also makes a point of the attachment of the peasant gaoler Manuel.

Even in this much condensed outline, the ambitions of Glissant's play should be evident. Although enriched with the swirl of shifting layers of action and reflection, and heightened by a number of laments, chants and effects of light and sound, the play tests the stamina. It is couched predominantly in a formal register of French which gives little distinctive voice to the range of characters deployed.[9] The historical information is considerable, and a satisfying shape is created by the control of dominant tone and mood for each stage in the unfolding tale. But from the outset this is a doomed hero, trapped in the web of his fatal destiny, despite his brilliance destroyed by a superhuman task; there is a numbing bitter irony (*"Toussaint-la-Fermeture"* ["Toussaint-closing-down"] says Langles, the unsympathetic deputy commander of the Fort) in Glissant's conception.

Glissant enmeshes his hero so thoroughly that he seems to prophesy the continued ambivalent dependency of so many Caribbean states, an underlying personal despondency despite all the images of heroism. No doubt the revolutionary period in France supplies an extreme metaphor to illuminate the vulnerability of the periphery: changes in policy in the colonizing power were so rapid and radical. However, in 1961 the internal issues of decolonization raised by the play – persistent suspicions of race and class in a plantation society, the quality and problematic transmission of leadership, and, for factions campaigning for independence by revolutionary violence, how to manage the transition to social order and peaceful development – were still subject to intensive debate.

Glissant's text of 1961 is so complex that a shorter version for the stage appeared in 1978, produced in Paris by the Théâtre Noir, and it is apparently only on French radio that the full script has been produced.[10] His essays dealing with theatre circle around the notion that in Martinique an alienated society does not share the myths that would nourish serious drama; trivialized folklore or borrowed French modes prevail. In *Monsieur Toussaint*, by staging at length an "ambiguous morality where the values and the nothingness of human effort are equally uncertain" (Silenieks quoted by Dash), Glissant seems to foreshadow a deepening pessimism; as he wrote bitterly after Carifesta 1976 in Jamaica, "Our heroes, of necessity, are primarily those of other people."[11]

II

J'ai voulu . . . leur apprendre à bâtir leur demeure
I wanted to teach them to build their dwelling place
                                        - Aimé Césaire, *Roi Christophe*

When we turn to the dramatic work of Aimé Césaire, we are looking at a particular phase in the work of a man who has achieved ountstanding success both in literature and in politics. Once elected to represent Martinique as a Communist *député* in the French National Assembly in 1945, he was continuously re-elected until he chose to retire, and even in 1995, at the age of eighty-two, the municipal electorate of Fort-de-France voted him into power yet again as mayor, under the slogan "We already have the best". Such a long career has contained plenty of controversy and compromise, including a resounding rejection of the French Communist Party in order to found his own Parti Progressiste Martiniquais (PPM), encapsulated in the 1956 *Lettre à Maurice Thorez*, and the 1981 announcement of a *'moratoire'* which, in the wake of François Mitterand's election to the presidency, effectively suspended any active pursuit by the PPM of independence from France. But however diverse the responses to his political leadership, Césaire as a writer has been the object of worldwide admiration and critical analysis. The *négritude* epic *Cahier d'un retour au pays natal* (first published in part in 1939) remains his most important work, and is now prescribed among the canonic texts studied by young people all over the French-speaking world.

Drama in Césaire's output corresponds to a period in his career when he sought to reach a broader public than the readers of his often abstrusely erudite poems, and speaks both to the growing fragmentation of left-wing politics within Martinique and to newly independent African nations forging their identities after colonial domination by France. A more abstract and incantatory symbolist drama, evoking the rebel who slays his white master, was published in a volume of early poetry in 1946, but *La Tragédie du roi Christophe* (1963) stages Césaire's vision for a liberated nation and plays out to a tragic end a leader's urgently clumsy desire to remould the citizens. This play was followed by a rather more didactic and unwieldy play on Patrice Lumumba, *Une Saison au Congo* (1965), and a more stylized study of the colonial dilemma in *Une Tempête* (1970), based on Shakespeare's *Tempest*.

Césaire responded early to the inspirational quality of Haitian history, hailing in the *Cahier "Haiti où la négritude se mit debout pour la première fois"* ("Haiti where negritude stood up for the first time") and dwelling imaginatively on the death of Toussaint *"un homme seul emprisonné de blanc"* ("a man alone, imprisoned by whiteness"). In 1944, just before embarking on a political career, Césaire visited Haiti for an extended lecture tour. His play bears the imprint of a personal visit to the Citadel at Le Cap, and responses to the vitality of oral history and folk art which keep alive the presence of the revolution in the popular imagination.[12] Césaire published a documented biographical study of Toussaint in 1961, which draws comparisons with Martinique, and concludes recalling the revolutionary principles, the recognition of the rights of man for which Toussaint mobilized in battle the Haitian people, but which prevailed in Martinique only through a long erratic process of bargaining and sporadic unrest.

The protagonist of Césaire's *Tragédie du roi Christophe* is, like Glissant's hero, a complex figure, the centre of a play which offers multiple images of post-colonial leadership, some positive, some negative, and seems in an intimate way to body forth Césaire's own ambivalence about his political power and relationship with the people of Martinique.

By taking an outline modelled on the 'Shakespearean' chronicle, the rise and fall of a monarch, Césaire can celebrate Henry Christophe's triumphs while posing critically the issues raised by his failure and death. Christophe is first shown positively as a rising proud black general, rejecting constitutional power-sharing with the coloured Pétion, acclaimed by the 'masses' (the marketplace where his agents manipulate the mob). Ardently he strives to structure, out of the anomie he inherits (symbolized by metaphors of clay and shit, mud and dust), a social order. In his northern kingdom, he institutes orders of nobility, compels his subjects to marry, and seeks to crown a social hierarchy (imitated from the English court) with himself as monarch, and fittingly magnificent public works. Césaire clarifies the symbolic pattern of the 'Negro ascending' by laying great stress on the construction of the Citadel on a peak in the northern mountains. Out of the rubble of the slave regime, its ruined estate houses and town mansions, the cut stones are retrieved, workers toil up the impossible gradients to build a towering Citadel. Supreme irony: the monument to freedom demands forced labour. The central sections of this play tend to be over-weighted with overt didacticism on the need to mobilize the will to work at all levels of the society, both inspirational, as in the much-recited tirade: *"Je demande trop aux hommes! Mais pas assez aux nègres, Madame!"* ("I ask too much of men? But not enough of black men, Madame!", I, 8), officially proclaimed *"la liberté ne peut subsister sans le travail. / Signé: Christophe"* ("Freedom cannot endure without labour. / Signed: Christophe", II, 1), or, more frantically, descending into megalomania: *"Ah! Quel métier! Dresser ce peuple!"* ("Ah! What a trade! Training this people!", II, 4). Having posed for his audience Christophe's dilemma, a labour force knowing only coercion and skilled in passive resistance, a social and political order to be constructed at speed (and using what tainted models?) from an exhausted and divided people, Césaire seems to retreat from pursuing these issues. In the final act Christophe is weakened and isolated, his gesture of self-immolation projects him beyond an insoluble social and political situation (his difficult manouevring with overseas enemies and patrons, and with the Catholic hierarchy, is also sketched in). All Césaire's considerable gifts of poetic rhetoric are mobilized to distract and dazzle as the king invokes Africa, mediated by chants to the voodoo *loa* and the figure of Baron-Samedi. A suicidal pistol shot rings out, reverberating in a solemn tribute of drumbeats and cannons, he is hailed on the mountain top as a phoenix who will rise again from the ashes of his hopes.

Liberation, especially black revolutionary liberation, in its pure ideal state, finds potent expression in Christophe's vision of the luminous Citadel glowing in the darkness, in the emblematic golden phoenix, in the figure of Hope leading Metellus and his men onward, dancing in the wild mountain terrain. The ideal inspires by remaining preserved from daily reality: Metellus is executed and his intransigent purity, like Che Guevara's, is preserved from aging. Christophe by contrast struggles to cause freedom to take root in the intractable human material he inherits.

This play is rich in the varied cultural forms of the Caribbean, with scenes in market and field, cathedral and court, and, unlike Glissant's sober text, offers abundant scope to the director. Its first production benefitted from the suggestions of the African and Caribbean cast assembled by director Jean-Marie Serreau who developed the music and voodoo elements during rehearsals.[13] The kaleidoscopic surface is designed, however, to build up a portrait of the king that puzzles by its contradictions, thought provoking in the Brechtian manner. Lightning shifts of mood and manner, a central figure fitfully illuminated, now oppressive, now inspirational, jovial and tormented by turns, render the play extraordinarily difficult to meld into a satisfying whole. It is much more often read than performed. The majority of critical studies[14] have come from Césaire's African, American or European admirers, and it was thirteen years before the play was performed in Martinique, on the occasion of an official visit by Senegal's President Léopold Senghor. The 1991 production at the Comédie Française sums up the uneasy status of the work: a director, Idrissa Ouedraogo, from Burkina Faso, mainly known for his films, a cast all of French classical actors with the sole exception of Haitian Toto Bissainthe, a humourless and truncated script, and very mixed reviews. Today, most local productions, not only of the plays but also attempted dramatizations of such texts as *Discours sur le colonialisme*,[15] take place under the aegis of the SERMAC, the cultural arm of the Fort-de-France municipality, with critical reactions polarized predictably according to political affiliation.

When Césaire's four dramatic works are considered as a sequence, the clash between visionary leader and external and internal forces of opposition is all the clearer. As he said in a 1964 interview, after decolonization: *". . . se pose le problème positif de former des Nations qui à la fois gardent certaines traditions, maintiennent leur autonomie et s'adaptent aux exigences du monde moderne"* ("... the problem has to be tackled constructively of creating nations which simultaneously maintain some of their traditions, preserve their autonomy and adapt to the demands of the modern world").[16] Rather like the generous project recalled in the epigraph to this article – founding a nation open to all the islands, to all blacks in the world[17] – it is a doomed ideal for small, poorly endowed societies. In his controversial 1993 study, *Aimé Césaire: Une traversée paradoxale du siècle*, Raphaël Confiant seeks to recombine the poet and the politician, to test the rhetoric against the daily action. He stresses Césaire's distance from the creole reality of ordinary Martinicans: *"tout comme les héros de ses pièces de théâtre, il n'a aucune confiance en ce peuple"* ("just like the heroes of his plays, he has no confidence in the [our] people"),[18] and a tendency to strike attitudes on a world stage when at home he is betrayed by the shortcomings of the political apparatus. Christophe's solitary struggle, culminating in self-sacrifice and apotheosis, is a consoling way of transcending the day to day effort of reconciling French dominance and Martinican pride. Césaire remains a lonely leader; he presides over a more prosperous and equitable society, but at the cost of ever greater economic dependency on transfers from France, fickle tourist gleanings and declining productivity. Full 'Liberation' is still no more than a luminous mirage gleaming over the hills.

III

Si je titube et que mes pas glissent, c'est qu'une terre orageuse me transporte et que je suis habité par l'hallucination de la vie que je porte en mes mains . . .

If I stagger and my feet slip, that's because I am borne on a stormy land and possessed by the vision of the life that I carry in my hands

- Vincent Placoly, *Dessalines*

Some twenty years after Césaire and Glissant, Vincent Placoly composed a historical play spanning the interval between Toussaint and Henry Christophe: *Dessalines*. Placoly belongs to a later generation, he was born in 1946, the year Césaire's bill achieved departmental status for Martinique, and as a militant student was in Paris in May 1968. His play was awarded an official prize and first published by the Cuban Casa de las Américas in 1983, signalling radical Caribbean solidarity, not the usual publishing ties with Paris. The author's premature death in 1992 has redirected attention to his work, and a new edition has appeared.[19] The play was produced by Henri Melon for the Centre Dramatique Régional in 1994, but proved rather less popular with the Martinican public than Placoly's commemorative historical pageants and comedies.

A high school teacher of French language and literature, broadcaster, journalist and writer, Placoly adapted or composed a number of works for local theatre groups, especially José Alpha's Teat Lari. His literary work reflects with conscious indirectness the political loyalties explicit in his journalism. His choice to portray the May uprising and the abolition of slavery in 1848 through the journal of a progressive white planter, as in *Frères volcans* (1983), foregrounds the problematic diversity of perspectives on any historical 'event'. In the 1970s he was a founder member of the Groupe Révolution Socialiste (GRS), Trotskyist in thinking, a small splinter group composed mainly of intellectuals, but through its meetings and regular news-sheet, a forum for independent far-left positions. It has survived only uncertainly in the post-Mitterand era, suffering when its most credible leader, Edouard Délépine, defected to the PPM, and voters' support for independence mainly mobilized around the Mouvement Indépendantiste Martiniquais (MIM) under Alfred Marie-Jeanne in his fief of Rivière Pilote.[20] The radicals of Placoly's generation have thinned out, some to espouse the cultural and ecological platform of *créolité*, some migrating, others joining the majority parties.

The text of *Dessalines*, subtitled ambiguously "The passion (calvary) of/for independence", was completed about 1982. The brilliant general, called a "one-sided genius" by C.L.R. James, brought Toussaint's work to its bloody conclusion, matching the French in intransigence and brutality. Placoly, like Glissant, situates Dessalines in the Maroon tradition, as a rebel of the forest, waging *"ma guerre de nègre"* to the death. He is very conscious of the opposing images: for white tradition Dessalines is a barbarous monster, emblem of black revenge; for Haitian tradition and black rulers like François Duvalier, he is hailed as the liberating emperor who finally triumphed over the colonial powers. In Glissant's play he is the archetypal black militant, itching to strip off his shirt and display the scars of the whip, his flesh etched indelibly with the white man's oppression which must be avenged. Dessalines' "scorched earth" policies aimed only at defeating the enemy. He is credited with tearing out the white strip from the *tricouleur* to create the Haitian flag of independence in red and blue, just as his regime excluded whites from ownership of land or property.[21]

Césaire had remodelled the historical Christophe to motivate more positively his authoritarian rule. Placoly is also reluctant to deal in a stereotype either of bloodthirsty monster or heroic Black Power ideologue. As he discussed in a lecture given in Cuba in 1991, when writing the play, the sparse if controversial realities of Dessalines' human existence were subsumed in a more general image of Caribbean resistance against the European invader. He relates Dessalines to Columbus landing in 1492, to Carpentier's novels and Césaire's reworking of Caliban's challenge to Prospero.[22] Placoly is much less concerned than Glissant to lead his audience towards detailed and specific historical understanding.

This Dessalines mainly speaks in an elevated register of formal French, apart from quoting a few creole proverbs, and demonstrates a thoughtful and statesmanlike cast of mind. His military strategies aimed to exterminate the enemy, to devastate the land, but in Act II he is shown as emperor, hearing petitions, seeking to reimpose control, looking forward to a new world fashioned out of a ravaged countryside. Already Pétion's faction is muttering, distancing itself from his policies, but Dessalines wills a future independent of all external exploitation. A telling scene shows the humiliation of a Belgian seeking to export hard wood (Act II, 5). When opposition culminates in the Emperor's assassination, Placoly nevertheless shows Pétion ordering a salvo in honour of the founder of independence. Though his discourse is that of the high French theatrical tradition, "Dessalines-Congo" both mocks the image of himself as wild man of the woods and affirms his black inheritance by a *yanvalou*, a night of African song and dance. As in Césaire's scenes at the court of King Christophe, tokens of French civilization, here Sèvres and

Limoges porcelain, are sample ingredients to demonstrate the creolization process of cultural fusion.

However, Placoly virtually decentres the historical narrative by creating the character of Coquille des Cayes, wordsmith and musician in the tradition of Césaire's griot/Joueur de Sanza in *Saison au Congo*, or the Fool Hugonin in *Christophe*. This chorus figure is close to an alter ego, in love with language (*coquille* means, among other things, 'misprint') as well as strong liquor. Through this character, Placoly introduces a new and stimulating dimension into his play, problematizing historical truth. Thus *Dessalines* raises not only the already well-rehearsed topics of Haiti's relationships with European powers, strategies for reconstruction once the army has overcome the enemy, the difficulty of securing solidarity among the rival generals, but also a postmodern concern: What is the status of our knowledge of these events? Coquille as scribe is ordered to write France out of the story, to show Bonaparte as defeated, but also to 'blacken' Dessalines' reputation. The emperor is shown musing over the role of song and fable in representing his rule, led to reflect on the validity of any 'history', with its selective bias and manufactured heroes and villains. Using a main protagonist and a moment particularly subject to divergent racial or national views, Placoly's play questions the status of Caribbean historical narrative, both scribal and oral.

A second invented main character also shows Placoly's originality. The rather heedless patriarchal attitudes found in Césaire and Glissant,[23] casting Madame Toussaint and Madame Christophe with dismaying conventionality as anxious mothers and spouses urging the claims of family life against politics, are jettisoned. The *vivandière* Defilée, caring for weary and wounded young soldiers, rising to the heights of palace living, then a crazed woman whose plaintive creole songs concentrate all the futile suffering, comes to stand for war-torn Haiti itself. With a poignant irony, the role was taken by the author's widow, Mina.

Placoly's *Dessalines* is somewhat too worthy and wordy to create a convincing revisionist portrait, it remains indebted to Césaire's *Christophe* (which he had seen as a student in Serreau's production) for some of its liveliest scenes. However, in its focus on the role of the writer/musician, it reflects the displacement of the political debate towards the cultural sphere which is a feature of today's Martinique. A greater awareness of the wider Caribbean also strikes the reader, not only through the Cuban connection but by references to Dessalines' support for Miranda and aid to Bolívar and Delgrès. Placoly was often nicknamed 'the American' in recognition of his will to distance himself from France in order to inhabit the real space of his hemisphere.

IV

It is a sobering thought that none of these three historical dramas has proved a viable play for popular performance, they have usually enjoyed a respectful '*succès d'estime*' and a much more extensive life as literary texts. Each tries to do justice to the unique complexity of revolutionary Haiti and pay tribute to the founding and early years of the first black republic. But in every case, the author's respect for the intricacies of event and motivation leads to a reflective ambivalent attitude, keen to celebrate the extraordinary valour of the combatants, but too emotionally close to the ironic contrast with Martinique to resist tracing complexities which overwhelm the heroes and open up a sombre climate of admiration and fear. Placoly casts himself as the tippling troubadour who plays with the French language and muses on history, Césaire identifies with the sacrificial victim, soaring back to Africa and leaving a disgruntled people muttering behind, Glissant's hero sinks into frozen immobility as the opaque grip of fatality settles on a tortured past and an uncertain future.

Rejoining a consecrated tradition of French high culture, the tragic drama reflecting on kingship and nationhood, each author struggles with a resistant form and a resistant content. The 'quarrel with history' remains unresolved. Perhaps in the very concept of the formal historical tragedy we are looking at a symptom of the oppressive hold of French cultural models on the Antillean literary imagination.

Notes

Notes to the Introduction

The authors would like to thank Alejandro de la Fuente for his comments on this Introduction.

1. Joseph Zobel, *Black Shack Alley*, trans. by Keith Q. Warner (Washington, DC: Three Continents Press, 1980 [1950]), 32–33.
2. Donald Wood, *Trinidad in Transition: The Years After Slavery* (London: Oxford University Press, 1968), 10.
3. For a good, recent review of the literature on emancipation in the British Caribbean, see Kevin D. Smith, "A Fragmented Freedom: The Historiography of Emancipation and its Aftermath in the British West Indies", *Slavery and Abolition* 16, no. 1 (April 1995): 101–30. Probably the best general work in English on the Hispanic Caribbean is Manuel Moreno Fraginals, Frank Moya Pons and Stanley L. Engerman, eds., *Between Slavery and Free Labor The Spanish-speaking Caribbean in the Nineteenth Century* (Baltimore: The Johns Hopkins University Press, 1985). For a recent comparative overview, see Franklin W. Knight, "The Disintegration of the Caribbean Slave Systems, 1772–1886", in Franklin W. Knight, ed., *UNESCO General History of the Caribbean, Vol. III: The Slave Societies of the Caribbean* (London: UNESCO/Macmillan, 1997), 322–45.
4. For an excellent recent discussion of this process focusing on Jamaica, Trinidad, and Haiti, see Richard D.E. Burton, *Afro-Creole: Power, Opposition, and Play in the Caribbean* (Ithaca: Cornell University Press, 1997).
5. For these issues, see Verene Shepherd, Bridget Brereton and

Barbara Bailey, eds., *Engendering History: Caribbean Women in Historical Perspective* (Kingston: Ian Randle; London: James Currey, 1995).

6. Barry W. Higman, "Theory, Method and Technique in Caribbean Social History", *Journal of Caribbean History* 20, no. 1 (1985–86): 1–29.

7. Richard Frucht, "A Caribbean Social Type: Neither 'Peasant' nor 'Proletarian' ", *Social and Economic Studies* 16, no. 3 (1967): 295–300.

8. See Veront M. Satchell, *From Plots to Plantations: Land Transactions in Jamaica, 1866–1900* (Mona: Institute of Social and Economic Research, UWI, 1990).

9. See R.W. Beachey, *The British West Indies Sugar Industry in the late-Nineteenth Century* (Oxford: Basil Blackwell, 1957).

10. *Report of the Commission on the Juvenile Population of Jamaica*, 1879, cited in F.R. Augier and Shirley C. Gordon, *Sources of West Indian History* (London: Longman, 1962), 188–89.

11. James Cummings, "Barrack Rooms", *Beacon* (Trinidad) 1, no. 7 (October 1931): 21.

12. Sidney W. Mintz long ago pointed out that the peasantry was 'reconstituted', established *after* the advent of capitalistic production that characterized the sugar estates. See his *Caribbean Transformations* (Chicago: Aldine, 1974).

13. Bonham C. Richardson, "Depression Riots and the Calling of the 1897 West India Royal Commission", *Nieuwe West-Indische Gids* 66, nos. 3 & 4 (1992): 185. See, also, Richard A. Lobdell, "British Officials and the West Indian Peasantry, 1842–1938", in Malcolm Cross and Gad Heuman, eds., *Labour in the Caribbean: From Emancipation to Independence* (London: Macmillan, 1988), 195–207.

14. Jean Besson has written widely on family land. For example, see her "Symbolic Aspects of Land in the Caribbean: The Tenure and Transition of Land Rights among Caribbean Peasantries", in Malcolm Cross and Arnaud Marks, eds., *Peasants, Plantations and Rural Communities in the Caribbean* (Guilford: Department of Sociology, University of Surrey; Leiden: Department of Caribbean Studies, Royal Institute of Linguistics and Anthropology, 1979), 86–116; "Family Land and Caribbean Society: Toward an Ethnography of Afro-Caribbean Peasantries", in Elizabeth M. Thomas-Hope, ed., *Perspectives on Caribbean Regional Identity* (Liverpool: Centre for Latin American Studies, University of Liverpool, 1984), 57–83; and "Land, Kinship and Community in the Post-Emancipation Caribbean: Regional Perspectives and Societal Variations", in Karen Fog Olwig, ed., *Small Islands, Large Questions: Society, Culture and Resistance in the Post-Emancipation Caribbean* (London: Frank Cass, 1995), 17–37. For an important study of the relation between peasants and

international economic forces, see Michel-Rolph Trouillot, *Peasants and Capital: Dominica in the World Economy* (Baltimore: Johns Hopkins University Press, 1988).

15. For this period in Trinidad, see Bridget Brereton, *A History of Modern Trinidad, 1783–1962* (London: Heinemann, 1981), chs. 8 and 9; and Alvin Magid, *Urban Nationalism: A Study of Political Development in Trinidad* (Gainesville: University Presses of Florida, 1988). On *"la guerre du Diamant"*, see Richard Price, *The Convict and the Colonel* (Boston: Beacon Press, 1998), ch. 1. For the Martinican political context, see Cécile Celma, "La vie politique en Martinique des années 1910–1939", in Roland Suvélor, ed., *Historial Antillais* (Pointe-à-Pitre: Société Dajani, 1981), 5:318–59.

16. Of the various works on the US interventions and the general nature of US-Caribbean relations during this period, see, for example, Edward J. Berbusse, *The United States in Puerto Rico, 1898–1900* (Chapel Hill: University of North Carolina Press, 1966); Bruce J. Calder, *The Impact of Intervention: The Dominican Republic during the US Occupation of 1916–1924* (Austin: University of Texas Press, 1984); Truman R. Clark, *Puerto Rico and the United States, 1917–1933* (Pittsburgh: University of Pittsburgh Press, 1975); James L. Deitz, *Economic History of Puerto Rico: Institutional Change and Capitalist Development* (Princeton: Princeton University Press, 1986);

Cathy Duke, "The Idea of Race: The Cultural Impact of American Intervention in Cuba, 1898–1912", in Blanca G. Silvestrini, ed., *Politics, Society and Culture in the Caribbean* (San Juan: University of Puerto Rico, Association of Caribbean Historians, 1983), 87–109; Lester D. Langley, *The United States and the Caribbean in the Twentieth Century* (Athens: University of Georgia Press, 1982); Anthony P. Maingot, *The United States and the Caribbean* (London: Macmillan, 1994); Arturo Morales Carrión, ed., *Puerto Rico: A Political and Cultural History* (New York: Norton, 1983); Louis A. Pérez, Jr., *Cuba Between Empires, 1878–1902* (Pittsburgh: University of Pittsburgh Press, 1983), and Pérez, *Cuba Under the Platt Amendment, 1902–1934* (Pittsburgh: University of Pittsburgh Press, 1986); Hans Schmidt, *The United States Occupation of Haiti, 1915–1934* (New Brunswick: Rutgers University Press, 1971); and Teresita Martínez Yglesia, *Cuba, primera república, secunda ocupación* (Havana: Editorial de Ciencias Sociales, 1976). On the United States' increasing cultural hegemony, see Franklin W. Knight, "United States Cultural Influence on the English-Speaking Caribbean During the Twentieth Century", in Silvestrini, ed., *Politics, Society and Culture*, 17–35. On the theme of the complex US relations with Caribbean strongmen, see, for example, G. Pope Atkins and Larman C. Wilson, *The United States and the*

Trujillo Regime (New Brunswick: Rutgers University Press, 1972).

17. Of the many works on inter-regional migration, see, for example, Philippe I. Bourgois, *Ethnicity at Work: Divided Labor on a Central American Banana Plantation* (Baltimore: Johns Hopkins University Press, 1989); Aviva Chomsky, *West Indian Workers and the United Fruit Company in Costa Rica, 1870–1940* (Baton Rouge: Louisiana State University Press, 1996); Michael L. Conniff, *Black Labor on a White Canal: Panama, 1904–1981* (Pittsburgh: University of Pittsburgh Press, 1985); Ronald N. Harpelle, "The Social and Political Integration of West Indians in Costa Rica: 1930–50", *Journal of Latin American Studies* 25, no. 1 (1993): 103–20; Franklin W. Knight, "Jamaican Migrants and the Cuban Sugar Industry, 1900–1934", in Moreno Fraginals, Moya Pons, and Engermann, eds., *Between Slavery and Free Labor*, 94–114; Velma Newton, *The Silver Men: West Indian Labour Migration to Panama, 1850–1914* (Mona: Institute of Social and Economic Research, UWI, 1984); Karen Fog Olwig, *Global Culture, Island Identity: Continuity and Change in the Afro-Caribbean Community of Nevis* (Philadelphia: Harwood Academic Publishers, 1993); Trevor W. Purcell, *Banana Fallout: Class, Color, and Culture Among West Indians in Costa Rica* (Los Angeles: Center for Afro-American Studies, University of California, Los Angeles, 1993); Bonham C. Richardson, *Caribbean Migrants: Environment and Human Survival on St Kitts and Nevis* (Knoxville: University of Tennessee Press, 1985), Richardson, *Panama Money in Barbados, 1900–1920* (Knoxville: University of Tennessee Press, 1985), and Richardson, "Caribbean Migrations, 1838–1985", in Franklin W. Knight and Colin A. Palmer, eds., *The Modern Caribbean* (Chapel Hill: University of North Carolina Press, 1989), 203–28.

18. Of the works on the 'race war of 1912', see, for example, Duke, "The Idea of Race"; Rafael Fermoselle, *Política y color en Cuba: la guerrita de 1912* (Montevideo: Géminis, 1974); Aline Helg, *Our Rightful Share: The Afro-Cuban Struggle for Equality, 1886–1912* (Chapel Hill: University of North Carolina Press, 1995); Louis A. Pérez, Jr., "Politics, Peasants, and People of Color: The 1912 'Race' War in Cuba Reconsidered", *Hispanic American Historical Review* 56 (1986): 509–39; and Serafín Portuondo Linares, *Los independientes de color: Historia del Partido Independiente de Color* (Havana: Ministerio de Educación, Dirección de Cultura, 1950). For discussions that place the *guerrita* in Afro-Cuban history, see Tomás Fernández Robaina, *El negro en Cuba, 1902–1958* (Havana: Editorial de Ciencias Sociales, 1990); Alejandro de la Fuente, " 'With All and For All': Race, Inequality and Politics in Cuba, 1900–1930" (PhD dissertation, University of Pittsburgh, 1996);

and Thomas T. Orum, "The
Politics of Color: The Racial
Dimension of Cuban Politics
During the Early Republican
Years, 1900–1912" (PhD
dissertation, New York University,
1975).

19. On Garvey, see Rupert Lewis,
*Marcus Garvey: Anti-Colonial
Champion* (Trenton, NJ: Africa
World Press, 1988); Rupert Lewis
and Patrick Bryan, eds., *Garvey: His
Work and Impact* (Mona, Jamaica:
Institute of Social and Economic
Research, UWI, 1988); Rupert
Lewis and Maureen Warner-Lewis,
eds., *Garvey: Africa, Europe, the
Americas* (Mona, Jamaica: Institute
of Social and Economic Research,
UWI, 1986); Tony Martin, *Race
First: The Ideological and
Organizational Struggles of Marcus
Garvey and the Universal Negro
Improvement Association* (Westport,
Conn.: Greenwood Press, 1976);
Judith Stein, *The World of Marcus
Garvey: Race and Class in Modern
Society* (Baton Rouge: Louisiana
State University Press, 1986); Tony
Sewell, *Garvey's Children: The Legacy
of Marcus Garvey* (1987; reprint,
London: Macmillan, 1990); as well
as a special issue of *Jamaica Journal*
to mark the centenary of his birth
(20, no. 3 [August–October 1987]).
A wealth of primary sources has
been collected. See Robert A. Hill,
ed., *The Marcus Garvey and Universal
Negro Improvement Association Papers*,
7 vols. (Berkeley: University of
California Press, 1983–85); and
Amy Jacques-Garvey, ed.,
Philosophy and Opinions of Marcus
Garvey, vols. 1 and 2 (New York:
Antheneum, 1969) and Jacques-
Garvey and E.U. Essien-Udom,
eds., *More Philosophy and Opinions of
Marcus Garvey*, vol. 3 (London:
Frank Cass, 1977).

20. On Bedward, see W.F. Elkins,
*Street Preachers, Faith Healers and
Herb Doctors in Jamaica, 1890–1925*
(New York: Revisionist Press,
1977); Martha Warren Beckwith,
*Black Roadways: A Study of Jamaican
Folk Life* (Chapel Hill: University
of North Carolina Press, 1929),
165–71; Patrick Bryan, *The Jamaican
People, 1880–1902: Race, Class and
Social Control* (London: Macmillan,
1991), 41–45; Burton, *Afro-Creole*,
115–19; and Roscoe M. Pierson,
"Alexander Bedward and the
Jamaica Native Baptist Free
Church", in Randall K. Burkett
and Richard Newman, eds., *Black
Apostles* (1969; reprint Boston:
G.K. Hall, 1978), 1–10. On the
'religious idiom' in Jamaican
popular protest, see, for example,
Abigail B. Bakan, *Ideology and Class
Conflict in Jamaica: The Politics of
Rebellion* (Montreal and Kingston:
McGill-Queen's University Press,
1990); Burton, *Afro-Creole*, ch. 3;
Trevor Munroe, "The Impact of
the Church on the Political
Culture of the Caribbean: The
Case of Jamaica", *Caribbean
Quarterly* 37, no. 1 (1991): 83–97;
and Ken Post, *Arise Ye Starvelings:
The Jamaican Labour Rebellion of
1938 and its Aftermath* (The Hague:
Martinus Nijhoff, 1978). Some
important works which take a
historical perspective on Rastafari

are Horace Campbell, *Rasta and Resistance: From Marcus Garvey to Walter Rodney* (Trenton, NJ: Africa World Press, 1987); Barry Chevannes, *Rastafari: Roots and Ideology* (Syracuse: Syracuse University Press, 1994); Frank Jan van Dijk, *Jahmaica: Rastafari and Jamaican Society, 1930–1990* (Utrecht: ISOR, 1993); and Robert A. Hill, "Dread History: Leonard P. Howell and Millenarian Visions in Early Rastafari Religions in Jamaica", *Epoché: Journal of the History of Religions at UCLA* 9 (1981): 30–71, among others. A good contextualization of Jamaican religions is George Eaton Simpson, *Religious Cults in the Caribbean: Jamaica, Trinidad and Haiti* (Río Piedras: Institute of Caribbean Studies, University of Puerto Rico, 1970), while a recent collection comparing Caribbean religions is Margarite Fernández Olmos and Lizabeth Paravisini-Gebert, eds., *Sacred Possessions: Vodou, Santería, Obeah and the Caribbean* (New Brunswick: Rutgers University Press, 1997). See, also, Shirley C. Gordon, *God Almighty Make Me Free: Christianity in Preemancipation Jamaica* (Bloomington: Indiana University Press, 1996); Monica Schuler, "Myalism and the African Religious Tradition in Jamaica", in Margaret C. Crahan and Franklin W. Knight, eds., *Africa and the Caribbean: The Legacies of a Link* (Baltimore: Johns Hopkins University Press, 1979), 65–79; and Robert J. Stewart, *Religion and*

Society in Post-Emancipation Jamaica (Knoxville: University of Tennessee Press, 1992).

21. Mervyn C. Alleyne, "A Linguistic Perspective on the Caribbean", in Sidney W. Mintz and Sally Price, eds., *Caribbean Contours* (Baltimore: The Johns Hopkins University Press, 1985), 160. Of the many works tracing the African influence on Caribbean languages, see Alleyne's *Comparative Afro-American* (Ann Arbor, Mich.: Karoma Press, 1980) and *Roots of Jamaican Culture* (London: Pluto Press, 1989), and Maureen Warner-Lewis, *Guinea's Other Suns: The African Dynamic in Trinidad Culture* (Dover, Mass.: The Majority Press, 1991), among others. On Caribbean festivals, Carnival, steelband, and calypso, see John W. Nunley and Judith Bettelheim, *Caribbean Festival Arts: Each and Every Bit of Difference* (Seattle: St Louis Art Museum and the University of Washington Press, 1988); Errol Hill, *The Trinidad Carnival: Mandate for a National Theatre* (Austin: University of Texas Press, 1972); Stephen Stuempfle, *The Steelband Movement: The Forging of a National Art in Trinidad and Tobago* (Philadelphia: University of Pennsylvania Press, 1995); Gordon Rohlehr, *Calypso and Society in Pre-Independence Trinidad* (Port of Spain: Gordon Rohlehr, 1990); and Donald R. Hill, *Calypso Calaloo: Early Carnival Music in Trinidad* (Gainesville: University Press of Florida, 1993). Caribbean religions have received a

tremendous amount of attention, especially from anthropologists. Some work that provides some history on the cases mentioned in the text include, on *santería*, George Brandon, *Santería from Africa to the New World: The Dead Sell Memories* (Bloomington: Indiana University Press, 1993). On the *cabildos*, see the early work of Fernando Ortíz Fernández, "Los cabildos Afro-cubanos", *Revista Bimestre Cubana* 26 (1921): 5–39; as well as, more recently, Philip Anthony Howard, "Culture, Nationalism, and Liberation: The Afro-Cuban Mutual Aid Societies in the Nineteenth Century" (PhD dissertation, Indiana University , 1988). On the relations between the Catholic Church and *vaudou* in Haiti, see Anne Greene, *The Catholic Church in Haiti: Political and Social Change* (East Lansing: Michigan State University Press, 1993) and for the politics of *vaudou* in general, see Michel Laguerre, *Voodoo and Politics in Haiti* (New York: St Martin's Press, 1980).

22. On Indian nationalism and the rise of middle class Indians, see, for example, Clem Seecharan, *'Tiger in the Stars': The Anatomy of Indian Achievement in British Guiana, 1919–29* (London: Macmillan, 1997). For an introduction to the literature of this period, see Roberto Márquez, "Nationalism, Nation, and Ideology", in Knight and Palmer, eds., *The Modern Caribbean*, 293–335. For the role of race and ethnicity, see the early classic study by G.R. Coulthard, *Race and Colour*

in Caribbean Literature (London: Oxford University Press, 1962). A recent provocative book on Afro-Cubanism is Vera M. Kutzinski's *Sugar's Secrets: Race and the Erotics of Cuban Nationalism* (Charlottesville: University of Virginia Press, 1993). On Price-Mars, see Magdaline W. Shannon, *Jean Price-Mars, the Haitian Elite and the American Occupation, 1915–35* (London: Macmillan; New York: St Martin's Press, 1996).

23. While the works on labour in this period are too numerous for us to mention here, for a sense of the variety of labour organizations in the Caribbean from the postemancipation period up through the 1930s, see the chapters in Cross and Heuman, *Labour in the Caribbean*. For this period in more historical perspective, see Mary Turner, ed., *From Chattel Slaves to Wage Slaves: The Dynamics of Labour Bargaining in the Americas* (Bloomington: Indiana University Press; London: James Currey, 1995). For a discussion of ethnicity, class, and workers in the broader Latin American context, see George Reid Andrews, "Black Workers in the Export Years: Latin America, 1880–1930", *International Labor and Working-Class History* 51 (1997): 7–29.

24. For example, see Glen Richards, "Masters and Servants: The Growth of the Labour Movement in St Christopher-Nevis, 1896 to 1956" (PhD thesis, University of Cambridge, 1989), ch. 2, for a discussion of the St Kitts sugar

industry, and Roy Thomas, "The Profit Situation in the Oil Industry Around 1937", in Roy Thomas, ed., *The Trinidad Labour Riots of 1937: Perspectives 50 Years Later* (St Augustine: Extra-Mural Studies Unit, UWI, 1987), 183–222, for rich data on the oil industry in Trinidad during this period.

25. Bridget Brereton, "Society and Culture in the Caribbean: The British and French West Indies, 1870–1980", in Knight and Palmer, eds., *The Modern Caribbean*, 98.

26. For example, see Thomas C. Holt, *The Problem of Freedom: Race, Labor, and Politics in Jamaica and Britain, 1832–1938* (Baltimore: Johns Hopkins University Press, 1992) and O. Nigel Bolland, *On the March: Labour Rebellions in the British Caribbean, 1934–39* (Kingston: Ian Randle; London: James Currey, 1995) on the English-speaking Caribbean. For Martinique and Guadeloupe, see Cécile Celma, "Le mouvement ouvrier aux Antilles de la Première Guerre Mondiale à 1939", in Suvélor, ed., *Historial Antillais*, 168–234, and Edouard de Lépine, *La crise de février 1935 à la Martinique: La marche de la faim sur Fort-de-France* (Paris: L'Harmattan, 1980). For Cuba, see Alejandro de la Fuente, "Two Dangers, One Solution: Immigration, Race, and Labor in Cuba, 1900–1930", *International Labor and Working-Class History* 51 (1997): 30–49; Barry Carr, "Mill Occupations and Soviets: The Mobilisation of Sugar Workers in

Cuba 1917–1933", *Journal of Latin American Studies* 28, no. 1 (1996); Samuel Farber, *Revolution and Reaction in Cuba, 1933–1960: A Political Sociology from Machado to Castro* (Middletown, Conn.: Wesleyan University Press, 1976); and for the role of tobacco workers, see Jean Stubbs, *Tobacco in the Periphery: A Case Study in Cuban Labour, 1860–1958* (Cambridge: Cambridge University Press, 1985). On Trujillo-ordered massacre of Haitians, see Lauren Derby, "Haitians, Magic, and Money: *Raza* and Society in the Haitian-Dominican Borderlands, 1900–1937", *Comparative Studies in Society and History* 36, no. 3 (1994): 488–526 and Thomas Fiehrer, "Political Violence in the Periphery: The Haitian Massacre of 1937", *Race & Class* 32, no. 2: 1–20.

27. For the Moyne Commission, see *West India Royal Commission Report* (London: HMSO, 1945, Cmd. 6607). The Comptroller's remarks can be found in *Development and Welfare in the West Indies, 1946–47* (London: HMSO, 1948). For more contemporary report on poverty, see *Labour Conditions in the West Indies* (London: HMSO, 1939, Cmd. 6070 [the Orde Browne report]) and, for Jamaica, Claus F. Stolberg, ed., *The Living Conditions of the Urban and Rural Poor: Two Social Surveys* (Mona: The Social History Project, Department of History, UWI, 1990). On British welfare policy toward the Caribbean colonies, see Stolberg, "British Colonial Policy and the

Great Depression - the Case of Jamaica", *Journal of Caribbean History* 23, no. 2 (1989): 142–60. For the effect on women of the Moyne Commission's recommendations and colonial welfare policy, see Joan French, "Colonial Policy Towards Women after the 1938 Uprising: The Case of Jamaica", *Caribbean Quarterly* 34, nos. 3 & 4 (1988): 38–59. On women's public role during this time period, see Rhoda E. Reddock, *Women, Labour and Politics in Trinidad and Tobago: A History* (London: Zed Books, 1994) and K. Lynn Stoner, *From the House to the Street: The Cuban Women's Movement for Legal Reform, 1898–1940* (Durham: Duke University Press, 1991). For the Mass Marriage Movement, see Lady Molly's memoir: Molly Huggins, *Too Much to Tell* (London: Heinemann, 1967). For Simey's view, which launched a generation of anthropological investigations, see his *Welfare and Planning in the West Indies* (Oxford: Clarendon Press, 1946). For the theoretical and political context, see the work of R.T. Smith, especially his *Kinship and Class in the West Indies: A Genealogical Study of Jamaica and Guyana* (Cambridge: Cambridge University Press, 1988) and *The Matrifocal Family: Power, Pluralism, and Politics* (London: Routledge, 1995). Smith argues that the family is not the cause of poverty, but, rather, its particular shape is part of the social practice of class relations.

28. Three works on nationalist movements and independence in the British Caribbean are Trevor Munroe, *The Politics of Constitutional Decolonization: Jamaica, 1944–62* (Mona: Institute of Social and Economic Research, UWI, 1972); Ivar Oxaal, *Black Intellectuals Come to Power: The Rise of Creole Nationalism in Trinidad and Tobago* (Cambridge, Mass.: Schenkman, 1968); and Selwyn D. Ryan, *Race and Nationalism in Trinidad and Tobago* (Toronto: University of Toronto Press, 1972). For the status of the French islands, see Philippe Alain Blérald, "Guadeloupe-Martinique: A System of Colonial Domination in Crisis", in Fitzroy Ambursley and Robin Cohen, eds., *Crisis in the Caribbean* (New York: Monthly Review Press, 1983), 148–65 and Richard D.E. Burton and Fred Reno, eds., *French and West Indian: Martinique, Guadeloupe and French Guiana Today* (London: Macmillan, 1995). There is a voluminous literature on Puerto Rico's relationship with the United States. Some sources on the history of the relationship are cited in note 16 above. Another good place to start is Blanca G. Silvestrini, "Contemporary Puerto Rico: A Society of Contrasts", in Knight and Palmer, eds., *The Modern Caribbean*, 147–67. Some recent work on the tourist industry includes Polly Pattulo, *Last Resorts: The Cost of Tourism in the Caribbean* (Kingston: Ian Randle; London: Latin American

Bureau, 1996); D. Gail Saunders, "The Changing Face of Nassau: The Impact of Tourism on Bahamian Society in the 1920s and 1930s", *Nieuwe West-Indische Gids* 71, nos. 1 & 2 (1997): 21–42; and Frank Taylor, *To Hell With Paradise: A History of the Jamaican Tourist Industry* (Pittsburgh: University of Pittsburgh Press, 1993).

Notes to Chapter 1

1. Noam Chomsky, *Deterring Democracy* (London and New York: Verso, 1991), 369–70.
2. R.W. Smith, "The Legal Status of Jamaican Slaves before the Anti-Slavery Movement", *Journal of Negro History* 30 (1945): 295.
3. See Richard Price, *First-Time, The Historical Vision of an Afro-American People* (Baltimore: Johns Hopkins University Press, 1983).
4. Mary Turner, *Slaves and Missionaries: The Disintegration of Jamaican Slave Society 1787–1834* (Urbana: University of Illinois Press, 1982), 81. The conviction that each spirit released by death returned to Africa to feast with the ancestors also endured for generations and substituted in the minds of slave converts for the hope of heaven.
5. Ibid., 53. Among the Saramaka and Maroon communities priests, mediums, diviners and doctors had specialized functions; slave village conditions precluded this degree of specialization.
6. One such chapel was observed by the resident attorney on a Jamaican plantation in 1829 among slaves who, despite his encouragements and the efforts of the local Anglican clergyman, remained firmly dismissive of Christianity. Mary Turner, "Chattel Slaves into Wage Slaves", in Mary Turner, ed., *From Chattel Slaves to Wage Slaves, The Dynamics of Labour Bargaining in the Americas* (London: James Currey; Bloomington: Indiana University Press, 1995), 40.
7. Bronislaw Malinowski, *Magic, Science and Religion* (Boston: Beacon Press, 1948), 78, 83.
8. Price, *First-Time*, 43–47.
9. Ibid., 48.
10. Richard B. Sheridan, *Doctors and Slaves: A Medical and Demographic History of Slaves in the British West Indies, 1680–1834* (New York: Cambridge University Press, 1985), 76–77, 81, 83–84.
11. Charles Leslie, *A New and Exact Account of Jamaica*, 3rd ed. (Edinburgh, 1740), 323–24, quoted in Roger D. Abrahams and John F. Szwed, eds., *After Africa: Extracts from British Travel Accounts and Journals of the Seventeenth, Eighteenth, and Nineteenth Centuries concerning the Slaves, their Manners, and Customs in the British West Indies* (New Haven: Yale University Press, 1983), 141.
12. Michael Craton, *Testing the Chains* (Ithaca and London: Cornell University Press, 1982), 127.
13. Bryan Edwards, *The History, Civil and Commercial of the British Colonies in the West Indies*, 3 vols. (London: J. Stockdale, 1801), 1:92.
14. J.R. Ward, *British West Indian Slavery, 1750–1834: The Process of*

Amelioration (Oxford: Oxford University Press, 1988); Turner, "Chattel Slaves into Wage Slaves".

15. Turner, *Slaves and Missionaries*, 9-10.
16. The black Baptists were orthodox Christians and must be distinguished from the syncretic sects such as, for example, the Native Baptists which under the leadership of self-appointed leaders, both slave and free, combined elements of Christian and traditional religion. This distinction is not always recognized in the literature. See, for example, Thomas C. Holt *The Problem of Freedom: Race, Labor, and Politics in Jamaica and Britain, 1832–1938* (London and Baltimore: Johns Hopkins University Press, 1992), 415, who mistakenly identifies the Native as black Baptists. Abigail B. Bakan, *Ideology and Class Conflict in Jamaica: The Politics of Rebellion* (Montreal and Kingston: McGill-Queen's University Press, 1990), 52–53, makes the same error.
17. Hope M. Waddell, *Twenty-Nine Years in the West Indies and Central Africa 1829–1858* (London: Nelson, 1863), 37; Turner, *Slaves and Missionaries*, 20.
18. Waddell, *Twenty-Nine Years*, 83.
19. Wesleyan Methodist Missionary Society Letters (W.M.M.S.), Ratcliffe, Kingston, 9 April 1818, Box 113, f. 44, quoted Turner, *Slaves and Missionaries*, 76.
20. W.M.M.S. Letters, Wiggins, Morant Bay, 20 August 1817, Box 113, f. 25; Duncan, Montego Bay, 1 June 1829, Box 128, f. 14, quoted Turner, ibid., 90.

21. Public Record Office, Colonial Office (C.O.) 137/267, Bp. Lipscomb to Bathurst, 17 Oct. 1825, f. 59, Enclosure 4, Revd H. Beams to Archdeacon Pope, July 1825, quoted Turner, ibid., 68.
22. Ibid., 104, 110–11.
23. *Parliamentary Papers* (P.P.) 47 (C. 480) 345 (1831–32), Finlayson to Bullock, 5 October 1830; Turner, *Slaves and Missionaries*, 139–40.
24. W.M.M.S. Letters, Whitehouse, 1 July 1829, Box 128, f. 21a; P.P. 16 (C. 91) 240–42 (1830–31), quoted Turner, ibid., 134–35.
25. Chomsky, *Deterring Democracy*, 369–70.

Notes to Chapter 2

1. In a study completed in 1992, Anthony de Verteuil used the "Spanish Protocols", 1787–1838. These must be notarial in character, but do not appear to include wills. See Anthony de Verteuil, *Seven Slaves and Slavery, Trinidad 1777–1838* (Port of Spain: Anthony De Verteuil, 1992), 424.
2. The first two paragraphs owe something to F.P. Bowser, "The Free Person of Color in Mexico City and Lima: Manumission and Opportunity 1580–1650", in Stanley Engerman and Eugene Genovese, eds., *Race and Slavery in the Western Hemisphere: Quantitative Studies* (Princeton: Princeton University Press, 1975), 331–32.
3. The wills are to be found in the Registrar General's Office, in the Red House, Port of Spain, Trinidad.

4. See Carl Campbell, *Cedulants and Capitulants: The Politics of the Coloured Opposition in the Slave Society of Trinidad 1783–1838* (Port of Spain: Paria Publishing Company, 1992), ch. 3.

5. Ibid.

6. See Stephanie Goodenough, "Race, Status and Ecology in Port of Spain, Trinidad", in Colin Clarke, ed., *Caribbean Social Relations* (Liverpool: Centre for Latin American Studies, University of Liverpool, 1978), 17–45.

7. For some figures suggesting a favourable rate of manumission, see Eric Williams, ed., *Documents on British West Indian History 1807–1838* (Port of Spain: Trinidad Publishing Company, 1952), 391. See, also, de Verteuil, *Seven Slaves*, 50–54 and Barry W. Higman, *Slave Populations of the British Caribbean, 1807–1834* (Baltimore: Johns Hopkins University Press, 1984), 381–85.

8. Under the Cédula of 1783, free non-whites were entitled to five quarrées each, and 2.5 quarrées for each slave. See Campbell, *Cedulants and Capitulants*, 86–98.

9. Will no. 65 of 1872, Marie Angelique.

10. See Carl Campbell, "Jonas Mohammed Bath and the Free Mandingos in Trinidad: The Question of their Repatriation to Africa 1831–1838", *Journal of African Studies* 2, no. 4 (Winter 1975–76): 467–93.

11. Spanish civil law was abolished in the 1840s in favour of English civil law. See Carl Campbell, "The Transition from Spanish law to English law in Trinidad before and after Emancipation", *Lawyer* 3, no. 2 (January 1989): 15–28.

12. Examples from the Slave Registers are: McClean Crooked, Watford Aged, Marie MiLord, Ferdinand Watch, Betsy Brandy, Tom True, Cherubin Sylbie, Patrick Whisky, Yorkshire Ham, Mary Shovel, Hippolyte Venus, Mary Sansraison, Clarisse Bigmouth. Such names, however, are in a small minority.

13. For some observations on slave names, see Higman, *Slave Populations*, 15–16.

14. Will No. 4 of 1832, Nancy Rivers alias Bruce.

Notes to Chapter 3

1. See Kenneth N. Bell and W.P. Morrell, eds., *Select Documents on British Colonial Policy, 1830–1860* (Oxford: Clarendon Press, 1928), 389–94.

2. See James Millette, ed., *Freedom Road* (Havana, 1988), 49ff.

3. See, for example, Monica Wilson and Leonard Thompson, *The Oxford History of South Africa*, 2 vols. (Oxford: Oxford University Press, 1969), 2:297ff; and G. R. Mellor, *British Imperial Trusteeship, 1783–1850* (London: Faber and Faber, 1951).

4. W.K. Marshall, "Metayage in the Sugar Industry of the British West Indies, 1838–65", *Jamaican Historical Review* 5 (1965): 28–55.

5. See W.E. Riviere, "Labour Shortage in the British West Indies after Emancipation", *Journal of*

Caribbean History 4 (May 1972): 1–30; and Donald Wood, *Trinidad in Transition: The Years After Slavery* (London: Oxford University Press, 1968), ch. 3.

6. *Parliamentary Papers* (P.P.) XXIX, 379 (1842). Select Committee on the West Indian Colonies, Q. 599.

7. Ibid., Q. 600.

8. Ibid., Q. 603.

9. Ibid., Qs. 610, 603, 605.

10. Ibid., Q. 602.

11. Ibid., Qs. 613, 616, 618.

12. Ibid., Q. 618.

13. Ibid., Qs. 613, 617.

14. Ibid., Q. 619.

15. Ibid., Q. 612.

16. Ibid.

17. See, for example, Riviere, "Labour Shortage"; and Wood, *Trinidad in Transition*, ch. 3.

18. Wood, *Trinidad in Transition*, 54.

19. *P.P.* XLVI (1848–49). Lord Harris to Earl Grey, 19 June 1848.

20. See William A. Green, *British Slave Emancipation: The Sugar Colonies and the Great Experiment 1830–1865* (Oxford: Clarendon Paperbacks, 1991), 187. Also, see Public Record Office, Colonial Office (C.O.) 318/169, Memorandum by Henry Taylor, 15 February 1846.

21. Marianne D. Ramesar, "Indentured Labour in Trinidad, 1880–1917", in Kay Saunders, ed., *Indentured Labour in the British Empire, 1834–1920* (London: Croom Helm, 1984). See, also, Raphael Sebastien, "The Development of Capitalism in Trinidad, 1845–1917" (PhD dissertation, Howard University, 1978), 252–61.

22. *West India Royal Commission* (*WIRC*), 1897, Appendix C, Part IV, Trinidad, 312.

23. Judith Ann Weller, *The East Indian Indenture in Trinidad* (Río Piedras: Institute of Caribbean Studies, University of Puerto Rico, 1968), 1.

24. *WIRC*, Appendix C, Part IV, Trinidad, 319. Memorandum on Indian Immigration.

25. Ibid., 320.

26. Ibid., 312. Return submitted by W.W. Coombs, Protector of Immigrants.

27. Ibid., 319. Memorandum on the Present Depression in the Colony.

28. Charles Kingsley, *At Last: A Christmas in the West Indies* (London: Macmillan and Co., 1871), 70.

29. *WIRC*, 343. Memorandum of Charles Mitchell, late Protector of Immigrants. See, also, Statistics of Cocoa Cultivation, Ibid., 308, and Memorandum of H.J. Clark, Government Statistical Office, 324.

30. See, for example, *Labour Committee Report, 1906.* Evidence of F.C. McClean, and passim. Also, D.W.D. Comins, *Notes on Emigration from India to Trinidad* (Calcutta, 1893).

31. See, P.N. Fedoseyev, et al., *Karl Marx: A Biography,* trans. by Yuri Sdobnikov (Moscow: Progress Publishers, 1973), 129–30.

32. *WIRC*, 344.

33. Ibid.

34. Ibid., Tables I and II, 327–28.

35. H. de R. Walker, *The West Indies and the Empire: Study and Travel in the*

Winter of 1900–1901 (London: T.F. Unwin, 1902), 93.

36. This information was derived from a reading of contemporary newspapers, directories, registers and the like.

37. G.P. Wall and J.G. Sawkins, *Report on the Geology of Trinidad; or, Part I of the West Indian Survey* (London: Longman, Green, Longman, and Roberts for H.M. Stationery Office, 1860).

38. *WIRC*, 324. Memorandum of H.J. Clark.

39. *Trinidad Blue Book* (1879).

40. C.O. 298/117/62880. Report of A.P. Catherall, Acting Inspector of Mines, 31 March 1921, Appendix A.

41. Ibid., Appendix C.

42. C.O. 295/24798/123/1917. "Labour Disturbances at the Oilfields".

43. See W.R. Jacobs, "The Role of the Labour Movement in the Political Process of Trinidad and Tobago" (M.Sc. thesis, University of the West Indies, Mona, Jamaica, 1967). See, also, Kelvin Singh, *Race and Class Struggles in a Colonial State: Trinidad 1917–1945* (Kingston: The Press UWI, 1994), ch. 2.

44. C.O. 295/526/11224, Governor Chancellor to Secretary of State Milner (Confidential), 24 January 1920, and enclosures III, Sub-Inspector, Tobago Division to Inspector-General of Constabulary, 11 December 1919, and IV, District Engineer, Tobago, to Senior District Engineer, 24 January 1920.

45. Ibid., see enclosures.

46. C.O. 295/464/62712, No. 4023. Draft Colonial Office correspondence of February–March 1911.

47. Singh, *Race and Class Struggles*, ch. 2. See, also, Trinidad and Tobago, Council Paper No. 125 of 1920.

48. C.O. 537/458/62453, Governor to Secretary of State Crewe, 28 May 1910.

49. C.O. 295/526, No. XCA/62964, Petition of Civil Servants to Governor, August 1919, enclosed in Despatch No. 55, 4 February 1920.

50. See Brinsley Samaroo, "Constitutional and Political Development of Trinidad, 1898–1925" (PhD thesis, University of London, 1969).

51. Sahadeo Basdeo, *Labour Organisation and Labour Reform in Trinidad, 1919–1939* (St Augustine: Institute of Social and Economic Research, UWI, 1983).

52. C.O. 295/526/11224, Governor Chancellor to Secretary of State Milner (Confidential), 24 January 1920.

53. C.O. 295/523/62805. Telegram from Secretary of State to Governor, 16 December 1919.

54. C.O. 295/526, No. XCA/62964, Petition of Civil Servants.

55. See Malcolm Cross and Gad Heuman, eds., *Labour in the Caribbean: From Emancipation to Independence* (London: Macmillan, 1988).

56. Jacobs, "The Labour Movement"; and Singh, *Race and Class Struggles*.

57. Jacobs, "The Labour Movement", Appendices 2, 3 and 4.

58. See, *Report on the Disturbances in Trinidad and Tobago* (London:

HMSO, 1938, Cmd 5641 [the
Forster Report]). Also, Trinidad
and Tobago Council Paper No. 92
of 1938.

59. Forster Report, 24.
60. Council Paper No. 32 of 1938,
"Mines", Appendix D, 16, in
Jacobs, "The Labour Movement",
Appendix 2.
61. J.A. Hobson, *Imperialism: A Study*
(New York: J. Pott and Company,
1902), 248–49.
62. S.H. Roberts, *The History of French
Colonial Policy, 1870–1925* (London:
Frank Cass, 1963 [1929]), 401–2.
63. L.C.A.T. Knowles, *The Economic
Development of the British Overseas
Empire* (London: G. Routledge &
Sons, 1924), 244, 247.
64. See George Padmore, *Africa:
Britain's Third Empire* (New York:
Negro Universities Press, 1969
[1949]), 20.
65. Ibid., 20–22.
66. *WIRC*, 302 (Q. 1836), 305 (Q.
1883).

Notes to Chapter 4

My thanks to Nigel Bolland and Kevin
Yelvington for helpful comments on
an earlier draft of this chapter.

1. Public Record Office, Colonial
Office (C.O.) 137/242, No. 74,
Special Magistrates' (SMs) Report
for St George's Parish, Jamaica, 20
March 1839.
2. R.T. Smith, "Race, Class and
Gender in the Transition to
Freedom", in Frank McGlynn and
Seymour Drescher, eds., *The
Meaning of Freedom: Economy, Politics*

and Culture after Slavery (Pittsburgh:
University of Pittsburgh Press,
1992), 267–68, 278; W.G. Sewell,
*The Ordeal of Free Labour in the
British West Indies* (New York,
1860), 79.
3. M. Morrissey, *Slave Women in the
New World* (Lawrence, Kan.:
University Press of Kansas, 1990),
especially ch. 2 and 74–79, 140–43;
Barbara Bush, *Slave Women in
Caribbean Society, 1660–1838*
(London: James Currey, 1990), ch.
4; Hillary Beckles, *Natural Rebels: A
Social History of Enslaved Black
Women in Barbados* (New
Brunswick, NJ: Rutgers University
Press, 1989), ch. 2; Lucille
Mathurin Mair, *Women Field
Workers in Jamaica during Slavery*
(Mona: Department of History,
UWI, 1987).
4. H. Cateau, "Natural Increase: The
Planter's Last Hope for Survival in
the British West Indies" (Paper
presented to the 28th Conference
of Caribbean Historians,
Barbados, 1996).
5. These issues were often bitterly
contested between women slave
workers and estate managements.
For pertinent examples from
Berbice (in modern Guyana)
between 1819 and 1823, see Mary
Turner, "The 11 O'clock Flog:
Women, Work and Labour Law in
the British Caribbean" (Paper
presented to a conference at Tulane
University, November 1996).
6. W.K. Marshall, "Apprenticeship
and Labour Relations in four
Windward Islands", in David
Richardson, ed., *Abolition and its*

Aftermath: The Historical Context (London: Frank Cass, 1985), 203–24.

7. For Grenada, see C.O. 101/87, Monthly Reports of SMs for 1838, ff. 216, 218, 250, 252, 255; for Jamaica, Mathurin Mair, *Women Field Workers*; for Trinidad, C.O. 295/121, Hill to Glenelg 28 June 1838, No. 66 and *Port-of-Spain Gazette*, 15 June 1838, Proclamation dated 13 June 1838; for the SPG estates, *Port-of-Spain Gazette*, 29 June 1838, extract from *Barbadian*, n.d. See, also, J. Sturge and T. Harvey, *The West Indies in 1837* (1838; reprint London: Frank Cass, 1968), 347–48.

8. Marshall, "Apprenticeship and Labour Relations", 211–12; C.O. 101/87, Grenada SMs' Monthly Reports for 1838, ff. 218, 250; R.A. McDonald, "The Journal of John Anderson, St Vincent Special Magistrate 1836–39" (Paper presented to the 22nd Conference of Caribbean Historians, Trinidad, 1990), 21; S.E. Craig, "Tobago, 1763–1838" (Seminar paper, University of the West Indies, St Augustine, Trinidad, 1988).

9. Mathurin Mair, *Women Field Workers*; W.A. Green, *The Great Experiment* (Oxford: Clarendon Press, 1976), 134–35; H. Beckles, *A History of Barbados* (Cambridge: Cambridge University Press, 1990), 97.

10. For instance, Douglas Hall, *Free Jamaica, 1838–65* (New Haven: Yale University Press, 1969), 19.

11. *Parliamentary Papers* (*P.P.*) XIII, 479 (1842), Select Committee on West India Colonies (*P.P.* 1842). Evidence of W. Sharpe; C.O. 28/130, No. 56, Replies from Barbados Police Magistrates (April 1839); J. Davy, *The West Indies, Before and Since Slave Emancipation* (London, 1854), 92–94; G. Chester, *Transatlantic Sketches in the West Indies, South America, Canada and the United States* (London, 1869), 64–65; C. Levy, *Emancipation, Sugar and Federalism: Barbados and the West Indies, 1833–1876* (Gainesville: University Presses of Florida, 1980), 113.

12. *Port-of-Spain Gazette*, 28 August 1838, extract from *Gazette* (St Kitts), 27 July 1838; *P.P.* 1842, evidence of N. Nugent (Antigua) and G. Estridge (St Kitts); F. Lanagan, *Antigua and the Antiguans* (London, 1844), 2:142–47; K.B. Smith and F.C. Smith, *To Shoot Hard Labour The Life and Times of Samuel Smith, an Antiguan Workingman, 1877–1982* (Scarborough, Ont.: Edan's, 1986), ch. 1.

13. *P.P.* 1842, Appendix. Report of J.V. Drysdale, St Lucia SM, January, 1842, 732, and of R. Sutherland, St Vincent SM, January, 1842, 748; C.O. 290/4, Tobago SMs' Half-Yearly Report for 1847, f. 159; G. Brizan, *Grenada: Island of Conflict: From Amerindians to People's Revolution, 1498–1979* (London: Zed Books, 1984), 180.

14. C.O. 137/232, No. 189, SMs' Reports (Jamaica) for October 1838; C.O. 137/242, No. 74,

Trelawney SMs to R.Hill, 27
March 1839, and *Falmouth Post*, n.d.
(March 1839); C.O. 137/242, No.
83, Table and Statement by Revds
Burchell and Dendy, 15 April 1839.

15. C.O.111/182, No. 10, Reports by
SMs in Berbice (British Guiana),
December 1840; A. Young, *The
Approaches to Local Self-Government
in British Guiana* (London:
Longmans, Green, 1958), 221–22.

16. *Port-of-Spain Gazette*, 27 August
1839, Letter from Candidus, n.d.,
and editorial; W.H. Burnley,
*Observations on the Present Condition
of the Island of Trinidad* (Port of
Spain, 1842), 51–52, 77; K.
Haraksingh, "Sugar Estates and
Labour in Trinidad, 1838–1845"
(Paper presented to the 11th
Conference of Caribbean
Historians, Curaçao, 1979).

17. Lanagan, *Antigua*, 2:42, 142–47;
C.O. 28/130, No. 56, Inspector of
Police's Reply (Barbados), 15 April
1839.

18. W.K. Marshall, "The Ex-Slaves as
Wage Labourers on the Sugar
Estates in the British Windward
Islands, 1838–1846" (Paper
presented to the 11th Conference
of Caribbean Historians, Curaçao,
1979); P.P. 1842, Evidence of
H.M. Grant (St Vincent); S.E.
Craig, "The Popular Struggle to
Possess the Land in Tobago,
1838–1855" (Paper presented to
the 22nd Conference of
Caribbean Historians, Trinidad,
1990); C.O. 290/4, Tobago SMs'
Half-Yearly Tabular Returns, f. 205
(1847), f. 281 (1848), f. 614 (1852).

19. P.P. 1842, evidence of John Scoble
(British Guiana); C.O. 111/182,

No. 10, Reports of Berbice SMs
(British Guiana), December 1840;
Trinidad Standard, 4 January 1839,
Agricultural Report for December
1838; *Port-of-Spain Gazette*, 27
November 1838, Report of
Council of Government, 24
November 1838.

20. For Smith's address, C.O. 137/231,
Proclamation of 9 July 1838. The
controversy can be followed in
voluminous enclosures in C.O.
137/243, No. 99 and C.O. 137/
244, 124; P.P. XXXV (1839),
Appendices C and D; *Port-of-Spain
Gazette*, 21 September 1838.

21. S. Wilmot, " 'Females of
Abandoned Character?' Women
and Protest in Jamaica, 1838–
1865", in Verene Shepherd,
Bridget Brereton and Barbara
Bailey, eds., *Engendering History:
Caribbean Women in Historical
Perspective* (Kingston: Ian Randle,
1995), 279–95; C.O. 137/232, No.
189, SMs' Reports, Jamaica,
October 1838; C.O. 137/242, No.
53, SMs' Reports, Hanover,
January 1839.

22. C.O. 137/242, No. 47, Report
upon the state of the labouring
population of Hanover, January
1839; No. 74, Report of SMs, St
George's parish, 20 March 1839; V.
Shepherd, "Alternative Husbandry:
Slaves and Free Labourers on
Livestock Farms in Jamaica in the
18th and 19th Centuries", *Slavery
and Abolition* 14, no. 1 (April 1993):
57–60.

23. C.O. 137/242, No. 74, Report of
SM, St Catherine and St Dorothy
parish, Jamaica, 3 April 1839.

24. Marshall, "The Ex-Slaves"; W.K. Marshall, ed., *The Colthurst Journal* (Millwood, NY: KTO Press, 1977), 228–30; C.O. 260/57, St Vincent SMs' Replies to Queries, Case of Adam and Trum, 16 August 1838; *P.P.* 1842, Appendix, Report of R. Sutherland, SM of St Vincent, 1 January 1842.

25. *Port-of-Spain Gazette*, 18 January 1839, : Extract from the St Lucia *Royal Gazette and Times*, 1 December 1838; *Port-of-Spain Gazette*, 13 August 1839, Notice, Grand Bras estate, Grenada, of 30 July 1839; C.O. 295/125, No. 12, Replies of Trinidad SMs to Questions, October–November 1838; C.O. 111/158, No. 112, Tabular Returns from British Guiana SMs, August–November 1838.

26. Wilmot, " 'Females of Abandoned Character?' "; C.O. 137/232, No. 182, Report of Trelawney SM, 15 September 1838.

27. C.O. 137/232, No. 182, Report of SM, St Catherine, 20 September 1838, and No. 216, Report of SM, Hanover, 3 December 1838 (italics in original); C.O. 137/242, No. 41, SMs' Reports, January 1839; C.O. 137/243, No. 113, SMs' Reports, April–May 1839. See also *P.P.* XXXV (1839), 602–3.

28. O.N. Bolland, "The Politics of Freedom in the British Caribbean", in McGlynn and Drescher, eds., *The Meaning of Freedom*, 140–43.

29. Smith, "Race, Class and Gender", 279; W. Rodney, "From Nigger Yard to Village" (1978 lecture, published Georgetown, 1988). For comparisons with the United States, see J. Jones, *Labor of Love, Labor of Sorrow* (New York: Basic, 1985), ch. 2.

30. *P.P.* 1842, evidence of J. Scoble, W. Knibb, H.M. Grant; evidence to 1848 Select Committee quoted in A. Adamson, *Sugar Without Slaves* (New Haven: Yale University Press, 1972), 40; C.O. 101/92, No. 3, Grenada SMs' Reports for 1841, f. 18; C.O. 260/57, St Vincent SMs' Replies, August 1838, f. 44; C.O. 137/242, No. 53, R. Hill to Governor of Jamaica, 20 February 1839, and No. 74, Report of SM, St Mary's, 1 April 1839. See Turner (note 5 above) for examples of pregnant women being brutally punished in Berbice in the late slavery period.

31. W.K. Marshall, " 'We Be Wise to Many More Tings': Blacks' Hopes and Expectations of Emancipation", in H. Beckles and V. Shepherd, eds., *Caribbean Freedom* (Kingston: Ian Randle, 1993), 17–19; Smith and Smith, *To Shoot Hard Labour*, ch. 1; *Trinidad Standard*, 2 November 1838, Agricultural Report for October; Burnley, *Observations*, 116.

32. Among many other works, see B.W. Higman, "Household Structure and Fertility on Jamaican Slave Plantations", *Population Studies* 27, no. 3 (1973): 527–50; "The Slave Family and Household in the British West Indies, 1800–1834", *Journal of Interdisciplinary History* 6, no. 2 (1975): 261–87;

"African and Creole Slave Family Patterns in Trinidad", in Margaret C. Crahan and Franklin W. Knight, eds., *Africa and the Caribbean: The Legacies of a Link* (Baltimore: Johns Hopkins University Press, 1979), 41–64.

33. R. Sheridan, "From Chattel to Wage Slavery in Jamaica, 1740–1860", *Slavery and Abolition* 14, no. 1 (April 1993): 35–37; C.O. 253/78, No. 22, St Lucia, Report of SM, Third District, 10 January 1843.

34. A great deal of evidence on these points is to be found in the testimony given to the 1842 Select Committee, and in the various SMs' reports already cited. For the St Lucia quotation, C.O. 253/78, No. 22, St Lucia, Report of SM, Second District, 26 December 1842; for the British Guiana quotation, C.O. 111/183, No. 111, Report of SM, District D (Demerara), for January to June 1841.

35. *P.P.* 1842, evidence of J. Bascom, R.H. Church, W.H. Burnley, G. Carrington; C.O. 111/182, No. 10, Berbice SM's Report, December 1840; *Port-of-Spain Gazette*, 23 November 1838, Letter from "A Planter", 19 November 1838; C.O. 28/130, No. 56, Return of Police Magistrate, St Thomas, Barbados, April 1839.

36. C.O. 265/3, St Vincent SMs' Tabular Returns for 1849, f. 337; C.O. 106/13, Grenada SMs' Tabular Returns for 1845, f. 11.

37. *P.P.* 1842, evidence of R.H. Church; C.O. 28/130, No. 50, Memo on Meeting with Deputation of Labourers of St George, Barbados, 23 April 1839.

38. For the US, see C. Robertson, "Africa into the Americas? Slavery and Women, the Family, and the Gender Division of Labour", in David Barry Gaspar and Darline Clarke Hine, eds., *More than Chattel: Black Women and Slavery in the Americas* (Bloomington: Indiana University Press, 1996), 29; C.O. 137/232, No. 189, Report of SM, St George's, 15 October 1838; C.O. 13/244, No. 160, Report of SM, St George's, 7 August 1839; Smith and Smith, *To Shoot Hard Labour*, 48; C.O. 290/4, Tobago SMs' Reports for 1848, f. 268.

39. *P.P.* 1842, evidence of H.M. Grant and Appendix, Report of SM R. Sutherland, 1 January 1842, 748; C.O. 253/78, No. 22, St Lucia, SMs' Reports for 1842; C.O. 290/4, Tobago SMs' Reports for 1850, f. 457–58; *Trinidad Standard*, 15 March 1839, Extract from *Grenada Free Press*, 27 February 1839.

40. *P.P.* 1842, Appendix, Report of Police Magistrate, Christ Church, Barbados, for 1841, 755; C.O. 28/125, No. 220, various enclosures; Marshall, " 'We Be Wise' ", 18–19.

41. Mrs A.C. Carmichael, *Domestic Manners and Social Condition of the White, Coloured and Negro Population of the West Indies* (New York, 1969), 2:181–86; C.W. Day, *Five Years' Residence in the West Indies* (London, 1852), 2:55; *Trinidad Standard*, 28 September 1838.

42. C.O.253/74, St Lucia SMs' Reports for 1841; M. Louis, " 'An

Equal Right to the Soil': The Rise of a Peasantry in St Lucia, 1838–1900" (PhD thesis, Johns Hopkins University, 1981), 197–99; Lanagan, *Antigua*, 1:202–3 and 2:145–46; C.O. 106/13, Grenada SMs' Tabular Returns for 1846, f. 127.

43. Louis, " 'An Equal Right' ", 186–93; O.N. Bolland, *Struggles for Freedom* (Belize City, 1997), 59–60; Adamson, *Sugar without Slaves*, ch. 3.

44. Bonham C. Richardson, *Caribbean Migrants: Environment and Human Survival on St Kitts and Nevis* (Knoxville: University of Tennessee Press, 1985), ch. 4; Richardson, "Freedom and Migration in the Leeward Caribbean, 1838–1848", *Journal of Historical Geography* 6, no. 4 (October 1980): 391–408; Beckles, *History of Barbados*, 113; Karen Fog Olwig, "The Migration Experience: Nevisian Women at Home and Abroad", in Janet H. Momsen, ed., *Women and Change in the Caribbean* (Bloomington: Indiana University Press; London: James Currey; Kingston: Ian Randle, 1993), 150–66.

45. Diane J. Austin-Broos, "Redefining the Moral Order: Interpretations of Christianity in Post-Emancipation Jamaica", in McGlynn and Drescher, *The Meaning of Freedom*, 221–43; Smith, "Race, Class and Gender", 277–79; Robertson, "Africa into the Americas?", 18–24; C. Hall, "Gender Politics and Imperial Politics: Rethinking the Histories of Empire", in Shepherd,

Brereton and Bailey, *Engendering History*, 48–59. See, also, D. Paton, "Decency, Dependency and the Lash: Gender and the British Debate over Slave Emancipation, 1830–34", *Slavery and Abolition* 17, no. 3 (1996): 163–84, esp. 173–80.

46. C. Buxton, *Slavery and Freedom in the British West Indies* (London, 1860), 47–48; *Port-of-Spain Gazette*, 15 April 1839, Lecture by Captain Stewart, 10 April 1839; C.O. 111/158, No. 46, Light to Glenelg 4 September 1838.

47. C.O. 111/158, No. 30, Governor's Address to Free Labourers of First August, 13 August 1838; *Trinidad Standard*, 15 February 1839, Speech by Governor Light to Free Labourers, 1 January 1839.

48. C.O. 28/125, No. 134, Proclamation of Governor of Barbados, 22 May 1838; C.O. 137/231, Proclamation of Sir Lionel Smith, 9 July 1838. Smith's advice about "sparing" wives heavy field work was bitterly attacked. See note 20 above.

49. Marshall, *Colthurst Journal*, 166–67; Lanagan, *Antigua*, 2:146. Lanagan's last remark suggests that black Antiguans did not accept this view of femininity. For similar comments about US female field labourers, see Robertson, "Africa into the Americas?", 23–24.

50. C.O. 137/244, No. 124, J. Kingdom, Manchioneal, to Governor's Private Secretary, 27 June 1839; E.B. Underhill, *The West Indies* (London, 1862), ch. 3; S. Copland, *Black and White; Or, the Jamaica Question* (London, 1866), 59.

51. *P.P.* 1842, evidence of H.M. Grant, and Appendix, Report by J. Macleod, SM of Demerara, for 1841, 662; C.O. 137/244, No. 160, Report of SM of St George (Jamaica), 7 August 1839; C.O. 137/232, No. 216, Report of SM of Hanover (Jamaica), 3 December 1838.

52. Hall, "Gender Politics", 54–57; Sidney W. Mintz, "Black Women, Economic Roles and Cultural Traditions", in Beckles and Shepherd, *Caribbean Freedom*, 238–44.

Notes to Chapter 5

1. Stanley Parker, *The Sociology of Leisure* (London: George Allen & Unwin, 1976), 17–18.

2. Joffre Dumazedier, *Sociology of Leisure* (Amsterdam: Elsevier, 1974), 13–16.

3. Ibid., 67–76. Dumazedier classifies different definitions of leisure based on whether they include four principal criteria: remunerated work, family obligations, sociospiritual and sociopolitical obligations, and activities oriented towards self-fulfilment. The first definition considers all activities, including remunerated work, to be permeated by leisure which may in some instances even dominate them. By this so-called psychological definition leisure is regarded as "a style of behaviour, which may occur in any activity". This approach, however, does not clearly delineate the difference between leisure and other activities such as pleasure and play; nor does it "illuminate the relationship, basic to the dynamics generating leisure, between the decrease in the time devoted to institutional obligations and the growth of the time freed for personal activity in the context of new social norms". The second defines leisure directly in relation to work. In other words, all non-work activity is considered leisure. The main weakness of this definition is that it does not take into account non-leisure activities or duties in the home, for instance, those related to the family. While excluding work and family obligations, the third definition incorporates sociospiritual and sociopolitical obligations "whose decrease favours the development of activities pertaining to a new type, as well as these activities themselves". Dumazedier notes, however, that although sociospiritual and sociopolitical activities are "free time" (spare time) activities, they should not be considered leisure phenomena because they are obligations owed to society. A third definition favoured by Dumazedier is discussed in the text of this chapter.

4. Edward Jenkins, *The Coolie; His Rights and Wrongs* (London, 1871), 63.

5. Brian L. Moore, *Race, Power and Social Segmentation in Colonial Society: Guyana after Slavery 1838–1891* (New York: Gordon and Breach, 1987), 39–41.

6. Ibid., 42–46.

7. By 1862, the actual contract period was fixed at five years, but many immigrant workers were induced to reindenture for another five-year term. In any event Indian workers were only entitled to a paid return passage if they completed ten years' "industrial residence" which effectively meant plantation work.

8. Moore, *Race, Power and Social Segmentation*, 164–65; Public Record Office, Colonial Office (C.O.) 111/379, *The Report of the Commissioners Appointed to Inquire into Treatment of Immigrants in British Guiana* (London: H.M.S.O., 1871), Sec. 14.

9. Brian L. Moore, *Cultural Power, Resistance and Pluralism: Colonial Guyana 1838–1900* (Kingston: The Press UWI, 1995), 26–30.

10. Ibid., 109–17, 137–42. Cumfo is an Afro-Creole religion akin to Shango in Trinidad, Kumina in Jamaica and Macumba in Brazil.

11. Barton Premium, *Eight Years in British Guiana* (London, 1850), 12–13; L. Crookall, *British Guiana* (London, 1898), 87–88.

12. Moore, *Cultural Power*, 21–23, 41–43, 53, 66–67.

13. R. Schomburgk, *Travels in British Guiana, 1840–44* (First published Leipzig, 1847. The Guiana edition, trans. by W.E. Roth, Georgetown, 1922), 43.

14. Moore, *Cultural Power*, 68–82.

15. H. Kirke, *Twenty Five Years in British Guiana* (London, 1898), 24–25; J. Amphlett, *Under a Tropical Sky* (London, 1873), 75; *Colonist*, 11 March 1871; *Royal Gazette*, 18 March 1875.

16. Kirke, *Twenty Five Years*, 19, 62-64, 97–98.

17. *Colonist*, 21 March 1875, 13 June 1876; *Royal Gazette*, 9 October 1880.

18. Moore, *Cultural Power*, 73–75.

19. J.A. Heatley, *A Visit to the West Indies* (Alnwick, 1891), 45.

20. Moore, *Cultural Power*, 61, 63–66.

21. Letter to the editor by "Paterfamilias", in *Royal Gazette*, 1 December 1874; "Mr. Pepps' Diary in Georgetown", in *Royal Gazette*, 14 April 1877.

22. Heatley, *A Visit*, 54.

23. Moore, *Cultural Power*, 39–40.

24. Moore, *Race, Power and Social Segmentation*, 132–33.

25. See, for instance, C.O. 111/224, No. 143, Light to Stanley, 2 July 1845; *Creole*, 28 March 1860; and *Berbice Gazette*, 22 July 1882.

26. *Creole*, 27 July 1863; *Royal Gazette*, 27 November 1855; *Demerara Daily Chronicle*, 14 August 1884; Schomburgk, *Travels*, 49–50.

27. Kirke, *Twenty Five Years*, 49.

28. Creole women also played cricket. See Moore, *Cultural Power*, 132.

29. Ibid., 124–26.

30. Schomburgk, *Travels*, 47; J.G. Cruickshank, "Among the 'Aku' (Yoruba) in Canal No. 1, West Bank, Demerara River", *Timehri* IV, 3rd. series (1917): 77–78.

31. Premium, *Eight Years*, 13–14; Schomburgk, *Travels*, 47; "H.R.", "Local Sketches: Dancing Parties", in *Royal Gazette*, 25 September 1880.

32. H.V.P. Bronkhurst, *The Colony of British Guiana and its Labouring Inhabitants* (London, 1888), 387;

"H.R."; *Creole*, 15 September 1858 and 24 August 1864.

33. J. van Sertima, *Scenes and Sketches of Demerara Life* (Georgetown, 1899), 99–102; *Echo*, 30 December 1893.

34. *Argosy*, 11 April 1885; *Royal Gazette*, 15 May 1883; *Daily Chronicle*, 4 April 1888.

35. Moore, *Cultural Power*, 253–61.

36. Father Woollett's "Notes", 1858–1860, Society of Jesus papers, BG/9; *Royal Gazette*, 8 January 1866 and 4 January 1877; *Colonist*, 2 January 1883.

37. *Colonist*, 15 February 1875, 6 June 1876, 19 May 1877 and 26 February 1878.

38. *Demerara Daily Chronicle*, 29 August 1882; *Colonist*, 17 August 1883.

39. M. Menezes, *Scenes from the History of the Portuguese in Guyana* (London: M. Menezes, 1986), 111–53.

40. *Royal Gazette*, 13 March 1875.

41. Moore, *Cultural Power*, 73, 254–56, 261–62.

42. C.O. 111/379, *The Report of the Commissioners*, Sec. 13; *Demerara Daily Chronicle*, 13 July and 16 October 1884, 18 and 20 October 1888.

43. Letter to the editor, *Creole*, 29 December 1858; *Royal Gazette*, 1 January 1880; H.V.P. Bronkhurst, *The Origin of the Guyanian Indians Ascertained* (Georgetown, 1881), 20.

44. D.W.D. Comins, *Notes on Emigration from India to British Guiana* (Calcutta, 1893), 80.

45. Ibid.

46. Ibid., 82; Bronkhurst, *The Colony*, 389.

47. H.V.P. Bronkhurst, *Among the*

Hindus and Creoles of British Guiana (London, 1888), 122–23.

48. C.O. 111/380, *The Report of the Commissioners*, Sec. 25.

49. Moore, *Cultural Power*, 218–26.

50. C.O. 111/297, No. 102, Walker to Newcastle, 20 October 1853; *Daily Chronicle*, 11 May 1888.

51. Comins, *Notes on Emigration*, 80, 82.

52. Ibid., Appendix, 31.

53. Yen Ching-Hwang, "Early Chinese Clan Organizations in Singapore and Malaya, 1819–1911", *Journal of Southeast Asian Studies* 12 (1981): 79–80.

54. C.O. 111/382, *The Report of the Commissioners*, Appendix C.

55. Brian L. Moore, "The Settlement of Chinese in Guyana in the Nineteenth Century", in Howard Johnson, ed., *After the Crossing: Immigrants and Minorities in Caribbean Creole Society* (London: Frank Cass, 1988), 45–47.

56. *Berbice Gazette*, 17 June 1865.

57. C.O. 111/379, *The Report of the Commissioners*, Sec. 13; *Argosy*, 5 April 1884.

58. Moore, *Cultural Power*, 289–91.

59. Kirke, *Twenty Five Years*, 160; *Royal Gazette*, 14 February 1854 and 10 March 1874.

60. Moore, "The Settlement of Chinese", 50–51.

61. *Daily Chronicle*, 19 February 1885; Kirke, *Twenty Five Years*, 49.

Notes to Chapter 6

1. See, for instance, Lord Stanley's attitude toward emancipation in *Hansard*, Third Series, XXI, 28

February 1834, 943–55. This
chapter is based on part of my
thesis "East Indians and Negroes
in British Guiana, 1838–1880"
(DPhil, University of Sussex,
1970). Here, I have not attempted
to update the secondary sources
published since this time, but have
relied on the primary sources that
were originally used for the thesis.

2. Lord Grey asserted that "the
progress of civilization among the
Negroes is entirely dependent
upon their continuing to have the
advantage of European
superintendence and example of
which they must necessarily be
deprived if sugar cultivation in the
West Indies is abandoned. The
true interest of all classes of the
inhabitants of Guiana is therefore
the same." Public Record Office,
Colonial Office (C.O.) 111/264,
Grey to Barkly, 1 June 1849. See
also *The Report of the Commissioners
Appointed to Inquire into Treatment of
Immigrants in British Guiana*
(London: H.M.S.O., 1871), 199.

3. H. Dalton, *The History of British
Guiana*, 2 vols. (London, 1855),
2:458.

4. Ibid., 467.

5. Ibid., 467. See also G.W. Des
Voeux, *My Colonial Experience*, 2
vols. (London, 1903), 1:28, on the
black reaction to the term 'nigger':
"Liar, blackguard, thief, and even
unmentionable words were usually
received with comparatively
equanimity. But the climax of
"nigger" almost invariably led to
blows and this though the object
of the language was as black as
Erebus."

6. *Creole*, 29 November 1856. Letter
by "S".

7. Ibid., 27 November 1858.

8. See for instance the petition of
the planters of Demerara and
Berbice against manumission in
1823 in which it was maintained
that the free black "being so
averse to work in the field . . .
cannot be induced to work for
hire or to carry on the cultivation
of the country in a regular and
effectual manner". *The Petition and
Memorial of the Planters of Demerara
and Berbice of the subject of
Manumission Examined* (London:
Pamphlet published by the Society
for the Gradual Abolition of
Slavery, 1827), 28.

9. Soon after the end of
apprenticeship the *Royal Gazette*
contrasted the 'good' black with
the worthless one. The good one
stayed near his plantation and
worked hard; the worthless one
went up river to become a wood
cutter and became vicious and
barbarous. *Royal Gazette*, 28 August
1838. In 1848, one of the
Stipendiary Magistrates bracketed
those blacks who had become
woodcutters and fishermen with
those who pursued "any idle way
of living" and described them as
retrograding physically, morally,
and in outward circumstances.
C.O. 111/254, Walker to Grey, 13
June 1848, Report of Stipendiary
Magistrate for District D.
Woodcutting was usually
associated with vagrancy and
squatting both of which implied
idleness to the planters.

10. Barton Premium, *Eight Years in British Guiana* (London, 1850), 12.
11. Ibid., 14.
12. C.O. 111/267, Barkly to Grey, 18 June 1849.
13. C.O. 111/284, Barkly to Grey, 28 November 1851.
14. Ibid.
15. C.O. 111/253, Light to Grey, Blue Book Despatch, 3 May 1848.
16. J. Brummell, *Demerara after Fifteen Years of Freedom* (London, 1853), 15. See also Premium, *Eight Years*, 90.
17. In 1859, this theory was expressed by all but two of the Stipendiary Magistrates in their reports on the state of the labour market. *Parliamentary Papers (P.P.)* XX, 39 (1859), Accounts and Papers. Correspondence on the State of the Labour Market in British Guiana.
18. Brummell, *Demerara*, 63.
19. Premium, *Eight Years*, 71.
20. *Creole*, 24 January 1857. Editorial.
21. See the report of the commission. C.O. 111/280, Barkly to Grey, 25 January 1851, 12.
22. Ibid. In particular the blacks living on the west bank of the Demerara River, near Georgetown, were, in the 1850s, frequently castigated by the planters for indolence and barbarism. Yet as *Creole* pointed out they were in fact the main suppliers of the Georgetown market with food as well as charcoal and shingles and their goats laden with provisions were in evidence at the main market every Saturday. Their robust independence of the sugar estates and their refusal to play the role of docile black Victorians particularly horrified the planters. See *Creole*, 24 January 1857.
23. Edward Jenkins, *The Coolie; His Rights and Wrongs* (London, 1871), 68.
24. A variation of this view was that the blacks' laziness made them content with the minimum subsistence. A remark often repeated during the period was that, if the East Indians were taking bread out of the mouths of the Creoles, it was because the latter did not desire to eat it. See *People*, 13 January 1866, Editorial, which replies to the editor of *Colonist* who originated this saying.
25. Anthony Trollope, *The West Indies and the Spanish Main* (London, 1860), 150–51.
26. Joseph Beaumont, *The New Slavery* (London, 1871), 83. Beaumont pointed out that 500 cubic feet of such work was set down as a "short task" in the schedule of labour drawn up by the committee of planters in 1837.
27. *Colonist*, 22 June 1880. Letter by William Russell entitled "Squatting Made Easy".
28. *Royal Gazette*, 1 July 1880. Some blacks accepted the idea that their race lacked all the qualities which made Europeans powerful and successful. For instance the Revd J.R. Moore, a black clergyman, in 1875 wrote a pamphlet entitled *Causes of the Non-Success of the Negro Race in British Guiana* in which he stated that the black suffered from "a want of those sterling qualities which are to be

found in a great people and which are the primary elements to success but which my race in this colony has not". And then he enumerated industry, energy, thrift and combination. See N.E. Cameron, *The Evolution of the Negro*, 2 vols. (Georgetown, 1928), 2:73. On the other hand, a local doctor with more perception pointed to the insanitary condition of most black villages as a reason for creole lassitude: "Very often it was said that the people were lazy and no doubt they were, but he often saw them come out in the morning after having slept close to the ground; they were suffering from a low fever and required to go to the rum shop to take a stimulant before they could throw off the depression that operated upon them, and in that way they laid the foundation for much evil in the community." Statement of Dr Hackett quoted by the Attorney General, proceeding of the Court of Policy, 4 July 1880, in *Colonist*, 5 July 1880.

29. The universal improvidence indicated by the stereotype was subject to considerable modification, when the facts were taken into account. In 1884, the amounts deposited in the government savings bank were as follows: 6,286 East Indians - £107,404.18.0d; 6,622 Creoles - £83,760.18.3d. The comment on these tables was "although they [the blacks] as a body are not frugally disposed, still a large amount of savings banks deposits

are made by the black and coloured labourers and artisans and of late several Friendly Societies had been established among them . . .". See Colonial and Indian Exhibition, *Special Catalogue of Exhibits on British Guiana*, with introductory notes by G.H. Hawtayne (London, 1884), 11.

30. The blacks' improvidence in their private life was linked with their attitude towards the plantation and the question of wages. *Colonist* expressed it thus: "They cannot be made to see that though it may serve the purpose of the manager to employ them at exorbitant rates of wages this year, rather than allow his crops to rot on the ground or his cut cane to spoil unground, he will not place himself in the same position again and that they are consequently discounting the future at a ruinous rate. To make a feast today they will kill the goose that lays the golden eggs though starvation stares them in the face tomorrow. Such a thriftless, unreflective creature is the common Creole labourer." *Colonist*, 21 December 1871. One writer to the *Colonist* maintained that the blacks' employment on the estates grew with the increasing immigration but they possessed nothing of value because of their lack of thrift. "They are mere day labourers who have hardly a shilling in their pockets." *Colonist*, 8 March 1870. Letter by "Agricola".

31. *Colonist*, 28 May 1874. Report on the Proceedings of the Anglican Synod.

32. H.V.P. Bronkhurst, *The Origin of the Guyanian Indians Ascertained* (Georgetown, 1881), 46. See also *Colonist*, 18 March 1875, where the Creoles are styled foolish and frivolous because it was said they "spend the whole of their earnings in worthless finery and in the gratification of their sensual appetites".

33. Report by R.T. Veness to the Secretary of the S.P.G., 24 July 1871. Reports from British Guiana, 1870 to 1871, U.S.P.G. Archives, Rhodes House Library, University of Oxford.

34. Bronkhurst, *Among the Hindus and Creoles of British Guiana* (London, 1888), 148–49.

35. Competition not control was the great belief of the nineteenth century. Hence when the blacks complained about the high price of Portuguese goods they were told to start cooperative shops to compete with the Portuguese. No attempt was made to control Portuguese prices. But the planters themselves did not believe in free and full competition as their insistence on aid from the Colonial Treasury in paying for East Indian and Chinese immigration showed.

36. Blacks sometimes replied that they could not compete with Portuguese rascality. See *Colonist*, 18 November 1881. "The Rev. Ketley and West Bank Villagers".

37. *Colonist*, 20 October 1875. Letter by "Sugar Cane".

38. Bronkhurst, *The Colony of British Guiana and its Labouring Inhabitants* (London, 1888), 103.

39. Although the blacks were constantly berated for their thriftlessness, the moment business was dull in Water Street, the merchants complained that a fall in the blacks' wages, their best customers, was responsible for the depression in trade and the consequent dullness of commercial life in the colony. The black could be forgiven a certain confusion over the values his "civilizers" wanted him to hold. For a discussion of the merchants' complaints and the paucity of black spending on account of low wages, see *Colonist*, 17 November 1874.

40. Trollope, *The West Indies*, 190–91.

41. Report of Revd R.T. Veness to the Secretary of the SPG, 16 July 1869. S.P.G. Volume of Reports 1869–70.

42. Bronkhurst, *Among the Hindus and Creoles*, 200.

43. They wanted a peasantry like that of the European countries; industrious, conservative and respectful. *Creole*, 29 January 1874. Editorial.

44. R. Schomburgk, *Travels in British Guiana, 1840–44* (First published Leipzig, 1847. The Guiana Edition, trans. by W.E. Roth, Georgetown, 1922), 27.

45. Brummell, *Demerara*, 64. A writer later in the century stated much the same view - except that he found the blacks who had experienced slavery much more docile. He found the black labourers to be insolent and rude; education had made them worse;

he advised other whites that the stricter one was with the black the more respect he gave one. "Familiarity with them is to be avoided. With almost every other class of labourer you may sometimes be free and kind; but my advice is – keep quashie in his place." J. Thompson, *The Overseer's Manual* (Demerara, 1887), 73. He did not realize that black impudence was the result of the expressed desire to keep "quashie in his place".

46. Quoted in Bronkhurst, *Among the Hindus and Creoles*, 25.
47. *Daily Chronicle*, 12 July 1882.
48. H. Kirke, *Twenty Five Years in British Guiana* (London, 1898), 36–37. See also, *The Report of the Inspector of Schools, 1894–5*. Administration Reports 1895. National Archives of Guyana.
49. E.E. Im Thurn, *Notes on British Guiana* (London, 1892), 8.
50. *Argosy*, 12 August 1888.
51. C.O. 111/253, Light to Grey, 18 May 1848. Enclosure.
52. See for instance C.O. 111/266, Barkly to Grey, 1 June 1849.
53. *Colonist*, 21 December 1871.
54. Ibid., 30 June, 1881.
55. Quoted in Bronkhurst, *British Guiana and its Labouring Population*, 128.
56. Bronkhurst, *Among the Hindus and Creoles*, 186.
57. C.O. 111/253, Light to Grey, 18 May 1848. Enclosure.
58. Brummell, *Demerara*, 54.
59. Ibid.
60. *Royal Gazette*, 25 August 1849. Letter addressed to the governor by "A Planter".
61. C.O. 111/273, Barkly to Grey, 18 April 1850. Elsewhere the same governor noted: "I have ever found the coolies the most easily managed people in the world, when they are once convinced you are in earnest." C.O. 111/294, Barkly to Newcastle, 14 April 1853.
62. These fears were described by Governor Scott as totally unfounded. See *P.P.* XLIX, 935 (1873), Accounts and Papers. Correspondence on the Disturbance amongst Indian Immigrants Employed on Devonshire Castle Estate.
63. C.O. 111/375, Scott to Earl Granville, 27 April 1870.
64. Ibid.
65. See Pierre van den Berghe, *Race and Racism* (New York: Wiley, 1967), for an excellent discussion of this issue. In any case, as Sir Henry Barkly had argued earlier, the immigrants were accustomed to institutions which encouraged servility - even the Portuguese to some degree - therefore forced labour would be no hardship to them but a kindness which they would understand. See C.O. 111/272, Barkly to Grey, 1 February 1850.
66. Jenkins, *The Coolie*, 94–95.
67. Thompson, *The Overseer's Manual*, 76–78.
68. *The Report of the Commissioners*, 85.
69. Ibid., 78.
70. G.W. Des Voeux, "Letter to Earl Granville", bound with *The Report of the Commissioners*, 3.
71. Jenkins, *The Coolie*, 94–95.

72. See for instance the statement of Robert Smith, an experienced and influential planter and member of the Court of Policy who justified the whole basis of East Indian immigration thus: "The seeking out of fresh and more productive fields of labour, must always have been a strong actuating motive [for migration]. At no time has it been more extensively practiced than in the present, when so many thousands are annually leaving the mother country and the continent of Europe for America, New Zealand and Australia. In many cases the hardy artisan or labourer of northern Europe can only accomplish his object after years of patient toil and careful saving, and often of heroic self denial, a home for himself in the new world. The same energies and the same endurance we cannot expect from the inhabitants of the tropics. Hence it is that which is only attained after much painstaking efforts by the inhabitants of more temperate regions we give gratuitously to the East Indian. All trouble, care and expense are saved to him; and all the security and protection which the most beneficent of governments can extend to him in the persecution of his desires after a fresh location and an improvement in his condition he receives without consideration." *Colonist*, 15 June 1874. Proceedings of the Court of Policy. A correspondent to *Colonist* referred to indenture "as the natural and best state of the coolie in Demerara - guaranteed good wages, medical care and dry and warm houses". *Colonist*, 13 July 1872. Letter by "B.M.S." on "The Proposed East Indian Settlement".

73. *The Report of the Commissioners*, 162–65.

74. Thompson, *The Overseer's Manual*, 38.

75. *The Report of the Commissioners*, 183.

76. *Royal Gazette*, 18 August 1869.

77. Jenkins, *The Coolie*, 67.

78. See *Colonist*, 15 January 1876. Letter by "G.H." on "Reindenturing the Immigrants". This writer claimed that the free Indians became degraded creatures like the blacks, while those on the estates were forced to work hard and live decently. See, also, *Colonist*, 6 September 1877. Proceedings of the Combined Court. Governor Longden felt that the Indian had no place off the estate: Guyana was not a small farmer's country. The importance of European control for the Indian was emphasized by *Colonist* in an illuminating passage: "If indenture were abolished, in place of a permanent, peaceable, contented and moderately industrious resident population on the estates, you will have wandering hordes of restless, discontented men without local ties or interests, working now here and now there, bent on making the best bargain they can for the moment, heedless of future consequences; turbulent, dangerous, reckless and

rapacious." *Colonist*, 21 December 1871. Editorial.

79. Trollope, *The West Indies*, 190–91.

80. See, for instance, *Colonist*, 18 March 1876. Letter by "H" on "Savings Banks".

81. *Daily Chronicle*, 12 July 1882. Letter by William Russell.

82. Thompson, *The Overseer's Manual*, 78; Kirke, *Twenty Five Years*, 250.

83. *Colonist*, 21 August 1880.

84. Ibid., 9 March 1881.

85. Ibid., 18 March 1875.

86. In 1880, 2,746 Indians applied for return passages and 1,583 were sent back. Minutes of the Court of Policy, *Report by the Immigration Agent General*, March 1881. Between 1 January and 30 April 1881, 2,441 were registered for return to India. Letter by the Immigration Agent General to the Court of Policy printed in *Colonist*, 15 May 1881. Eventually 1,416 were repatriated. *Report of the Immigration Agent General for 1880*. Administration Reports 1881.

87. *Colonist*, 16 December 1881. In the 1890s, this idea had strong apologists, for example W. Alleyne Ireland, *Demerariana: Essays Historical, Critical, Descriptive* (Georgetown, 1897). He saw Guyana as the safety valve of India. He felt that it was the frugality of the Indians which made them so valuable and he foresaw millions of them settled in the colony, flourishing and outstripping the other races. He did not believe the blacks had the capacity for developing the colony. "If a large settlement of the East Indians takes place, what is to become of the improvident, thriftless black labourer who is such a good citizen when viewed from the standpoint of the rum shop . . .?" (31).

88. *Report of the Immigration Agent General for 1905*. Administration Reports, 1906.

89. E.R. Davson, "British Guiana and its Development", *Royal Colonial Institute* (1908), 6–7.

90. *The Report of the Commissioners*, 158. See, also, *Creole*, 28 January 1874.

91. *Working Man*, 18 May 1872. Editorial.

92. C.O. 111/386, Scott to Kimberley, 18 July 1871; *Watchman*, 28 April 1876.

93. *Watchman*, 19 November 1875. Editorial.

94. This idea emerged very early in the 1850s. After a fight between the newly arrived Chinese and the blacks on Plantation Blankenburg, West Coast, Demerara, the governor enjoined the Creoles to be patient with the strangers. The former replied that they had no objection to living at peace with the Chinese, as they considered them more "respectable" than the Indians. What was meant by "respectable" was explained by the governor in this way: "They [the Chinese] have . . . purchased already several articles of European attire and seem disposed - unlike the natives of India - to spend their money very freely on such things, or even on mere luxuries and dainties." C.O. 111/293, Barkly to Newcastle, 26 February 1853.

95. *Watchman*, 14 April 1876. Editorial.
96. Ibid., 14 November 1875. Letter by "Veritas".
97. Ibid., 19 November 1875. Editorial.
98. Ibid., 14 September 1872. Editorial.
99. See for instance *Creole*, 11 October 1871. Letter by "Statist".
100. *Watchman*, 21 November 1873.
101. *Creole*, 28 January 1874. Editorial.
102. *Colonist*, 17 November 1874. Editorial.
103. *Royal Gazette*, 27 October 1849.
104. *Creole*, 10 November 1873. Editorial.
105. *Working Man*, 6 July 1872.
106. *Watchman*, 28 July, 1876.
107. *Working Man*, 6 July 1872. Contrast this writer's view of the Indian with that of the Barbadian immigrant: "He speaks the same language as we, adores the same God as we, boasts of being the subject of the same Crown as his loyalty is as great as ours, and he looks upon all those places over which England's Queen reigns as his home, because protected by the same laws and constitution."
108. *Working Man*, 16 June 1872. It was even claimed that the blacks prevented the planters from losing their labour force because, by repressing the riotous Indians, they prevented the police from shooting them. See *Working Man*, 10 June 1872.
109. *Working Man*, 30 October 1872.
110. Ibid., 14 September 1872. See also *Weekly Penny*, 5 March and 19 March 1870.
111. *Working Man*, 14 September 1872.
112. Bronkhurst, *Among the Hindus and Creoles*, 22–23.

Notes to Chapter 7

1. In over one hundred estates with a total population of 2,099, 158 had died, or 7.8 percent. See Papers of the Stipendiary Magistrates, December 1841 in *Papers Relative to the Affairs of British Guiana*. See, also, Public Record Office, Colonial Office (C.O.) 111/83, Report of the Commissioners in *Royal Gazette*, 13 October 1841, Appendix I.
2. C.O. 111/83, *Report of the Commission of Enquiry, 1841*, Treatment and Condition of the Madeira Emigrants; see *Royal Gazette*, 13 October 1841.
3. Charles R. Boxer, *Four Centuries of Portuguese Expansion, 1415–1825: A Succinct Survey* (Johannesburg: Witwatersrand University Press, 1968), 61.
4. Sarah Bradford, *Portugal* (London: Thames and Hudson, 1973), 139.
5. Francis M. Rogers, *Atlantic Islanders of the Azores and the Madeiras* (North Quincy, Mass.: The Christopher Publishing House, 1979), 34. *"Quem manda em casa é ela, quem manda nala sou eu"* ("She's the boss at home, but I am her boss") was a popular saying. See Bradford, *Portugal*, 139.
6. John Farrow and Susan Farrow, *Madeira, Pearl of the Atlantic* (London: Robert Hale, 1987), 54–55.
7. Ibid., 115–16.
8. Return of Immigrants, 1 April 1842, enclosed in Governor H. Light to Lord Stanley, No. 28, 19 April 1842. *Parliamentary Papers*

(*P.P.*), Colonies: West Indies, 727–30.

9. Results of the *Census of the Population of British Guiana, 1841* and the Census of 1851.

10. See Walter Rodney, *The History of the Guyanese Working People, 1881–1905* (Baltimore: Johns Hopkins University Press, 1981), 108; M.J. Wagner, "Structural Pluralism and the Portuguese in Nineteenth-Century British Guiana: A Study in Historical Geography" (PhD thesis, McGill University, 1975); and Brian L. Moore, "The Social Impact of Portuguese Immigration into British Guiana after Emancipation", *Boletín de estudios latinoamericanos y del caribe* 19 (December 1975).

11. Wagner, "Structural Pluralism", 45.

12. In the huckstering trade the Portuguese rivalled but never really supplanted the blacks. In 1842, of 1,179 licensed hucksters in Guyana, the majority were blacks and coloureds. See *Local Guide of British Guiana* (1843). In July 1852, of 618 rural huckster licences the Portuguese held 238. See the *Official Gazette of British Guiana*, 15 August 1852.

13. *Official Gazette of British Guiana*, 15 August 1852. See M. Noel Menezes, *The Portuguese of Guyana: A Study in Culture and Conflict* (Bombay: The Anand Press, 1994), 42.

14. *Registo de Passaportes* (Funchal, Madeira, 1853).

15. Menezes, *The Portuguese of Guyana*, 43, 65.

16. Petition of Manuel Pereira, *Minutes of the Court of Policy*, 20 January 1847.

17. Although this custom is no longer the rule in Madeira today, there are some instances where young men and women can still be seen showing this mark of respect to their parents.

18. *Watchman*, 15 September 1876.

19. BG/11, Bishop J. Etheridge to Father Provincial, 10 July 1857.

20. See *The Frederician Code* (Edinburgh, 1761), Part 1, Bk. 1, Title VIII, 37–39; Sir William Blackstone, *Commentaries on the Laws of England*, 11th edn. (London, 1791), Bk. 1, 433, 442–45; and *The Napoleonic Code, 1804*.

21. Bradford, *Portugal*, 135.

22. *British Guiana Directory, 1862*.

23. Menezes, *The Portuguese of Guyana*, 112.

24. *Watchman*, 15 September 1876.

25. *Daily Chronicle*, 5 April 1888.

26. *Daily Liberal*, 5 April 1893.

27. Menezes, *The Portuguese of Guyana*, 114.

28. Ibid., 115.

29. *Daily Chronicle*, 12 February and 13 April 1888.

30. C.O. 111/526, J. McArthur, Barrister-at-Law, to Government Secretary, enclosed in Lord Gormanston to Rt. Hon. J. Chamberlain, No. 18, 15 January 1901. No record was found showing whether the claim was upheld or denied.

31. Charles A. Le Power, *Power's Guide to the Island of Madeira: The Pride of Portugal* (London: George Philip & Son, n.d.), 11.

32. *Daily Chronicle*, 2 September 1902.

33. Menezes, *The Portuguese of Guyana*, 105. See, also, Cecil H. Miles, *A*

Glimpse of Madeira (London: Peter Garnett, 1949), 60, for premarriage practices of the Madeirans.

34. Menezes, *The Portuguese of Guyana*, 124.

35. Ibid., 125. See, also, *Creole*, 12 December 1870, which highly praised the singing reputation of Miss Vasconcellos.

36. A great musical star was the mezzo-soprano, Elsa Fernandes. *Daily Chronicle*, 13 February 1932.

37. It was not known whether this play was ever produced in nineteenth-century Demerara. On the occasion of the 150th Anniversary of the arrival of the Portuguese in Guyana in 1985 this play was translated and presented over Radio Demerara by the staff and students of the University of Guyana.

38. *Daily Chronicle*, 12 September 1886.

39. Ibid., 14 June 1902.

40. The Portuguese Club, Nonpareil Park, was founded on 29 May 1924. There were no ladies among the Founding Committee but five out of the eight Honorary Members elected by the Founding Committee were ladies; one sole lady graced the group of twenty-eight members elected by the Founding Committee while there were nine Lady Subscribers.

41. *The Christmas Annual* (1934). The local newspapers of the 1930s devoted regular sections to men and women in sports. Portuguese ladies were prominent among the tennis champions, such as Doris Baptista, Muriel Delgado, Agnes De Caires, Erna Pestano, and Elvie Matthias. In 1932, there was even a Portuguese Beauty Queen. Miss Genevieve D'Abreu was crowned Miss Guiana in the beauty contest. *Daily Chronicle*, 15 October 1932.

42. Very few Portuguese became British subjects. They were unwilling to forego their Portuguese nationality while, at the same time, the colonial government was reluctant to grant them certificates of naturalization. Only their desire to move into politics necessitated their becoming naturalized as one had to be a British subject either to vote or to become a candidate. Not until J.P. Santos and F.I. Dias were on the brink of their political campaign did they become naturalized in 1906.

43. The first women's political organization, the WPEO, was created jointly by Winifred Gaskin and Janet Jagan and launched on 12 July 1946 at the Georgetown Town Hall. Its aim was "to ensure the political organisation and education of the women of British Guiana in order to promote their economic welfare and their political and social emancipation and betterment". See WPEO files, Constitution, as quoted in Roberta Walker-Killkenny, "Women in Social and Political Struggle in British Guiana, 1946–1953", *History Gazette* 49 (October 1992), 6. For a more detailed discussion on the WPEO, see Hazel Woolford, "Gender and Women in Guianese Politics,

1812–1964", *Guyana Historical Journal* 3 (1991): 13–26.

Notes to Chapter 8

1. Well-known books on this subject are Morton Klass, *East Indians in Trinidad: A Study in Cultural Persistence* (New York: Columbia University Press, 1961) and A. Niehoff and J. Niehoff, *East Indians in the West Indies* (Milwaukee: Milwaukee Public Museum, 1960). Two other informative, though less popular, works are: J.C. Jha, "The Indian Heritage in Trinidad", in J. G. LaGuerre, ed., *Calcutta to Caroni: The East Indians of Trinidad* (Port of Spain: Longman Caribbean, 1974); and Singaravélou, *Les Indiens de la Caraïbe* (Paris: L'Harmattan, 1987).

2. Klass, *East Indians*, 81.

3. Ibid., 80.

4. Niehoff and Niehoff, *East Indians*, 34.

5. Klass, *East Indians*, 244.

6. Between 1869 and 1890, about 5,800 adults and at least as many children were settled in the following, government-sponsored East Indian villages: Coolie Block (Patna), Couva, Caratal, Lengua, Barrackpore, Cucurite, Rousillac, Peparo, Cocorite, Caracas, Coromandel, Malabar, Calcutta, Mausica, Madras, Simla, Chandernagore, Chin Chin, Caurita, Demson, Guaracara, Coolie Town, Cunaripo, Fyzabad, and Philipine. Public Record Office, Colonial Office (C.O.)

298/79, Memorandum on East Indian Settlements in Trinidad by the Revd Dr. Morton, 178. Council Paper (C.P.) No. 13 of 1906.

7. Bonham C. Richardson, "Livelihood in Rural Trinidad in 1900", *Annals of the Association of American Geographers* 65, no. 2 (June 1975): 245.

8. Richardson, "Livelihood".

9. *Parliamentary Papers* (P.P.) L (C. 8657) (1898), 792.

10. C.O. 298/60, Summary of Reports by the Wardens. C.P. No. 176 of 1897.

11. C.O. 298/74, Annual Reports of the Wardens, 1902–3. C.P. No. 114 of 1903.

12. C.O. 298/79, Evidence of Revd K.J. Grant. C.P. No. 13 of 1906.

13. *P.P.* L (C.8656) (1898), 395.

14. *P.P.* L (C.8657) (1898), 814.

15. C.O. 298/74, Annual Reports of the Wardens, 1902–3, 23. C.P. No. 114 of 1903. In India a *denkhi* consisted of a pestle attached to a wooden pole six to eight feet long placed on a fulcrum. By alternately stepping on and off the end of the pole, the pestle was repeatedly dropped into a wooden mortar fixed in the ground and containing paddy. A *denkhi* was used for both dehusking and polishing.

16. *Port-of-Spain Gazette*, 21 October 1903, 3.

17. C.O. 298/62, Annual Reports of the Wardens, 1897, 26. C.P. No. 136 of 1898.

18. *P.P.* L (C.8657) (1898), 814.

19. C.O. 298/71, Annual Reports of the Wardens, 1901–2, 23. C.P. No. 132 of 1902.

20. C.O 298/74, Annual Reports of the Wardens, 1902–3. C.P. No. 114 of 1903.
21. C.O. 298/79, Evidence of Revd K.J. Grant. C.P. No. 13 of 1906.
22. C.O. 298/79, Evidence of J.J. Mcleod. C.P. No. 13 of 1906.
23. J.R. Mandle, *The Plantation Economy: Population and Economic Change in Guyana 1838–1960* (Philadelphia: Temple University Press, 1974), 42. See also T. Ramnarine, "The Growth of the East Indian Community in British Guiana, 1880–1920" (DPhil thesis, University of Sussex, 1977). In ch. 5, Ramnarine points out that at sowing and reaping seasons, Indian peasants earned higher wages from rice than from sugar.
24. Mandle, *Plantation Economy*, 42.
25. Ramnarine, "The Growth of the East Indian Community".
26. *Report on the Labour Question.* C.P. No. 20 of 1905.
27. C.O. 298/77, Letter from the Honourable A.P. Marryat fowarding a *Report on the Labour Question*, 6. C.P. No. 20 of 1905.
28. C.O. 298/79, Evidence of S. Henderson, 33. C.P. No. 13 of 1906.
29. C.O. 298/79, Labour Question in Trinidad, viii. C.P. No. 13 of 1906.
30. Donald Wood, *Trinidad in Transition: The Years After Slavery* (London: Oxford University Press, 1968).
31. S. Morton, ed., *John Morton of Trinidad* (Toronto, 1916), 319–20.
32. C.O. 298/85, Annual Reports of the Wardens, 1907–8, Appendix I.2, 31. C.P. No. 144 of 1908; C.O. 298/96, Annual Reports of the Wardens, 1911–12, Appendix I.2, 29. C.P. No. 184 of 1912.
33. C.O. 298/85, Annual Reports of the Wardens, 1907–8, Appendix I.3, 32–33. C.P. No. 144 of 1908; C.O. 298/104, Annual Reports of the Wardens, 1913–14, Appendix I.3, 26–27. C.P. No. 9 of 1916.
34. The warden of Naparima, in his report for 1906–7, stated that the figures he was including for rice production were only estimates since accurate information had proved impossible to obtain, "the people being suspicious that it is being asked for the purpose of imposing extra taxation". See: C.O. 298/83, Annual Reports of the Wardens, 1906–7,18. C.P. No. 149 of 1907.
35. *Trinidad and Tobago Blue Book*, 1911–12, Section W, 4.
36. C.O. 298/100, Annual Report of the Protector of Immigrants, 1913–14, 11. C.P. No. 114 of 1914.
37. C.O. 298/109, Annual Reports of the Wardens, 1917. C.P. No. 103 of 1918.
38. *Trinidad Guardian*, 11 January 1918.
39. C.O. 298/113, Annual Reports of the Wardens, 1918. C.P. No. 103 of 1919.
40. C.O. 298/104, Annual Reports of the Wardens, 1914–15, Appendix I.2, 23. C.P. No. 14 of 1916; C.O. 298/113, Annual Reports of the Wardens, 1918, Appendix I.2, 20. C.P. No. 103 of 1919. Note that the *Trinidad and Tobago Blue Book* cites the higher figure of 13,369 acres in 1914–15.
41. C.O. 298/104, Annual Reports of

the Wardens, 1914–15, Appendix I.3, 24–25. C.P. No. 14 of 1916; C.O. 298/113, Annual Reports of the Wardens, 1918, Appendix I.3, 21. C.P. No. 103 of 1919.

42. *Trinidad Guardian*, 11 January 1918, 6.

43. Ibid., 12 September 1918.

44. Ibid., 11 September 1918, 6.

45. Ibid., 27 October 1918, 3.

46. This conclusion is based on a close examination of the statistics for acreage and production in the years 1904–5, 1907–8, 1911–12, 1914–15 and 1918.

47. *Trinidad and Tobago Blue Book*, 1914–21.

48. C.O. 298/113, Annual Reports of the Wardens, 1918, Appendix I.2, 20. C.P. No. 103 of 1919; C.O. 298/119, Annual Reports of the Wardens, 1920, Appendix I.2, 21. C.P. No. 96 of 1921; C.O. 298/129, Annual Reports of the Wardens, 1923, Appendix I.2, 15. C.P. No. 66 of 1924.

49. C.O. 298/113, Annual Reports of the Wardens, 1918, Appendix I.3, 21. C.P. No. 103 of 1919; C.O. 298/119, Annual Reports of the Wardens, 1920, Appendix I.3, 23. C.P. No. 96 of 1921; C.O. 298/129, Annual Reports of the Wardens, 1923, Appendix I.3, 16. C.P. No. 66 of 1924.

50. *Trinidad Guardian*, 16 September 1934.

51. Ibid., 16 September 1934, 3.

52. C.Y. Shephard, *Agricultural Labour in Trinidad* (St Augustine: Imperial College of Tropical Agriculture, 1929).

53. C.C. Parasinos, "An Agro-Economic Survey of Peasant Agriculture in the Las Lomas Area" (Thesis, Imperial College of Tropical Agriculture, Trinidad, 1943), 20.

54. Klass, *East Indians*, 84.

55. Ibid.,83.

56. Ibid., 66.

57. Ibid., 83.

58. Shephard, *Agricultural Labour*.

59. *Trinidad Guardian*, 7 January 1932, 4.

60. Ibid., 20 January 1934, 3.

61. Ibid., 18 September 1934.

62. Ibid., 23 June 1934.

63. Ibid., 16 September 1934.

64. Ibid., 23 September 1934.

65. Ibid., 15 September 1940, 14.

66. Ibid., 23 September 1934, 8.

67. Ibid., 15 September 1940.

68. C.O. 950/951, Memorandum by the Presbyterian Church, 1938.

69. C.O. 950/951, Memorandum by the East Indian Advisory Board, 1938.

70. C.O. 298/129, Annual Reports of the Wardens, 1923, Appendix 1.2, 15. C.P. No. 66 of 1924; *Trinidad and Tobago Blue Book*, 1929 and 1938–39.

71. C.O. 950/953, Memorandum by the Government of Trinidad and Tobago, 1938, Section IIb, 3.

Notes to Chapter 9

Funding for research was provided by two Mellon Foundation-Latin American and Caribbean Center (LACC), Florida International University grants, for which I am grateful to Mark B. Rosenberg, director of LACC, by a Library Travel Grant from the Center for Latin American Studies (CLAS), University of Florida, for which I am grateful to Helen I. Safa and Deborah Pacini Hernández of CLAS, and by a Presidential Young Faculty Award from the University of South Florida (USF), for which I am grateful to the USF Division of Sponsored Research and to Amos Webster for all of his help. For their valuable assistance, I would like to thank Richard F. Phillips and the staff at the Latin American Collection of the University of Florida Libraries, André Elizée and the staff at the Schomburg Center for Research in Black Culture of the New York Public Library, Georgia Garbo-Noel and the staff at the National Archives, Port of Spain, Trinidad, the officials of the British Newspaper Library, Colindale, London, and those at the Public Record Office, Kew, London. A special thanks is due to the staff of the Interlibrary Loan department at the USF library for their incredible cheerful competence in dealing with a torrent of hard to locate requests. An earlier version of this paper was presented to the Tenth Annual Meeting of the Association of Third World Studies, Gainesville, Florida, 1–3 October 1992. I would like to thank Bridget Brereton, René Lamarchand, and the late François Manchuelle for their comments on earlier versions of this chapter, and Rupert Lewis, Richard Pankhurst, Glen Richards and William R. Scott for their advice on the research process. I would like to thank Garth L. Green who diverted his busy PhD dissertation research schedule to provide sources on Trinidad Carnival, and Neill Goslin for his research assistance with primary and secondary sources. And I would especially like to thank my wife, Dr Bárbara C. Cruz, who took time out from her own career to put in long hours helping me to collect primary sources.

1. On the large (re)emerging literature on 'race', see for a concise treatment Roger Sanjek, "Race", in Alan Barnard and Jonathan Spencer, eds., *Encyclopedia of Social and Cultural Anthropology* (London and New York: Routledge, 1996), 462–65.

2. Rhoda Reddock, *Elma François, the NWCSA, and the Worker's Struggle for Change in the Caribbean* (London: New Beacon Books, 1988), 18.

3. Brian L. Friday, "The Impact of the Italo-Ethiopian Crisis on Trinidad, 1934–1937" (MA thesis, Dalhousie University, 1986). The results of Friday's thesis were never published as he died in a tragic accident in 1986. I became aware of his thesis only long after the primary research and most of the writing for this chapter was completed (see Kevin A. Yelvington, " 'West Indian Blacks Rally to the Fatherland!': Ethnicity and the West Indian Reaction to the 1935 Italian Invasion of Abyssinia" [Paper presented to the 10th Annual Meeting of the Association of Third World Studies, Gainesville, Florida, USA, 1–3 October 1992]) when I saw it cited in Joseph E. Harris's 1994 book *African-American Reactions to War in Ethiopia, 1936–1941* (Baton Rouge: Louisiana State University Press, 1994, 37, n. 9), where it is

erroneously referred to as a PhD dissertation. This error is understandable as Friday's impressive thesis shows a substantial amount of work and a seriousness and thoughtfulness in his analysis. It turns out that we have culled many of the same primary sources, but there are also a number of areas where we diverge, in both the historical materials we utilize and in our interpretations. My own chapter here is dedicated to the memory of Brian L. Friday, a promising scholar whose contributions to Caribbean history writing will be sorely missed.

4. Among book-length studies see, for example, Sahadeo Basdeo, *Labour Organisation and Labour Reform in Trinidad, 1919–1939* (St Augustine: Institute of Social and Economic Research, UWI, 1983); O. Nigel Bolland, *On the March: Labour Rebellions in the British Caribbean, 1934–39* (Kingston: Ian Randle; London: James Currey, 1995); Bridget Brereton, *A History of Modern Trinidad 1783–1962* (London: Heinemann, 1981); Susan Craig, *Smiles and Blood: The Ruling Class Response to the Workers Rebellion of 1937 in Trinidad and Tobago* (London: New Beacon Books, 1988); Ron Ramdin, *From Chattel Slave to Wage Earner: A History of Trade Unionism in Trinidad and Tobago* (London: Martin, Brian & O'Keefe, 1982); Reddock, *Elma François*; Reddock, *Women, Labour and Politics in Trinidad and Tobago: A History* (London: Zed Books, 1994); Bukka Rennie, *The History*

of the Working Class in the 20th Century (1919–1956): The Trinidad and Tobago Experience (Toronto and Trinidad: New Beginning Movement, 1973); Kelvin Singh, *Race and Class Struggles in a Colonial State: Trinidad 1917–1945* (Kingston: The Press UWI; Calgary: University of Calgary Press, 1994); and the chapters in W. Richard Jacobs, ed., *Butler Versus the King: Riots and Sedition in 1937* (Port of Spain: Key Caribbean Publications, 1976) and in Roy Thomas, ed. *The Trinidad Labour Riots of 1937: Perspectives 50 Years Later* (St Augustine: Extra-Mural Studies Unit, UWI, 1987).

5. Daniel A. Segal, " 'Race' and 'Colour' in Pre-Independence Trinidad and Tobago", in Kevin A. Yelvington, ed., *Trinidad Ethnicity* (Knoxville: University of Tennessee Press; London: Macmillan, 1993), 83.

6. *Beacon* 1, no. 4 (July 1931): 1.

7. *Beacon* 1, no. 10 (January/February 1932): 18.

8. Ernest A. Carr, "The Negro Child and its Environment", *Beacon* 1, no. 7 (October 1931): 14–15.

9. "Race Admixture", *Beacon* 1, no. 4 (July 1931): 25–29.

10. "The Intelligence of the Negro: A Few Words with Dr. Harland", *Beacon* 1, no. 5 (August 1931): 7.

11. Alfred H. Mendes, "Is the Negro Inferior?", letter, *Beacon* 1, no. 6 (September 1931): 27. Mendes was the son of a wealthy Portuguese merchant. Educated in England, he returned to Trinidad in 1920, articulating socialist ideals, after fighting in World War I. His

position on the matter was ironic considering his novels set in Trinidad and his later interactions with African American writers during his time in New York. Sander claims that in *Black Fauns* (1934) Mendes was "able to attack the racial and social prejudices of the colonial middle class" and that in *Pitch Lake* (1935) Mendes "step by step explodes the myth that racial prejudice in a society such as Trinidad is inevitable". Reinhard W. Sander, *The Trinidad Awakening: West Indian Literature in the Nineteen-Thirties* (Westport, Conn.: Greenwood Press, 1988), 77, 82. See Harland's reply to James, "Magna est Veritas et Praevalebit: A Reply to Mr. C.L.R. James", *Beacon* 1, no. 7 (October 1931): 18–20, where he concludes: "I wish that the evidence has indicated equality of negro with the white: my task in endeavouring to secure equality of opportunity irrespective of race would thereby be made easier. But let Mr. James take note of this. Throughout my period of residence in the West Indies I have fought against untutored race prejudice as much as I possibly could, and in future I shall continue to do so. When Mr. James attacks me let him rather consider the spirit which animates my first article, and let him admit at any rate that I put up a good fight against race prejudice, and for a square deal based on germ plasm." In this exchange Harland maintained that he had worked against racism. It is interesting in

this connection to note that, when the legislature approved the £25,000 gift for the United Kingdom in 1931 Harland wrote a letter to the *Port-of-Spain Gazette* decrying the decision, saying that the money should have been used locally to provide free milk, meals, and "many other things which our children will have to go without. Are our legislators", he asked, "wilfully blind to the appalling misery, degradation, malnutrition and disease among our own children?", *Port-of-Spain Gazette*, 31 October 1931, cited in Brinsley Samaroo, "The Trinidad Disturbance: of 1917–20: Precursor to 1937", in Thomas, ed., *The Trinidad Labour Riots*, 44. Harland was threatened with dismissal for this outburst.

12. W.V. Tothill, letter, *Beacon* 2, no. 2 (May 1932): 38. After spending seven years in East Africa, Tothill arrived in Trinidad in the early 1920s to work as a doctor for the Trinidad Leaseholds oil company. He moved into private practice in San Fernando and spent from 1925 until 1928 working for the Usine Ste. Madeleine Sugar Company, after which he returned to private practice. Ironically, like Harland, Tothill too maintained he was not racist. Throughout his Trinidad memoirs, *Doctor's Office* (London and Glasgow: Blackie and Son, 1939), he repeats that he had no "colour prejudice", explaining at one point that "if you don't possess it, it is very difficult to find out what it is all

about" (54). Indeed, in the Foreword, Owen Rutter calls him "the one European I met in the West Indies who had no colour complex" (vi). However, Tothill's book is rife with degrading ethnic stereotypes, not without irony and contradiction. At one point he says "I have never yet met a Negro who refused his rum" (223), when throughout the book Tothill reports himself going from one drinking session to another. And when his personal debts mount up to the point that he seriously contemplates leaving Trinidad to seek employment, a delegation of black and East Indian patients in San Fernando came to him to offer him office space rent free for six months and to guarantee his practice will earn $300 per month. "I did not know what to do," he writes. "These people had come to me entirely off their own bat. The coloured people had come to my rescue. I accepted" (59).

13. "Truth is Mightier than Fiction [Part 1]", *Beacon* 1, no. 10 (January/February 1932): 11.

14. "Truth is Mightier than Fiction [Part 2]", *Beacon* 1, no. 11 (March 1932): 11.

15. Ibid. See also Mentor's article "Facts More Convincing than Theory: A Reply to Dr. W.V. Tothill", *Beacon* 2, no. 2 (June 1932): 12–13, as well as Gomes's own comments: "Germ Plasm: Some Comments on Dr. Harland's Articles", *Beacon* 1, no. 7 (October 1931): 23–24.

16. For a succinct discussion, see Ellis Cashmore, "Ethiopianism", in

Dictionary of Race and Ethnic Relations, by Ellis Cashmore with Michael Banton, James Jennings, Barry Troyna, and Pierre L. van den Berghe (London: Routledge, 1994, third edition), 99–100. The classic discussions are provided by George Shepperson. See, for example, his "Ethiopianism and African Nationalism", *Phylon* 14, no. 1 (1953): 9–18; "Pan-Africanism and 'Pan-Africanism': Some Historical Notes", *Phylon* 23, no. 4 (1962): 346–58; and "Ethiopianism: Past and Present", in C.G. Baëta, ed., *Christianity in Africa* (London: Oxford University Press, 1968), 249–64. In addition, see William R. Scott, " 'And Ethiopia Shall Stretch Forth Its Hands': The Origins of Ethiopianism in Afro-American Thought, 1767–1896", *Umoja* 2, no. 1 (Spring 1978): 1–14. See, also, St Clair Drake, *The Redemption of Africa and Black Religion* (Chicago: Third World Press, 1970), 54–75, for a discussion of the role of Edward Wilmot Blyden, born in the Danish West Indies, in making Ethiopianism intellectually respectable. In his discussion of the phenomenon in Jamaica, Ken Post writes that "Jamaican Ethiopianism was a general view of the relationship between the black man and the white, its past, present and future, which in its most political form had implications akin to those of 'Africa for the Africans'. Mixed up with such ideas were also views upon the significance of the actual country Ethiopia, and . . . the two bodies of ideas merged into one another." Ken Post, "The Bible as Ideology: Ethiopianism in Jamaica, 1930–38", in Christopher Allen and R.W. Johnson, eds., *African Perspectives* (Cambridge: Cambridge University Press, 1970), 188.

17. For example, see Andrew T. Carr, "A Rada Community in Trinidad", *Caribbean Quarterly* 3, no. 1 (1953): 36–54; Melville J. Herskovits and Frances S. Herskovits, *Trinidad Village* (1947; reprint, New York: Octagon Books, 1964); and George Eaton Simpson, *The Shango Cult in Trinidad* (Río Piedras: Institute of Caribbean Studies, University of Puerto Rico, 1965) for the time period discussed in this chapter, and Stephen D. Glazier, *Marchin' the Pilgrims Home: Leadership and Decision-Making in an Afro-Caribbean Faith* (Westport, Conn.: Greenwood Press, 1983), James T. Houk, *Spirits, Blood, and Drums: The Orisha Religion in Trinidad* (Philadelphia: Temple University Press, 1995) and Maureen Warner-Lewis, *Guinea's Other Suns: The African Dynamic in Trinidad Culture* (Dover, Mass.: The Majority Press, 1991) for other important studies in general.

18. Quoted in Tony Martin, *Race First: The Ideological and Organizational Struggles of Marcus Garvey and the Universal Negro Improvement Association* (Westport, Conn.: Greenwood Press, 1976), 77.

19. Amy Jacques-Garvey, ed., *Philosophy and Opinions of Marcus Garvey* (New York: Atheneum, 1969), 1:44.

20. Ibid., 140–41.

21. By around 1926, there were at least 30 UNIA branches in Trinidad and Tobago, second in the Caribbean only to 52 in Cuba, nearly three times the number of branches (11) in Jamaica, Garvey's birthplace. In Trinidad, as elsewhere, a large number of women participated and many held executive posts in the UNIA branches. See Martin, *Race First*, 16, 370–73; Reddock, *Women, Labour and Politics*, 106-08. Herskovits and Herskovits, *Trinidad Village*, 263, report that, in 1939, women were members of a UNIA 'lodge' in Cumana.

22. Friday, "The Impact of the Italo-Ethiopian Crisis", 52–55.

23. Public Record Office, Colonial Office (C.O.) 318/418/4, Letter from Godfrey A. Philip to the Colonial Secretary, 2 September 1935, enclosure in Trinidad Despatch No. 460 of 19 September 1935.

24. *People*, 1 May 1935, 5.

25. Ibid., 10 August 1935, 5.

26. Ibid., 3 August 1935, 10.

27. For example, the sermon by Revd J. Caddy was published in the *Trinidad Guardian*, 3 September 1935, 2.

28. *People*, 20 July 1935, 9.

29. Ibid., 16 November 1935, 10.

30. Ibid., 3 August 1935, 6.

31. *Port-of-Spain Gazette*, 26 July 1935, 6.

32. For the Caribbean, see Robert G. Weisbord, "British West Indian Reaction to the Italian-Ethiopian War: An Episode in Pan-Africanism", *Caribbean Studies* 10, no. 1 (1970): 34–41. For West

Africa, see S.K.B. Asante, *Pan-African Protest: West Africa and the Italo-Ethiopian Crisis, 1934–1941* (London: Longman Group, 1977), and for North America, see William R. Scott, *The Sons of Sheba's Race: African-Americans and the Italo-Ethiopian War, 1935–1941* (Bloomington: Indiana University Press, 1993), and Harris, *African-American Reactions*.

33. For an example from North America, see Scott, *Sons of Sheba's Race*, ch. 16. Selassie sent emissaries to the United States to help encourage the assistance of black Americans. These emissaries forged bonds of cooperation with blacks in the United States and expressed solidarity as 'Africans'. On the other hand, many Ethiopians considered the New World term 'Negro' an insult, an invention of white rulers in order to classify and subjugate African slaves and their descendants.

34. Jeffrey T. Sammons, *Beyond the Ring: The Role of Boxing in American Society* (Urbana: University of Illinois Press, 1988), 101-2. According to Craig in *Smiles and Blood*, "Down to the 1970s, in many homes of working class people who survived from the 1930s, two photographs were commonly seen: those of Haile Selassie and Joe Louis, showing the importance of these figures in the formation of their political consciousness" (56, n 34). As Gordon Rohlehr reports in *Calypso and Society in Pre-Independence Trinidad* (Port of Spain: Gordon

Rohlehr, 1990), between 1937 and 1939 there was a number of 'black pride' calypsoes extolling Joe Louis and chronicling his major fights.

35. *Port-of-Spain Gazette*, 1 August 1935, 6.

36. Segal, " 'Race' and 'Colour' in Pre-Independence Trinidad", 83.

37. Ibid., 87.

38. See Reddock, *Elma François, Women, Labour and Politics*, and "Women in Revolt: Women and the Radical Workers' Movement in Trinidad, 1934–1937", in Thomas, *The Trinidad Labour Riots*, especially 237–39.

39. Reddock, *Elma François*, 44.

40. Interview by Friday with Barrette, 21 March 1985, cited in Friday, "The Impact of the Italo-Ethiopian Crisis", 74.

41. *People*, 13 July 1935, 11.

42. C.O. 318/418/4, "Italo-Abyssinian Relations: West Indies Reaction", 1935 & 1936, 275–57, letter (number 406, with enclosure) from Governor Hollis to Malcolm MacDonald, the Secretary of State for the Colonies, 17 August 1935. Enclosure of a letter from A.E. James, secretary, AWIL, dated 9 August 1935. The AWIL also sent the following cable directly to Selassie: "AFRO-WEST INDIANS, TRINIDAD, ADMIRE YOUR MAJESTY'S FIRM STAND ETHIOPIAN SOVEREIGNTY FREEDOM, PLEDGE SUPPORT" (*Port-of-Spain Gazette*, 4 August 1935, 8).

43. C.O. 318/418/4, Resolution in letter from Godfrey A. Philip to

the Colonial Secretary, 2
September 1935, enclosure in
Trinidad Despatch No. 460 of 19
September 1935, 2.

44. Friday, "The Impact of the Italo-
Ethiopian Crisis", 80.

45. George Padmore, "Ethiopia
Today: The Making of a Modern
State", in Nancy Cunard, ed.,
Negro: An Anthology (1934; reprint,
New York: Frederick Ungar,
1970), 390.

46. *People*, 27 July 1935, 6.

47. *Trinidad Guardian*, 5 September
1935, 3, cited in Friday, "The
Impact of the Italo-Ethiopian
Crisis", 87.

48. *Trinidad Guardian*, 3 September
1935, 8.

49. Friday, "The Impact of the Italo-
Ethiopian Crisis", 85.

50. *Trinidad Guardian*, 3 September
1935, 4.

51. Interview with the author, St
Augustine, Trinidad, 19 March
1993.

52. *Daily Gleaner* (Jamaica), 22 July
1935, 6.

53. *Trinidad Guardian*, 6 October 1935,
9.

54. See the notice for broadcast in
C.O. 318/418/4, "Italo-Abyssinian
Relations: West Indies Reaction",
1935–1936, 133–34, 31 August
1935.

55. *Port-of-Spain Gazette*, 27 November
1935, 6, cited in Friday, "The
Impact of the Italo-Ethiopian
Crisis", 122. See Friday, 120–22 for
Trinidadian efforts to fight on
behalf of Ethiopia.

56. *Port-of-Spain Gazette*, 8 October
1935, 7. This news was reported

elsewhere in the Caribbean. See,
for example, *West Indian*
(Grenada), 10 October 1935, 4.

57. *Trinidad Guardian*, 11 October
1935, 11, cited in Friday, "The
Impact of the Italo-Ethiopian
Crisis", 98.

58. Reddock, *Elma François*, 19–20.

59. *Port-of-Spain Gazette*, 11 October
1935, 7, cited in Friday, "The
Impact of the Italo-Ethiopian
Crisis", 99.

60. *Census of the Colony of Trinidad and
Tobago, 1931* (Port of Spain:
Government Printery, 1932), 15.

61. *People*, 9 November 1935, 7. See
People of 16 November 1935, 7
when "Junius" again said Ristori
"must go". See the commentary
by "Ethiopian", possibly a
Colonial Hospital employee, in
People, 16 November 1935, 7.

62. *West Indian*, 20 October 1935, 7.

63. C.O. 318/418/4 "Italo-Abyssinian
Relations: West Indies Reaction",
1935–1936, 235, Copy of Reuters
wire story, 12 October 1935.

64. *Trinidad Guardian*, 23 October
1935, 1.

65. *Port-of-Spain Gazette*, 16 November
1935, 13.

66. *West Indian*, 18 October 1935, 7.
Guisto's case was followed in the
Trinidadian press. He said he would
apply for naturalization as a British
subject. When this was granted, it
made front-page news. A
Certificate of Naturalization was
issued to Guisto on 18 December
1935. See *Trinidad Guardian*, 20
December 1935, 1. For Guisto's
Certificate of Naturalization, see
the *Trinidad Royal Gazette*, 19
December 1935, 1397.

67. *Census*, 17–18.

68. For some of the background to religious diversity of Trinidad, as well as the origins of Catholic and anti-Catholic elite conflict, see Donald Wood's classic work *Trinidad in Transition: The Years After Slavery* (London: Oxford University Press, 1968), chs. 9 and 10.

69. *People*, 19 October 1935, 6. The next week many letter-writers congratulated *People* on the editorial. These letters were signed by "A Coloured Catholic", "Anti-Jesuit", "Constant Reader", "Pax", and "Pro Pax". Another editorial was entitled "Judas in the Vatican". A letter-writer, "Pro-Selassie", wrote to congratulate a Mr. Rufus Garcia who announced in the *Gazette* (17 November 1935, 11) that he had quit the Catholic Church "in consequence of the conduct of His Holiness the Pope", saying "in my opinion all persons of pigmentation who are followers of that church, should take the step I have taken". See *People*, 23 November 1935, 6–7.

70. *People*, 19 October 1935, 6, cited in Friday, "The Impact of the Italo-Ethiopian Crisis", 113.

71. *Catholic News*, 13 September 1935.

72. *Port-of-Spain Gazette*, 3 November 1935, 18.

73. *Port-of-Spain Gazette*, 3 September 1935, 10, cited in Friday, "The Impact of the Italo-Ethiopian Crisis", 112–13.

74. *Port-of-Spain Gazette*, 9 November 1935, 11.

75. Reddock, *Women, Labour and Politics*, 110.

76. Friday, "The Impact of the Italo-Ethiopian Crisis", 101–3.

77. *Trinidad Guardian*, 20 November 1935, 1.

78. Ibid., 15 November 1935, 1–2. See Proclamation 84 in the *Trinidad Royal Gazette*, 31 October 1935, 1172 and Proclamation 86 in the *Trinidad Royal Gazette*, 14 November 1935, 1211–12.

79. Friday, "The Impact of the Italo-Ethiopian Crisis", 106. See also *Trinidad Guardian*, 16 October 1935, 2, and other papers of the time.

80. *Trinidad Guardian*, 30 October 1935, 2.

81. Ibid., 19 October 1935, 3.

82. Reddock, *Women, Labour and Politics*, 109–10.

83. *Port-of-Spain Gazette*, 27 November 1935, 6, cited in Friday, "The Impact of the Italo-Ethiopian Crisis", 110.

84. *Trinidad Guardian*, 22 December 1935, 10.

85. *Port-of-Spain Gazette*, 27 November 1935, 7, cited in Friday, "The Impact of the Italo-Ethiopian Crisis", 108.

86. *People*, 7 December 1935, 8, cited in Friday, "The Impact of the Italo-Ethiopian Crisis", 109.

87. Foreign Office (F.O.) 371/20154/28930, Report of Sergeant-Major N. Johnston to Inspector, Southern Division, San Fernando, 29 October 1935, enclosure 2 in Trinidad Despatch No. 4 of 6 January 1936.

88. F.O. 371/20154/28930, Resolution enclosed in Trinidad Despatch No. 4 of 6 January 1936.

89. *Trinidad Guardian*, 11 December 1935, 9.

90. Ibid., 18 January 1936, 3.

91. On the involvement of these Trinidadians in pro-Ethiopia organizations and activities, see Robert A. Hill's article on James, "In England, 1932–1938", *Urgent Tasks* 12 (Summer 1981), especially 22; George Padmore, *Pan-Africanism or Communism?* (Garden City, NY: Doubleday, 1971 [1956]); John Gaffar LaGuerre, *The Social and Political Thought of the Colonial Intelligentsia* (Mona, Jamaica: Institute of Social and Economic Research, UWI, 1982); James R. Hooker, *Black Revolutionary: George Padmore's Path from Communism to Pan-Africanism* (New York: Praeger, 1967); S.K.B. Asante, "The Impact of the Italo-Ethiopian Crisis of 1935–36 on the Pan-African Movement in Britain", *Transactions of the Historical Society of Ghana* 8, no. 2 (1972), especially 218–19; and Paul Buhle, *C.L.R. James: The Artist as Revolutionary* (London: Verso, 1988).

92. *New York Times*, 14 December 1935, 8.

93. See William R. Scott, "Malaku E. Bayen: Ethiopian Emissary to Black America, 1936–1941", *Ethiopia Observer* 15, no. 2 (1972): 132–38; Scott, *Sons of Sheba's Race*, and Harris, *African American Reactions.*

94. Of the many newspaper reports in the United States, especially in the black press, see "Ethiopia Glad to be Rid of Julian", *Pittsburgh Courier*, 21 March 1936, 3.

95. *New York Times*, 19 June 1936, 2.

96. Information on Julian was gleaned from the following sources: Colonel Hubert Julian, as told to John Bulloch, *Black Eagle* (London: The Adventurers Club, 1965); William R. Scott, "Hubert F. Julian and the Italo-Ethiopian War: A Dark Episode in Pan-African Relations", *Umoja* 2, no. 2 (Summer 1978): 77–93; Scott, *Sons of Sheba's Race*, ch. 7; and John Peer Nugent, *The Black Eagle* (New York: Stein and Day, 1971).

97. Malaku E. Bayen, ed., *The March of Black Men* (New York: Voice of Ethiopia Press, 1939), 6, cited in Scott, *Sons of Sheba's Race*, 95.

98. *Port-of-Spain Gazette*, 29 November 1935, 3, cited in Friday, "The Impact of the Italo-Ethiopian Crisis", 115–16.

99. *Trinidad Guardian*, 6 December 1935, 2.

100. For a discussion, see Herskovits and Herskovits, *Trinidad Village*, Appendix II, 340–48. They report that, during a period of four months in 1939, two convictions of 'Shouters' (Spiritual Baptists) were obtained in the village of Toco (184).

101. *Trinidad Guardian*, 4 January 1936, 3.

102. Rohlehr, *Calypso and Society*, 288–315.

103. *Port-of-Spain Gazette*, 20 November 1935, 6, cited in Friday, "The Impact of the Italo-Ethiopian Crisis", 119.

104. Rohlehr, *Calypso and Society*, 316.

105. *Trinidad Guardian*, 28 November 1935, 8.

106. Cited in Donald R. Hill, *Calypso Calaloo: Early Carnival Music in Trinidad* (Gainesville: University Press of Florida, 1993), 251–52.

107. Rohlehr, *Calypso and Society*, 316–17.
108. See Friday, "The Impact of the Italo-Ethiopian Crisis", 118, citing contemporary newspapers.
109. *Trinidad Guardian*, 26 February 1936, 1.
110. Ibid., 27 February 1936, 2.
111. F.O. 371/20155 (1936), Letter to the Colonial Secretary from Hugo Mentor, the president of the Afro-West Indian League, of 5 May 1936. Enclosure in Trinidad Despatch No. 258 of 13 May 1936.
112. *People*, 30 November 1935, 12, cited in Friday, "The Impact of the Italo-Ethiopian Crisis", 125.
113. F.O. 371/20155 (1936), letter to the Acting Governor A. Wallace Seymour from A.E. James, secretary of the Friends of Ethiopia Committee of 9 May 1936. Enclosure in Trinidad Despatch No. 259 of 13 May 1936.
114. *People*, 6 June 1936, 12 and Rennie, *The History of the Working Class*, 69, cited in Reddock, *Women, Labour and Politics*, 109. See, also, Reddock, *Elma François*, 20–21.
115. Friday, "The Impact of the Italo-Ethiopian Crisis", 106.
116. Arthur Calder-Marshall, *Glory Dead* (London: Michael Joseph, 1939), 254.
117. *Hansard*, 9 July 1937, 255.
118. C.O. 295/599/76297 II, Fletcher to Ormsby-Gore, confidential, 7 July 1937, cited in Singh, *Race and Class Struggles*, 170.
119. Calder-Marshall, *Glory Dead*, 169.
120. Ibid., 168–69.
121. Ibid., 171.
122. Rohlehr, *Calypso and Society*, 318–19.
123. *Trinidad Village*, 186.
124. *New Times and Ethiopia News*, 7 October 1939, 2. See Ibid., 11 March 1939, for another letter from a Trinidadian well-wisher.
125. See *Black Man* 2, no. 2 (July–August 1936): 6.
126. See the reports in the *Daily Herald* (4 June 1936, 2) and the *Daily Express* (4 June 1936, 11), for example.
127. Of many broadsides against Selassie on this count, see, for example, *Black Man*, 6 no. 6 (March–April 1937): 8–9.
128. *Sunday Guardian*, 29 August 1937, 1, 3.
129. Reddock, *Women, Labour and Politics*, 111. The reasons for this may have had to do with his need to placate the Colonial Office in order to obtain permission for the visit. Indeed, the Colonial Office expressed a belief in his sincerity, although articles in his *Black Man* magazine showed support for striking workers in the West Indies. See Tony Martin, "Marcus Garvey and Trinidad, 1912–1947", in Rupert Lewis and Maureen Warner-Lewis, eds., *Garvey: Africa, Europe, the Americas* (Mona: Institute of Social and Economic Research, UWI, 1986), 75–76.
130. See the *Trinidad Guardian*, 21 September 1937, 3; 21 October 1937, 2; *Sunday Guardian*, 24 October 1937, 21; *Trinidad Guardian*, 27 October 1937, 2; and 28 October 1937, 12, 14 for reports of Garvey's visit and speeches.

131. *People*, 13 November 1937, 6, cited in Reddock, *Women, Labour and Politics*, 111.

132. *Voice of St Lucia*, 2 November 1937, 1. Garvey's remarks had been reported there. See the *Voice of St Lucia*, 14 September 1937, 4.

133. Herskovits and Herskovits, *Trinidad Village*, 265.

134. Post, "The Bible as Ideology", 186.

135. Talal Asad, "A Comment on Ajaz Ahmad's *In Theory*", *Public Culture* 6, no. 1 (1993): 32.

136. See Patrick Joyce, "The End of Social History?", *Social History* 20, no. 1 (1995): 73–91. For a more philosophical treatment of problems related to this issue, see Raymond Williams, "Base and Superstructure in Marxist Cultural Theory", in his *Problems in Materialism and Culture* (London: Verso, 1980), 31–49.

Notes to Chapter 10

1. W.A. Lewis, *Labour in the West Indies* (London: Fabian Pamphlet No. 44, 1939).

2. *House of Commons Debates*. 5th Series, 1937. Col. 3311.

3. M.R. Pocock, *Out of the Shadows of the Past* (London: The Author, 1993), 256–57.

4. Ralph de Boissière, *Crown Jewel* (London: Allison and Busby, 1981). Actually, versions of this book started appearing from 1952. This is discussed later.

5. Mrs. H. Nankivell, Memorandum for the West India Royal Commission (The Moyne Commission), 1938, 7 (hereafter referred as Nankivell Memo).

6. This account of Woodbrooke is based on Robert Davis, ed., *Woodbrooke 1903–1953: A Quaker Experiment in Religious Education* (London: Bannisdale Press, 1953).

7. *Hansard* (Trinidad and Tobago), 1937, 263.

8. *Report on the Disturbances in Trinidad and Tobago* (London: HMSO, 1938, Cmd. 5641 [the Forster Report]), paragraph 246.

9. *Petit Parisien* (France), 24 December 1938, 3.

10. An account of Florence Nankivell's trip to Jamaica and Trinidad, 3 January–24 February 1966. Nankivell Family Papers.

11. Nankivell Memo, 9.

12. Ibid., 4.

13. Speech to Mother's Day Celebration, Coterie of Social Workers, Port of Spain, 1933. Nankivell Family Papers.

14. Public address by Mrs. Nankivell, c. 1940, paragraph 7. Nankivell Family Papers.

15. Ibid., paragraph 14.

16. Public Record Office, Colonial Office (C.O.) 295/600, Enclosed with Fletcher to Ormsby-Gore, 20 August 1937.

17. Nankivell Memo, 6.

18. Nankivell Family Papers.

19. Arthur Calder-Marshall, *Glory Dead* (London: Michael Joseph, 1939), 58.

20. Kenneth Ramchand, "Interview with Ralph de Boissère: back to Kangaroos", *CRNLE Reviews Journal* (Flinders University of South Australia) 1 (1994), 11. This paragraph is based on that interview.

21. Ibid.

22. Ibid., 19–20.

23. Ibid., 9.

24. Ibid., 25.

25. C.O. 295/599, Enclosed with Fletcher to Ormsby-Gore, 5 July 1937.

26. Here de Boissière uses the name of an actual leader, Clem Payne, who was in fact not killed during the riots.

27. Forster Report, paragraphs 263 and 265.

28. Ibid., paragraph 265.

29. Ibid., paragraph 269.

30. Rhoda Reddock, "Women in Revolt: Women and the Radical Workers' Movement in Trinidad, 1934–1937", in Roy Thomas, ed. *The Trinidad Labour Riots of 1937: Perspectives 50 Years Later* (St Augustine: Extra-Mural Studies Unit, UWI, 1987), 233.

31. Ramchand, "Interview", 24.

32. Rhoda Reddock, *Elma François, the NWCSA, and the Worker's Struggle for Change in the Caribbean* (London: New Beacon Books, 1988), 33–34.

33. Ibid., 11.

34. Ibid., 14.

35. Ibid., 15.

36. Ibid., 22.

37. Ibid., 37.

38. Ibid., 35.

39. Coterie of Social Workers to Mrs Nankivell, 4 June 1938. Nankivell Family Papers.

40. *West India Royal Commission Report* (the Moyne Commission). Cmd. 6607. (London: HMSO, 1945), 218–19.

41. *Rum and Coca-Cola* (London: Allison and Busby, 1984).

42. For details on the arrangements see Fitz Baptiste, *War, Co-Operation and Conflict: The European Possessions in the Caribbean, 1939–45* (New York: Greenwood Press, 1988), ch. 8.

Notes to Chapter 11

1. Exemplified when Derek Walcott's chronicle, *Drums and Colours*, which includes Toussaint in "Rebellion", was commissioned for the 1958 celebration of the West Indies Federation (reprinted in *Caribbean Quarterly* 38, no. 4 [December 1992]: 22–135).

2. John Conteh-Morgan, *Theatre and Drama in Francophone Africa* (Cambridge: Cambridge University Press, 1994), especially the section of ch. 3 entitled "The Dramatist as Historian".

3. See VèVè Clark, "Haiti's Tragic Overture: (Mis)Representations of the Haitian Revolution in World Drama (1796–1975)", in James Hefferman, ed., *Representing Revolution: Essays on Reflections of the French Revolution in Literature, Historiography and Art* (Hanover: University Press of New England, 1991). Marie-José N'Zengou-Tayo in "Re-Imagining History: The Caribbean Vision of the Haitian Revolution and of the Early Independence [sic] Days", *Espace caraïbe* 3 (1995): 105–20, surveys the mythification of history and complex rewriting at work in fiction and drama in English, Spanish, and French.

4. See Richard D.E.Burton's incisive analysis in his *La Famille coloniale: La Martinique et la mère patrie 1789–*

1992 (Paris: L'Harmattan, 1994).

5. H. Salandre and R. Cheyssac, *Les Antilles françaises: Histoire et civilisation* (Paris: Fernand Nathan, 1962), 69. My translation.

6. J. Michael Dash, *Edouard Glissant* (Cambridge: Cambridge University Press, 1995), 20. This lucid study can be consulted for bibliographical details on Glissant.

7. Haitian painters use the severed arm to identify Mackandal, and a lost limb is incorporated into Glissant's symbolism for Africa in the Caribbean.

8. Writer and activist Daniel Blérald erased his patronym in order to take on the name of the slave leader and voodoo priest who presided over the legendary ceremony in the Bois Caïman cemetery on the eve of the revolution.

9. The shortened version, devised with the Théâtre Noir company, gives a greater place to creole dialogue.

10. The English translation edited by Juris Silenieks (Three Continents Press, 1981) supplies much useful supporting information on the play and its content.

11. *Caribbean Discourse* (Charlottesville: University Press of Virginia, 1989), 69. Selected essays from *Le discours antillais* (Paris: Du Seuil, 1981), translated with preface by J. Michael Dash.

12. A number of the murals celebrating Aristide's election to the presidency portrayed him in the company of the revolutionary heroes.

13. See Pierre Laville in *Les voies de la création théâtrale* (Paris: Editions du C.N.R.S., 1970), vol. 2, especially 255 ff.

14. See a valuable analysis of *Le roi Christophe* by Régis Antoine in the Bordas "Lectoguide" series, 1984, and book-length studies of Césaire's plays by Rodney E. Harris, *L'Humanisme dans le théâtre d'Aimé Césaire* (Sherbrooke: Naaman, 1973); Clément M'Bom, *Le Théâtre d'Aimé Césaire* (Paris: Nathan, 1979); Rémy S. Bouelet, *Espaces et dialectique du héros césairien* (Paris: L'Harmattan, 1987); Marianne Wichmann Bailey, *The Ritual Theatre of Aimé Césaire* (Tübingen: Narr, 1992); as well as numerous articles and studies of individual texts. A useful bibliography exists in Daniel Delas *Aimé Césaire* (Paris: Hachette, 1991).

15. Staged by the Turkish director Mehmet Ulusoy, as a collage with other poetic texts under the title *Equateur funambule* at the Fort-de-France festival of 1995. There was much ingenuity in visual effects but the debate, forty years on, seemed dated. Césaire, though present, declined to acknowledge applause.

16. A 1964 interview quoted in M.M. Ngal, *Aimé Césaire: Un homme à la recherche d'une patrie* (Dakar/Abidjan: Nouvelles Editions Africaines, 1975), 220.

17. Part of Metellus' speech evoking the rigours and glory of the freedom struggle in the hills. Unrestricted movement between

the Caribbean islands remains, however, a major demand of ordinary citizens, as recent West Indian Commission surveys have shown.

18. See p. 171 (Paris: Stock, 1993). Confiant's *'démystification'* of Césaire reflects the attitudes of the *'créolité'* group (including Patrick Chamoiseau and Jean Bernabé) which promote creole language and cultural synthesis. His polemic rather lacks a historical sense.

19. Martinique: L'Autre mer, 1994.

20. For an informative short account of recent political developments in Martinique, see Richard D.E. Burton, "Towards 1992: Political-Cultural Assimilation and Opposition in Contemporary Martinique", *French Cultural Studies* 3 (1992): 61–86.

21. See David Nicholls, *From Dessalines to Duvalier*, 3rd ed. (London: Macmillan, 1996).

22. Text in *Tranchées*, Revue politique et culturelle du Groupe Révolution Socialiste, No. hors-série, January 1993, 29–34, which also contains a bibliography of Placoly's work.

23. Research by Mimi Sheller (see "Sword-Bearing Citizens: Militarism and Manhood in Nineteenth-Century Haiti", *Plantation Society in the Americas* 4, nos. 2 and 3 [1997]: 233-78) highlights the masculine imagery permeating the rhetoric of the Haitian Revolution. It is striking that drama by Antillean women such as Simone Schwartz-Bart (*Ton beau capitaine*, 1987) and

Maryse Condé (*Pension les Alizés*, 1988) deals sympathetically with the dilemmas of ordinary contemporary Haitian citizens, not male heroics.

Index